PSYCHOLOGY OF DI

Democracy was forged in the furnaces of oppression, whether combatting tyranny or affirming the rights of the individual. As democracy is under threat in many parts of the world, there has never been a more urgent need to understand political thoughts and behaviours. This lucid and accessible book brings together a global group of scholars from psychology, political science, communication, sociology, education and psychiatry. The book's structure, based on Abraham Lincoln's well-known phrase 'Of, by and for' the people, scrutinises the psychological factors experienced by politicians as representatives 'of' the electorate, the political institutions and systems devised 'by' those we elect, and the societies that influence the context 'for' us as citizens. From trust to risk, from political values to moral and religious priorities, from the personality and language of leaders to fake news and anti-democratic forces, this book provides vital new insights for researchers, politicians and citizens alike.

ASHLEY WEINBERG is Senior Lecturer in Psychology at the University of Salford, UK. He is the founding chair of the Political Psychology Section of the British Psychological Society (BPS) and a BPS winner of the Excellence in Occupational Psychology Policy Impact award. He is the editor of *The Psychology of Politicians* (Cambridge, 2012) and *Brexit in the Workplace* (2020).

PSYCHOLOGY OF DEMOCRACY

Of the People, By the People, For the People

EDITED BY

ASHLEY WEINBERG

University of Salford

CAMBRIDGE
UNIVERSITY PRESS

CAMBRIDGE
UNIVERSITY PRESS

Shaftesbury Road, Cambridge CB2 8EA, United Kingdom

One Liberty Plaza, 20th Floor, New York, NY 10006, USA

477 Williamstown Road, Port Melbourne, VIC 3207, Australia

314–321, 3rd Floor, Plot 3, Splendor Forum, Jasola District Centre, New Delhi – 110025, India

103 Penang Road, #05–06/07, Visioncrest Commercial, Singapore 238467

Cambridge University Press is part of Cambridge University Press & Assessment, a department of the University of Cambridge.

We share the University's mission to contribute to society through the pursuit of education, learning and research at the highest international levels of excellence.

www.cambridge.org
Information on this title: www.cambridge.org/9781108745093

DOI: 10.1017/9781108774871

First published 2022
First paperback edition 2024

A catalogue record for this publication is available from the British Library

Library of Congress Cataloging-in-Publication data
NAMES: Weinberg, Ashley, editor.
TITLE: Psychology of democracy : of the people, by the people, for the people / edited by Ashley Weinberg.
DESCRIPTION: Cambridge, United Kingdom ; New York, NY : Cambridge University Press, 2022. | Includes bibliographical references and index.
IDENTIFIERS: LCCN 2021024876 (print) | LCCN 2021024877 (ebook) | ISBN 9781108477758 (hardback) | ISBN 9781108745093 (paperback) | ISBN 9781108774871 (epub)
SUBJECTS: LCSH: Democracy–Psychological aspects. | Behaviorism (Political science) | Personality and politics.
CLASSIFICATION: LCC JC423 .P88353 2022 (print) | LCC JC423 (ebook) | DDC 320.01/9–dc23
LC record available at https://lccn.loc.gov/2021024876
LC ebook record available at https://lccn.loc.gov/2021024877

ISBN   978-1-108-47775-8   Hardback
ISBN   978-1-108-74509-3   Paperback

Contents

Figures

Tables

Contributors

GIZEM ARIKAN, Department of Political Science, Trinity College Dublin

PAZIT BEN-NUN BLOOM, Department of Political Science, The Hebrew University of Jerusalem

BENJAMIN BOWMAN, Manchester Centre for Youth Studies, Manchester Metropolitan University

PETER BULL, Directorate of Psychology, University of Salford

GIAN VITTORIO CAPRARA, Dipartimento di Psicologia, Sapienza Università di Roma

JUAN CARLOS CASTILLO, Instituto di Sociologica, Pontificia Universidad Católica de Chile

SHARON COEN, Department of Psychology, University of Salford

JOSÉ DANIEL CONEJEROS, Instituto di Sociologica, Pontificia Universidad Católica de Chile

RODERICK DUBROW-MARSHALL, Department of Psychology, University of Salford

JOAKIM EIDENFALK, School of Humanities and Social Inquiry, University of Wollongong

SARAH HARRISON, Electoral Psychology Observatory, Department of Government, London School of Economics and Political Science

HELEN HASTE, Department of Psychology, University of Bath

THALIA MAGIOGLOU, School of Social Science, Humanities and Languages, University of Westminster; and IIAC, Centre Edgar Morin, Ecole des hautes études en science sociale, Paris

KYLE MATTES, Department of Political Science, Florida International University

KAROL SOLÍS MENCO, Department of Political Science, Florida International University-Universidad del Norte

CATALINA MIRANDA, Instituto di Sociologica, Pontificia Universidad Católica de Chile

DANIEL MIRANDA, Centro de Medición MIDE UC, Pontificia Universidad Católica de Chile

RUKMINI BHAYA NAIR, Department of Humanities and Social Sciences, Indian Institute of Technology Delhi

DAVID P. REDLAWSK, Department of Political Science and International Relations, University of Delaware

JANE ROBERTS, Faculty of Business and Law, Open University

JO SILVESTER, School of Business and Economics, Loughborough University

SJOERD STOLWIJK, Department of Political Science and Public Administration, Vrije Universiteit Amsterdam

PETER SUEDFELD, Department of Psychology, The University of British Columbia

BARBARA VIS, Faculty of Law, Economics & Governance, Utrecht University School of Governance

MAURICE WADDLE, Department of Psychology, University of York

ASHLEY WEINBERG, Department of Psychology, University of Salford

JAMES WEINBERG, Department of Politics, University of Sheffield

STUART WOODCOCK, School of Education and Professional Studies, Griffith University, Queensland

MADELEINE WYATT, King's Business School, King's College London

KARL TURGUT MALONEY YORGANCI, Department of Psychology, University of Salford

YIDA ZHAI, School of International and Public Affairs, Shanghai Jiao Tong University

Preface

Democracy was forged in the furnaces of oppression. Its history has been colourful and its varieties plentiful. Values of freedom and opportunity have been its bywords, yet whatever the perceptions, practices and experiences of democracy, its systems have been flouted all too frequently by power-hungry play-makers. Designated historically as government 'of', 'by' and 'for' the people, perhaps it should be surprising that the processes by which it operates are not by the design of the wider population, that information about policies and perspectives is routinely relayed via media over which citizens have little control, and that school-age education on the nature of citizenship is rarely prioritised. Each of these threatens public understanding or agency over how democratic nations are governed, despite the wars and battles their publics have fought to win such rights.

The intent of this observation is not to toll a bell of doom but to excite the need for engagement with what we hold dear – whatever one's political persuasions. Whether in combatting tyranny in the city state of Athens in ancient Greece or ushered in by ages of revolution against despotism around the world, democracy has sought to enshrine principles and rights we have come to associate with aspiring and successful struggles for rights as well as survival, in turn refined by ongoing progress and definition. Yet, in affirming the rights of the individual – as expressed historically by Paine, Voltaire and others – the challenge remains in how best to recognise the wishes and political potential of populations. Failure to give this proper consideration runs risks foreshadowed by political upheaval – whether quiet or loud – and at worst the undoing of what may have been achieved historically. Such risks are not confined to one system of government – democratic or otherwise. As such, in early 2021, minds were drawn to 'Brexit' by which the UK withdrew from the European Union, the attack by an outgoing US president on the outcome of the presidential election, as well as threats to opposition voices in Uganda and Russia. All are different in their own way, but suggest that democracy as understood globally faces constant challenges. History confirms this is not an unusual pattern of events and so, when the Psychology of Democracy conferences began in 2015 at the University of Salford, they did not predate such events by design – despite the temptation to claim considerable foresight. The lessons of the past were there for all to see – the cycle of events would bring them back to the centre of our attention.

Democracy, as a process, is founded on hard-won principles of freedom, equality and commonality of peoples, yet in turn can founder on the rocks of counter-revolution from within or indeed from outside. Naturally, opposing views are succour to healthier political debate and ultimately to recognition of a need for consensus – provided there is respect for the perspectives of all parties concerned. The success of democratic process also depends on effective forms of representation. Such are the general rules of deliberative and participatory democracy, but neither is without flaw. The form of democracy represented by referenda can make for difficulties in consensus-building, yet the majority view is required to prevail. The functioning of political parties and their manifestos means that the ideas of one side can be moulded over time or indeed adopted by others. However, consensus is not always possible or desirable, and as nations approach such 'political black holes', the energy – and sometimes with it the lifeblood – is sucked from the protagonists, with potentially disastrous consequences for all citizens.

The emergence of democracy as a political system over the last 2,500 years has involved the battle for hearts and minds of the rulers and the ruled. While electoral rights and universal suffrage are currently enshrined in law in many countries and federations with democratic systems, these have taken anywhere between decades and centuries to reach fruition. This reflects psychological as well as physical conflicts, from which nations with either long-standing or more recent commitments to the principles of democracy have endeavoured to heal and recover. Recognising that the opportunity to vote is only one part of democratic process, the shaping of healthy democracy – what it might look like and how it may be actualised in practice by citizens and nations – is both ongoing and variably experiences poorer or better outcomes, with potential pitfalls as old wounds are reopened. The role of emotions and all that motivates them cannot be ignored. Trust and its betrayal are obvious touchstones for electorates.

However, time is not necessarily the friend of well-considered political options in democracies, as the crunch point in the cycle of elections inevitably returns. A focus on the short term may be politically expedient for retaining power but unhelpful for longer-term strategies for the public good. The delay and failure in grasping the actions demanded by climate change is a case in point. Understandably, democracy is a tool for the expression of political will, but the actions taken by political actors – leaders and parties – are not necessarily practical or popular, and where this becomes a consistent pattern, discontent and potentially unrest can follow. From this perspective, the nature of democracy – in assuming that it does seek the utilitarian best deal for the majority – means that its standing is always under question and potentially under threat. As British prime minister Winston Churchill pointed out in 1947, 'Democracy is the worst form of government, except for all the others that have been tried from time to time!'

Despite this less-than-ringing historical endorsement and indeed the regular tribulations faced by it, democratic forms of government are widespread and more numerous than forty years ago, making up almost 60 per cent of worldwide political systems according to the (non-partisan) Pew Research Centre in 2017.[1] The remainder comprise approaches which combine elements of democracy with autocracy (28 per cent) or are dictatorships (13 per cent). Within a context that adopts aspects of democratic and non-democratic government, such as Morocco, it is revealing that prospective legislation is more likely to reflect interests of the ruling elite, whereas questions raised in parliament are statistically more likely to reflect wider public concerns.[2] Within more clear-cut autocracies, such as China, perceptions of democracy certainly differ from Western perspectives but are not ignored.[3] This use of the term is not new and led Sir Bernard Crick to note in 1962, 'Democracy is perhaps the most promiscuous word in the world of public affairs'.[4]

The opportunity – whether presented or not – to participate in elections raises its own questions about the efficacy of democracy. Many citizens are prepared to vote and this covers those who are alternatively excited, disenchanted or disenfranchised by poor quality systems of voter registration, or, who as minors in the eyes of the law (under the age of twenty-one in Lebanon and Singapore), are excluded – despite the likely impacts on their futures. There are proportions who decide not to vote

[1] Pew Research Centre (2019) Available at www.pewresearch.org/fact-tank/2019/05/14/more-than-half-of-countries-are-democratic/.

[2] M. Shalaby and A. Aydogan (2020) Elite-citizen linkages and issue congruency under competitive authoritarianism. *Parliamentary Affairs*, 73(1), 66–88.

[3] Y. Zhai (2020) Popular perceptions of democracy in China: Characteristics and longitudinal changes. *Asian Survey*, 60(3), 557–582.

[4] B. Crick (1962) *In defense of politics*, p. 12. University of Chicago Press.

and, as a potential rejoinder, there are many nations with laws obliging citizens to participate, including the possibility of a financial penalty in Australia. For those successful in gaining eligibility to vote, there is hopefully a choice of candidate or outcome, but, once cast, how the vote is counted is swiftly taken beyond the realm of the individual, either as part of a 'first past the post' system or as a form of transferable vote. After that, whether the citizen feels their vote has made a difference can depend on the outcome. Whatever the level of satisfaction, the notion of participation retains its appeal; yet as political scientist Matt Flinders observes, the overarching system in which this plays out is viewed less positively: 'Maybe the problem with democracy – at a deeper level – is that you cannot have democracy without the politics'.[5]

Nevertheless, at a societal level, such operations – whether considered democratic or not – seem beyond our individual scope to influence, even for those who at times have been part of the apparatus that designed or modified them! For political activists, conceiving an image of votes adding up to make majorities is less difficult, while, for others, the sheer effort of trying to visualise thousands or millions of votes prohibits the feeling they have a role to play, when their individual contribution is weighed on such a grand scale. Perhaps the opportunity to stand in the room where paper votes are counted and see and hear the computations, with batches building up behind the names of political candidates, is one that all citizens should have. Here, at least, it is clear how one vote can make a difference. Here is the chance to experience votes being unloaded from ballot boxes, counted, checked, placed in order and assembled on tables. Here are the wheels of democracy in action – it is no more important than the casting of the vote by the individual citizen, yet it is salutary in what it represents and to what it leads.

Democracy comes in many forms. Protest has been the lifeblood of its struggle for survival and recognition and counter-protest has ensured its continuing need for reflection. Democracy comes without guarantees and we do not always get the outcomes we wish, but a democratic backdrop provides a necessary forum for discussion and debate whatever one's views. As American poet Amanda Gorman observed with hope in 2021 following tumult at the heart of government, 'we weathered and witnessed a nation that isn't broken, but simply unfinished'.[6] So, will democracy ensure our

---

[5] M. Flinders (2016) The problem with democracy. *Parliamentary Affairs*, 69, 181–203. Quote on p. 181.
[6] A. Gorman (2021) The hill we climb. Poem recited by the author at the inauguration of the 46th president of the United States, Joe Biden, and vice president, Kamala Harris, 20 January.

survival and produce the actions and solutions we feel are necessary? Whatever your view on climate change or on abuses of human rights or a sense of belonging to a nation or a broader collective of nations, it is clear that democracy, as a means to providing a voice for the views of all peoples, plays a vital part.

Globally the impacts of environmental change, of inefficient and insufficient provision of basic resources for living and of ongoing unrest with established systems of government highlight the scale of the challenges facing our species. The unpreparedness of nations for combatting a viral pandemic has thrown these considerations into stark relief. No respecter of forms of government globally or nationally, COVID-19 wrought havoc. The answer to such a threat remains the power and ingenuity of people helping others. Yet how best can the people's potential be fulfilled? The pandemic opened wider the cracks of inequalities in societies worldwide, while proffered solutions remain vociferously debated and desperately needed. Whether rooted in popular dissatisfaction with the daily reality of governments, or in attempts by a range of stakeholders to shock or manipulate outcomes to their own benefit, the issues for all who wish to live within 'democratic' systems are shared: striving to ensure a relatively safe and productive existence for all. We have little option in this particular choice. While we can be sure that progress is slow, change is possible, but persistence is the key!

Acknowledgements

I would like to dedicate this volume to my wonderful family. To Anne, for all her love and companionship and guidance, as well as supporting my literary endeavours. To my inspiring children, for their talent and passion in making a positive difference to the world: James, as a champion for citizenship education and advancing understanding of political behaviour, and Lottie, through her therapeutic work that empowers the lives of countless others in their times of need. To my Dad for a lifetime of encouragement and belief and stimulating discussions about politics. To my Mum, who we miss in many ways, not least for nurturing my love of language and the written word.

I am particularly grateful to Janka Romero, commissioning editor at Cambridge University Press, for supporting the concept and creation of this book and for her kind patience while it has taken shape, and also to her colleagues Emily Watton, Santosh Laxmi Kota and Jessica Norman for all their help and assistance. I would like to thank Divya Arjunan and her team for producing this book during such challenging times and Paul Martin for his splendid copy-editing.

Naturally this book would not exist without the endeavours of its contributors from around the world, whose research shines light on the psychology of politics and in particular on what makes democracy tick. Thanks to each of you for trusting me with your work and for giving so generously of your time.

My thanks go also to those who have participated in our biannual Psychology of Democracy conferences at Salford since 2015 and supported the establishment of the Political Psychology section of the British Psychological Society.

Thank you to you, the reader: the book, as well as the future, is in your hands!

CHAPTER I

Psychology of Democracy

Ashley Weinberg

Democracy is in danger. Consider these questions if you are unsure whether this is the case. Do you trust others? Do you believe others will act on your behalf? Would you take up a cause on others' behalf? These are fundamental questions of democracy and how it is practised across the world. For many, democracy represents political freedom, access to justice and an assumed range of esteemed values, while, for others, it is a political system that, at its basest level, needs to be navigated at all costs to achieve desired goals. For some, democracy represents an impediment to achieving their desired aims. Where there is attraction to power in the minds of those involved, there are clear challenges for democracy and for the populations it purports to represent. The reason such motivations can differ is simple: it is because we are human.

One paradox of democracy appears to lie in how the power it confers is used. If we are interested in the common good, why would a nation claim to have a system that looks like it involves everyone, but teems with examples in which it does not necessarily serve them? This situation results in negative perceptions of politics and elected representatives that undermine belief in democracy, unless democracy is seen to deliver results with which the majority can agree. It has been suggested by the Cambridge University Centre for the Future of Democracy (2020) that there is a 'global democratic recession' (Foa et al., 2020). Perhaps it should come as no surprise that democracy – as a system of government – is facing its greatest challenges and, at the same time, the standing of politicians as assessed by polls and academic studies is invariably low (e.g., Clarke et al., 2016; Hansard Society, 2019; Stoker and Evans, 2016). Furthermore, it has been suggested that the 'third wave of autocratization' in the early part of the twenty-first century, characterised by gradual erosion of democratic functions, is a legitimate cause for concern (Lührmann and Lindberg, 2019).

This book explores relevant individual, social and political psychological mechanisms and processes that contribute, not only to our experiences of democracy, but also to its relative success or failure. At this stage in human evolution, the stakes in forms of government that can deliver our survival could not be higher.

Naturally, the roles and responsibilities of those elected to act on behalf of the population are brought into sharp focus. Yet, the study of those who become elected representatives is relatively scarce, so attitudes tend to rely rather unhelpfully on popular perceptions in which a range of media play an influential role. In considering, 'Of the people, by the people, for the people', this book seeks to analyse the key factors that shape and determine our involvement in the government of our lives and of our communities and nations. Examining democracy, from an emerging awareness of citizenship among young people right through to our involvement with political processes and institutions and to the experience of those serving and leaving political office, the psychology of politics is a window to our future, whoever we are. Seen through the lens of democracy, we ask how bright is that future?

Who Counts?

The survival instincts of humans have not changed in millennia and, in order to guarantee continuing success, we need to co-exist effectively within groups, whether these are the size of family units, communities or entire nations. As political philosophers have acknowledged, such tasks are not only daunting for citizens struggling with the challenges and exigencies of daily life, but also for those who seek and take responsibility for making democratic systems work: 'What we require in a democratic society is enlightened individuals who will be mature and responsible because they reflect upon the issues which face them' (Mill, 1859). Yet, it is at the individual, community and national levels that we take steps to exert some control over our environments, whether at home, at work or in government. Hopefully, this control is expressed in ways that add positively to our own and others' experiences and in so doing lies an important realisation: in a democracy, we are all politicians, whether we like it or not.

So, how could we organise society for the better? Naturally everyone will have a differing view or preference, but it is equally likely that – when it comes to such weighty matters – arrangements do not meet hopes and expectations. People starve, are deprived or neglected, lose their homes, are obliged to yield to mightier forces – and without fair reason in a world supposedly knowing more than before. Yet, while citizens can conceive of the ideal state of affairs for our families and communities, nations struggle to achieve them. The difficulties in agreeing and implementing measures to combat climate change are a case in point.

Politicians complain of responsibility without real power to effect change, yet people take a stand where they can – unless they feel disinclined by a sense of inevitable failure. So, how would you devise a political system? Would it be one that serves the interests equally of all, or one that tends to favour some over others? Power-holders – as though wearing the ring from Tolkien's tales – know the temptations all too well. As Lord Acton observed in 1887, 'Power tends to corrupt and absolute power corrupts absolutely'. Even the prospect of it can tempt those who seek power towards dubious actions – perhaps to load the dice of the electoral gamble, whether over-spending on a political campaign or manipulating information about promised outcomes or political opponents.

These considerations beg an important question: Can we be dispassionate about democracy or indeed about the exercising of power? Walter Bagehot's *The English Constitution* (1873) considers both colourfully and enthusiastically the definition of one parliamentary system and perhaps herein lies a major dilemma. It is not only knowing what we really want that is important, but how we would know what this resembles? In part, this depends on how our knowledge of our political systems is shaped. Bagehot recognised that, in changing times, the conundrum about the best shape of government faces both those in power 'and. . . a people neither of whom are guided by a different experience' (p. 6). After all, how can we live outside of the era of our existence to judge what is best? As a species, we often learn through trial and error – of our own or others – but the turn of events decides whether this learning is put into practice.

Consensus and committees that abound in parliaments reasonably give the appearance of scrutinising policies and actions that should promote the common good, arguably much more so where these bodies are purportedly representative of the wider population. However, this itself begs further major questions for democracy. Just how many and how involved are people in democracy and how could everyone be engaged in the ways things are run? For example, where are the voices of those deemed outside the system? As we have seen in climate change protests, many children are keen for and deserving of a voice, the logic and fairness of which few can deny, yet they are without political representation. Similarly, for citizens without a home or regular dwelling, or access to the Internet, there is no clear system for registering to vote and they are frequently denied the franchise. Furthermore, many disenchanted with politics and politicians are overwhelmed by the prospect of getting to grips with such contested

matters or feel disinclined to participate or perceive their part too insig-
nificant – finding themselves instead on the receiving end of a 'democratic'
deal. For those who hope that political parties will represent and safeguard
their interests, there are options to join or facilitate their impact in some
way, yet how influential can individuals be? An example of financial
political contributions makes for interesting reading. In 2019, the year of
the UK's Brexit General Election, £24.9 million was donated to the
Conservative Party from among its fifty largest party donors; this compares
to the main opposition Labour Party's total campaign fund from all donors
of just over £5 million (*Sunday Times*, 2020).

Who Has Power in a Democracy?

If politics is about power, then it is naturally about control as well. There
are claims that the way democracy works is rooted in manipulation by a
privileged minority for their advantage, while others point to the practical
challenges in politics of suiting everyone at every turn and to the progress
achieved in areas of one policy or another. Whether these are narratives
with which one concurs or not, the outcome for democracy is the same:
there are seeds of unhappiness in how we feel about it. Hopefully, there are
causes for optimism, too, yet uneasy emotions may lead us to become
either disenchanted with the system of democracy, distrustful and even
angry with the politicians and voters involved or apathetic to hopes we
may have previously held about the future. As David Runciman, author of
How Democracy Ends, suggests, 'Democracy works best when we take it in
turns to complain about the system. . . [but] ecumenical distrust is something new' (*The Economist*, 2018).

Our efforts to meet or exceed the demands of daily life are shaped by
our individual thoughts and behaviours. Yet, the notion of running a
country – even though likened by one former prime minister to running
a household – is something harder to grasp. The responsibility carried on
behalf of millions in order to exercise power should make the process of
democracy different from dictatorship, yet there may well be rulers who
nevertheless feel it is their destiny to do so and see no need for recourse to
their wider country-folk. The wielding of power in such an autocratic
manner has gained in pace around the world. Showcasing, garnering and
even creating their own popularity and public persona has variously helped
leaders in recent times in Russia, China, the United States of America and
India in trying to tighten their grip on power. Some observers have harked
back to dictators emerging in Germany and Italy in the 1920s and 1930s,

whose use of military might and populist rhetoric was key to their tenure, perhaps after initially using the democratic system to gain office (e.g., Hett, 2018). Scanning across the last 100 years allows us to compare snapshots of leaders' behaviour: from leading a rally chanting against a labelled 'common enemy' to sitting astride their chosen mode of transport – perhaps a motorcycle or armoured vehicle – while accepting the plaudits of cheering crowds. Particular parallels are also evident in steps taken to remove barriers to ruling for life. Not only do these suggest unbridled ambitions to stay atop the political 'greasy pole', but show that public affirmation – either by superficially democratic means or social approval from a political in-group – need only be to 'rubber-stamp' the legitimacy of their leadership. It is in this context that concerns about the viability and survivability of democracy more globally are raised.

Much has been written about the psychological motivations of leaders of all guises in taking power, whether drawing on political legitimacy or none at all. Perhaps just as concerning is how the use or manipulation of a democratic apparatus by an autocrat to gain power may reflect on voters who, initially at least, lend their support, but then find the wheel controlling power pushed beyond their reach. This raises the question of our own psychological needs as electorates. A sense of justice might have us believe it is only a matter of time before dictators fall foul of their own self-belief or delusions and that, at some point, popular uprising – within or from outside their boundaries – consigns them to the history books. However, the notion of ruling without the need to consult meaningfully or to genuinely foster the support of others is a perennial source of fear for the majority and a tempting prospect for the power-hungry, yet it remains a risk in democratic and non-democratic societies. In the fifth century BCE, Athenian safeguards against such abuse of the political system included ostracism for up to ten years! Of course, one difficulty for humankind is the length of time and scale of suffering peoples are forced to endure waiting for abuse by leaders to be exposed or addressed.

So, how can we be sure that democracy is preferable? How can rule for the many be carefully and efficiently realised? First, it requires a shared desire that it should work and, second, a commitment from those holding political office to the welfare of current and future generations, which is hopefully supported by the population. In such a way, history will judge the role of governments in combating the COVID-19 pandemic. Communication between the power-holders and the electorate is key to this understanding and places considerable influence in the hands of the media and its sponsors and owners. Therefore, overly comfortable relations between politicians and the purveyors of media can create problems of their own.

Whatever one's role in a democratic system – as a voter, party member or political decision-maker – the need for control, the search for the empowerment of oneself or others, the notion of freedom of choice in what happens next and an ongoing commitment to citizenship are characteristics that shape our perception of its relative success or failure. Each of these represents a range of psychological constructs that underpin attitudes towards democratic behaviours in society as well as in exercising political power at a national level. In order to understand what makes democracy tick, we must also examine our own motives, expectations and emotions as individuals.

People as Politicians

Unease with politics is an understandable consequence of decisions being made away from the public eye or beyond the easy influence of our lives as citizens. Yet, we should not lose sight of our own role as politicians in daily life, seeking to influence our immediate environments – families, communities and workplaces – by communicating, persuading and acting to achieve change. This can range from efforts to put food on the table to successfully navigating the worlds of work, study and relationships. In addition, each of us may find ourselves operating along a continuum – whether oriented towards our own needs or, indeed, seeking to represent the needs of those around us. One could argue that this is no different a scenario for professional politicians, yet, whether we see politicians as serving themselves or others, it plays an important role in how they are perceived. Naturally, the transparency of the systems in which we and they operate influences such perspectives and, in part, the openness of political processes to public view is due to the nature of representative democratic systems by which politicians are elected to decide on actions on behalf of the electorate. Attention to such dynamics is bound to inspire a range of emotions.

Democracy means something slightly different to so many, but, on any given day, we are aware of actions that run counter to its prized principles. As basic human rights, we are affronted and distressed by attempts to curb freedoms. In response to a brutal crackdown on civilian protests and the arrests of leaders of the political opposition, marches by huge numbers of an unsettled population, carrying white flags and flowers, echoes the same sentiments across 200 years of history from Peterloo to Belarus. Collective action and peaceful protest as expressions of democratic principle demonstrate that political awareness is within all of us and the propensity towards emotion over democratic values should come as no surprise.

It is natural that these emotions should have a voice, for, without their expression, resentment simmers and, with their expression, an uneasy legacy lingers. For the dictator, autocrat or unaccountable government official, here is a conundrum: whether to risk the free expression of emotion by public protest or to contend with the consequences if it is ignored or suppressed? In a democracy, there are expectations of greater tolerance of expression of views, as its essence lies with political freedom and chances of progress, which in turn support advances towards equality. The risk for any democratically elected government is that, once elected, should it ignore its electors' wishes, the chances of re-election are reduced; yet, frustratingly for the electorate, this brings no guarantees of a responsive government. In such cases, what public protest against unpopular policies symbolises can be far stronger than one may assume. For what remains are troubling questions: how does a democratically elected government make such gross errors that it is at odds with the people who originally voted for it? 'Events' (as lamented by former UK Prime Minister Harold Macmillan) play their part, of course, but where the gap in mismatched expectations and the trap of undelivered promises exists, the more a gulf in democratic functioning is apparent. The discretion afforded to leaders to make choices may seem politically necessary, but how well does this serve democracy? Democracy may be the game, but politics are the rules by which it is played – as they are in any autocracy or other system of government.

Achieving procedural democracy, by which the rules with which we live are subject to democratic principles, rather than to political manoeuvrings for those in power, is one difference between having a democratic form of government and a fully functioning democracy (Moghaddam, 2018). In considering the psychological factors involved in successful steps towards democracy, Fathali Moghaddam (2016) has charted the roles of first-, second- and third-order change, following on from his modern-day observations of Iran and the United States of America. Respectively, these point first to large-scale political reform, second to institutional structures to support such reform and finally to the development of democratic characteristics at the level of individual cognitive styles and behaviours. Accordingly, he proposes, 'the psychological citizen can become capable of constructively participating in, and supporting, a democracy through acquiring a variety of cognitive and behavioural skills and practices'

(Moghaddam, 2018, p. 26). Such 'political plasticity', Moghaddam (2018) argues, is needed to cement in place the values that might guarantee the psychological foundations for ensuring the success of democracy, not necessarily from the viewpoint of only one form is right – but from one that minimises the risks of incumbents of any political shade from perpetrating anti-democratic deeds. Therefore, 'For democratic actualisation to occur, the democratic citizen must develop the appropriate social skills to implement action based on the following convictions' (Moghaddam, 2016, p. 50): recognising one's fallibility, questioning societal assumptions, changing opinions based on evidence, seeking knowledge from a range of sources and understanding and learning from people with other life courses, being open to new experiences and to sharing one's own with others, being guided by ethical principles and undertaking pursuit of activities 'of higher value' while recognising the differing worth of experiences. On reading these, one's mind may consider with interest our own habits – as well as those of elected and unelected politicians. This is not to say that people are naturally without the capacity to act democratically in everyday life, but, as Helen Haste and colleagues point out later in this volume, the role of educating for citizenship and meaningfully nurturing such values in society is vital for the future survival of democracy.

From Sabres to Umbrellas: The Fortunes of Democracy

Why does the perception of a threat to democracy evoke strong emotion? For many, ignoring the will of the people represents injustice and is reminiscent of wars necessitated by would-be invaders who care little for the right to vote and free speech. Either way, the unwritten message 'you do not matter' is a powerful call to arms in both material and metaphorical terms. Perhaps it is a more powerful motivator than any subtext suggesting that 'you do matter'!?

Of course, as voters we recognise that policies will not suit everyone equally and, in voting for candidates or supporting a proposition at referendum, we are probably aware of wider considerations than a political party or movement with which we may not agree entirely. So, voting often represents a compromise between what we think and what is on offer and, in this way, can be considered an act of reasonableness on our behalf. Not surprisingly, we expect those we support to treat our vote and our faith in them fairly and with respect. Where such a psychological contract goes unrewarded, we are likely to feel aggrieved or worse. It is fair to say that unmet expectations are the enemies of happiness.

The pro-democracy protests in Hong Kong in August 2019 transformed from largely peaceful gatherings, objecting to reforms shifting the territory towards compliance with the rest of China's non-democratic government system. Huge crowds faced armed police in demonstrations over the proposal to transport those accused of crimes to China, with accompanying concerns about their legal rights. In other words, what appeared to be at stake were the rights of the individual, not only to vote, but to have a voice enshrined in the administration of the law – an issue that formed a cornerstone of the Magna Carta signed in England almost 800 years previously and that is recognised by those denied fair trial around the world. The symbolic use of umbrellas by pro-democracy protesters in Hong Kong to combat the teargas fired by police gave rise to depiction of their action as 'The Umbrella Movement'.

What may not have been apparent to those involved was that, in August 1819 – almost exactly 200 years before the Hong Kong protests, a peaceful demonstration in Manchester, England of 60,000 workers and their families saw calls for political rights and became a symbol of democratic struggle. The marchers, including women wearing white and carrying flowers (also echoed in Belarus in 2020), were met by militia deployed by local magistrates fearful of disorder. Charging through neighbouring streets and into the crowd on horseback with sabres drawn, the soldiers injured over 700 and killed 15 unarmed civilians, including a baby. The bicentenary of what became known as the Peterloo Massacre – so named after the defeat of Napoleon in 1815 and the location in Manchester of St Peter's Fields – was commemorated by a monument, events and marches, in turn characterised by the Brexit-related politics of modern-day Britain. Limited media coverage meant that the significance of the event was less than might have been expected. However, within days, the importance of what had been the largest gathering of UK citizens found resonance with demonstrations for democracy over 5,000 miles away. Not only is democracy a worldwide phenomenon, but so is the struggle to maintain it over time, as well as across the globe.

Similarly, the action of populations taking to the streets is seen across many contexts and countries, voicing concern and protests against threats and destruction of political rights and resources. From the Arab Spring risings of the early 2010s, which sought to overthrow established autocratic regimes, to long-running street battles in Chile in 2019–2020 over proposals to raise transport fares, extreme expressions of emotion about how we are governed and treated as citizens are universally evident. Furthermore, considering the global impact of political emergencies is vital, as these tend not to exist in isolation, but influence events elsewhere, as evidenced by the figure that 3.5 per cent of the world's population are considered migrants (IOM, 2020). It is salutary that 'voting with one's feet', as a result of conflicts in Afghanistan, Iraq, Syria and central Africa, has fuelled a far-reaching diaspora. Similarly, mass migration from nineteenth-century Russia came in response to pogroms and a Tsar who presided over mass hunger and programmes of persecution. For those seeking refuge or economic stability, the precious commodity of political rights can be hard to maintain or – indeed – regain.

Emotions and the Principles of Democracy

In the context of the evolution of democracy, demonstrations of fear and anxiety and tussles fuelled by the prospect of losing valuable commodities and thereby a measure of control are variously echoed across history. Political resources available to the population are frequently rooted in access to natural and essential resources and, therefore, such capital is a critical issue. Conservation of Resources Theory (Hobfoll, 1989) describes the negative psychological impact of the threat of losing what one has. It follows that direct links can be observed between perceptions of threat, associated political rhetoric and motivations to seek redress. If the price of negative emotion is undeliberative attitudes in resolving political matters, how far can positive outcomes for democracy be guaranteed? This is not to suggest that negative political change must flow from the experience of negative emotions. The titles of the pamphlets of Thomas Paine, whose words fuelled the zeal of American uprising against British imperial rule and were used to defend revolutionary ideals in France, exemplify the strategy of evoking and harnessing emotion. 'Common sense' (1776) sold 500,000 copies in the United States of America and 'The rights of man' (1792) is thought to have sold 1.5 million copies by the time of Paine's death in 1809 (National Archives, nd). In such ways, concepts of freedom and equality were given a voice and used as rallying cries for major political change across the Atlantic and, over time, in calling for revolution and experimentation in new forms of government. Marx and Engels' Communist Manifesto (1848) played a similar role in mid-nineteenth century European revolutions and found various expressions in twentieth-century upheaval across the globe, whether for democracy or against it. However, for continuity and progress of a political system, John Stuart Mill (1859), as noted earlier in this chapter, suggested that reflection more than emotion is a prerequisite for successful practice in a democratic society. So, who was right?

It has been argued that support for Brexit (the UK's withdrawal from the European Union) represented a popular backlash against the system and a clawing back of resources with the slogan 'Take back control'. It produced far more than a war of words in Parliament, but also acts of violence against Members of Parliament (MPs) – including murder – and a General Election that put pro-Brexit politicians (known as 'Brexiteers') into a majority government. Amid this, aspersions cast by the prime minister on Parliament and his capacity for provocative comments fanned the flames of discord. While the history of one is not the history of all, such upheaval finds resonance in other countries, including – for example – in the United States of America, where a rise of populism was harnessed by a president uncritically harking back to a so-called 'golden age' and carried significant risks for how democracy was enacted. The advent of a super-ordinate goal – a threat to survival of our species by a virus – certainly provided motivation for all to refocus on a common enemy, for, as history confirms, we do not thrive where division rules.

In recognising that democracy finds expression in a variety of forms, it is important to understand that, however it is manifest, it can in turn influence how we feel about its use and misuse. Accordingly, the role of emotions in narrating the battle for democratic traditions deserves scrutiny, not only for understanding political discourse, but the impact of that discourse on subsequent events. For example, the establishment of the Icelandic parliament (the 'Althing') around 930 CE was notable, not only for what it represented in a proto-democratic form of law-making based on an annual fortnight's gathering of the island's whole community (Byock, 2002), but in the choice of location – on land forfeited following the outlawing of a farmer who had murdered a slave (Bronowski, 1973).

In current times, we are frequently bombarded with information about political events and perspectives likely to arouse a range of accompanying emotions, especially where we perceive criticism of or threats against the political group with which we identify (Huddy, Mason and Aarøe, 2015). It is not surprising that emerging empirical studies shed light on how uncivil verbal attacks against a viewpoint can promote combative partisanship on the part of the listener (Gervais, 2019) and, more widely, the venerated philosopher Martha Nussbaum (2015) has sought to promote understanding of the role of emotions in politics. As the history of democracy necessitates such a focus on relations among and between the rulers and the ruled, traditionally philosophy has promoted values that, in turn, are used to justify that scrutiny and, sometimes, the overthrow of regimes – whether violently or peacefully. These are evident from many sources: from the premise of Hobbes and Locke that governments should safeguard the welfare of the populace, from Voltaire's elucidation of civil liberties, from Wollstonecraft's calls for rights for men and women and from Rousseau's social contract in which law-making was seen as expressing the people's will. Furthermore, the utilitarianism of Bentham and Mill espoused the promotion of the greatest happiness for the greatest number – a concept most apparently resonant with that of democracy.

The Fourth Estate

Casting a retrospective eye over history, it is not fanciful to view the fortunes of democracy as often in flux, whether in conflict within or between parties of rival influence or, indeed, whole populations. One key to the success of this form of government lies with the checks and balances incorporated into the political system or invoked to restore equilibrium and faith in its underlying values. These take a variety of forms and include the notion of a 'free press' or, these days, 'media' – by which political processes and decisions can be scrutinised and relayed to the public – as a cornerstone of democratic functioning. Yet, the last fifty years have seen some of the best and worst fortunes for news reporting. Such a spectrum spans the Watergate revelations of US presidential wrong-doing in the early 1970s to the closure of the 168-year-old UK-based *News of the World* in 2011 following the hacking of a murder victim's phone. It encompasses sacrifices – sometimes by assassination – of reporters' lives in a number of countries worldwide amid regime pressures to advance their own propaganda. As such, the global challenge of political objectivity in search of publicising the 'truth' continues to be played out in public view. 'A check on behalf of the governed and not the governors', a free press was envisioned as giving 'them [the people] full information of their affairs' (Jefferson, 1787). Yet, it is much clearer in modern times that the relationships between media and the people are subject to a range of influences. Not least is the role of those who own and sponsor media outlets, from newspaper proprietors to state outlets and social media entrepreneurs and the algorithms they employ. The potential for cosiness, collaboration and conflicting interests raises questions such as, 'Whose news is this?'

Decisions about which stories to cover and how to cover them are constant in a fast-paced 24/7 media culture with dedicated channels providing rolling news stories and instant commentary. Competition for 'space' is pushed to a premium as complex decisions are reached by unelected individuals about which issues to cover 'in the public interest'. Naturally, journalists work as hard as any occupation to keep audiences informed and relationships with editors are likely to play a key part, but the premium of accuracy remains a cause for vigilance and, sometimes, concern. Not dissociated from this, the labelling of fake news and 'alternative facts' (as described by a US presidential aide) does not signify the birth of the underlying concept of misleading information. There have always been temptations to use propaganda at many levels in politics, whether considered 'spin' to promote positive perceptions or flagrantly misleading messages to stir more extreme emotions. However, the ubiquity of social media serves to emphasise the impact and impetus of information, as it means anyone can become a news source.

At one time considered a democratising force for the expression of opinion, concerns that the Internet is subject to forces of manipulation have been fuelled by the behaviour of some social media organisations, where user profiling of personalised information for political ends has itself brought reputations into question (e.g. use of citizens' data during the 2015 US presidential election). This offers a worrying insight into the potential for exploitation of information, however, the targeted marketing of social media users is commonplace and also widely seen as an extension to political campaigning processes (Dommett and Temple, 2018). Aside from this, there is widespread disquiet over the potential influence via cyber-espionage of 'unfriendly' governments during democratic electoral campaigns.

As consumers of news, how conscious are we of the processes underlying its production and selection for our consumption, or indeed how comfortable are we with its commodification? Do we worry that what we learn from any medium is 'true' or does a level of scepticism or acceptance guide us? Perhaps more importantly for the processes of democracy, how much does the news we feel more comfortable believing actually influence our own political behaviours and, specifically, determine how we vote? We play more than a passive role in using the news, by processing information in ways shaped by psychological as well as political preferences and we would not easily wish to see ourselves 'tricked'. Arguably, news organisations can take a share in the responsibility for political outcomes, yet, in a democracy, government-sponsored attempts to address potential wrong-doing by the media are rare and, as the UK's Leveson inquiry showed in 2012, also require careful handling for fear of undermining the freedom of the media and this cornerstone of democracy itself.

The Structure of This Book

There is no doubt that ours is a future with challenges – yet, challenges are also the history of our species. Naturally, we need to consider how best to proceed and certainty is not always plentiful. Systems of government can underpin successful survival on a large scale, however, the search for answers is by its very nature an optimistic goal and the endeavours of those who have been kind enough to contribute to this book demonstrate a wonderful commitment to sharing understanding. Their generosity comes at an important juncture and stands to provide a great service to us all. Faced with our ongoing personal decisions about democracy, whether to engage, stand back or walk away, this book aims to shed light on the hidden political psychological processes and to interrogate a range of issues that characterise democracy and how (well) it works. We hope you will share this enthusiasm!

Psychology of Democracy: Of the People, By the People, For the People is divided into three sections in recognition of three levels of political and psychological experience suggested by theoretical and practical consider-ations. Established ecological frameworks for contemplating influences upon the lives of individuals (Bronfenbrenner, 1979) have been refined with reference to democracies and clearly indicate the need to understand political experience at a range of levels. Indeed, the structure of this book reflects these levels of consideration proposed by Moghaddam (2018) and explores the psychological conditions and motivations for what he describes as first-, second- and third-order change at the macro-, meso- and micro-levels of our existence. Beginning with the last of these, the book seeks to apply this structured approach to relevant psychological and political factors, using the nomenclature suggested by Abraham Lincoln's oft-quoted Gettysburg address. Organising the content in this way – as outlined below – permits the opportunity to consider political micro-level characteristics of politicians as representatives 'of the people', actions within political meso-level systems enacted 'by the people' and the role of wider macro-level influences of religion, education and media, which set the context 'for the people'.

Of the People

'Of the people' focuses on the psychological characteristics '**of**' individuals who serve as politicians and, at the micro-level of individual, cognitive and social functioning, this section considers politicians from each of these perspectives on the human condition.

In seeking to share an empirically-driven knowledge base, this portion of the book examines the roles and influence of a range of psychological factors – in studies with politicians – that shape and impact on all of our abilities to function. Through focusing on the influence of major personality traits on politicians in their career development, Jo Silvester and Madeleine Wyatt highlight the importance of the role of attributes ascribed to them and, in particular, implications for the emergence of leaders and how personality shapes their success in office, as well as indications for future directions in research. In considering the aspect of personality characterised by basic values, James Weinberg investigates the role of psychological predispositions in the political attitudes held by politicians, examining how far those who run as candidates and become politicians differ in their values from the wider public and how important the public consider these values to be. Turning the focus to what is more clearly visible of politicians at work, Peter Bull and Maurice Waddle review research in which the UK showpiece parliamentary confrontations known as 'Prime Minister's Questions' are analysed for their adversarial nature, use of equivocation in dealing with questions and the impact of this often-lively political interchange on public perceptions of Parliament and politics.

In order to aid our understanding of how politicians think, Peter Suedfeld explores 'cognitive interactionism' in which individual capacities to process information, make decisions, adopt perspectives and perceive the social world can vary depending on the political contexts in which these occur; taking into account viewpoints across the political spectrum, positions of relative power as well as the influence of stress. Given the importance of decision-making in politics, Barbara Vis and Sjoerd Stolwijk use data drawn from experiments with politicians and members of the public in the Netherlands to ask whether and how they differ and consider the roles of cognitive shortcuts and political experience in the judgements at which they arrive. In an arena where politicians are less often considered, Ashley Weinberg reflects on the significance and prevalence of politicians' experiences of psychological ill health, drawing on international studies assessing symptoms and reviewing the potentially damaging impact of sources of pressure on MPs and the functioning of political workplaces.

By the People

If there is a key to answering the big challenges for survival then arguably it lies in the capacity to harness the combined abilities of our species to do so. Government '**by**' systems that comprise people tends to underpin the success of such efforts and, traditionally, democracy has garnered a reputation as a more inclusive – although far from perfect – approach than alternatives (Flinders, 2016). Nevertheless, the fortunes of democracy are mixed, as research and events have borne out. Despite the increased proportion of the world's nations adopting democratic systems of government over the last thirty years, levels of public distrust with these political processes are high (van Prooijen and van Lange, 2014). Efforts to meet global challenges for survival depend on systems of government and the people within them, whether as citizens, elected politicians or employees of political institutions, yet our understanding of the psychological factors that underpin the functioning of democracy is relatively limited (Conover, Searing and Crewe, 2002). This section of the book considers how democracy operates at the level of institutions and processes charged with maintaining the political system. Tracing the chronology of political involvement that brings voters and politicians into the same arena, 'By the people' examines social and political experiences and behaviours in the democratic process at the meso-level.

This section seeks insights into the psychology of democracy as its biggest stakeholders – the voters and the politicians – contemplate one another around the globe. Beginning with the development of the relationship between would-be voters and political institutions and processes, this section opens with Daniel Miranda, Juan Carlos Castillo, Catalina Miranda and José Conejeros considering whether civic knowledge affects trust in political institutions among school-age students surveyed in Latin America, where positive attitudes towards aspects of authoritarianism suggest concerning trends in advance of reaching voting age. Seeking to capitalise on what appeals to the electorate, perhaps it is not surprising to learn of the assertive styles of communication observed in use by would-be leaders – including the subsequent prime minister – on the campaign trail in India, as the detailed analysis by Rukmini Bhaya Nair reveals politicians' extensive use of linguistic and gestural devices in seeking to influence voters in the world's largest democracy. Yet, how do political tactics such as negative campaigning and false information impact on potential voters in the context of the United States of America? David Redlawsk, Kyle Mattes and Karol Solis Menco simulated a presidential primary election to test the impact of online campaigns and fact-checking – they confirm that negative campaigns grab attention, but, in this study, it was not attention of the desired kind and lying politicians were indeed punished at the virtual ballot box.

This begs the important question, what really happens to us when we vote? Drawing on surveys conducted in the United States of America, South Africa, the UK, France, Germany and Georgia, Sarah Harrison argues for electoral psychology as representing a major shift from focusing on what political institutions require to what matters to citizens. This necessitates a new understanding of positive and negative emotions as experienced before, during and after voting, as well as of the roles of identity and collective assumptions about other voters in exercising these. Once in office, what can leaders do to safeguard their political futures? The background of selected policy areas of immigration and climate change set the scene for frequent changes in leader in Australia, where attempts to rebuild trust through a triad of integrity, competence and responsiveness are analysed by Joakim Eidenfalk and Stuart Woodcock in case studies of three prime ministers. This brings the section to its natural conclusion: leaving office. The psychological impact of the end of political careers is examined by Jane Roberts, drawing on her in-depth interviews that probe the experience of loss and potential dislocation in UK MPs and council leaders, whether deciding to go or forced by circumstances. Yet, she asks, is democracy too easily discarding the skills of its servants, as well as the need to treat politicians with more compassion and inadvertently obliging political survivors to tighten their grip?

For the People

This section of the book considers social-psychological factors operating 'for' all of us, shaping the macro-level contexts within which we live and the degree to which these significantly underpin the relative success or failure of democratic systems.

While humankind faces enormous threats to its existence, clearly there is no democratic mandate for an ongoing age of species extinctions. However, it is widely held that – ultimately – these cataclysmic possibilities are the cumulative result of everyday behaviours of citizens, organisations and nations. This attests to the associated behavioural challenge faced in our daily lives – when the problems are owned by us alone, it can be difficult enough to address, but, when these are global in their impact, it is far harder to envision how we might make the difference and swim against the tide. Democracy faces a similar challenge. 'How does my vote make any difference?' is a common question posed at elections. At this level, self-worth and possessing a sense of agency play important roles in our perceptions – perhaps far more so than has been acknowledged. So, what are the factors that shape the psychological backdrop to our political experience?

Understandably, our focus tends to be drawn to issues that define our daily concerns – whether preoccupations with ongoing conflicts or trade, or personal access to health, social care and education. Yet, the psychological processes that shape our beliefs and feelings about such weighty matters are often hidden from view. 'For the people' assesses wider societal influences on our psychological experiences of politics and democracy in particular.

Beginning with an examination of the links between personality and the moral underpinnings of democracy, Gian Vittorio Caprara highlights the significance of both individual and collective moral responsibility upon citizens living in a democracy and how our relative successes in this endeavour are rooted in relevant values and self-knowledge. Benjamin Bowman, Thalia Magioglou and Helen Haste trace the fortunes of civic engagement in school-age students, drawing on qualitative data from the UK and Greece, recognising the real and potential challenges facing young people and their aspirations in times of dramatic change. The wider societal context is further examined in the four remaining chapters of this section, with consideration of religion and media, as well as prevailing political contexts – both national and group-based – which are not widely considered democratic.

Gizem Arikan and Pazit Ben-Nun Bloom draw on worldwide survey data to focus on the relationship between religious identity and support for democracy, which appears to be influenced, not only by belonging to a religious minority, but by how the minority community is treated by the state, with clear implications for the strength of their religious identity. Media provide another important lens through which we experience politics and major technological advances have reshaped how and where we access political news and information. Sharon Coen and Karl Turgut Maloney Yorganci consider how political knowledge is manifest, as well as ways in which it is developed through interaction with the Internet and traditional news media, proposing a self-regulated learning model that shapes what we view as political knowledge, how it makes us feel and what it means for how we see ourselves.

China, with the world's largest national population, is not generally viewed as a democracy outside of the country. However, democracy is widely considered within China and Yida Zhai uses a social-psychological framework to analyse the impact of economic modernisation and political culture on popular perceptions of democracy and the potential for democratisation. The creation and operation of cultural norms and what implications these have for political reasoning are examined by Roderick Dubrow-Marshall in unpicking radicalised conceptions of democracy, as envisioned by extremist groupings, whether political or not.

What This Book Does

In seeking to further our understanding of the links between psychology and politics, this is the first book written by scientists from many disciplines about the functioning of democracy and the influences upon our experiences of it, based on research findings from around the world. Contributors also include participants of the Psychology of Democracy conferences that began as biannual events at the University of Salford in 2015 – these inspired the book and curiously predated the political phenomena that saw the UK retreat from the European Union and the election of a populist president in the United States of America.

This volume expands its focus to feature new research findings from researchers on the influences of relevant public and political behaviour in North and South America, Asia, Africa and Australia, as well as Europe. In recognition of the many different perspectives and influences involved in the wide-ranging concept of democracy, it is important to consider its worldwide context. As such, *Psychology of Democracy* is unique in providing an empirically informed psychological analysis of our capability to address global political turmoil and change.

The book brings together academics from multi-disciplinary specialities including psychology, political science, communication, sociology, linguistics, education and psychiatry to consider human aspects of democratic government and citizenship. Using empirical data gathered through research using a range of methodological paradigms at international, national and regional levels, these academics aim to address the key questions of how well democracy works and how well it can work, taking into account the psychology of political organisations, political processes, societal influences such as education, religion, culture, media and new technology and the people involved, including politicians, voters and non-voters in democratic and non-democratic contexts.

The Psychology of Politicians (Weinberg, 2012), published by Cambridge University Press, was the first research-based book to examine the hidden processes that influence how politicians behave, showcasing insights from European researchers into their functioning. *Psychology of Democracy* casts the research net globally, shedding new light on how social, cultural and other psychological processes impact on the democratic experiences of those who govern and are governed, as well as examining the factors that shape behaviour in a range of political arenas. As the significance of the motivations and behaviours that characterise systems of government gathers pace, it is becoming more evident that, while the public remains sceptical of politics, a failure to understand how it operates can impact on us all and on the effective functioning of democracy, whether actualised or not.

Jacob Bronowski helped to summarise this dilemma in *The Ascent of Man* (1973):

> If we are anything, we must be a democracy of the intellect. We must not perish by the distance between people and government, between people and power, by which Babylon and Egypt and Rome failed. And that distance can only be conflated, can only be closed, if knowledge sits in the homes and heads of people with no ambition to control others, and not up in the isolated seats of power (p. 435).

Similarly, Rajni Kothari, during his last interview, given in 2012, echoed these sentiments: 'I also suggest that intellectuals must intervene in the political process by linking critical ideas to political ideas. If we close the possibility of criticism, the gap between ideas and processes will increase.' Recognising the role and threat of inequality in our experiences of government, Ruth Bader Ginsburg (2014) went further: 'I think the notion that we have all the democracy that money can buy strays so far from what our democracy is supposed to be.' Taken in the round, the words of such eminent thinkers serve to emphasise the role to be played by the citizenry, including politicians, media and academics, in raising awareness and promoting good practice in government of the people, by the people, for the people.

REFERENCES

Lord Acton. Lord Acton to Archbishop Mandell Creighton, 5 April 1887. Accessed at: https://oll.libertyfund.org/quote/lord-acton-writes-to-bishop-creighton-that-the-same-moral-standards-should-be-applied-to-all-men-polit ical-and-religious-leaders-included-especially-since-power-tends-to-corrupt-and-absolute-power-corrupts-absolutely-1887.

Bader Ginsburg, R. (2014). Interview. The New Republic, 28 September.

Bagehot, W. (1873). *The English constitution*, 2nd Edition. London: Little, Brown and Company.

Bronfenbrenner, U. (1979). *The ecology of human development: Experiments by nature and design*. Cambridge, MA: Harvard University Press.

Bronowski, J. (1973). *The ascent of man*. London: British Broadcasting Corporation.

Byock, J. (2002). The Icelandic Althing: Dawn of parliamentary democracy. In J. M. Fladmark (Ed.), *Heritage and identity: Shaping the nations of the north* (pp 1–18). The Heyerdahl Institute and Robert Gordon University. Donhead St. Mary, Shaftesbury: Donhead. Available at: www.viking.ucla.edu/publica tions/articles/icelandic_allthing.pdf

Clarke, N., Jennings, W., Moss, J. and Stoker, G. (2016). *The rise of anti-politics in Britain*. Southampton: University of Southampton.

Conover, P. J., Searing, D. D. and Crewe, I. M. (2002). The deliberative potential of political discussion. *British Journal of Political Science*, 32(1), 21–62.

Dommett, K. and Temple, L. (2018). Digital campaigning: The rise of Facebook and satellite campaigns. *Parliamentary Affairs*, 71(1), 189–202. doi:10.1093/pa/gsx056

Flinders, M. (2016). The problem with democracy. *Parliamentary Affairs*, 69, 181–203.

Foa, R. S., Klassen, A., Slade, M., Rand, A. and Collins, R. (2020). *The global satisfaction with democracy report 2020*. Cambridge, UK: Centre for the Future of Democracy.

Gervais, B. T. (2019). Rousing the partisan combatant: Elite incivility, anger and anti-deliberative attitudes. *Political Psychology*, 40, 637–655.

Hansard Society (2019). Audit of political engagement: The 2019 report. Available at: www.hansardsociety.org.uk/publications/reports/audit-of-politi cal-engagement-16

Hett, C. H. (2018). *The death of democracy: Hitler's rise to power*. London: William Heinemann.

Hobfoll, S. E. (1989). Conservation of resources: A new attempt at conceptualizing stress. *American Psychologist*, 44(3), 513–524.

Huddy, L., Mason, L. and AarØe, L. (2015). Expressive partisanship: Campaign involvement, political emotion and partisan identity. *American Political Science Review*, 109(1), 1–17.

International Organization for Migration (United Nations) (2020). World migration report 2020. Accessed at: www.un.org/sites/un2.un.org/files/wmr_2020.pdf

Jefferson, T. (1787). Jefferson's preference for 'newspapers without government' over 'government without newspapers'. Available at: https://oll.libertyfund.org/quotes/302

Kothari, R. (2012). Interview with Rajni Kothari, Founder-Director, Centre for the Study of Developing Societies by Hilal Ahmed, Priyadarshini Vijaisri and Abhay Kumar Dubey, CSDS, Delhi. Available at: www.india-seminar.com/2012/639/639_interview_kothari.htm

Lührmann, A. and Lindberg, S. I. (2019). A third wave of autocratization is here: What is new about it? *Democratization*, 26(7), 1095–1113. doi:10.1080/13510347.2019.1582029

Mill. J. S. (1859/1983). *On liberty (Reprinted)*. Middlesex: Penguin.

Moghaddam, F. (2018). *The road to actualized democracy: A psychological explanation*. Niels Bohr Lecture in Cultural Psychology, Aalborg University. Available at: www.ccp.aau.dk/digitalAssets/150/150776_niels-bohr-lecture-road-to-actualized-democracy.pdf

(2016). *The psychology of democracy*. Washington, DC: American Psychological Association Books.

National Archives (n.d.) Thomas Paine's Rights of Man. www.nationalarchives
.gov.uk/pathways/citizenship/struggle_democracy/docs/rights_man.htm
Accessed 30 April 2020.

Nussbaum, M. (2015). *Political emotions: Why love matters for justice.* Cambridge,
MA: Harvard University Press.

Stoker, G. and Evans, M. (Eds.) (2016). *Evidence-based policy making in the social
sciences: Methods that matter.* Bristol: Policy Press.

The Economist (2018). The death of democracy and birth of an unknown beast;
interview with David Runciman, 13 September. Available at: www.economist
.com/open-future/2018/09/13/the-death-of-democracy-and-birth-of-an-unknown-
beast

The Sunday Times (2020). The Sunday Times rich list. 17 May.

van Prooijen, J. W. and van Lange, P. A. M. (2014). *Power, politics and paranoia.*
Cambridge, UK: Cambridge University Press.

Weinberg, A. (Ed.) (2012). *The psychology of politicians.* Cambridge, UK:
Cambridge University Press.

PART I

Of the People

CHAPTER 2

Personality, Politics and Strong Democracy
A Review of Research and Future Directions

Jo Silvester and Madeleine Wyatt

Introduction

US presidential elections in recent years have been dominated by media discussion of candidates' personal qualities, such as 'conciliatory' or 'sleepy' Joe Biden and 'bold' versus 'messiah complex' Trump. Supporters and opponents alike appear equally keen to identify, celebrate and vilify the personalities of candidates, as well as of those who achieve office. Likewise, candidates and their supporters expend significant effort (and resources) in attempts to influence and shape how members of the public perceive their personality as well as that of their opponents – and, with growing use of social media, they have more opportunity than ever to do so.

The United States of America is certainly not alone: interest in the personalities of political elites is a global phenomenon – and one that shows little sign of diminishing. Researchers have argued that politics has become increasingly personalised across many Western democracies (Caprara and Zimbardo, 2004; Garzia, 2011), with candidate characteristics such as personality, integrity and appearance becoming more important for voters, and a more dominant focus in the overall evaluation of candidates and political elites (Caprara et al., 2006; Nai, Martínez and Maier, 2019; Wattenberg, 1991). Although personalisation applies to many prominent leaders in business, sport and the public sector, the personalities of political leaders appear to have a special hold over our imagination, and an important impact on our engagement with democratic process. Unsurprisingly, perhaps, such deep-rooted interest has also generated a wealth of research in political science and psychology (c.f. Caprara and Silvester, 2018). One popular question is whether strong democracy can be developed by identifying and nurturing individuals with the characteristics needed to become good political leaders capable of delivering responsible government.

Our aims in this chapter are to introduce and provide an overview of existing research on personality and political leadership, identify gaps and consider areas for future studies investigating relationships between personality characteristics of political leaders and the development of strong democracy. We begin by examining what is meant by personality, how it has been conceptualised by researchers and why it is considered important for political leadership. Next, we draw on existing studies from political science and psychology to examine evidence that personality contributes to political leadership, and the theories and methods used to generate this evidence. Building synergies with the broader leadership literature, we divide our focus into two areas. First, we consider *leadership emergence* in politics, by examining research that explores whether personality characteristics influence an individual's attraction to politics, their desire – or motivation – to become a politician, how politicians' characteristics are perceived during elections and their success in political campaigns. In short, we ask, 'Do personality characteristics contribute to the likelihood that an individual will be elected to political office?' Second, we consider *leadership effectiveness* (i.e. the success of an elected member in political office) by examining evidence that personality characteristics influence how politicians behave in office, including their decision-making and their likelihood of gaining more senior positions within their political party or legislature. Finally, we consider future directions for research and practice in this area, including the development of new methods for examining personality in political elites, as well as likely challenges, including research that accommodates the need for political leaders to balance authenticity with efforts to present in different ways to appeal to and persuade diverse groups of voters.

Personality and Politics

Although there are many different ways of studying and thinking about personality, psychological approaches to its understanding and examination are broadly concerned both with what makes us different and what makes us similar to others. Personality can be conceptualised as the characteristic sets of behaviours, cognitions and emotional patterns that evolve from biological and environmental factors (Corr and Matthews, 2009). Caprara and Cervone (2000) describe personality as the patterns of behavioural habits and qualities expressed through physical and mental activities that characterise individuals as purposive agents and distinguish them from others with whom they interact.

Studies of personality and political leadership have been similarly diverse. These have explored many different individual characteristics, such as personality traits, motives, cognitive style, values and biological traits (e.g. facial appearance), of different populations (e.g. political candidates, elected members in local, national and international legislatures, and leaders of political parties, presidents, prime ministers) and in the context of multiple political outcomes (campaign performance, voter perceptions, successful legislation, contribution to debates, avoidance of war). We begin with a brief introduction of the aspects of personality studied in political elites.

Trait theories are among the oldest and most researched aspects of personality. Defined as 'dimensions of individual differences in tendencies to show consistent patterns of thought, feelings, and actions' (McCrae and Costa, 1990, p. 23), personality traits are relatively stable, enduring dispositions that influence how individuals experience, interact and, potentially, change their environment. It is assumed that, within a population, people vary in the extent to which they possess particular traits. Psychologists also differentiate between single- and multi-trait theories of personality. Single traits relevant to political research include Machiavellianism, a personality disposition reflecting an individual's willingness to control or manipulate others (Christie and Geis, 1970); Authoritarianism, an individual difference originally identified by Adorno et al. (1950) associated with predisposition to conform and obey authority (Duckitt, 2020); and Narcissism (Raskin and Hall, 1979), where those scoring high tend to lack consideration for others, and engage in bragging and exaggeration of personal accomplishments (Hart, Adams and Burton, 2016).

Since the 1970s, personality researchers have sought to identify the small number of core personality traits that can explain personality across populations and cultures. A substantial body of evidence now exists to support a five-factor model (FFM) of personality (McCrae, 2009) that comprises Extraversion, Conscientiousness, Openness to Experience, Agreeableness and Neuroticism. According to Costa and McCrae (2006), extraverts tend to be more outgoing, sociable, persuasive and energetic than introverts; conscientious individuals tend to be achievement-oriented, reliable and likely to persevere in the face of setbacks; openness to experience relates to individuals' need for variety, novelty and change; agreeableness refers to an individual's level of compliance, altruism and trust; neuroticism (also referred to as emotional stability) is typically associated with being more anxious and less able to deal effectively with conflict and criticism. Researchers (e.g. Mondak, 2010) have theorised the importance of the FFM for understanding political leadership.

All of these traits are normally distributed, with people varying along a continuum on each, and have been found to predict a diverse range of outcomes, including leadership emergence and effectiveness in non-political work contexts (e.g. Judge et al., 2002). Paradoxically, in some instances, the same trait may predict different political leadership outcomes (Wyatt and Silvester, 2018).

Other individual characteristics included within a broader psychological conception of personality, and considered important for leadership, include intelligence or cognitive ability and cognitive style (Judge, Colbert and Ilies, 2004); motivation and ambition; empathy and charisma. All have been explored in relation to political leadership. However, psychologists also differentiate between biological traits (e.g. facial appearance, height), psychological traits (e.g. personality, intelligence), or 'basic tendencies', and also characteristic adaptations, which are considered the consequences of traits, such as needs, values and motives (McCrae and Sutin, 2018). Values are relevant for political leadership because values refer to what an individual considers important and will therefore drive their actions, determine how they judge others and justify their choices (Caprara et al., 2006). Needs, motives and values are features of personality that relate to the nature of goals set by individuals and how these goals are pursued.

Leader Emergence

In leadership research more widely, psychologists differentiate between 'leader emergence' and 'leader effectiveness' – emergence focuses on the factors that differentially impact on whether an individual is likely either to be identified as someone with the qualities needed to be appointed as a leader (e.g. leader selection) or to become a future leader (e.g. supported as a prospective parliamentary candidate). Similarly, in business, leader emergence may occur when an employee is identified as having the potential to move to a more senior role with managerial responsibilities or when an individual from outside the company is recruited into a leadership role. In both cases, the individual is perceived to possess the 'right' qualities by one or more with the power to promote or appoint them to a leadership role. However, in politics, leader emergence is more complicated because it requires that an individual gains support and therefore legitimacy through the democratic process of an election. In this section, we examine the relevance of personality for political leadership emergence in four areas:

(i)   How does personality influence the likelihood that an individual will stand for election and become a political leader?

(ii) How does personality impact on what sort of political leader an individual wants to become (i.e. what they stand for)?

(iii)   How do the judgements of personality made by party selectors impact whether individuals are chosen to stand as a political candidate?

(iv)   How do personality attributes influence political campaigning and voter perceptions of political candidates?

Political Engagement

It has long been recognised that the desire to become a politician can begin at a very young age. Studies of political socialisation point to the importance of family, upbringing, schooling and networks on the emergence of political elites (Langton, 1969). However, psychologists – and, increasingly, political scientists – are exploring how personality contributes to leadership emergence by examining whether politicians demonstrate personalities that differ from those of the general public. These studies utilise standardised questionnaire measures of personality and compare 'typical' or average personalities of politicians with those of members of the public. For example, Best (2011) asked German members of the federal, state and European parliaments (n = 1,223) to self-rate themselves on an FFM personality measure, and then compared their scores with self-ratings on the same measure provided by the general public (n = 17,300). In a similar study, Caprara et al. (2010) compared the self-rated personality of Italian politicians with that of the general public. Both studies found that politicians score higher on extraversion and openness to experience than members of the public, and lower than members of the public on neuroticism, agreeableness and conscientiousness. More recently, Schumacher and Zettler (2019) replicated these results in Denmark; yet, they also found that politicians rated themselves higher on honesty–humility, which prompts questions about the possibility of impression management. Importantly, however, research shows that personality traits may only contribute some of the variance in political outcomes, with situational variables, followers, levels of support and observer characteristics also being important.

Motivation to Stand for Election

A key question often asked of political candidates is *why* they want to stand for election: are there personality traits that make individuals more predisposed to seek political office? Dietrich, Lasley, Mondak, Remmel and Turner (2012) found that US legislators were more interested in standing for higher political office if they reported being extroverted and emotionally stable, with the authors suggesting these individuals relish the limelight of the political stage and are able to manage the stressful, combative nature of the campaign and cope with potential defeat.

Political motivation has also been linked to McClelland's (1987) trait-like need for achievement (nAch: to excel, compete and achieve potential), need for power (nPow: to be influential) and need for affiliation (nAff: to form close personal relationships). NPow is most often associated with politicians because individuals driven by power are likely to prefer engaging in competitive campaigns and seek contexts that grant status and control over others; they are also likely to appeal to the electorate because they are persuasive, make strong decisions and are therefore viewed as charismatic (Rohrer, 2014). Accordingly, US presidents and UK prime ministers high on a need for power are more likely to be rated as 'great' by observers (Suedfeld, Cross and Brcic, 2011; Winter, 1987).

Individuals' propensity to seek power is a key feature of research on political will. In political science, political will is considered a collective phenomenon that gauges support among decision-makers for a particular issue (Post, Raile and Raile, 2010). However, in the organisational literature, political will represents individual political motivation, where individuals engage in political activity to either achieve their own personal goals (self-serving) or support others (benevolence: Kapoutsis et al., 2017; Treadway, 2012), and both forms are related to successful political behaviour in the workplace (Kapoutsis et al., 2017). Although individual political will has not yet been studied in politicians, it is conceivable that self-serving and benevolent motivations guide different campaign strategies, with the former being less appealing to voters if made apparent.

In the political literature, this ties to the notion of 'character'. Political candidates who are perceived to lack character are also perceived to be motivated by self-serving goals such as the perks that come with political office (Callander, 2008); in contrast, candidates perceived to have character are considered motivated by the opportunity to implement policy they care about (Kartik and McAfee, 2007). Accordingly, voters are assumed to prefer policy-motivated candidates, because they are authentic and put greater effort into achieving political goals. The implication is that candidates motivated by political privileges may be more strategic in their campaigns by imitating policy-motivated candidates to conceal their opportunistic and surface-level ambitions. In a study of US governors, Fredriksson, Wang and Mamun (2011) argued they found evidence of this strategy because governors who won repeated elections and ended up as 'lame ducks' (i.e. with a binding term limit) set significantly less challenging environmental policy goals than governors eligible for re-election, suggesting this group of governors is largely office-motivated. However, Callander (2008) found office-motivated candidates did not dominate elections, giving hope that numerous political candidates have character and are standing because they are sincere in implementing the policies they espouse.

Values are also likely to be important for understanding why politicians choose to stand for election or re-election, because they inform politicians' political message (or vision), which explains what they stand for, what they hope to achieve in office and why they want the public to vote for them to become their democratically elected leader. Values are cognitive representations of desirable, abstract, trans-situational goals that serve as guiding principles in a person's life (Schwartz, 1992, 2017). Schwartz (1994) argued that sets of basic personal values underlie political ideologies and attitudes and ten values have demonstrated predictive validity for political orientation and activism (Schwartz et al., 2014; Vecchione et al., 2015). Basic personal values are important because they act as standards and guiding principles for how people live their lives, what they strive to achieve and how they are prepared and willing to act. Basic personal values also serve as standards for judging behaviour, events and people, finding expression in all domains of life and, therefore, underlying our attitudes and opinions (Rokeach, 1973; Schwartz, 2006). However, values are important in politics because they help in deciding how an individual will act in power, and in communicating their political values these values act as a guide for voters to understand what they believe is important and how they will behave if elected. In short, values communicated as part of a candidate's and political party's vision and manifesto are key to gaining support and, therefore, leadership emergence via election (see Chapter 3 by James Weinberg).

Becoming a Candidate

In democracies, most elected members belong to a political party; these can have considerable power over who becomes a political candidate and campaigns for election as the party's representative in a local constituency. Indeed, party selection procedures have been described as 'the secret garden of politics' (Gallagher and Marsh, 1988). In the British context, political party control takes two forms. First, political parties exert central control when members of the central executive or candidates committee assess potential candidates and approve (or not) individuals as prospective parliamentary candidates (PPCs) for the party. Next, PPCs can apply to local associations with a vacancy for a candidate, where they compete alongside other applicants to be chosen by members of a local party selectorate. Personality is relevant for leadership emergence in candidate selection, because, in judging an individual as a potential candidate, selection panels are concerned with whether they possess the characteristics needed to appeal to voters, win votes and improve the party's chances of retaining or winning the seat; whether they possess characteristics deemed necessary to be an effective political leader; and the integrity and values to remain loyal to the party and their constituents once in office.

Silvester and Dykes (2007) describe the use of critical thinking skills as part of the UK Conservative Party selection process, as well as competencies such as leading and motivating and political conviction (see Silvester, 2012). However, a particular challenge for those responsible for political selection processes is ensuring that the personality traits being assessed are relevant to the role and free from bias. Traditionally, political parties have sought representatives who exhibit charisma, gravitas and good media presence, with a bias towards typically masculine qualities (Murray, 2010). More informal practices can also be imbued with gender bias: candidates may be required to demonstrate strong networks, notwithstanding structural disadvantages that can mean women are less likely to have access to powerful networks of political contacts because they are dominated by men (Bjarnegård and Kenny, 2015). Yet, despite efforts to standardise and reduce bias in candidate selection at a party level (Krook and Childs, 2010; Silvester and Dykes, 2007), there is still evidence that women can experience barriers to their political participation. Worldwide, only 25 per cent of national parliamentarians, and just 6 per cent of heads of state, are women (UN Women, 2018).

Getting Elected: Candidate Effects

Not surprisingly, a substantial number of studies have investigated what candidate characteristics might improve a candidate's chances of being elected. In political science, this is often referred to as 'candidate effects' (i.e. what is it about a political candidate that means they are more likely to win votes?) as opposed to 'campaign effects' (i.e. how can a campaign be run in order to increase votes received?). Most studies consider voters' beliefs about desirable personality characteristics in political candidates, or voter perceptions of candidate personality inferred from their behaviour or communication (DeVries and van Prooijen, 2019). Some experimental studies reveal a preference for certain types of candidates based on stereotypes relating to the gender or perceived sex of a candidate or ethnicity (Campbell and Cowley, 2014). Political science studies of candidate effects have broadened characteristics to include candidate education, income, occupation and whether they are local to the constituency (e.g. Campbell and Cowley, 2014; Campbell and Lovenduski, 2015; Vivyan and Wagner, 2015). Deluga (2001) found that voters identify the ability to empathise as a key trait required by political leaders. Caprara, Vecchione and Schwartz (2012) also found that people who vote are more likely to have congruence with the values of politicians. Other studies have also shown that electoral success depends on voters judging a candidate to be trustworthy and have integrity (Deluga, 1998; Pillai et al., 2003).

Notably few studies have captured self-report personality data from political candidates ahead of elections (see, for example, Costantini and Craik, 1980). However, in a recent study of candidate effects, we found that political skill, self-efficacy and campaign intentions, self-reported by parliamentary candidates three months before polling day, had a small but significant positive effect on their performance in the 2010 British general election (Silvester et al., 2020). Therefore, while self-report data can be very difficult to access (particularly from candidates ahead of elections), these findings suggest this is a potentially rich source of information for researchers investigating personality and political elites.

There are a number of biological traits that voters use to make judgements. Interestingly, height appears to predict the number of votes presidential candidates receive (Stulp et al., 2013), potentially explaining why many US presidents, including Trump, Obama and Kennedy, measure above six foot, with Abraham Lincoln being tallest at six foot four (POTUS.com, 2020: we assume they measured him without the stovepipe hat). Election losers are also estimated to be less 'formidable' in terms of height and strength (Knapen, Blaker and Pollet, 2017). Yet, while there might be evolutionary reasons why we would want tall leaders (Murray and Schmitz, 2011), there are few reasons why height is relevant for contemporary political roles.

Likewise, a great deal of research has examined how individuals may use facial appearance to make judgements about the characteristics of aspiring and incumbent leaders. Facial images have been found to predict hypothetical and actual votes in political elections (Sussman, Petkova and Todorov, 2013). Factors such as facial symmetry, jaw line and eyebrow distance influence whether candidates are rated as charismatic, honest, likeable, trustworthy, aggressive, intelligent or competent (Olivola and

Todorov, 2010). Faces that look competent (i.e. intelligent, reliable) have the strongest relationship with electoral outcomes. When asking participants to guess the winners and runners-up of US Senate elections from photographs, Todorov et al. (2005) found that faces rated as competent were the election winners in 70 per cent of races. Although facial appearance does not seem to impact performance in political office (Wyatt and Silvester, 2018), these findings do suggest that the way images and photographs are used in campaigns might impact elections (Schill, 2012).

The predictive impact of biological traits on electoral outcomes demonstrates that it is not just traits that politicians actually possess that impact their leadership emergence, it is also important to examine characteristics inferred from, or attributed to, politicians by voters. As voters have little interaction with candidates, they are likely to rely on 'implicit leadership theories' about what makes political candidates 'leader-like' (Lord, Foti and De Vader, 1984). This can mean that candidates are evaluated on characteristics that seem to matter for leadership, but are not actually relevant for political office (Antonakis, 2011).

Gender is one such characteristic that has received a great deal of interest in political and leadership research (McLaughlin et al., 2018). Although women are often as likely as men to win elections (Lawless, 2015), they need to overcome the challenges of voters ascribing them traits that are often based on stereotypes, or cognitive shortcuts that lead individuals to assign characteristics to others based on their social identity. Accordingly, Eagly's Role Congruity Theory (Eagly and Karau, 2002) research on political leadership finds that the expected requirements of political roles tend to relate to masculine stereotypes (e.g. capable, assertive, dominant), rather than the traits typically ascribed to women (e.g. caring, cooperative, likeable), meaning men are viewed as better equipped to take on such leadership roles (Aaldering and Van Der Pas, 2018). Yet, in an analysis of political stereotypes, Schneider and Bos (2014) found that female politicians are also perceived as not possessing the strengths stereotypical of women (e.g. empathetic, sensitive) and are instead evaluated negatively (e.g. uptight, ambitious) and assessed on deficits in masculine traits (e.g. lack of leadership, low competence).

These findings reflect media coverage of high-profile women political candidates, such as that labelling Hillary Clinton as being cold, aloof and lacking in stamina and strength during the 2016 US presidential campaign (Casesse and Holman, 2018). It also explains why female politicians are often attacked on their lack of femininity and bearing of feminine roles such as 'mother' (Campbell and Childs, 2010). For example, UK Prime

Minister Teresa May and Australian Prime Minister Julia Gillard were both criticised for not being able to relate to policy issues because they do not have children. It is, therefore, more straightforward for male political candidates to manage impressions during campaigns, whereas women need to work hard to break down stereotypes that do not match with voters' notions of the personality characteristics required of successful political leaders.

Leader Effectiveness

Having considered evidence that personality characteristics contribute to nascent political careers and success in achieving political office (i.e. *leadership emergence*), we next turn to the concept of how well individuals perform their roles and achieve success once elected to political office (i.e. *leader effectiveness*). In traditional work contexts, leadership effectiveness might be considered in relation to a manager's success in achieving or exceeding the objectives or targets set for them in their role, or the extent to which a chief executive, for example, improves company performance. In these situations, performance is articulated and operationalised in terms of observable and agreed outcomes (e.g., human resource targets, shareholder dividends). Performance of leaders in more traditional work contexts has been the focus of much research, including the contribution of personality characteristics. Identification and measurement of personality traits originally prompted a number of studies concerned with exploring whether specific traits increase the likelihood of individuals becoming and being effective as leaders (Judge et al., 2002), although studies have also shown that the contribution of traits is relatively small, and that no one set of these guarantees successful leaders.

The contribution of personality to leader effectiveness is even more difficult to determine in politics for two reasons: (1) politicians are more difficult to access and (2) the nature of good and poor role performance is more contested and therefore difficult to operationalise. In this section, we consider theorised relationships between personality and behaviour in political office (e.g. decision-making), and evidence that personality characteristics influence how well politicians perform their roles (e.g. re-election, achieving senior positions in their political party or legislature). We also draw comparisons and identify differences with studies of leadership in non-political work contexts.

Personality and Political Leadership

There is a long history of researchers seeking to identify personality characteristics associated with success in political roles (c.f. Barber, 1972;

George and George, 1998; Hermann, 1980; House, Spangler and Woycke, 1991; Kowert, 1996; Lyons, 1997; McCann, 1992; Simonton, 2006; Spangler and House, 1991). Perhaps not surprisingly, however, most studies have utilised at-a-distance ratings provided by observers of elected officials, and personality ratings provided by experts based on analysis of biographical materials. For example, Simonton (1986) obtained expert ratings of personality for thirty-nine US presidents based on the adjectives used to describe each president when in office. Using this method, he found a positive correlation between Machiavellianism and the total number of acts passed by a president during their administration and with the number of their legislative victories. Deluga (2001) also found a positive relationship between Machiavellianism and charismatic leadership when he asked raters to assess anonymised profiles of US presidents. Deluga suggests that higher levels of Machiavellianism may help presidents to depersonalise their decision-making, becoming more detached and thus acting more confidently when advancing their goals. Yet, as already noted, voters are less likely to approve candidates with high Machiavellianism (Deluga, 1998). As a recent meta-analysis of employees in other work contexts also found a small *negative* correlation between Machiavellianism and job performance (Forsyth, Banks and McDaniel, 2012), it is possible that the ability to hide a propensity for Machiavellianism is important for achieving success in politics.

Political actors must also be able to recognise, understand and interpret the events and behaviour they encounter in order to navigate political environments (Silvester and Wyatt, 2018). Political cognition therefore involves making sense of the political landscape in order to decide what or who needs to be influenced and how. Studies have also analysed transcripts of speeches, interviews and political debates in order to examine personality in political elites (e.g. Tetlock, 1984). For example, Suedfeld (2010) (see also Chapter 5 by Peter Suedfeld) found that integrative complexity is important for performing aspects of political roles that involve the necessity to scrutinise complex information and to reconcile competing arguments.

Rubenzer, Faschingbauer and Ones (2000) asked observers to rate personality traits of US presidents using established measures based on the FFM and found different trait profiles related to eight presidential types, which reflected how they enacted the role. For instance, 'dominator' presidents (e.g. Nixon) were rated as having low agreeableness, 'maintainers' (e.g. Ford) were rated as having low openness and 'good guys' (e.g. Washington) were given average ratings across all five traits. Although observers' ratings provide an important perspective on the personality of political elites, they tell us little about how political leaders perceive their own personalities and whether these self-perceptions are similar to how others see them (Silvester, 2008; with Wyatt and Randall, 2014).

Politicians' motives have been linked to their behaviour and effectiveness in office. House, Spangler and Woycke (1991) found that differences in nPow, nAff and nAch explained 59 per cent of variance in measures of presidential performance. Of these motives, need for power has been most associated with political success because it relates to forceful actions, an energy or 'zest' for the job and effective persuasion and influence skills (Winter, 2010). Winter (2003), who rated transcripts of presidential campaign speeches and inaugural addresses to study presidential motivation, found that US presidents whose inaugural addresses were rated as high in nPow were more likely to be perceived as 'great' leaders by historians, whereas those with a higher nAff were more associated with scandal. Likewise, Rohrer (2014) analysed verbal records of British prime ministers and found that those who were power motivated were viewed by British historians and political scientists as significantly more effective.

The dominance of power motivation in predicting political effectiveness is noteworthy because one would imagine achievement-striving (nAff) should also be important for political roles, i.e. to implement policy and enact change. However, Winter (2010) argues that politicians who are achievement-oriented may experience frustration when political wrangling makes policy implementation difficult to control. He suggests this frustration leads achievement-focused individuals to employ authoritarian tactics, such as micro-managing, bypassing legislators with appeals to the people and avoiding democratic decision-making. This could explain why Donald Trump, who exhibited a need for achievement over other motives (Jordan and Pennebaker, 2017), demonstrated a propensity for issuing executive orders to bypass Congress. Winter (2010) claims that individuals who strive for achievement are unlikely to enjoy political roles and may also be viewed negatively by their colleagues, whereas power-motivated politicians may be more effective because they enjoy the 'scrimmages' and political tussles required to progress their plans and ambitions.

The predominant focus on personality of elites as rated by observers and experts makes the small number of studies that have captured self-report personality data from large numbers of politicians especially notable (see earlier). These studies typically compare generic profiles of politicians with those of the general population and do not consider performance – albeit with the exception of potential links between personality and ideology. Moreover, in order to demonstrate a relationship between leader personality and effectiveness, there is a further need to define good performance in the context of political roles. This, as we will see, is a lot more complicated than using election performance as an outcome in studies of leader emergence.

Personality and the Contested Nature of Political Performance

Leadership effectiveness broadly refers to how successful an individual is once elected to office. In other work settings, effectiveness is often defined in terms of how well the individual delivers on the role objectives, i.e. do they achieve organisational targets for sales, performance, etc? However, defining effectiveness in politics is more difficult: perhaps accounting for the extent to which the individual is able to enact their personal political vision and achieve their political goals, while also navigating the pluralistic needs of their party and different groups within their constituency.

Although traditional theories of representative democracy have tended to assume politicians care only about winning elections (Diermeier, Keane and Merlo, 2005), being a 'good' politician by performing well in their role also increases their likelihood of being re-elected. Although politicians have the right to define how they perform their role, their performance can be *judged* good, bad or both by different stakeholders, depending on how each believes the elected representative *should* enact their role (Silvester, 2008; Silvester, Wyatt and Randall, 2014). The tension between how different audiences define performance can be seen with evaluations of 'professional' politicians, who are those pursuing careers solely in politics. Having developed politically related experience in internships or as party advisers, such career politicians are adept at networking, have been socialised into the legislative rules and procedures of government, are ambitious and more assertive than amateur politicians and thus deemed very effective by political insiders (Allen and Cairney, 2017; Allen et al., 2020). However, they also have limited 'real world' experience, and are thought to lack common sense and knowledge about important policy areas, so may be regarded as ineffective by the electorate (Campbell and Cowley, 2014; Valgarðsson et al., 2020).

Definitions of performance, therefore, have important implications for what we know about political personality. Although researchers (e.g. Best, 2011; Caprara et al., 2010) have found that politicians score higher on extraversion and openness to experience, and lower on neuroticism, agreeableness and conscientiousness than members of the public, this does not necessarily imply effectiveness in political roles because the researchers do not examine in-role performance. In fact, very few studies have investigated politicians' self-rated characteristics and role performance, although Dietrich et al. (2012) – in finding that US legislators scoring higher on extraversion and emotional stability were also more likely to express interest in standing for higher political office – speculate that these traits may influence political ambition and, therefore, performance. However, *interest* in higher office does not necessarily imply the *competence* to perform it well.

The trait most associated with good performance across numerous types of work, including political roles, is conscientiousness (Dudley et al., 2006). More conscientious individuals tend to be achievement-oriented, reliable and likely to persevere in the face of setbacks (Bono and Judge, 2004; Costa and McCrae, 2006). Mondak and Halperin (2008) also argue that, to be successful, politicians need the strong sense of duty often associated with conscientiousness, which may manifest as being committed to attend political meetings and keep up to date with new information. Wyatt and Silvester (2018) found that conscientiousness was related to UK local politicians' resilience – the ability to cope with the competing and challenging demands of political roles – as rated by their political colleagues.

Outside politics, neuroticism has been shown to be a negative predictor of performance in traditional work settings (Judge et al., 2002) and it has been theorised that, as political roles are characterised by high levels of conflict, opposition and interpersonal challenge (Simonton, 1988), high neuroticism may be negatively associated with political effectiveness. In a study examining the traits important for the performance of UK local politicians standing for re-election, Silvester et al. (2014) collected 360-degree performance ratings, provided by the politicians' political peers, and found that individuals who were more emotionally stable (i.e. low in neuroticism) were rated as better in dealing with complex information, balancing public needs and policy, and coping with complex role demands.

In a related study, Wyatt and Silvester (2018) went on to examine how personality traits might differentially impact leadership emergence (i.e. votes in an election) and leadership effectiveness (i.e. in-office performance ratings from political colleagues). An important finding from this work was that agreeableness – thought to be a useful trait for politicians because it helps them build relationships, listen to others and build trust with the electorate (Caprara et al., 2003; Roets and Van Hiel, 2009) – was found to positively predict leadership emergence, but *negatively* predict effectiveness. In what Judge et al. (2009) call a 'trait paradox', this suggests that – while voters value agreeableness – politicians who are compliant, altruistic and cooperative may find it difficult to engage in the strategic and darker sides of political roles, because they may be less comfortable with challenging others, debating and fighting for policy. This finding poses a conundrum for those selecting political candidates – and potentially for achieving strong democracy – because the traits that help get people elected may be different to the ones required to be politically effective and might even lead to poorer performance in political office.

Future Directions

Despite its long and illustrious history, research concerned with personality and political leadership continues to be a popular topic for psychology and political science researchers. Given the advance of social media and the opportunity for political leaders to communicate instantaneously with millions of voters, it is also likely that there has never been a more important time to understand the impact of personality characteristics on political outcomes and performance. In this section, we consider areas worthy of future study, both because they represent key challenges (and opportunities) for research in this area, and because we believe there is a need to broaden the focus of research by incorporating new theories of personality that may better explain leader emergence and leader effectiveness in politics. To conclude our chapter, we reflect on two areas: (1) methodology and measurement in political leadership research and (2) personality as a dynamic social construct and its relationship with authenticity.

Methodology and Measurement

As our chapter has shown, researchers have adopted a diverse range of methods to assess the personality of political elites, including analysis of historical documents, political speeches and verbal records, expert and voter observation, as well as self-reported and peer/other-ratings. In comparison with leadership research in other contexts, where it has been possible to capture data from large numbers of leaders in similar roles – together with self-report and observer personality and performance ratings – and longitudinal data to better examine causal relationships, studies of personality and political leadership research are more limited; not only by their ability to access populations but, excepting election performance (where a large amount of public information is available), by the difficulty in capturing comparable in-role performance data. As a consequence, much of the research utilises at-a-distance methods to rate generic personality factors for political leaders with a significant public profile. This ignores the relevance of personality for political leaders in less prominent roles (e.g. as state or local government representatives), as well as for less observable aspects of a political leader's work, for example, activities outside the debating chamber or scrutiny committees, and within political groups.

Moreover, in order to access this hard-to-reach population, the vast majority of studies using self-report measures of personality have utilised much shortened versions of questionnaires that lack the capacity for a more nuanced exploration of how personality impacts political leadership at a facet level. For example, extraversion includes the facets sociability and dominance that may differentially impact political outcomes such as engaging with the public or winning gladiatorial presidential debates respectively. Using longer and more detailed measures of personality also provides greater opportunity to identify how combinations of traits form leader personality profiles, rather than the variable approach typically used in political personality research, which considers traits separately (Foti et al., 2012).

There has been a number of efforts recently to innovate the methods used to study the personality of politicians. For example, Rice, Remmel and Mondak (2020) have advanced a new strategy for improving the validity of measuring the personality traits of US Senators by combining ratings from different groups of expert assessors (i.e. individuals working in Senate), able to observe Senators in various aspects of their work. Other approaches to capturing personality information on political elites include more recent developments in machine learning, an application of artificial technology that uses traditional psychometric personality inventories in conjunction with written texts and auditory transcriptions to train predictive models for personality. For example, Ramey, Klingler and Hollibaugh (2016) used linguistic modelling of floor debates to infer the personality of participants in US Congress and found legislators with higher conscientiousness proposed fewer symbolic bills (e.g. renaming a local post office), yet more substantive bills that put forward real change (e.g. new legislation).

However, one methodological issue that is particularly relevant for examining the relationship between personality and political outcomes is the problem of endogeneity (Antonakis et al., 2010). To date, endogeneity, which is discussed extensively in the wider leadership and personality literature (Antonakis, Bastardoz and Rönkkö, 2019), has received little attention from researchers studying personality and political leadership.

Endogeneity is broadly concerned with causality. More specifically, when estimating an outcome that is measured and not manipulated in an experimental setting, it is important that researchers ensure that the relationship between the predictor and the outcome does not stem from causes that are not controlled for (Sajons, 2020). This is important for at-a-distance measures of personality, such as expert ratings from historical documents, which might be influenced by causes such as the economic context and party-political pressures of the time and the experts' own biases. Likewise, perceptions of political effectiveness might stem from politicians' personality and their appearance, but also from factors such as the state of the economy and party allegiance. It is, therefore, important that researchers identify omitted variables and include them in analytical models where possible.

Authenticity: Personality as a Social Construct

The second area worthy of attention from researchers is the extent to which leaders can vary how they present aspects of their personality according to the situation or audience. As Klingler, Hollibaugh and Ramey (2019) note, studies typically rely on an implicit assumption that public personality profiles are not strategic in nature, and that elites do not tailor their personalities in strategic ways to try to appeal to their constituencies. The concept of authenticity is important to political leadership research for several reasons. First, as Stiers et al. (2021) argue, authenticity, which relates broadly to concepts of 'trueness to origins' (Buendgens-Kosten, 2014) – being 'true to self' and 'transparent about one's views and values' (Jones, 2016), has important implications for voter trust and, therefore, political support. The more a political candidate is perceived as authentic, the more likely they will also be seen as sincere and trustworthy. Likewise, individuals who engage in political spin and 'twist words' are often labelled Machiavellian, disingenuous and immoral (Allen and Cairney, 2017). Authenticity has been conceptualised as a desirable character (i.e. personality) trait for politicians (Klingler et al., 2019; Valgarðsson et al., 2020) although, at its core, authenticity also implies the ability to adapt behaviour to the needs of an audience or situation. Ironically, in politics, the need to *present* as authentic may be more important than the need to *be* authentic.

The paradox of authenticity also presents challenges for personality researchers in political leadership research, because how the public perceive a candidate or politician's personality (i.e. observed traits) may be more important for certain outcomes (e.g. elections). Yet, personality in these circumstances is socially constructed through the interaction of actor and observer. For example, the presence of a crisis has long been discussed as a primary determinant of charismatic leadership (Bligh, Kohles and Pillai, 2011; Davis and Gardner, 2012). Likewise, observer ratings of politicians' personalities suffer from evaluative and value-related biases (de Vries and van Prooijen, 2019). Thus, we argue that future studies of personality and political leadership need to reconcile basic assumptions about the nature of personality as innate characteristics that predict behaviour versus a socially constructed public persona that can be shaped, developed and adapted to different needs.

Social media provides an avenue for future research to examine the complexity of authenticity. Platforms such as Twitter, Instagram and YouTube allow politicians to bypass editorial media to have direct contact with the electorate and, therefore, analysis of such content has been espoused as important for better understanding the true characteristics of politicians (Dumitrica, 2014). Apparent authentic use of social media certainly seems to lead to electoral success: for example, research on the 2016 US presidential election finds that Trump's 'authentic style' on Twitter helped give him the advantage in the campaign (Enli, 2017). Blunders on Twitter have also been found to enhance perceived authenticity of politicians (Lee, Lee and Choi, 2020). However, researchers need to remain mindful that, despite the window that social media offers into most people's lives, its use in political campaigns may be a one-way marketing tool, where candidates carefully manipulate content, limit discussion with actual voters and use elements of 'real talk' to *seem,* but not actually *be*, authentic.

Conclusion

Recent studies have shown that the relationship between personality and political leadership is more nuanced and complex than traditional 'great man' theories of leadership might have us believe. Researchers have advanced our understanding of personality and its relationship with leadership – differentiating between leadership emergence (i.e. how individuals progress towards and attain leadership positions) and leadership effectiveness (i.e. how successful an individual is in a leadership role once attained). Likewise, we know much more about the influence of followers and their perceptions of individuals' fit with leadership roles – as well as the proactive way in which individuals seek to create and project an image of leadership qualities and character to enhance their suitability and success in a role. Yet, politics poses particular challenges: politicians are not selected or appointed to their positions, they are elected. As such, public perceptions matter far more, particularly given that a large majority of voters will only observe candidates from afar, usually via television or social media and, increasingly, through secondary reporting.

REFERENCES

Aaldering, L. and Van Der Pas, D. J. (2018). Political leadership in the media: Gender bias in leader stereotypes during campaign and routine times. *British Journal of Political Science*, 50(3), 1–21.

Adorno, T. W., Frenkel-Brunswik, E., Levinson, D. J. and Sanford, N. J. (1950). Types and syndromes. In *The authoritarian personality* (Studies in Prejudice Series, American Jewish Committee). New York: Harper.

Allen, N., Magni, G., Searing, D. and Warncke, P. (2020). What is a career politician? Theories, concepts, and measures. *European Political Science Review*, 12(2), 199–217.

Allen, P. and Cairney, P. (2017). What do we mean when we talk about the 'political class'? *Political Studies Review*, 15(1), 18–27.

Antonakis, J. (2011). Predictors of leadership: The usual suspects and the suspect traits. In A. Bryman, D. Collinson, K. Grint, B. Jackson and M. Uhl-Bien (Eds.), *Sage handbook of leadership* (pp. 269–285). Thousand Oaks, CA: Sage.

Antonakis, J., Bastardoz, N. and Rönkkö, M. (2019, July). The endogeneity problem in random intercept models: Are most published results likely false? *Academy of Management Proceedings*, 2019(1), 18927.

Antonakis, J., Bendahan, S., Jacquart, P. and Lalive, R. (2010). On making causal claims: A review and recommendations. *The Leadership Quarterly*, 21(6), 1086–1120.

Barber, J. D. (1972). *The presidential character: Predicting performance in the White House*. Englewood Cliffs, NJ: Prentice-Hall.

Best, H. (2011). Does personality matter in politics? Personality factors as determinants of parliamentary recruitment and policy preferences. *Comparative Sociology*, 10(6), 928–948.

Bjarnegård, E. and Kenny, M. (2015). Revealing the "secret garden": The informal dimensions of political recruitment. *Politics and Gender*, 11(4), 748–753.

Bligh, M. C., Kohles, J. C. and Pillai, R. (2011). Romancing leadership: Past, present, and future. *The Leadership Quarterly*, 22(6), 1058–1077.

Bono, J. E. and Judge, T. A. (2004). Personality and transformational and transactional leadership: A meta-analysis. *Journal of Applied Psychology*, 89(5), 901.

Buendgens-Kosten, J. (2014). Authenticity. *ELT Journal*, 68(4), 457–459.

Callander, S. (2008). Political motivations. *The Review of Economic Studies*, 75(3), 671–697.

Campbell, R. and Childs, S. (2010). 'Wags', 'wives' and 'mothers'... but what about women politicians? *Parliamentary Affairs*, 63(4), 760–777.

Campbell, R. and Cowley, P. (2014). What voters want: Reactions to candidate characteristics in a survey experiment. *Political Studies*, 62(4), 745–765.

Campbell, R. and Lovenduski, J. (2015). What should MPs do? Public and parliamentarians' views compared. *Parliamentary Affairs*, 68(4), 690–708.

Caprara, G. V., Barbaranelli, C., Consiglio, C., Picconi, L. and Zimbardo, P. G. (2003). Personalities of politicians and voters: Unique and synergistic relationships. *Journal of Personality and Social Psychology*, 84(4), 849–856.

Caprara, G. V. and Cervone, D. (2000). *Personality: Determinants, dynamics, and potentials*. New York: Cambridge University Press.

Caprara, G. V., Francescato, D., Mebane, M., Sorace, R. and Vecchione, M. (2010). Personality foundations of ideological divide: A comparison of women members of parliament and women voters in Italy. *Political Psychology*, 31(5), 739–762.

Caprara, G. V., Schwartz, S., Capanna, C., Vecchione, M. and Barbaranelli, C. (2006). Personality and politics: Values, traits, and political choice. *Political Psychology*, 27(1), 1–28.

Caprara, G. V. and Silvester, J. (2018). The personality attributes of political elites. In H. Best and J. Higley (Eds.), *The Palgrave handbook of political elites* (pp. 467–488). London: Palgrave Macmillan.

Caprara, G. V., Vecchione, M. and Schwartz, S. H. (2012). Why people do not vote: The role of personal values. *European Psychologist*, 17, 266–278.

Caprara, G. V. and Zimbardo, P. G. (2004). Personalizing politics: A congruency model of political preference. *American Psychologist*, 59(7), 581–594.

Cassese, E. C. and Holman, M. R. (2018). Party and gender stereotypes in campaign attacks. *Political Behavior*, 40(3), 785–807.

Christie, R. and Geis, F. L. (1970). *Studies in Machiavellianism*. New York: Academic Press.

Corr, P. J. and Matthews, G. (Eds.). (2009). *The Cambridge handbook of personality psychology*. Cambridge, UK: Cambridge University Press.

Costa, P. T., Jr. and McCrae, R. R. (2006). Trait and factor theories. In J. C. Thomas and D. L. Segal (Eds.), *Comprehensive handbook of personality and psychopathology* (Vol. I). Personality and everyday functioning 36. New York: Wiley.

Costantini, E. and Craik, K. H. (1980). Personality and politicians: California party leaders, 1960–1976. *Journal of Personality and Social Psychology*, 38, 641–661.

Davis, K. M. and Gardner, W. L. (2012). Charisma under crisis revisited: Presidential leadership, perceived leader effectiveness, and contextual influences. *The Leadership Quarterly*, 23(5), 918–933.

de Vries, R. E. and van Prooijen, J. W. (2019). Voters rating politicians' personality: Evaluative biases and assumed similarity on honesty-humility and openness to experience. *Personality and Individual Differences*, 144, 100–104.

Deluga, R. J. (2001). American presidential Machiavellianism: Implications for charismatic leadership and rated performance. *The Leadership Quarterly*, 12(3), 339–363.

(1998). American presidential proactivity, charismatic leadership, and rated performance. *The Leadership Quarterly*, 9(3), 265–291.

Diermeier, D., Keane, M. and Merlo, A. (2005). A political economy model of congressional careers. *American Economic Review*, 95(1), 347–373.

Dietrich, B. J., Lasley, S., Mondak, J. J., Remmel, M. L. and Turner, J. (2012). Personality and legislative politics: The Big Five trait dimensions among US state legislators. *Political Psychology*, 33(2), 195–210.

Duckitt, J. (2020). Authoritarianism. In V. Zeigler-Hill and T. K. Shackelford (Eds.), *Encyclopedia of personality and individual differences*. Springer, Cham. doi:10.1007/978-3-319-24612-3_1046

Dudley, N. M., Orvis, K. A., Lebiecki, J. E. and Cortina, J. M. (2006). A meta-analytic investigation of conscientiousness in the prediction of job performance: Examining the intercorrelations and the incremental validity of narrow traits. *Journal of Applied Psychology*, 91(1), 40.

Dumitrica, D. (2014). Politics as "customer relations": Social media and political authenticity in the 2010 municipal elections in Calgary, Canada. *Javnost-The Public*, 21(1), 53–69.

Eagly, A. H. and Karau, S. J. (2002). Role congruity theory of prejudice toward female leaders. *Psychological Review*, 109(3), 573.

Enli, G. (2017). Twitter as arena for the authentic outsider: Exploring the social media campaigns of Trump and Clinton in the 2016 US presidential election. *European Journal of Communication*, 32(1), 50–61.

Forsyth, D. R., Banks, G. C. and McDaniel, M. A. (2012). A meta-analysis of the Dark Triad and work behavior: A social exchange perspective. *Journal of Applied Psychology*, 97(3), 557.

Foti, R. J., Bray, B. C., Thompson, N. J. and Allgood, S. F. (2012). Know thy self, know thy leader: Contributions of a pattern-oriented approach to examining leader perceptions. *The Leadership Quarterly*, 23(4), 702–717.

Fredriksson, P. G., Wang, L. and Mamun, K. A. (2011). Are politicians office or policy motivated? The case of US governors' environmental policies. *Journal of Environmental Economics and Management*, 62(2), 241–253.

Gallagher, M. and Marsh, M. (1988). *Candidate selection in comparative perspective: The secret garden of politics* (Vol. 18). London: Sage Publications Ltd.

Garzia, D. (2011). The personalization of politics in Western democracies: Causes and consequences on leader–follower relationships. *The Leadership Quarterly*, 22(4), 697–709.

George, A. L. and George, J. L. (1998). *Presidential personality and performance*. Boulder, CO: Westview.

Hart, W., Adams, J. M. and Burton, K. A. (2016). Narcissistic for the people: Narcissists and non-narcissists disagree about how to make a good impression. *Personality and Individual Differences*, 91, 69–73, ISSN 0191-8869.

Hermann, M. G. (1980). Explaining foreign policy behavior using the personal characteristics of political leaders. *International Studies Quarterly*, 24(1), 7–46.

House, R. J., Spangler, W. D. and Woycke, J. (1991). Personality and charisma in the US Lombardo, MM, Ruderman, MN, and McCauley, CD (1988). Explanations of success and derailment in upper-level management positions. *Journal of Business and Psychology*, 2, 199–216.

Jones, B. (2016). Authenticity in political discourse. *Ethical Theory and Moral Practice*, 19(2), 489–504.

Jordan, K. N. and Pennebaker, J. W. (2017). The exception or the rule: Using words to assess analytic thinking, Donald Trump, and the American presidency. *Translational Issues in Psychological Science*, 3(3), 312.

Judge, T. A., Bono, J. E., Ilies, R. and Gerhardt, M. W. (2002). Personality and leadership: A qualitative and quantitative review. *Journal of Applied Psychology*, 87(4), 765–780.

Judge, T. A., Colbert, A. E. and Ilies, R. (2004). Intelligence and leadership: A quantitative review and test of theoretical propositions. *Journal of Applied Psychology*, 89(3), 542–552.

Judge T. A., Piccolo R. F. and Kosalka T. (2009). The bright and dark sides of leader traits: A review and theoretical extension of the leader trait paradigm. *Leadership Quarterly*, 20, 855–875.

Kapoutsis, I., Papalexandris, A., Treadway, D. C. and Bentley, J. (2017). Measuring political will in organizations: Theoretical construct development and empirical validation. *Journal of Management*, 43(7), 2252–2280.

Kartik, N. and McAfee, R. P. (2007). Signaling character in electoral competition. *American Economic Review*, 97(3), 852–870.

Klinger, J. D., Hollibaugh, G. E. and Ramey, A. J. (2019). What I like about you: Legislator personality and legislator approval. *Political Behavior*, 41, 499–525.

Knapen, J. E., Blaker, N. M. and Pollet, T. V. (2017). Size, skills, and suffrage: Motivated distortions in perceived formidability of political leaders. *PLoS ONE*, 12(12), e0188485.

Kowert, P. A. (1996). Where does the buck stop?: Assessing the impact of presidential personality. *Political Psychology*, 17(3), 421–452.

Krook, M. and Childs, S. (2010). *Women, gender, and politics: A reader*. Oxford, UK: Oxford University Press.

Langton, K. P. (1969). *Political socialization* (Vol. 1). Oxford, UK: Oxford University Press.

Lawless, J. L. (2015). Female candidates and legislators. *Annual Review of Political Science*, 18, 349–366.

Lee, E. J., Lee, H. Y. and Choi, S. (2020). Is the message the medium? How politicians' Twitter blunders affect perceived authenticity of Twitter communication. *Computers in Human Behavior*, 104, 106188.

Lord, R. G., Foti, R. J. and De Vader, C. L. (1984). A test of leadership categorization theory: Internal structure, information processing, and leadership perceptions. *Organizational Behavior and Human Performance*, 34(3), 343–378.

Lyons, M. (1997). Presidential character revisited. *Political Psychology*, 18(4), 791–811.

McCann, S. J. (1992). Alternative formulas to predict the greatness of U.S. presidents: Personological, situational, and zeitgeist factors. *Journal of Personality and Social Psychology*, 62(3), 469–479.

McLaughlin, H., Silvester, J., Sealy, R., Billimoria, D., Peters, K., Huse, M., Moltner, H., Jane, S. and Göke, J. (2018). Women in power: Contributing factors that impact on women in organizations and politics; psychological research and best practice. *Organizational Dynamics*, 47, 189–199.

McClelland, D. C. (1987). *Human motivation*. New York: Cambridge University Press.

McCrae, R. R. (2009). The Five-Factor Model of personality traits: Consensus and controversy. In P. Corr and G. Matthews (Eds.), *The Cambridge handbook of personality psychology* (pp. 148–161). Cambridge, UK: Cambridge University Press.

McCrae, R. R. and Costa, P. T. (1990). *Personality in adulthood*. New York: Guilford.

McCrae, R. R. and Sutin, A. R. (2018). A five-factor theory perspective on causal analysis. *European Journal of Personality*, 32(3), 151–166.

Mondak J. J. (2010). *Personality and the foundations of political behavior*. New York: Cambridge University Press.

Mondak, J. J. and Halperin, K. D. (2008). A framework for the study of personality and political behaviour. *British Journal of Political Science*, 38(2), 335–362.

Murray, G. R. and Schmitz, J. D. (2011). Caveman politics: Evolutionary leadership preferences and physical stature. *Social Science Quarterly*, 92(5), 1215–1235.

Murray, R. (2010). *Cracking the highest glass ceiling: A global comparison of women's campaigns for executive office*. Santa Barbara: Praeger Publishers.

Nai, A., Martínez i Coma, F. and Maier, J. (2019). Donald Trump, populism, and the Age of Extremes: Comparing the personality traits and campaigning styles of Trump and other leaders worldwide. *Presidential Studies Quarterly*, 49(3), 609–643.

Olivola, C. Y. and Todorov, A. (2010). Elected in 100 milliseconds: Appearance-based trait inferences and voting. *Journal of Nonverbal Behavior*, 34(2), 83–110.

Pillai, R., Williams, E. A., Lowe, K. B. and Jung, D. I. (2003). Personality, transformational leadership, trust, and the 2000 US presidential vote. *The Leadership Quarterly*, 14(2), 161–192.

Post, L. A., Raile, A. N. and Raile, E. D. (2010). Defining political will. *Politics and Policy*, 38(4), 653–676.

POTUS.com (2020). Presidential Heights. Accessed from www.potus.com/presidential-facts/presidential-heights/.

Ramey, A., Klingler, J. and Hollibaugh, G. (2016). Measuring elite personality using speech. *Political Science Research and Methods*, 7(1), 163–184.

Raskin, R. N. and Hall, C. S. (1979). A narcissistic personality inventory. *Psychological Reports*, 45(2), 590.

Rice, M. G., Remmel, M. L. and Mondak, J. J. (2020). Personality on the Hill: Expert Evaluations of US Senators' Psychological Traits. *Political Research Quarterly*, 74(3), 674–687. doi:10.1177/1065912920928587

Roets, A. and Van Hiel, A. (2009). The ideal politician: Impact of voters' ideology. *Personality and Individual Differences*, 46(1), 60–65.

Rohrer, S. R. (2014). What makes a prime minister great?: A leadership trait analysis of the effectiveness of British prime ministers from 1902 to 2004. *Research and Politics*, 1(3), 1–8.

Rokeach, M. (1973). *The nature of human values*. New York: Free Press.

Rubenzer, S. J., Faschingbauer, T. R. and Ones, D. S. (2000). Assessing the US presidents using the revised NEO Personality Inventory. *Assessment*, 7(4), 403–419.

Sajons, G. B. (2020). Estimating the causal effect of measured endogenous variables: A tutorial on experimentally randomized instrumental variables. *The Leadership Quarterly*, 31(5), 1–17.

Schill, D. (2012). The visual image and the political image: A review of visual communication research in the field of political communication. *Review of Communication*, 12(2), 118–142.

Schneider, M. and Bos, A. (2014). Measuring stereotypes of female politicians. *Political Psychology*, 35(2), 245–266.

Schumacher, G. and Zettler, I. (2019). House of Cards or West Wing? Self-reported HEXACO traits of Danish politicians. *Personality and Individual Differences*, 141, 173–181.

Schwartz S. H. (2017). Individual values across cultures. In: Chuch, A. T. (Ed.) *The Praeger handbook of personality across cultures*. Santa Barbara, CA: Praeger.

Schwartz, S. H. (2006). A theory of cultural value orientations: Explication and applications. *Comparative Sociology*, 5(2–3), 137–182.

(1994). Are there universal aspects in the structure and contents of human values? *Journal of Social Issues*, 50(4), 19–45.

(1992). Universals in the content and structure of values: Theoretical advances and empirical tests in 20 countries. *Advances in Experimental Social Psychology*, 25(1), 1–65.

Schwartz, S. H., Caprara, G. V., Vecchione, M., Bain, P., Bianchi, G., Caprara, M. G., Cieciuch, J., Kirmanoglu, H., Baslevent, C., Lönnqvist, J. E., Mamali, C., Manzi, J., Pavlopoulos, V., Posnova, T., Schoen, H., Silvester, J., Tabernero, C., Torres, C., Verkasalo, M., Vondráková, E.,

Welzel, C. and Zaleski, Z. (2014). Basic personal values underlie and give coherence to political values: A cross national study in 15 countries. *Political Behavior*, 36(4), 899–930.

Silvester, J. (2012). Recruiting politicians: Designing competency-based selection for UK parliamentary candidates. In A. Weinberg (Ed.), *The psychology of politicians* (pp. 21–38). Cambridge, UK: Cambridge University Press.

(2008). The good, the bad and the ugly: Politics and politicians at work. *International Review of Industrial and Organizational Psychology*, 23, 107–148.

Silvester, J. and Dykes, C. (2007). Selecting political candidates: A longitudinal study of assessment centre performance and political success in the 2005 UK General Election. *Journal of Occupational and Organizational Psychology*, 80(1), 11–25.

Silvester, J. and Wyatt, M. (2018). Political effectiveness at work. In D. S. Ones, N. Anderson, C. Viswesvaran and H. K. Sinangil (Eds.), *The SAGE handbook of industrial, work and organizational psychology: V1: Personnel psychology and employee performance*, 228–247. London: Sage.

Silvester, J., Wyatt, M., Ellen, B.P. III, and Ferris, G. R. (2020). Candidate effects on election outcomes: Political skill, campaign efficacy and intentions in a British general election. *Applied Psychology: An International Review* 1–41, doi.org/10.1111/apps.12292.

Silvester, J., Wyatt, M. and Randall, R. (2014). Politician personality, Machiavellianism, and political skill as predictors of performance ratings in political roles. *Journal of Occupational and Organizational Psychology*, 87(2), 258–279.

Simonton, D. K. (2006). Presidential IQ, openness, intellectual brilliance, and leadership: Estimates and correlations for 42 US chief executives. *Political Psychology*, 27(4), 511–526.

(1988). Presidential style: Personality, biography, and performance. *Journal of Personality and Social Psychology*, 55(6), 928–936.

(1986). Presidential personality: Biographical use of the Gough Adjective Check List. *Journal of Personality and Social Psychology*, 51(1), 149.

Spangler, W. D. and House, R. J. (1991). Presidential effectiveness and the leadership motive profile. *Journal of Personality and Social Psychology*, 60(3), 439.

Stiers, D., Larner, J., Kenny, J., Breitenstein, S., Vallée-Dubois, F. and Lewis-Beck, M. (2021). Candidate Authenticity: 'To Thine Own Self Be True'. *Political Behavior*, 43, 1181–1204.

Stulp, G., Buunk, A. P., Verhulst, S. and Pollet, T. V. (2013). Tall claims? Sense and nonsense about the importance of height of US presidents. *The Leadership Quarterly*, 24(1), 159–171.

Suedfeld, P. (2010). The cognitive processing of politics and politicians: Archival studies of conceptual and integrative complexity. *Journal of Personality*, 78(6), 1669–1702.

Suedfeld, P., Cross, R. W. and Brcic, J. (2011). Two years of ups and downs: Barack Obama's patterns of integrative complexity, motive imagery, and values. *Political Psychology*, 32(6), 1007–1033.

Sussman, A. B., Petkova, K. and Todorov, A. (2013). Competence ratings in US predict presidential election outcomes in Bulgaria. *Journal of Experimental Social Psychology*, 49(4), 771–775.

Tetlock, P. E. (1984). Cognitive style and political belief systems in the British House of Commons. *Journal of Personality and Social Psychology*, 46(2), 365.

Todorov, A., Mandisodza, A. N., Goren, A. and Hall, C. C. (2005). Inferences of competence from faces predict election outcomes. *Science*, 308(5728), 1623–1626.

Treadway, D. C. (2012). Political will in organizations. In G. R. Ferris and D. C. Treadway (Eds.), *Politics in organizations: Theory and research considerations*: 531–556. New York: Routledge, Taylor and Francis Group.

UN Women (2018). Facts and figures: Leadership and political participation. www.unwomen.org/en/what-we-do/leadership-and-political-participation/facts-andfigures. Accessed date: 2 July 2019.

Valgarðsson, V., Clarke, N., Jennings, W. and Stoker, G. (2020). The good politician and political trust: An authenticity gap in British politics? *Political Studies*. doi:10.1177/0032321720928257

Vecchione, M., Schwartz, S. H., Caprara, G. V., Schoen, H., Cieciuch, J., Silvester, J., Bain, P., Bianchi, G., Kirmanoglu, H., Baslevent, C., Mamali, C., Manzi, J., Pavlopoulos, V., Posnova, T., Torres, C., Verkasalo, M., Lönnqvist, J.-E., Vondráková, E., Welzel, C. and Alessandri, G. (2015). Personal values and political activism: A cross-national study. *British Journal of Psychology*, 106(1), 84–106.

Vivyan, N. and Wagner, M. (2015). What do voters want from their local MP? *The Political Quarterly*, 86(1), 33–40.

Wattenberg M (1991). *The rise of candidate-centered politics: Presidential elections of the 1980s*. Cambridge, MA: Harvard University Press.

Winter, D. G. (2010). Why achievement motivation predicts success in business but failure in politics: The importance of personal control. *Journal of Personality*, 78(6), 1637–1668.

(2003). Measuring the motives of political actors. In J. Post (Ed.), *The psychological assessment of political leaders* (pp. 153–177). Ann Arbor: University of Michigan Press.

(1987). Leader appeal, leader performance, and the motive profiles of leaders and followers: A study of American presidents and elections. *Journal of Personality and Social Psychology*, 52, 196–202.

Wyatt, M. and Silvester, J. (2018). Do voters get it right? A test of the ascription-actuality trait theory of leadership with political elites. *The Leadership Quarterly*, 29(5), 609–621.

CHAPTER 3

From Big Ben to the Breakfast Table
Basic Values and Political Attitudes among Politicians and the Public

James Weinberg

Politicians are central to representative democracy. In all of its formal and informal guises – liberal, authoritarian, populist, consensus, majoritarian – democracy relies on and is shaped by those who stand for political office. Among elite groups in modern society, politicians hold unique power in their ability to achieve far-reaching legislative outcomes with ramifications that stretch throughout different tiers of governance in any single democracy, as well as beyond its borders. In local, national and – increasingly – supra-national democratic parliaments and assemblies, politicians formulate and scrutinise policy directives; they hold executives to account and either grant or withhold support for sitting governments; they shape the tenor of political discourse and debate through discursive cues broadcast in print and news media; and they contribute to the incremental evolution of state institutions (see also Best and Vogel, 2018). Above all, politicians take on the formidable task of 'representing' the sovereign people at the heart of a democracy.

It is in the trappings of this principal-agent relationship that the importance of 'politicians as people' becomes starkly apparent. The institutions of democratic representation, elections in particular, involve a drastic transfer of democratic power from the many to the few. Elections decide 'who' has that power, but they do not necessarily decide 'what' is done with it. In the absence of imperative legal mandates, election candidates and elected representatives are judged according to their values, opinions and ideological discourse – elsewhere referred to as 'political fictions' (see Kelsen, 1992). Indeed, a constructivist turn in the study of representation focuses specifically on how political actors within and without formal parliaments and legislatures make 'representative claims' on behalf of real or imagined communities of interest (e.g., Näsström, 2015; Saward, 2006, 2010). In this sense, politicians not only respond to popular will, but they have the potential to shape it and bring broader palettes of public opinion into formal political debate that may, or may not, fit within the normative and ideological boundaries of 'being democratic'. For those students or concerned observers of the degenerative slide to mainstream populism and dog-whistle 'claim-making' seen in Western democracies (for an overview, see Dean and Maiguashca, 2020), the psychology of politicians has taken on new meaning and urgency.

This chapter does not focus, then, on the institutional mechanisms by which democracy is enacted, but rather the psychological characteristics of the people who are deemed eligible to act in citizens' best interests. Over the last decade, political scientists and political psychologists have made significant headway in this field by acquiring and analysing self-report data on the psychological predispositions of politicians in comparative contexts. In the United States of America, Canada, Germany, Italy, Denmark, Belgium and the UK, research has shown that politics is a job few 'ordinary' people care to enter (Best, 2011; Caprara et al., 2010; Hanania, 2017; Nørgaard and Klemmensen, 2018; Scott and Medeiros, 2020; Weinberg, 2020a). On personality characteristics such as traits and basic values, elected politicians (as well as those who stand for election) differ in a myriad of ways to those who elect them, as well as each other, when divided by party, gender and ethnicity. Psychological predispositions such as personality characteristics also influence who climbs the greasy pole of electoral politics to enter executive office (Joly et al., 2019; Weinberg, 2019), as well as how politicians act out a variety of legislative behaviours (Weinberg, 2020b).

While these findings raise a host of practical and theoretical questions about the conduct of democratic leadership and the accessibility of politics as a vocation, there has been relatively little attempt to understand how the unique psychologies of politicians might also precipitate and/or explain differences or similarities between their own political opinions and those of the citizens they govern. This research agenda matters for our collective understanding of the psychology of democracy and, by implication, for the successes and failures of democratic representation. If governor and governed fundamentally disagree in their political preferences, then why? If they do not, then why not? The rest of this chapter addresses this dilemma through theoretical engagement with existing studies of public opinion and personality in politics (specifically focusing on basic human values), and through empirical analysis of original data collected from over 900 elected politicians and unsuccessful political candidates (Table 3.1).

Table 3.1. *Sample characteristics (percentages rounded to the nearest whole number).*[1]

	Members of Parliament (N = 62)	Councillors (N = 415)	Unsuccessful Parliamentary Candidates (N = 134)	Unsuccessful Council Candidates (N = 331)	British Public – European Social Survey 9 (N = 2,204)
Gender					
Male	65	62	71	68	45
Female	35	38	29	32	55
Age					
18–30	4	4	9	18	13
31–45	23	18	16	28	24
46–60	37	34	45	27	27
60+	36	44	31	27	36
Education (highest qualification)					
Postgraduate Degree	31	31	31	34	13
Undergraduate Degree	57	47	52	43	20
A-Levels/Vocational Diploma	8	14	11	15	25
Apprenticeship	4	2	2	2	8
None of the above	1	6	5	6	34
Religion					
Christian	60	52	44	40	14
Non-Christian	5	6	7	10	1
Non-Religious	35	42	49	50	85
Party					
Labour	40	32	16	24	37
Conservative	27	17	8	10	42
Liberal Democrat	14	30	19	22	8
Green	< 1	7	20	21	2
Scottish National Party	8	< 1	0	< 1	4
UK Independence Party	< 1	< 1	7	4	3
Other	9	12	30	18	3

[1] Participants were identified through the Democracy Club database of political candidates, which contains details of all candidates that have stood in a UK election between 2010–2019 and who made their contact details available to the Electoral Commission at the time of standing. Surveys were fielded online in early 2019 and attitudinal questions were selected from the 2018 (ninth) round of the European Social Survey for elite-mass comparisons. Comparative data for the British public was downloaded here: www .europeansocialsurvey.org/data/.

This analysis shows that elites and masses (to use common parlance from political research) in UK politics do differ substantively in their political opinions and that these differences can be partly explained by dynamic models of individual preference formation that account for the effects of psychological predispositions as well as environmental factors.

Political Attitudes among Elites and Masses

In observing the democratic links between elites and masses, there has been a tendency to seek causal relationships between the public policy preferences of each. Put simply, who leads and who follows when it comes to defining the political zeitgeist? On one hand, a top-down approach to opinion formation has long contended that elites share a broad governing consensus that is transferred to a 'largely passive, apathetic and ill-informed' public (Dye and Ziegler, 1978, p. 6; see also Federico, 2015; Johnston, Lavine and Federico, 2017). On the other hand, a democratic-responsiveness model suggests that elected representatives act as delegates who follow the opinions of mass publics (for an extended discussion, see Page and Shapiro, 1983). Both models have been used to explain similar structures in elite and mass opinions: one accounting for the dissemination of elite preferences and the other suggesting sensitivity to public views by electorally attentive politicians.

Unsurprisingly, longitudinal studies of elite and mass opinion tend to support both of these theoretical (and tautologically interlinked) propositions. In the United States of America, Cunningham and Moore (1997) carried out time-series analysis of opinion polls conducted with American members of Congress and voters every four years between 1974 and 1994. Focusing specifically on foreign policy attitudes, Cunningham and Moore note that elites and masses share similar patterns of opinion change over time, while holding and maintaining very different opinions at any individual time point. Moreover, the time-lagged effects of elite and mass opinions linked to the attitude changes of each other were significantly weaker than the lagged effects over time of each group's own prior opinions. Of possibly more interest, elite *perceptions* of mass opinion over the time series were substantially different from *actual* mass opinion across four out of five issues polled. These nuanced dynamics of elite and mass opinion have been studied in greater detail in comparative contexts. In

France, for example, Tiberj and Kerrouche (2013) find that the distance between MPs and voters changes according to the hegemony of the opinion and its issue domain (whether social, cultural or economic), that MPs in certain parties are more alienated from public opinion than others (particularly those on the ideological fringe), and that MPs are more polarised in their political opinions than voters (see also Jost, 2006; Zaller, 1992). Taken together, this research base points to something more complex than either explanation offered by leader-follower models of representative democracy.

For the purpose of this chapter, elected politicians and unsuccessful political candidates in the UK (surveyed in early 2019) were asked to complete attitudinal items that had been fielded to the British public in the previous round of the European Social Survey (ESS) only months beforehand. Table 3.2 compares these subsamples across nineteen survey items that cover two diffuse and *affectively* oriented political opinions (trust in politics and satisfaction with democracy) and three specific and *cognitively* oriented political opinions (on immigration, climate action and inequality). The data show interesting, yet nuanced, similarities and differences between the political opinions of British politicians, candidates and the public. Elected politicians generally have higher levels of trust in politics than the public, especially regarding the European Parliament, the legal system, political parties and politicians themselves. However, the same cannot be said of unsuccessful candidates, who are equally – if not more – distrustful of political actors and institutions than the general public. At the same time, elected politicians and candidates are, on average, considerably less satisfied with UK democracy and domestic public services than the public (whose satisfaction remains lukewarm at best). On specific policy issues, politicians and candidates are both considerably more liberal than the public – at an aggregate level – in their attitudes towards the cultural and economic benefits of immigration, action on climate change and inequality.

Table 3.2 also reports the average distances between the self-reported attitudes of Labour and Conservative Party supporters in each subsample.[1] As anticipated by theories of elective affinity (Jost,

---

[1] To avoid confusion and in order to simplify the analysis, only the two main parties in British politics from the Left and Right are compared.

Federico and Napier, 2009) and the congruency principle (Caprara and Zimbardo, 2004) – which stipulate psychological and sociological determinants of partisanship at elite and mass levels – these differences run in the same direction across all of the subsamples reported here. For example, Labour Party politicians, candidates and voters are less trusting of and less satisfied with domestic politics (and its associated institutions and actors) than their Conservative Party counterparts, but much more supportive of immigration, climate action and social equality. These latter differences confirm longstanding comparative research on the organising principle of the Left-Right divide in elective democratic politics. Put simply, Left-wing preferences for greater equality and change tend to conflict with Right-wing preferences for social hierarchy and less social change (e.g., Benoit and Laver, 2006; Federico, 2015; Jost et al., 2003).

Within subsamples, the average distance between the substantive issue positions of Labour and Conservative elites (politicians *and* candidates) is much larger than between corresponding voters in the general public. Empirically, these findings support prior research showing greater polarisation of opinion among elites than publics around the Western world (e.g., Jost, 2006; Sood and Iyengar, 2014). Theoretically, the data also support seminal studies of attitude formation that suggest stronger ideological coherence and self-presentation among elites than voters, which is generally attributed to comparably higher levels of education, political interest and political expertise (Converse, 1964; Sniderman, Brody and Tetlock, 1991; Zaller, 1992). In a similar vein, these findings add empirical nuance to John May's (1973) classic descriptions of *leaders as extremists* and *deviants*. May argued that party leaders: (1) hold stronger ideological views than those lower down the party hierarchy because they are most likely to benefit from ideological conflict (i.e. '*leaders as extremists*') and (2) are more Right-wing than the median voter by virtue of gravitating to political leadership from positions of high social status (i.e. '*leaders as deviant rightists*'). On the first of these assumptions, the data presented in Table 3.2 suggest that UK citizens and elites *do* share patterns of opinion formation within samples, but *diverge considerably* between samples. On the second assumption, however, the data contradict May's proposition. Instead, UK politicians appear to be *deviant liberals*. This chapter now turns to the question of why these differences exist and how they might form.

Table 3.2. *Diffuse and specific political opinions among elected politicians, unsuccessful political candidates and the British public.*

	Members of Parliament (N = 62)		Councillors (N = 415)	
	Mean (Standard Deviation – SD)	Con-Lab distance	Mean (SD)	Con-Lab distance
Trust				
How much do you personally trust each the following? (0–10, where 10 = completely trust)				
...the UK Parliament.	**4.85** (2.59)	1.36	**4.74** (2.26)	0.11
...the legal system.	**6.35** (2.08)	−.11	**6.35** (2.12)	0.39
...the police.	**6.05** (1.95)	0.33	**6.23** (2.01)	**0.81**
... political parties.	**4.18** (1.94)	0.75	**4.13** (2.01)	−0.19
...the European Parliament.	**4.95** (2.54)	−2.94	**4.97** (2.78)	−**3.89**
...the United Nations.	5.5 (2.5)	−**2.25**	**5.79** (2.38)	−**1.66**
...politicians.	**4.84** (2.02)	0.38	**4.60** (2.16)	−0.45
Satisfaction				
On the whole, how satisfied are you with the following? (0–10, where 10 = completely satisfied)				
... the present state of the economy.	**3.40** (2.55)	**4.89**	**3.40** (2.42)	**4.59**
... the performance of the current UK government.	**1.56** (2.19)	**3.83**	**1.30** (1.87)	**3.12**
... the way democracy works in the UK.	**3.13** (2.42)	**2.75**	**3.26** (2.48)	**1.54**
... the state of education in the UK.	**3.84** (2.00)	**2.75**	**3.70** (2.16)	**2.25**
... the state of healthcare in the UK.	**4.47** (1.96)	**2.94**	**4.13** (2.43)	**2.43**
Immigration				
Would you say it is generally bad or good for the UK economy that people come to live here from other countries? (0–10, where 10 = good)	**8.06** (1.74)	−**1.39**	**7.77** (1.94)	−**2.29**
Would you say the UK's cultural life is generally undermined or enriched by people who come to live here from other countries? (0–10, where 10 = enriched)	**8.15** (1.87)	−**2.28**	**7.84** (2.19)	−**2.88**
Climate action[**]				
To what extent are you in favour or against the following policies in the UK to reduce climate change? (five-point Likert scale, where 5 = strongly in favour)				

Unsuccessful Parliamentary Candidates (N = 134)		Unsuccessful Council Candidates (N = 331)		British Public – ESS 9 (N = 2,204)	
Mean (SD)	Con-Lab distance	Mean (SD)	Con-Lab distance	Mean (SD)	Con-Lab distance
3.91 (2.59)	0.03	4.19 (2.55)	0.86	4.21 (2.51)	**0.72**
5.41 (2.66)	−1.14	5.86 (2.43)	**1.59**	5.72 (2.44)	0.17
5.02 (2.38)	−.62	**5.68** (2.40)	**1.76**	6.58 (2.39)	0.13
2.89 (2.08)	−.92	3.65 (2.14)	0.59	3.50 (2.24)	**0.27**
4.48 (2.85)	**−3.68**	**4.57** (2.88)	**−1.78**	3.39 (2.52)	**−1.01**
5.21 (2.73)	−1.75	**5.38** (2.59)	**−1.18**	5.07 (2.48)	0.04
3.21 (2.36)	−1.06	**3.78** (2.24)	0.59	3.43 (2.31)	**0.50**
3.10 (2.53)	**4.79**	2.92 (2.45)	**4.46**	4.65 (2.14)	**1.28**
0.96 (1.72)	**2.71**	**1.16** (1.88)	**4.11**	3.75 (2.40)	**1.81**
2.27 (2.32)	0.89	**2.79** (2.29)	**2.01**	4.99 (2.45)	**0.99**
3.23 (2.27)	**1.88**	**3.37** (2.40)	**3.38**	5.53 (2.14)	**0.28**
3.75 (2.56)	**2.69**	**3.97** (2.52)	**2.95**	5.73 (2.40)	**0.72**
7.74 (2.18)	**−2.12**	7.74 (2.09)	**−1.37**	5.89 (2.42)	**−0.61**
7.66 (2.72)	**−3.67**	7.78 (2.34)	**−2.08**	5.88 (2.64)	**−1.21**

Table 3.2. (*cont.*)

	Members of Parliament (N = 62)		Councillors (N = 415)	
	Mean (Standard Deviation – SD)	Con-Lab distance	Mean (SD)	Con-Lab distance
Increasing taxes on fossil fuels, such as oil, gas and coal.	**4.02** (1.05)	−0.92	**3.91** (1.19)	−**1.58**
Using public money to subsidise renewable energy such as wind and solar power.	**4.44** (.84)	−**1.08**	**4.35** (1.02)	−**1.34**
A law banning the sale of the least energy efficient household appliances.	**3.94** (1.10)	−**1.22**	**3.97** (1.14)	−**1.03**
Inequality *Please indicate how much you agree or disagree with each of the following statements. (five-point Likert scale)*				
Society is fair when hard-working people earn more than others. (0–5, *where 5 = strongly disagree*)	**3.27** (1.48)	−**2.72**	**3.57** (1.33)	−**2.34**
Society is fair when income and wealth are equally distributed. (0–5, *where 5 = strongly agree*)	3.44 (1.24)	−**1.19**	**3.74** (1.21)	−**1.59**

Note: coefficients in bold indicate statistically significant differences between a specific 'political' sample (i.e. MPs, councillors, unsuccessful parliamentary and council candidates) and the ESS public sample ($p < .05$ or less) **OR** statistically significant differences between Labour and Conservative (Left- and Right-wing) supporters within samples ($p < .05$ or less). Mean differences and associated p-values are calculated using independent samples t-tests with Bonferroni corrections. Standard deviations were not pooled to account for non-homogeneity of variance across subsamples. Negative Con-Lab distances indicate higher mean scores for Labour Party supporters, whereas positive Con-Lab distances indicate higher mean scores for Conservative Party supporters.

[**] Questions about climate action were not included in the ninth round of the ESS. Instead, public attitudes on climate action are calculated using data collected by the previous eighth (2016) round of the ESS (N = 1,557). These elite-mass comparisons are not robust to period effects on mass attitudes between 2016 and early 2019 when elite data were collected. These comparisons should be read as indicative only.

Unsuccessful Parliamentary Candidates (N = 134)		Unsuccessful Council Candidates (N = 331)		British Public – ESS 9 (N = 2,204)	
Mean (SD)	Con-Lab distance	Mean (SD)	Con-Lab distance	Mean (SD)	Con-Lab distance
3.85 (1.47)	**−1.55**	**3.98** (1.27)	**−0.99**	2.87 (1.16)	−0.09
4.18 (1.32)	**−1.53**	**4.34** (1.08)	**−1.16**	3.73 (1.05)	**−0.17**
3.70 (1.41)	−0.96	**3.95** (1.16)	**−0.84**	3.44 (1.14)	−0.01
3.60 (1.44)	**−2.42**	**3.51** (1.38)	**−2.32**	2.20 (0.80)	**−0.18**
3.69 (1.29)	**−1.97**	**3.75** (1.24)	**−1.85**	3.17 (1.13)	**−0.62**

Theories of Attitude Formation

For many decades, political psychologists have investigated those salient characteristics that may anchor, cause or moderate attitude formation and political behaviours. They have sought, in particular, to move beyond a Rational Choice Theory (RCT) of action, which typically draws on notions of utility maximisation and value expectancy to suggest that people form opinions (and later act upon them) that will optimise their own economic satisfaction and personal success (e.g., Binmore, 2009; Opp, 2017). In contrast, a 'Predisposition Model' in political psychology is concerned with delineating and testing the 'primary ingredients' of public opinion (see Kinder, 1998). These 'ingredients' include individuals' personality characteristics, ideologies, group attachments and social identity, genetic make-up and even evolution (for extended discussions, please see Huddy, Sears and Levy, 2013). Taken individually or together, these hidden phenomena provide blueprints by which to understand when and why citizens are predisposed to favour one policy, one candidate, one party or even one political opinion over another. For example, personality characteristics have now been used to explain political behaviours such as vote choice (Schoen and Schumann, 2007), party affiliation (Gerber et al., 2010), ideological self-placement (Jost, 2006), candidate preferences (Barbaranelli et al., 2007), as well as public policy preferences (Riemann et al., 1993).

The Predisposition Model does, however, suffer from an often-generalised assumption that citizens exist in a vacuum. In reality, predispositions only become meaningful and actionable in specific contexts. As McGraw (2000, p. 821) argues, '[t]he social context in political cognition research is largely ignored, even though citizens learn and think about the political world in complex environments'. At the same time, the mechanisms by which predispositions are translated from generic psychological principle to contextual application are not straightforward. The former often do not map neatly onto the messy and complex world of political reality and, as such, citizens require heuristics (or 'shortcuts' in processing information) to achieve cognitive or affective harmony between predispositions and political opinions or preferences (e.g., Feldman, 2003; Hatemi and McDermott, 2011). For this reason, there is merit to be found in conjoining top-down (e.g. elite cues) and bottom-up (e.g. individual personality) approaches to understanding political preferences.

The reconciliation of these theoretical and empirical approaches is captured in a 'Partisan Conflict-Predisposition Model' (see Leeper and Slothuus, 2014, p. 132). From this perspective, political parties (and the competition between them) facilitate the application of predispositions to political contexts by structuring the alternatives available to voters. Put another way, '[c]itizens can overcome informational shortfalls about politics, not because they (mysteriously) can simplify public choices effectively, but because these choices are systematically simplified for them' (Sniderman, 2000, p. 81). Unlike individual politicians and party leaders, who come and go at regular intervals, parties and their associated platforms, symbols and socio-political identities offer long-term bellwethers of political competition by which citizens are activated, mobilised, informed and persuaded (e.g. Lavine, Johnston and Steenbergen, 2012). At one step removed, it is citizens' predispositions that attract them to a party in the first place. A powerful congruency principle binds citizens (elites and voters) in partisan blocs; individuals seek and identify congruency between their own predispositions and those of the political 'families' available to them (Caprara et al., 2010; Weinberg, 2020b). This theoretical approach helps to make sense of parallel patterns in attitude formation such as those reported between elites and masses on the Left and Right of British politics (Table 3.2).

Similar 'dynamic' models of attitude formation might also help political scientists to understand the enduring differences between the discrete attitudes of political elites and masses. Giving primacy to neither person nor situation – and, by implication, understanding political attitudes and choices as the combination of individual predispositions as well as situational contexts, experiences and socialisation – it may be possible to determine when and why those with democratic power align or diverge from those on whose behalf they wield it. In terms of socialisation and situation, it is possible, for example, that unsuccessful candidates are less trusting of political institutions and actors than the average citizen because of the emotional rebuff of trying to enter the political world and being found wanting. Conversely, elected politicians may well be more trusting of 'the political' because of the *savoir faire* acquired in doing the job and seeing behind the curtain. Equally, politicians and candidates may well be less satisfied with the political system and more supportive of specific policy options than the public because of an asymmetry of information afforded by high-intensity political participation or, indeed, because they have experienced a system of otherwise opaque decision-making processes. On the flip side, a dynamic model of attitude formation suggests that differences in political attitudes between elites and masses will simultaneously rely on differences in psychological predispositions. It is to one such predisposition, basic values, that this chapter now turns.

Basic Values

In operationalising psychological predispositions to explain attitude formation and attitudinal differences between elites and masses, this chapter focuses on individuals' basic values. According to Schwartz (1992), basic values can be summarised as cognitive representations of sought-after, trans-situational targets that act as guiding principles in people's lives. Personality studies in psychology now advance an integrative view of the individual that gives greater attention to values alongside traits (see, for example, Barenbaum and Winter, 2008; Cervone, 2005; McAdams and Pals, 2006). There is growing evidence to suggest that values and traits capture distinct, yet complementary, data about personality (Parks-Leduc, Feldman and Bardi, 2015; Saroglou and Munoz-Garcia, 2008); people also find their own values more desirable than their traits and express less of a wish to change them (Roccas et al., 2014).

Schwartz's original theory (1992) identifies ten basic values that sit within four so-called 'higher-order' values on two orthogonals: Self-Enhancement values (Power, Achievement) oppose Self-Transcendence values (Benevolence, Universalism), and Conservation values (Security, Conformity, Tradition) oppose Openness to Change values (Hedonism, Stimulation, Self-Direction). Openness to Change values emphasise receptivity to change as well as independent thought, feeling and action, whereas Conservation values motivate submissive self-restriction, a desire to maintain stability and the preservation of traditional ideas, practices and customs. Self-Transcendence values encourage the acceptance of others as equals and place importance on regard for others' welfare, while Self-Enhancement values give weight to the pursuit of personal success and dominance over material and human resources.

The closer that values are situated to one another within the circle that encompasses the orthogonals, the greater the level of compatibility between their motivations and, by implication, it becomes more probable that they can be achieved or expressed through the same sentiments and actions. As values increase in distance around the circle, the greater the level of conflict between them and the more likely it is that the actions and attitudes used to express them will diverge. The content and structure of Schwartz's theory of basic values has been tested and reaffirmed across different socio-demographic and cultural contexts in a long list of studies worldwide (see Cieciuch, Schwartz and Vecchione, 2013, p. 1, 216). According to Borg (2019, p. 336) '[t]hese theorems have been replicated so many times in so many countries and cultures that they can almost be considered psychological laws' (see also Bilsky, Janik and Schwartz, 2011).

In politics, basic values have accounted for more variance in voting than personality traits, as well as demographic variables such as education, location and income (Caprara et al., 2006). Basic values have also been used to explain mass political attitudes and ideologies in a range of comparative contexts and political systems (Piurko, Schwartz and Davidov, 2011), as well as levels of political activism and participation among different publics (Pacheco and Owen, 2015; Vecchione et al., 2015). At an elite level, unique self-report data on the basic values of MPs have been studied in Italy and the UK (Caprara et al., 2010; Weinberg, 2020b). These studies suggest that: (a) basic values contribute to political ambition more so than socio-demographic factors and political opportunity structures; (b) MPs are psychologically distinct from those they govern; (c) politicians differ in their basic values according to gender, age, education and partisanship, but these differences are still smaller than those between MPs and their corresponding socio-economic and -demographic groups in the general population; and (d) congruence between the basic values of political elites and voters occurs to a much greater extent on the Right of British politics than the Left. Attesting to this personality gap between elites and citizens, Figure 3.1 compares the basic values of elected politicians, unsuccessful political candidates and the public in the UK.

In line with existing research, elites and masses in these samples show distinct differences in their basic values. Elected politicians and candidates attribute much more importance to Self-Transcendence and Openness to Change values than the general public, while the latter score higher for Conservation values. Elected politicians and unsuccessful candidates also display stronger motivations towards leadership and resource domination (Power values) than the British public. That these differences exist between

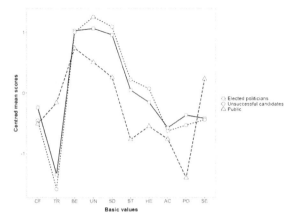

Figure 3.1   A comparison of basic values among political elites and citizens in the UK.
Note: CF – Conformity values; TR – Tradition values; BE – Benevolence values; UN –
Universalism values; SD – Self-Direction values; ST – Stimulation values; HE – Hedonism
values; AC – Achievement values; PO – Power values; SE – Security values. Politicians and
candidates completed the Twenty Item Values Inventory (TwIVI), which is a shortened
version of the Portrait Values Questionnaire (PVQ) designed to measure basic values
(Schwartz et al., 2001). All PVQs emphasise context-free thinking and contain short verbal
portraits of individuals, gender-matched with the respondent. For each portrait,
participants respond to the question 'How much like you is this person?' using a six-point
Likert scale that ranges from 'very much like me' to 'not like me at all'. A similar
instrument – the PVQ-21 – was administered to the British public by the ESS. A full
comparison of these survey instruments, including convergent and divergent validity, can
be found in Sandy et al. (2017). For a full discussion of robustness checks on the data used
here, please refer to Weinberg (2020b)

the public and both elected and unelected candidates reinforces prior
conclusions that personality characteristics delineate psychological differences between all those desiring a political career and those who would
never contemplate one. Put simply, these data circumscribe the political
animal. A small pool of research into elite and mass personality traits (the
Big Five in particular) finds parallel trends in comparative contexts (Best,
2011; Hanania, 2017; Nørgaard and Klemmensen, 2018; Scott and
Medeiros, 2020).

   The focus of this chapter is not, however, the differences between elite
and mass basic values, per se, but the explanatory potential of these
predispositions when it comes to understanding differences in political
attitudes. Existing research suggests that basic values are important as
central aspects of the self and as behavioural codebooks (e.g., Bardi and
Schwartz, 2003; Verplanken and Holland, 2002). Basic values are

theorised to predict behaviours and situational preferences through a series of 'linking processes': they can be activated by the external context in which an individual finds themselves (i.e. value activation); they can motivate individuals to reach value-associated goals through planned value-expressive behaviours (i.e. value planning); and they guide an individual's attention to or perception and interpretation of external stimuli (i.e. value guidance). In each case, the strength of these linking processes is heightened for an individual's most important basic values. There is no reason, then, why this same logic should not help to illuminate: (a) attitude formation in the context of politics generally and (b) differences in political attitudes between groups with varying value hierarchies (e.g. elites and masses).

To test the first of these assumptions, Table 3.3 presents univariate statistics for five attitudinal variables created from items fielded to politicians, candidates and the British public (see Table 3.2). These aggregate measures of opinion are correlated with all ten of participants' lower-order basic values. Bivariate correlations indicate meaningful and theoretically predictable associations between political attitudes and psychological predispositions across four of the five opinion domains.[2] At an aggregate level, Self-Transcendence values (Benevolence and Universalism) are positively associated with support for immigration, climate action and equality, and negatively associated with satisfaction with democracy. The opposite is true of Conservation values (Conformity, Tradition and Security). Only levels of political trust appear to be weakly correlated with participants' basic values.

A Dynamic Model of Attitude Formation among Elites and Masses

The previous section of this chapter showed that political elites (those who enter office as well as those who do not) are distinct in their psychological predispositions by comparison with the general UK public. It also demonstrated associations between basic values and political attitudes at an aggregate level. The purpose of the present section is to tease apart the implications of these findings vis-à-vis understanding and explaining differences in elite and mass political attitudes using dynamic theories of preference formation.

---

[2] Participants' mean scores for each basic value have been centred using their average response to all items on the survey in order to correct for individual differences in scale use.

Table 3.3. *Univariate statistics and correlation coefficients for latent political attitudes and basic values.*

	N	Mean	SD.	Cronbach alpha	(1)	(2)	(3)	(4)	(5)	CF	TR	BE	UN	SD	ST	HE	AC	PO	SE
(1) Political trust	3016	4.7	1.9	0.88	1	0.42	0.39	X	0.02	0.08	-0.08	-0.01	0.09	-0.05	-0.04	-0.04	0.12	0.08	-0.05
(2) Satisfaction with democracy	3065	4.3	2	0.84		1	-0.12	X	-0.43	0.09	0.32	-0.21	-0.36	-0.32	-0.24	-0.14	0.08	-0.15	0.21
(3) Immigration	3104	6.4	2.4	0.86			1	X	0.27	-0.11	-0.35	0.16	0.42	0.22	0.22	0.09	0.04	0.12	-0.28
(4) Climate action	2390	3.6	0.94	0.69				1	X	-0.14	-0.38	0.13	0.45	0.24	0.20	0.06	-0.03	0.02	-0.28
(5) Inequality	3124	3.0	0.98	0.54					1	-0.01	-0.28	0.22	0.37	0.22	0.19	0.11	-0.10	0.13	-0.19

Note: CF – Conformity values; TR – Tradition values; BE – Benevolence values; UN – Universalism values; SD – Self-Direction values; ST – Stimulation values; HE – Hedonism values; AC – Achievement values; PO – Power values; SE – Security values. Correlation coefficients in bold are statistically significant at $p < .05$ or less. Correlations between attitudes to climate action and basic values combine elite data with public responses collected in the eighth rather than the ninth round of the ESS.

A series of simple mixed models with random effects suggests that the strength of the connections between basic values and political attitudes differs across elected politicians, unsuccessful candidates and the public. Specifically, the examples illustrated in Figure 3.2 show that: (a) salient basic values may be activated when individuals are presented with political choices; (b) these basic values are correlated with meaningful variation in political attitudes regardless of subsample (i.e. changes in political attitudes mapped by basic values run in the same direction); but (c) basic values appear to share stronger associations with elite rather than public preferences. Even Security values – which are attributed [relatively] more importance by the public than political elites – have a broadly comparable predictive relationship with attitudes towards immigration across all three subsamples. As per existing research and earlier discussions in this chapter, it is possible that the differential strength of these relationships reflects an asymmetry of information and resource between political elites and masses, which in turn contributes to greater coherence in the activation and application of psychological predispositions to political choices among politicians as compared to the public.

In line with dynamic theories of attitude formation, it is probable that the effects of basic values upon political attitudes are dependent upon or work in conjunction with an individual's social identity and their exposure to partisan conflict in the political environment. To test the joint impact of these variables upon political attitudes, a series of nested ordinary least squares (OLS) regressions was conducted for each subsample. In each case, political attitudes are regressed on basic values (specifically the eight most highly correlated with the target attitude). Partisanship (coded broadly on the Left and Right) and sociodemographics are then added sequentially. Model statistics are reported for each of these iterations in Appendix A. At an aggregate level, these results support a dynamic approach to studying political attitudes: the addition of partisanship and socio-demographic controls increases the amount of variance in participants' political attitudes that is explained in these models by an average of 6 per cent for the public, 16 per cent for elected politicians and 10 per cent for unsuccessful candidates.[3] At the

---

[3] The Akaike Information Criteria (AIC) – which is a useful measure of prediction error and therefore the relative quality of statistical models – also decreases in all instances where partisanship and socio-demographics are added.

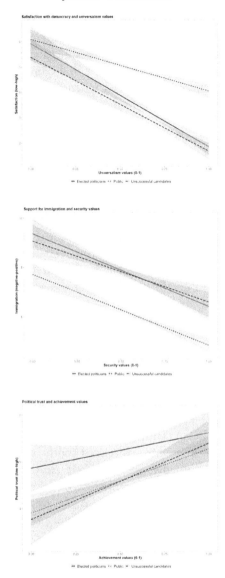

Figure 3.2   Basic values and political attitudes among elites and masses.
Note: basic values have been rescaled 0–1 so that the regression slopes extend from the lowest scores in the target population to the highest. Scores on the y axis run from low to high in the direction of the scale terms provided in parentheses. Shaded areas indicate 95 per cent confidence intervals.

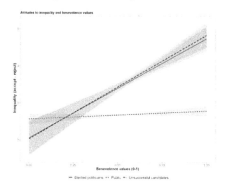

Figure 3.2 (*cont.*)

same time, it useful to note that basic values still account for as much or more variance in political attitudes, on average, than the additional controls: 6 per cent for the public, 19 per cent for elected politicians and 25 per cent for political candidates.

Two additional observations arise from these analyses (see Appendix A). First, basic values appear to explain considerably more variance in political attitudes among elites than masses. This supports the random effects reported in Figure 3.2 and suggests that public attitudes may rely to a greater extent on confounding variables that are not considered here. It is possible, for example, that public opinion is influenced more by elite cues or by media coverage of politics than predispositions, socialisation at the micro level or partisanship. These inferences cannot be tested here since they require reliable time-series data, but they may inform future research in this field. Second, the models reported in Appendix A are much better at explaining attitudes towards specific policy issues as opposed to diffuse attitudes about the state of politics and the political system. This may say something interesting about the applicability of basic values across a broader range of public opinion. It is possible that diffuse, system-level evaluations such as trust and satisfaction – as measured here – are either too broad to activate specific values or to allow for direct application of predispositions per se, or that these attitudes are more affective than cognitive and, therefore, based on intuition rather than conscious deliberation (the latter aids the predictive strength of basic values when explaining political behaviour; see Caprara et al., 2006).

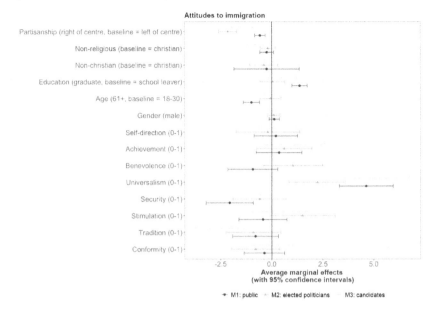

Figure 3.3   Predictors of support for immigration among UK politicians and the
UK public.

To illustrate the explanatory potential of these individual variables, the
average marginal effects of two 'dynamic' models are presented in
Figures 3.3 and 3.4.[4] These figures show the average change in response
scores for attitudes to immigration and climate action for each one unit
increase in any single independent variable, within each sample, while
controlling for the constant effects of all other variables in the model. In
terms of predispositions, Universalism values continue to exert positive
effects on both attitudes across all subsamples. For example, candidates
and members of the public most motivated by caring for others, engaging
with outgroups and protecting their environment scored, on average,
approximately five points (on a ten-point scale) more positively in their
attitudes to immigration than those who scored lowest for Universalism
values. In contrast, Power and Tradition values were negative predictors
of support for climate action, although these effects only reached

---

[4] Variance Inflation Factors (VIF) were calculated to rule out multicollinearity. Nearly all VIF scores
   were below two and none exceeded three.

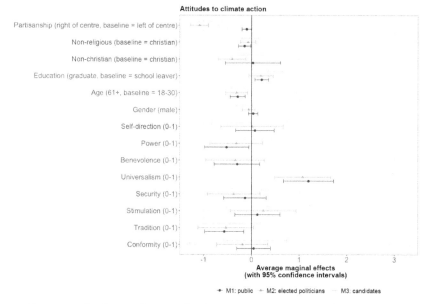

Figure 3.4   Predictors of support for climate action among UK politicians and the
UK public.

statistical significance among the public. It is possible that those most
psychologically wedded to 'the way things have always been' and most
motivated by control over their personal or material resources are less
likely to support system-level changes aimed at revolutionising how we
consume energy and how much we are allowed to consume. In both
models, additional controls also have meaningful effects on political
attitudes. In particular, partisans on the Right of British politics (those
who voted for or represented the Conservative Party or UKIP) are more
opposed to climate action and think more negatively about immigration than those on the Left (those who voted for or represent the
Labour Party, Scottish National Party, Green Party or the Liberal
Democrats). These partisan effects are also more pronounced among
elites than masses.

Conclusions

This chapter has attempted to add holistically to the central aims of this
edited collection: that is, to further the psychological study of

democracy and to add specifically to the study of political attitudes among elites and masses. Theoretical discussions have been matched with original empirical analysis of a unique dataset to show that: (a) psychological predispositions (particularly personality characteristics such as basic values) share meaningful relationships with people's political attitudes; (b) politicians and candidates differ from the public in their basic values; (c) basic values have a stronger effect upon political attitudes among elites than masses; but (d), in any case, the explanatory potential of a predisposition model is improved by accounting for partisan conflict and socialisation within politics.

At a broad level, this chapter adds theoretically and empirically to a specific research base on democratic elitism, largely conducted in the United States of America and touched upon earlier in this chapter, that has demonstrated the superficial and often illiberal nature of public opinion as compared to elites across a series of policy domains (see also Kinder and Kalmoe, 2017; Lupia, McCubbins and Popkin, 2000; McCloskey, 1964; Peffley and Rohrschneider, 2003). At an aggregate level, for example, UK politicians and candidates surveyed for this study are more liberal in their outlook than the public on policy domains such as immigration, climate action and inequality. At the same time, this chapter goes further in anchoring these claims of democratic elitism in a dynamic model of attitude formation. Unlike prior studies that start their analysis from the point of departure between self-reported elite and mass attitudes – and thus risk simply measuring an asymmetry of information or political interest between elites and masses – this chapter advances a joined-up approach that takes into account the psychological characteristics of politicians and those they govern. Put simply, politicians may be more liberally inclined in their political attitudes than the average citizen because their basic values are also uniquely oriented to such opinions. These assumptions obviously require qualification, not least given that prior research has demonstrated much larger differences between the basic values of voters and politicians on the Left than the Right of UK politics (see Weinberg, 2020b, chapter 4). As such, claims of democratic elitism undergirded by a predisposition model of attitude formation may require further ideological demarcation.

It is worth stressing that the findings in this chapter are offered as a preliminary foray into this line of inquiry and, as such, they suffer from a number of limitations. First, it is regrettable that the survey of politicians and candidates did not [and could not] take place simultaneously to the ninth round of the ESS. That said, the surveys were fielded just a matter of months apart and, in any case, variables like basic values remain remarkably stable after adolescence. Regardless of any fluctuations in political attitudes that could have occurred in the intervening months, it is thus highly unlikely that either sample changed their value priorities or orientations (for a related discussion, see Sagiv and Roccas, 2017). Second, the instruments used to measure basic values in each survey were slightly different in some of their item descriptors. It is not possible, therefore, to be entirely confident of measurement invariance across the two datasets. Third, only time-series data could account for the lagged/lead effects of each group's attitudes on the other (as per top-down and democratic-responsiveness models of public opinion). These challenges should be addressed in future research. Finally, it is worth reiterating, on one hand, that there are case studies within Western liberal democracies that defy the conclusions drawn above (the presidency of Donald Trump in the United States of America being a case in point) and, on the other hand, that these conclusions may not replicate in authoritarian regimes or even among political elites in extreme populist parties in liberal democracies.

Nevertheless, the arguments advanced in this chapter – that psychological peculiarities put elites out-of-step with actual popular political opinions – do raise a number of pertinent questions about the principal-agent relationship in representative democracies such as the UK. Can elites actually claim to represent the interests of their electors or some nebulous common good if, in fact, they do not place importance upon the same motivational goals? What does it say about the state of our political institutions and the accessibility of a political career if the people who enter the profession are comparatively unique in how they think and feel about politics, as well as life in general? Given that elites are more polarised from each other in their political attitudes than citizens – and these differences in attitudes in turn arise from distinct psychological predispositions on the Left and Right – then is it possible that the level of political conflict seen in the legislative arenas of contemporary democracies fails to reflect a popular psyche more attuned to consensus? These and many more questions will continue to fascinate scholars of democracy and, in particular, those studying the psychology of politicians.

REFERENCES

Barbaranelli, C., Caprara, G. V., Vecchione, M. and Fraley, C. R. (2007). Voters' personality traits in presidential elections. *Personality and Individual Differences*, 42, 1199–1208.

Bardi, A. and Schwartz, S. H. (2003). Values and behaviour: Strength and structure of relations. *Personality and Social Psychology Bulletin*, 29(10), 1207–1220.

Barenbaum, N. B. and Winter, D. G. (2008). History of modern personality theory and research. In O. P. John, R. W. Robins and L. A. Pervin (Eds.), *Handbook of personality: Theory and research* (3rd ed.) (pp. 3–26). New York: Guilford Press.

Benoit, K. and Laver, M. (2006). *Party policy in modern democracies*. London: Routledge.

Best, H. (2011). Does personality matter in politics? Personality factors as determinants of parliamentary recruitment and policy preferences. *Comparative Sociology*, 10, 928–948.

Best, H. and Vogel, L. (2018). Representative elites. In H. Best, J. P. Daloz, and U. Hoffman-Lange. (Eds.), *Palgrave handbook of political elites* (pp. 339–357). London: Palgrave.

Bilsky, W., Janik, M. and Schwartz, S. H. (2011). The structural organization of human values-evidence from three rounds of the European Social Survey (ESS). *Journal of Cross-Cultural Psychology*, 42(5), 759–776.

Binmore, K. (2009). *Rational decisions*. Princeton and Oxford: Princeton University Press.

Borg, I. (2019). Age- and gender-related differences in the structure and the meaning of personal values. *Personality and Individual Differences*, 138, 336–343.

Caprara, G. V., Francescato, D., Mebane, M., Sorace, R. and Vecchione, M. (2010). Personality foundations of ideological divide: A comparison of women Members of Parliament and women voters in Italy. *Political Psychology*, 31, 739–762.

Caprara, G. V., Schwartz, S., Capanna, C., Vecchione, M. and Barbaranelli, C. (2006). Personality and politics: Values, traits, and political choice source. *Political Psychology*, 27(1), 1–28.

Caprara, G. V. and Zimbardo, P. (2004). Personalizing politics: A congruency model of political preference. *American Psychologist*, 59, 581–594.

Cervone, D. (2005). Personality architecture: Within-person structures and processes. *Annual Review of Psychology*, 56, 423–452.

Cieciuch, J., Schwartz, S. H. and Vecchione, M. (2013). Applying the refined values theory to past data: What can researchers gain? *Journal of Cross-Cultural Psychology*, 44(8), 1215–1234.

Converse, P. (1964). The nature of belief systems in mass publics. In D. E. Apter (Ed.). *Ideology and discontent* (pp. 206–261). New York: Free Press.

Cunningham, J. and Moore, M. K. (1997). Elite and mass foreign policy opinions: Who is leading this charade? *Social Science Quarterly*, 78(3), 641–656.

Dean, J. and Maiguashca, B. (2020). Did somebody say populism? Towards a renewal and reorientation of populism studies. *Journal of Political Ideologies*, 25(1), 11–27. doi: 10.1080/13569317.2020.1699712

Dye, T. R. and Ziegler, H. (1978). *The irony of democracy*. Boston, MA: Duxbury.

Federico, C. M. (2015). The structure, foundations, and expression of ideology. In A. Berinsky (Ed.), *New directions in public opinion* (2nd ed.) (pp. 81–103). New York: Routledge.

Feldman, S. (2003). Values, ideology, and structure of political attitudes. In D. O. Sears, L. Huddy and R. Jervis (Eds.), *Oxford handbook of political psychology* (pp. 477–508). New York: Oxford University Press.

Gerber, A. S., Huber, G. A., Doherty, D., Dowling, C. M. and Ha, S. (2010). Personality and political attitudes: Relationships across issue domains and political contexts. *American Political Science Review*, 104, 111–133.

Hanania, R. (2017). The personalities of politicians: A Big Five study of American legislators. *Personality and Individual Differences*, 108, 164–167.

Hatemi, P. K. and McDermott, R. (2011). *Man is by nature a political animal: Evolution, biology and politics*. Chicago: University of Chicago Press.

Huddy, L., Sears, D. and Levy, J. (Eds.) (2013). *Oxford handbook of political psychology*. Oxford, UK: Oxford University Press.

Johnston, C. D., Lavine, H. G. and Federico, C. M. (2017). *Open versus closed: Personality, identity, and the politics of redistribution*. Cambridge, UK: Cambridge University Press.

Joly, J., Soroka, S. and Loewen, P. (2019) Nice guys finish last: Personality and political success, *Acta Polit*, 54, 667–683, doi:10.1057/s41269-018-0095-z

Jost, J. T. (2006). The end of the end of ideology. *American Psychologist*, 61, 651–670.

Jost, J. T., Federico, C. M. and Napier, J. L. (2009). Political ideology: Its structure, functions, and elective affinities. *Annual Review of Psychology*, 60, 307–337.

Jost, J. T., Glaser, J., Kruglanski, A. W. and Sulloway, F. (2003). Political conservatism as motivated social cognition. *Psychological Bulletin*, 129, 339–375.

Kelsen, H. (1992). *Introduction to the problems of legal theory*. Oxford, UK: Clarendon Press.

Kinder, D. R. (1998). Communication and opinion. *Annual Review of Political Science*, 1, 167–197.

Kinder, D. R. and Kalmoe, N. P. (2017). *Neither liberal nor conservative: Ideological innocence in the American public*. Chicago: University of Chicago Press.

Lavine, H., Johnston, C. and Steenbergen, M. (2012). *The ambivalent partisan*. New York: Oxford University Press.

Leeper, T. J. and Slothuus, R. (2014). Political parties, motivated reasoning, and public opinion formation. *Political Psychology*, 35(1), 129–156.

Lupia, A., McCubbins, M. and Popkin, S. L. (Eds.) (2000). *Elements of reason. Cognition, choice and the bounds of rationality*. Cambridge, UK: Cambridge University Press.

May, J. (1973). Opinion structure of political parties: The special law of curvilinear disparity. *Political Studies*, 21(2), 135–151.

McAdams, D. P. and Pals, J. L. (2006). A new Big Five: Fundamental principles for an integrative science of personality. *American Psychologist*, 61, 204–217.

McCloskey, H. (1964). Consensus and ideology in American politics. *American Political Science Review*, 58, 361–382.

McGraw, K. M. (2000). Contributions of the cognitive approach to political psychology. *Political Psychology*, 27(4), 805–832.

Näsström, S. (2015). Democratic representation beyond election. *Constellations*, 22(1), 1–12. doi:10.1111/1467-8675.12123

Nørgaard, A. S. and Klemmensen, R. (2018). The personalities of Danish MPs: Trait- and aspect-level differences. *Journal of Personality*, 87(2), 267–275. doi:10.1111/jopy.12388

Opp, K. (2017). Rational choice theory and methodological individualism. In P. Kivisto (Ed.), *The Cambridge handbook of social theory* (pp. 1–23). Cambridge, UK: Cambridge University Press.

Pacheco, G. and Owen, B. (2015). Moving through the political participation hierarchy: A focus on personal values. *Applied Economics*, 47(3), 222–238.

Page, B. I. and Shapiro, R. Y. (1983). Effects of public opinion on policy. *American Political Science Review*, 80, 1249–1270.

Parks-Leduc, L., Feldman, G. and Bardi, A. (2015). Personality traits and personal values: A meta-analysis. *Personality and Social Psychology Review*, 19(1), 3–29.

Peffley, M. and Rohrschneider, R. (2003). Democratization and political tolerance in seventeen countries: A multilevel model of democratic learning. *Political Research Quarterly*, 56(3), 243–257.

Piurko, Y., Schwartz, S. H. and Davidov, E. (2011). Basic personal values and the meaning of left-right political orientations in 20 countries, *Political Psychology*, 32, 537–561.

Riemann, R., Grubich, C., Hempel, S., Mergl, S. and Richter, M. (1993). Personality and attitudes towards current political topics. *Personality and Individual Differences*, 15, 313–321.

Roccas, S., Sagiv, L., Oppenheim, S., Elster, A. and Gal, A. (2014). Integrating content and structure aspects of the self: Traits, values, and self-improvement. *Journal of Personality*, 82(2), 144–157.

Sagiv, L. and Roccas, S. (2017). What personal values are and what they are not: Taking a cross-cultural perspective. In S. Roccas and L. Sagiv (Eds.), *Values and behaviour: Taking a cross-cultural perspective* (pp. 3–13). New York: Springer International Publishing.

Sandy, C. J., Gosling, S. D., Schwartz, S. H. and Koelkebeck, T. (2017). The development and validation of brief and ultrabrief measures of values. *Journal of Personality Assessment*, 99(5), 545–555.

Saroglou, V. and Munoz-Garcia, A. (2008). Individual differences in religion and spirituality: An issue of personality traits and/or values. *Journal for the Scientific Study of Religion*, 43, 83–101.

Saward, M. (2010). *The representative claim*. Oxford, UK: Oxford University Press.

(2006). The representative claim. *Contemporary Political Theory*, 5(3), 297–318.

Schoen, H. and Schumann, S. (2007). Personality traits, partisan attitudes, and voting behaviour: Evidence from Germany. *Political Psychology*, 28, 471–498.

Schwartz, S. H. (1992). Universals in the content and structure of values: Theory and empirical tests in 20 countries. In M. Zanna (Ed.). *Advances in experimental social psychology*. New York: Academic Press.

Schwartz, S. H., Melech, G., Lehmann, A., Burgess, S., Harris, M. and Owens, V. (2001). Extending the cross-cultural validity of the theory of basic human values with a different method of measurement. *Journal of Cross-Cultural Psychology*, 32(5), 519–542.

Scott, C. and Medeiros, M. (2020). Personality and political careers: What personality types are likely to run for office and get elected? *Personality and Individual Differences*, 152. doi:10.1016/j.paid.2019.109600

Sniderman, P. M. (2000). Taking sides: A fixed choice theory of political reasoning. In A. Lupia, M. D. McCubbins and S. L. Popkin (Eds.), *Elements of reason* (pp. 1–20). New York: Cambridge University Press.

Sniderman, P. M., Brody, R. A. and Tetlock, P. E. (1991). *Reasoning and choice*. New York: Cambridge University Press.

Sood, G. and Iyengar, S. (2014). *All in the eye of the beholder: Partisan affect and ideological accountability*. Unpublished manuscript [Online]. Available at: www.gsood.com/research/papers/inNout.pdf [Accessed: 14 February 2018].

Tiberj, K. and Kerrouche, E. (2013). Up and down, old and new: Values and value systems of MPs and voters in France. *The Journal of Legislative Studies*, 19(2), 160–177.

Vecchione, M., Schwartz, S., Caprara, G., Schoen, H., Cieciuch, J., Silvester, J., Bain, P., Bianchi, G., Kirmanoglu, H., Baslevent, C., Mamali, C., Manzi, J., Pavlopoulos, V., Posnova, T., Torres, C., Verkasalo, M., Lönnqvist, J., Vondráková, E., Welzel, C. and Alessandri, G. (2015). Personal values and political activism: A cross-national study. *British Journal of Psychology*, 106(1): 84–106.

Verplanken, B. and Holland, R. W. (2002). Motivated decision making: Effects of activation and self-centrality of values on choices and behaviour. *Journal of Personality and Social Psychology*, 82(3), 434–47.

Weinberg, J. (2020a). Who wants to be a politician? Basic values and candidate emergence in the United Kingdom. *British Journal of Political Science*, 51(4), 1565–1581. doi:10.1017/S0007123419000814

(2020b). *Who enters politics and why? Basic human values in the UK Parliament.* Bristol: Bristol University Press.

(2019). The winner takes it all? A psychological study of political success among UK Members of Parliament. *Parliamentary Affairs*, 73(4), 711–733. doi:10.1093/pa/gsz017

Zaller, J. R. (1992). *The nature and origins of mass opinion.* New York: Cambridge University Press.

Model statistics for OLS regressions of political attitudes among the British public (P), politicians (E) and unsuccessful candidates (C)

		Trust			Satisfaction			Immigration			Climate Action		
		P	E	C	P	E	C	P	E	C	P	E	C
Model 1	R²	.028	.054	.127	.040	.140	.128	.112	.247	.331	.088	.279	.355
	AIC	7885.673	1724.797	1726.805	7623.56	1765.481	1692.439	9242.336	1767.784	1760.743	3399.263	1069.789	1134.198
Model 2	R²	.025	.085	.230	.088	.371	.207	.169	.358	.368	.097	.476	.473
	AIC	5549.736	1711.502	1674.501	5392.811	1623.438	1652.057	6337.388	1695.866	1736.942	2306.241	788.621	783.097
Model 3	R²	.068	.106	.260	.093	.376	.210	.216	.367	.391	.127	.489	.499
	AIC	5435.03	1673.542	1640.585	5338.639	1594.847	1631.794	6203.566	1666.543	1706.661	2258.802	756.092	746.966

		Inequality		
		P	E	C
Model 1	R²	0.009	0.214	0.296
	AIC	4593.228	1338.524	1275.935
Model 2	R²	0.082	0.397	0.385
	AIC	3161.227	1217.826	1217.435
Model 3	R²	0.097	0.403	0.392
	AIC	3114.299	1194.383	1200.828

Note: Model 1 = Basic values only (up to eight salient predictors); Model 2 = Model 1 + Partisanship (Left–Right); Model 3 = Model 2 + Socio-demographics (age, gender, education, religion).

CHAPTER 4

Under the Microscope:
Prime Minister's Questions in the UK Parliament

Peter Bull and Maurice Waddle

In the UK, laws are passed by the House of Commons, which is supreme in legislative matters. The Prime Minister (PM) is answerable to the Commons, and must maintain its support to stay in power. Every Wednesday at noon while Parliament is sitting, the Commons is called to order by *the Speaker*,[1] who announces 'Order! Questions to the Prime Minister'. This heralds the start of the debate known as Prime Minister's Questions (PMQs). For at least the next half-hour, Members of Parliament (MPs) have the opportunity to pose questions to the PM on any topic of their choice, thereby bringing to the event a degree of political accountability. PMQs is the central British parliamentary institution and its highest profile parliamentary event. It has also become the focus of a burgeoning research literature. To review and evaluate this literature is the purpose of this chapter.

Notably, the tradition of questioning heads of government in parliamentary settings is not confined to the UK. In Canada, this convention is known as Question Period, in Australia and New Zealand as Question Time, in India as Question Hour. A fixed period for questions – Question Time – is a feature of many European parliaments. In some countries, such as Austria and Finland, the procedure for asking questions is even enshrined in the constitution. In the European Parliament, a Question Time, allowing members to ask questions in plenary sessions, was introduced in 1973 (Norton, 1993).

However, perhaps unsurprisingly in the self-styled 'mother of parliaments', the British version of PMQs was the first to appear (Norton, 1993), its tradition dating right back to the eighteenth century, to the era of the first and longest-serving British PM, Sir Robert Walpole (PM 1721–1742). In its modern form, the institution of PMQs dates from

---

[1] The Speaker, so-called because traditionally he spoke on behalf of other MPs, presides over debates in the House (including Prime Minister's Questions), determining, among other things, which members may speak.

1961, when it was formalised to two fifteen-minute events – on Tuesdays and Thursdays. In 1997, this procedure was changed by PM Tony Blair to just one weekly event every Wednesday, lasting for thirty minutes.

In PMQs, backbench MPs[2] who wish to ask a question must enter their names on the Order Paper. The names of entrants are then randomised in a ballot to produce a list from which they will be called by the Speaker. MPs who are not so selected may be chosen to ask a question by rising from their seat immediately before the PM's reply; this practice is known as 'catching the Speaker's eye' (House of Commons Information Office, 2010a, p. 8). PMQs always begins with the same tabled question, asking the PM to list his/her 'official engagements' for the day. At this point, the called member can then follow with a so-called *supplementary*, namely, a question on almost any topic of their choice relating to some aspect of the PM's responsibility or government policy. In addition to the official engagements question, *closed* questions on a particular topic can also be asked, which allow the PM to read out a prepared answer before a supplementary question on the same topic is posed. However, the Leader of the Opposition (LO) is not constrained by the same limitation and is allowed up to six questions, thereby having the opportunity for follow-ups.[3] Importantly, as there is no requirement for prior notice of the topic of supplementary questions, the proceedings retain the potential for unpredictability and surprise.

In PMQs, MPs must orient themselves to the expectation that the dialogue should follow a question-response pattern. However, they are expected to observe certain traditions and conventions, including the avoidance of what is termed *unparliamentary language*. Specifically, they should not be abusive or insulting, call another member a liar, suggest another MP has false motives or misrepresent another MP. These conventions are enforced by the Speaker, who may admonish members who break the rules of the House. For example, the Speaker may ask an MP to withdraw an objectionable utterance. Historically, they have objected to the use of abusive epithets such as coward, git, guttersnipe, hooligan, rat, swine, traitor and stoolpigeon (House of Commons Information Office, 2010b). An MP who refuses to comply with the Speaker may be suspended from the House (referred to in parliamentary procedure as *naming*).

---

[2] Backbench MPs are so called because, in the Chamber, they sit in the rows of benches behind their parties' spokespeople, who are known as frontbenchers.

[3] Currently, the only other member granted the opportunity to ask more than a single question is the leader of the second largest party of opposition (currently the Scottish National Party), who may ask two questions.

The stated purpose of a question to the PM is 'to obtain information or to press for action' (House of Commons Procedure Committee, 1995). This can be linked to the five broader objectives of parliamentary questions: 'a vehicle for individual backbenchers to raise the individual grievance of their constituencies'; 'an opportunity for the House. . . to probe. . . the Executive'; 'a means of illuminating differences of policy on major issues between the various political parties, or of judging the parliamentary skills of individual members. . .'; 'a combination of these or any other purposes, for example, a way of enabling the Government to disseminate information. . .'; and 'the obtaining of information by the House from the Government' (House of Commons Procedure Committee, 1991).

Although there has been praise for PMQs (e.g. Gimson, 2012; *The Guardian*, 2010; Sedgemore, 1980; Thatcher, 1993), it has often faced severe criticism from select committees, parliamentarians and commentators (e.g. Blair, 2010; Thomas, 2006). Such criticism is exemplified by one recent Speaker, John Bercow, who complained about the 'character, conduct, content and culture' of PMQs, arguing that it is dominated by questions from the LO to the exclusion of backbench questions, that MPs treat the PM as if 'a President in sole control of the. . . Government' and that MPs 'yell and heckle' in an 'unbecoming manner', providing 'scrutiny by screech' (Bercow, 2010).

PMQs has certainly become notorious for its political point-scoring. When David Cameron became Leader of the Conservative Party (6 December 2005), he pledged to bring an end to 'the Punch and Judy[4] politics of Westminster, the name-calling, backbiting, point-scoring, finger-pointing'. However, Cameron subsequently admitted in a BBC radio interview that he had not kept this pledge, blaming the adversarial nature of PMQs (BBC, 2008). Indeed, one distinguished political journalist (Hoggart, 2011) characterised the event thus:

> Prime Minister's Questions is increasingly like an unpleasant football match, in which the game played publicly is accompanied by all sorts of secret grudge matches, settlement of scores and covert fouls committed when the players hope the [referee] is not looking.

The most substantive recent academic analyses of PMQs have been conducted by Bates et al. (2014) and by Waddle, Bull and Böhnke (2019). The analysis by Bates et al. spanned thirty-one years, comprising the early

---

[4] Punch and Judy is a traditional popular British puppet show, which features domestic strife between the two central characters, Mr Punch and his wife, Judy.

periods of five recent PMs [Margaret Thatcher (Conservative PM 1979–1990), John Major (Conservative PM 1990–1997), Tony Blair (Labour PM 1997–2007), Gordon Brown (Labour PM 2007–2010) and David Cameron (Conservative PM 2010–2016)]. The analysis by Waddle et al. (2019) was based on the same five leaders, but focused on both their early and later periods as PMs – a span of thirty-seven years (1979–2016); the particular concern of their article was personal attacks in PMQs.

Overall, academic research on PMQs can be broadly summarised under four main headings: historical trends, adversarialism, equivocation and public perceptions. Each of these topics is reviewed in the following sections.

Historical Trends in PMQs Research

Historical analyses of PMQs in the House of Commons – from 1868 to 1987 – have been conducted by Dunleavy and colleagues, based on Hansard (the written record of proceedings in Parliament) (Dunleavy et al., 1993; Dunleavy, Jones and O'Leary, 1990). Their chosen starting point was 1868, following the 1867 *Representation of the People Act* that established the Commons in its recognisably modern form as a body of elected representatives directly accountable to a mass electorate.[5]

Notably, in the nineteenth century, questions to the PM were treated no differently to questions put to any other minister; they could be asked on any day when ministers were present, without notice, and were dealt with in whatever order MPs rose to ask them (Allen et al., 2014). Occasional piecemeal changes were then introduced from the late 1880s onwards. In 1881, as a mark of respect to the then PM, William Gladstone,[6] it was agreed that questions to the PM would be placed last on the day's list so that he could attend the House later in the day. However, in subsequent years, due in part to the growing number of questions to other government ministers, questions to the PM were rarely reached. Therefore, in 1904, it was agreed that they should commence no later than Question 45 on the day's list. Despite this, questions to the PM were often still not reached. In 1953, out of respect for another PM of advancing years – Winston Churchill[7] – it was agreed that he would answer questions only on Tuesdays and Thursdays. It was not until

---

[5] At that time, the mass electorate only included a minority of the population, given the property qualification for voting for adult males and the total exclusion of women.

[6] Gladstone was aged seventy-one at that time. He served as PM four times; his final term ended in 1894 at the age of eighty-four.

[7] Churchill continued as PM until 1955, when he resigned aged eighty.

1961 that the procedure was formalised into fifteen-minute slots on those two days each week (to be replaced in 1997 by just one thirty-minute slot on Wednesdays).

The analyses of Dunleavy and colleagues (1993, 1990) were focused on the premierships of nineteen PMs (from Benjamin Disraeli, who first became PM in 1868, to Margaret Thatcher). All these PMs were answerable to the House of Commons. Their parliamentary activities were categorised under four main headings: answering questions; making a ministerial statement; delivering a speech as part of a debate; and minor interventions in debates (e.g. impromptu debating responses to points initiated by other MPs). Historically, results showed that PMs engaged in all four such parliamentary activities, whereas, in modern times, especially since the mid-1970s, PMQs has come to the fore.

Historical analyses have also shown substantial increases in questions and changes to the pattern of question-asking in the House of Commons. In the first half of the twentieth century, Question Time stood out as a mechanism used by backbenchers, but not extensively (Chester and Bowring, 1962, as cited in Norton, 1993). Indeed, the number of oral questions tabled in the 1950s did not deviate much from the number tabled in the years of the Liberal government of 1906–1914, the daily average of tabled questions rarely exceeding 100. It seems that, when MPs had constituency matters they wished to pursue, they preferred to correspond in writing with ministers. Tabling questions was seen, not as a preference, but as a last resort.

However, between 1960 and 1990, the number of oral questions on the Order Paper dramatically increased – from 13,778 in the parliamentary session of 1960–1961 to 24,687 in the 1989–1990 session. By 1990, it was common for over 400 (sometimes over 500) questions for oral answer to be tabled on the two days when the PM (and other ministers) answered questions (Irwin et al., 1993).

Furthermore, there were marked changes in the pattern of question-asking and in the communicative functions the questions fulfilled. Three particular features were observed by Norton (1993). First, question-asking had become much more partisan. Notably, it was common for parties to hand out suggested questions to their backbenchers, a practice known as *syndication* (Giddings and Irwin, 2005). Syndication developed in the 1970s (Wilson, 1977), and burgeoned in the 1980s, as each side felt obliged to respond to the other (Norton, 1993). It was described by the Commons Procedure Committee in 1990 as an 'abuse', and the Committee proposed rule changes to try to discourage it. However, according to a questionnaire posed to MPs in 2001, requests to table questions from party advisers or *whips* (party officials whose role is to maintain the discipline of its members) were still frequent. As many as 30 per cent of MPs reported receiving such requests at least once a week, 52 per cent reported occasionally acceding to such requests, while only 20 per cent stated that they never acceded to such requests (Giddings and Irwin, 2005). A second important reported feature of question-asking was attention-seeking by MPs, especially since the televising of Parliament began in 1989. Posing questions in PMQs could raise a politician's status with their party hierarchy, their constituents and the public at large. A third development was the tabling of questions in response to increasing demands made on MPs by constituents and pressure groups (Norton, 1993).

In the recent historical analysis of thirty-one years of PMQs by Bates et al. (2014), a significant drop was found in the number of questions. While an average of 35.7 questions were asked during each of Thatcher's early PMQs, the equivalent for Blair was 25.9, for Brown 26.3 and for Cameron 26.5. Bates et al. also reported that, in 1979, Thatcher typically accounted for around 45 per cent of the words spoken per session of PMQs; by 2010, Cameron's equivalent figure was 60 per cent. In 1979, the average LO contribution was 4.1 per cent of the total spoken words; by 2010, that figure had increased almost threefold to 11.5 per cent. In contrast, opposition backbench questions to the PM during Thatcher's early premiership accounted for 28 per cent of words spoken, whereas the corresponding figures for Brown's and Cameron's were 14 and 16 per cent, respectively. This growing PM dominance of PMQs and, particularly, the increased focus on the LO-PM contest has been at the expense of the direct contribution of backbenchers. While that overshadowing may be inevitable, the scrutiny of government by backbench MPs is of equal importance to the democratic process.

Overall, these historical analyses show that PMQs has become by far the most prominent form of prime ministerial activity in the Commons, and that the interaction between the PM and the LO has become increasingly the dominant form of activity within PMQs.

Adversarialism

A number of authors have commented on the adversarial discourse of PMQs. Over thirty years ago, the interaction between the leaders of the two main parties was described as a form of 'gladiatorial combat', with both sides cheering their leader and booing their opponent (Irwin, 1988,

p. 82). Furthermore, at his election as Speaker on 17 June 1987, Bernard Weatherill told the House that he had been 'appalled' to hear the noises during the radio broadcast of PMQs and, in the 1983–1987 Parliament, he regularly appealed for better (and quieter) behaviour at Question Time. In this section, we review some key research on adversarialism at PMQs – considering various forms of impoliteness, potential functions, individual behaviours and approaches, and associated effects.

In a study entitled 'Being politically impolite', Harris (2001) argued that much of the discourse of PMQs is composed of intentional and explicitly face-threatening acts (FTAs). These are forms of speech that may either make a person look bad, or threaten their future freedom of action (Brown and Levinson, 1978, 1987). Harris analysed twelve sessions of PMQs from March to November 2000. She argued that systematic impoliteness at PMQs is not only sanctioned but rewarded in line with expectations in an adversarial and confrontational political system. Hence, even serious FTAs rarely, if ever, cause a breakdown in interpersonal relationships, nor is that the intention. MPs fully recognise that the main purpose of political opposition is to oppose, namely, to challenge, criticise, subvert, even ridicule the policies and actions of the government. Never is this more apparent than in these weekly exchanges between the PM and the LO. Indeed, the latter will know that his/her reputation as a skilful and effective adversary, whereby they can best enhance their own *face* by undermining that of the PM, is commensurate with their success as a leader. Arguably, the presence of television cameras has intensified this adversarial and confrontational process.

Harris (2001) identified a number of ways of performing FTAs, which often deride the competence of the PM (Bull and Fetzer, 2010). For example, one strategy is to pose a question requesting highly specific information, which the PM may not have to hand or may not wish to divulge. If (s)he declines or fails to answer, the LO may then provide the information in order to embarrass or attack the PM. Also common are questions containing loaded presuppositions, thereby triggering implicatures that contribute to the strength of the FTA. The question 'Doesn't he find it deeply disturbing that the Trade Secretary is a classic example of this all mouth and no delivery Government?' presupposes that the government is 'all mouth and no delivery'. Similarly, the question 'Will the PM promise straightforwardness and honesty in future health announcements?' implies that past announcements were not honest and straightforward. Harris observed that the latter example is particularly interesting, since conventions regarding unparliamentary language (see above) prohibit accusations of lying. An explicit accusation, unless retracted immediately, would result in the MP's expulsion from the Chamber.

A typology of FTAs in PMQs was devised by Bull and Wells (2012). In addition to detailed questions and contentious presuppositions, (Harris, 2001), Bull and Wells identified four further distinct means of performing FTAs in questions. First, questions typically take the form of one or more propositions followed by an interrogative, e.g., 'Is the PM aware that...' or 'Will the PM assure the House that...'? (Harris, 2001). These propositions that preface the interrogative may contain information with the potential to perform FTAs. A second is through conflictual questions – where all possible responses are potentially face-threatening, but a response is still expected (see Bull, 2008; Bull et al., 1996), e.g. 'Does the government accept systemic failure in this department?'[8] A third technique is to invite the PM to perform some kind of face-damaging act (e.g. issuing an apology, criticising a fellow party member, admitting that a particular policy has failed or conceding that a government department has been incompetent). Each of the above questioning techniques typically conforms to the question-response format expected in PMQs (for detailed examples, see Bull and Wells, 2012, pp. 36–40).

Finally, however, MPs may depart from this format to make asides, which may also be used to perform FTAs. In the following example (17 October 2007), Cameron (while LO) used an interruption from a Labour MP to make an aside accusing the Labour government of a lack of discipline. During his question, Cameron was twice interrupted by the shouting of a Labour MP, who then received the following reprimand from the Speaker: 'Order. I hope the Honourable Gentleman Mr. Austin you're not going to keep shouting again. You have a difficulty in Prime Minister's Questions. You keep shouting. Shouldn't do it'. Cameron then used the reprimand to quip: 'It comes to something when you have to tick off the Prime Minister's own PPS'.[9] Cameron's aside prompted laughter from MPs, as he resumed his original question.

In response to FTAs in questions, Bull and Wells (2012) identified five distinctive countermeasures used by PMs. First, the PM may talk up their own *positive face*,[10] or that of the government. Second, by way of a

---

[8] The quoted example, reported in Bull and Wells (2012), refers to the loss of computer discs containing the personal data of Child Benefit claimants. An affirmative response would indicate incompetence; a denial, due to the publicity the incident had generated, would lack credibility.

[9] Ian Austin was Parliamentary Private Secretary (PPS) to PM Brown.

[10] Positive face is defined as 'the want of every member that his wants be desirable to at least some others' (Brown and Levinson, 1987, p. 62).

rebuttal, the PM may explicitly refute the FTA performed by the questioner. A third way is to counter-attack; a fourth is simply to ignore the FTA. Finally, a fifth strategy is that of self-justification, whereby the PM offers reasons, explanations or excuses for the actions taken. Notably, all of these strategies can be used separately or in combination, and may or may not involve the performance of a FTA by the PM (for detailed examples of all five categories, see Bull and Wells, 2012, pp. 40–42).

Bull and Wells (2012) use the term *face aggravation* in the context of PMQs to refer to the aggressive use of facework (see Goffman, 1967), in which antagonists seek to score points over their opponent. Overall, they proposed that face aggravation between leaders is not just acceptable in terms of parliamentary discourse, it is both sanctioned and rewarded – thereby an opportunity for the LO to enhance their own status. They further argued that PMQs should be considered another of the situations identified by Culpeper (1996), where impoliteness is not a marginal activity, but central to the ongoing interaction.

Impoliteness in the form of personal attacks was the focus of the study by Waddle et al. (2019) via an evaluation of LO–PM exchanges, encompassing the early and latter periods of five premierships (from Thatcher through to Cameron). Using a coding system based on language characterised as personally disrespectful, they highlighted and provided examples of seven types of personal attacks in PMQs. The first of these was *negative personality statements*, for example 'The truth is he is weak and despicable and wants to crawl to power in Alex Salmond's[11] pocket' (PM Cameron to LO Ed Miliband on 11 March 2015). The other six types were: *implications of an enduring negative character trait, negative names* (e.g. 'He is just the nowhere man of British politics'), *disparaging insinuations, condescending remarks, mockery* and *badgering*. They showed that PM Cameron was more personally antagonistic towards the LO than the four PMs who preceded him. Each PM from Thatcher onwards showed an increase in personal antagonism over their respective premierships. A peak was reached in the penultimate year of Cameron's term of office, when, in the final ten PMQs sessions prior to the 2015 general election, almost 62 per cent of his responses to LO Miliband contained personal disrespect. Interestingly, however, Cameron's attacks reduced significantly at the end of his time in office in 2016, when responding to questions from Jeremy Corbyn (Labour LO since 2015), who himself used fewer personal attacks

[11] Alex Salmond is a former First Minister of Scotland, MP, and a former leader of the Scottish National Party (SNP).

than any other LO over the thirty-seven-year period of analysis (1979–2016).

Corbyn became leader of the Labour Party on 12 September 2015 and, four days after this appointment, he participated in his first PMQs as LO (16 September 2015). During his successful campaign for the leadership, Corbyn had called for a 'new kind of politics' (ITV, 2015). One feature of this 'new' approach, apparent during his early sessions, was to include questions to the PM sourced from members of the public, as illustrated in the following extract from his first PMQs:

> ... Many told me that they thought Prime Minister's Question Time was too theatrical, that Parliament was out of touch and too theatrical, and that they wanted things done differently, but above all they wanted their voice heard in Parliament. So I thought, in my first Prime Minister's Question Time, I would do it in a slightly different way... So I sent out an email to thousands of people and asked them what questions they would like to put to the Prime Minister and I received 40,000 replies. There is not time to ask 40,000 questions today – our rules limit us to six – so I would like to start with the first one, which is about housing. Two-and-a-half thousand people emailed me about the housing crisis in this country. I ask one from a woman called Marie, who says, 'What does the government intend to do about the chronic lack of affordable housing and the extortionate rents charged by some private sector landlords in this country?'

Cameron's response to Corbyn included:

> ... Let me now answer, very directly, Marie's question. We do need to see more affordable housing in our country. We delivered 260,000 affordable housing units during the last Parliament, and we built more council houses in our country than had been managed in the previous 13 years, but I recognise that much more needs to be done.... (Hansard HC Deb, 16 September 2015, col. 1037)

At his first session of PMQs as LO, all six of Corbyn's questions took the form of such 'public questions' (Bull and Waddle, 2019). At subsequent sessions, the number was reduced – down to three, then four, then just one or two for several weeks, until his twentieth session (13 April 2016), when none of his quota of six questions were of that type. The adversarial impact of these public questions was assessed by comparing them with LO–PM exchanges in which such questions did not feature (Bull and Waddle, 2019). Results showed that Cameron, when responding to non-public questions, made significantly more personal attacks than Corbyn; however, the level of such attacks by Cameron for public questions was as low as Corbyn's, with no significant difference between them. This revealed the potential for public questions to mitigate the ritualistic and customary adversarialism of PMQs.

A further analysis of personal attacks in PMQs was conducted in relation to question topic (Waddle and Bull, 2020a), in which the authors utilised the dataset from their previous study (Waddle et al., 2019). In addition to personal attacks, questions were coded according to policy topic, based on techniques used by John et al. (2013). A comparison was made of domestic and foreign policy topics, which showed that question-response sequences focused on foreign policy were significantly lower in personal attacks than exchanges on domestic policies. This apparent reduction in adversarialism during foreign policy debates may be considered a form of patriotism,[12] or at least a desire by leading politicians to avoid appearing unpatriotic.

Although PMQs is often castigated for its adversarialism – as no more than a worthless exercise in political point-scoring – adversarial questioning can play a significant role in political opposition. This was illustrated in an analysis of the way in which the then Labour LO Miliband challenged PM Cameron in PMQs regarding his handling of the British phone-hacking scandal[13] (Bull, 2013). Through his questions in PMQs, Miliband succeeded in getting Cameron to agree to setting up a public inquiry into the culture and practices of British newspapers. Thereby, the LO could be seen to have made a substantial political gain on this particular issue. These judicial proceedings were chaired by Lord Justice Leveson, and became known as the Leveson inquiry. In this inquiry, the general culture and ethics of the British media were reviewed and recommendations made for a new, independent body to replace the existing Press Complaints Commission. However, it should be noted, these recommendations were not subsequently implemented by the Conservative government, as confirmed by the then Culture Secretary Matt Hancock in a statement to the House of Commons (1 March 2018).

Equivocation

A third focus of research on PMQs has been the phenomenon known as equivocation, in particular, the extent to which the PM answers or evades questions. In this context, the term *reply rate* refers to the proportion of questions that are answered by the politician in full (Bull, 1994).

---

[12] Waddle and Bull (2020a) discussed their findings in relation to the *patriotism* explanation (Lee, 1977) for the phenomenon known in US political science as the *rally 'round the flag effect*.

[13] In the UK, phone-hacking represented an illegal intrusion into personal privacy by certain sections of the press, and which seemingly had not been rigorously investigated by the police.

An established procedure for analysing reply rate was devised by Bull – which includes identifying questions, answers and what are termed *non-replies* to questions – and this has been extensively applied to research on televised political interviews. Thus, analyses of thirty-three political interviews broadcast in the 1980s and 1990s showed an overall reply rate of 46 per cent (Bull, 1994). An independent study of interviews broadcast during a comparable period indicated a similar reply rate of 39 per cent (Harris, 1991). More recently, analyses of twenty-six interviews broadcast during the General Elections of 2015 and 2017 have also shown an overall reply rate of 38 per cent (Waddle and Bull, 2020b).

In the context of broadcast interviews, the evaluation of equivocation levels has been widespread, but parliamentary discourse has not been scrutinised to the same extent. However, some recent studies have addressed this shortfall. For example, an analysis focused on Question Time in the Australian Parliament (Rasiah, 2010) showed only eight of forty-eight questions were answered (a reply rate of 17 per cent). These findings might suggest that reply rates in parliamentary debates are far lower than those reported for political interviews, a view supported by two recent studies focused specifically on equivocation in PMQs in the UK, as discussed below.

First, in the aforementioned PMQs study of Corbyn's public questions (Bull and Waddle, 2019), further to evaluating the impact of his novel questioning technique on personal attack levels in the LO–PM exchanges, the PM's reply rate was also assessed. No significant difference was found between Cameron's responses to public and non-public questions (23 per cent and 20 per cent, respectively), but, notably, his overall reply rate was only 21 per cent, again highlighting a notably lower rate than those reported above for broadcast interviews.

A second study of equivocation was conducted of Cameron's successor as UK Prime Minister, Theresa May (Bull and Strawson, 2020). This analysis was focused on the PM's responses to LO Corbyn's questions across all twenty-three PMQs sessions held in May's first administration (July 2016–April 2017). The PM's low mean reply rate was subsequently reported in a front-page article in the UK national press (Hope, 2019), which prompted a comment by an opposition politician in PMQs later that day. Namely, MP Marion Fellows of the SNP in her question to the PM began 'May I be lucky enough to be one of the 27 per cent who get their question answered by this Prime Minister?' (In fact, the figure Fellows quoted in her thinly-veiled criticism of May was an actual over-estimation of the mean reply rate reported in the analysis by Bull and Strawson, which was just 11 per cent).

In addition to the analysis of reply rates, equivocation has also been analysed through a typology that identifies thirty-six different forms of equivocation, organised in terms of both superordinate and subordinate categories (Bull, 2003; Bull and Mayer, 1993; Bull and Strawson, 2020). So, for example, *attacks the question* is a superordinate category, divided into eight subordinate categories (*e.g. the question is based on a false premise, the question is factually inaccurate*). The application of this typology to the twenty-three PMQs sessions referred to above (Bull and Strawson, 2020) showed that May's distinctive equivocation style was characterised primarily by acknowledging questions without answering them, ignoring questions, stating or implying that she had already answered and modifying questions. Noticeably, these forms of equivocation may be regarded as essentially covert (Clayman, 2001). Thus, in acknowledging the question, May might give the misleading impression that an answer will be forthcoming. In ignoring the question, May does not even acknowledge that a question has been asked. In stating or implying that she has already answered the question, May attempts to conceal the fact that the question has not been answered. In modifying the question, May then goes on to answer her own version of it. This is perhaps the most covert of all four techniques, because thereby May seemingly gives the impression of answering the question, but not the actual question that was posed.

Undoubtedly, the general public regard equivocation by politicians as infuriating. Comments about public perceptions of political evasiveness are typically anecdotal, but recently the Hansard Society commissioned the first formal study of public attitudes to PMQs (Allen et al., 2014) entitled 'Tuned in or turned off: Public attitudes to Prime Minister's Questions'. The results of that study are summarised in the following section.

Public Perceptions of PMQs

The Hansard Society study (Allen et al., 2014) was based on two sources of information – focus groups and an *audit of political engagement* – outlined below, which are followed by the authors' proposals for reform of PMQs.

Focus Groups

Four online focus groups comprised thirty-eight participants, aged between nineteen and eighty-four. The groups included people who had voted in the 2010 general election for the Conservative Party, the Labour Party, the Liberal Democrats, the Green Party, the UK Independence Party or the British National Party. Across all four focus groups, there was a strong reaction to PMQs as 'childish'. The interaction between the politicians – likened by some to badly behaved children in a playground – was considered uncivilised and disrespectful. Overall, the process was described as 'pointless', a 'waste of time' and an exercise in 'futility'. Many respondents expressed anger over their perception of politicians' failure to answer questions and of their political point-scoring. A number of people questioned the authenticity of what they saw – whether the whole thing was rehearsed and pre-planned; and one speculated that politicians 'go down the pub afterwards and have a good laugh. . .' (p. 6). Overall, the focus group research clearly suggested that, while citizens recognised the value of PMQs in theory, they deplored how PMQs is played out in practice.

Audit of Political Engagement

A series of questions was posed in an opinion poll, based on the findings from the focus groups. These questions were put in face-to-face interviews to a representative sample of 1,286 adults (aged eighteen and above) living in Great Britain, conducted by Ipsos MORI (between 6 and 12 December 2013). Over half (54 per cent) of the respondents claimed to have watched or listened to PMQs in the preceding twelve months. On the basis of the focus group discussions, eight different statements were constructed about PMQs and respondents were asked the extent to which they agreed with them. These statements (showing percentages of agreement and disagreement; 'Don't knows' are excluded) were as follows: 'There is too much party political point-scoring instead of answering the question' (67 per cent agreed, 5 per cent disagreed); PMQs 'deals with the important issues facing the country' (40 per cent agreed, 20 per cent disagreed); PMQs is 'informative' (36 per cent agreed, 22 per cent disagreed); PMQs is 'exciting to watch' (20 per cent agreed, 44 per cent disagreed); MPs 'behave professionally at PMQs' (16 per cent agreed, 48 per cent disagreed); PMQs 'makes me proud of our Parliament' (12 per cent agreed, 45 per cent disagreed); PMQs 'puts me off politics' (33 per cent agreed, 27 per cent disagreed).

Overall, although some people liked the tone and format of PMQs, they were in a minority; for a higher proportion of respondents, the observed behaviour of MPs fostered negative perceptions of Parliament and damaged its reputation. Indeed, these negative perceptions may have serious political ramifications. If such behaviour infuriates large sections of the public, many may be turned off politics. Reduced engagement in the political process – voter apathy and poor electoral turnouts – is recognised as a serious problem for an effectively functioning democratic system.

Reform of PMQs

The authors of the Hansard report (Allen et al., 2014) discussed a number of proposals for the reform of PMQs. These were: (1) Rescheduling to a Tuesday or Wednesday evening [Wednesday lunchtime enables only viewers of retirement age to watch the event in full]; (2) Varying the format to facilitate a more discursive approach, pursuing genuine debate on a few topical areas, as well as the traditional rapid-fire question and answer sessions; (3) Including fewer open questions, with renewed emphasis on closed, subject-specific questions from backbenchers; (4) Reducing the number of questions asked by the LO, to allow more time for backbencher questions; (5) Introducing a 'sin-bin' – naming members for disorderly conduct (at the Speaker's discretion) and removing them from the Chamber for the remainder of the session; (6) Inviting citizens to submit questions for consideration at PMQs. Indeed, this final proposal was subsequently implemented by Jeremy Corbyn in 2015, as described above (Bull and Waddle, 2019).

Conclusions

PMQs has been described as a kind of political 'Marmite' (Allen et al., 2014) – people either love it or hate it. Hence, there are some who want to abolish PMQs, some who want to reform it and some who cherish it as it is. In the context of this ongoing debate, the emergence of a substantive research literature can contribute to fostering public understanding of the kind of interaction that takes in place in PMQs, and possibly even pinpoint and highlight ways in which it might be changed or improved. Notably, however, the UK PMQs remains the most famous event of any parliament worldwide (Allen et al., 2014). As such, in one form or another, its future looks assured, as indeed does its influence on public perceptions of the functioning of British democracy.

REFERENCES

Allen, B., Fox, R., Geis-King, I., Gibbons, V., Korris, M., Pavlova, P. and Raftery, M. (2014). *Tuned in or turned off? Public attitudes to Prime Minister's Questions*. London: Hansard Society.

Bates, S. R., Kerr, P., Byrne, C. and Stanley, L. (2014). Questions to the Prime Minister: A comparative study of PMQs from Thatcher to Cameron. *Parliamentary Affairs*, 67, 253–280.

Bercow, J. (2010). Speech to the Centre for Parliamentary Studies. Retrieved from www.johnbercow.co.uk./content/speech-centre-parliamentary-studies.

Blair, T. (2010). *A journey.* London: Arrow Books.

BBC (British Broadcasting Corporation). (2008, 29 April). Cameron 'unable to keep PMQs vow'. *BBC News.* Retrieved from http://news.bbc.co.uk/1/hi/uk_politics/7372660.stm.

Brown, P. and Levinson, S. C. (1987). *Politeness: Some universals in language usage.* New York: Cambridge University Press.

(1978). Universals in language usage: Politeness phenomena. In E. N. Goody (Ed.), *Questions and politeness: Strategies in social interaction* (pp. 56–289). Cambridge, UK: Cambridge University Press.

Bull, P. (2013). The role of adversarial discourse in political opposition: Prime Minister's questions and the British phone-hacking scandal. *Language and Dialogue, 3,* 254–272.

(2008). Slipperiness, evasion, and ambiguity: Equivocation and facework in noncommittal political discourse. *Journal of Language and Social Psychology, 27,* 324–332.

(2003). *The microanalysis of political communication: Claptrap and ambiguity.* London: Routledge.

(1994). On identifying questions, replies, and non-replies in political interviews. *Journal of Language and Social Psychology,* 13(2), 115–131.

Bull, P., Elliott, J., Palmer, D. and Walker, L. (1996). Why politicians are three-faced: The face model of political interviews. *British Journal of Social Psychology,* 35, 267–284.

Bull, P. and Fetzer, A. (2010). Face, facework and political discourse. *International Review of Social Psychology,* 23(2/3), 155–185.

Bull, P. and Mayer, K. (1993). How not to answer questions in political interviews. *Political Psychology,* 14(4), 651–666.

Bull, P. and Strawson, W. (2020). Can't answer? Won't answer? An analysis of equivocal responses by Theresa May in Prime Minister's Questions. *Parliamentary Affairs,* 73(2), 429–449.

Bull, P. and Waddle, M. (2019). 'Let me now answer, very directly, Marie's question': The impact of quoting members of the public in Prime Minister's Questions. *Journal of Language Aggression and Conflict,* 7(1), 56–78.

Bull, P. and Wells, P. (2012). Adversarial discourse in Prime Minister's Questions. *Journal of Language and Social Psychology,* 31, 30–48.

Chester, D. N. and Bowring, N. (1962). *Questions in Parliament.* Oxford, UK: Clarendon Press.

Clayman, S. E. (2001). Answers and evasions. *Language in Society,* 30(3), 403–442.

Culpeper, J. (1996). Towards an anatomy of impoliteness. *Journal of Pragmatics,* 25, 349–367.

Dunleavy, P., Jones, G. W., Burnham, J., Elgie, R. and Fysh, P. (1993). Leaders, politics and institutional change: The decline of prime ministerial account-ability to the House of Commons, 1868–1990. *British Journal of Political Science,* 23, 267–298.

Dunleavy, P., Jones, G. W. and O'Leary, B. (1990). Prime Ministers and the Commons: Patterns of behaviour, 1868 to 1987. *Public Administration, 68,* 123–140.

Giddings, P. and Irwin, H. (2005). Objects and questions. In P. Giddings (Ed.), *The future of Parliament* (pp. 67–77). Basingstoke: Palgrave Macmillan.

Gimson, A. (2012). PMQs: That's the way to do it! *British Journalism Review, 23,* 11–13.

Goffman, E. (1967). Where the action is. In E. Goffman (Ed.), *Interaction ritual: Essays on face to face behaviour* (pp. 149–270). New York: Anchor Books.

The Guardian. (2010, 14 October). Editorial: In praise of... prime minister's questions. Retrieved from www.theguardian.com/commentisfree/2010/oct/14/in-praise-of-prime-ministers-questions.

Harris, S. (2001). Being politically impolite: Extending politeness theory to adversarial political discourse. *Discourse and Society, 12,* 451–472.

(1991). Evasive action: How politicians respond to questions in political interviews. In P. Scannell (Ed.), *Broadcast talk* (pp. 76–99). London: Sage.

Hoggart, S. (2011, 14 December). Prime Minister's Questions – or an unpleasant football match. *The Guardian.* Retrieved from www.theguardian.com/politics/2011/dec/14/prime-ministers-questions-football-match.

Hope, C. (2019, 1 May). Theresa May is most evasive Tory leader in past 50 years, scientific study finds. *The Telegraph.* Retrieved from www.telegraph.co.uk/politics/2019/04/30/theresa-may-evasive-tory-leader-past-50-years-scientific-study/.

House of Commons Information Office. (2010a). *Parliamentary Questions.* (Factsheet P1, Procedure Series). Retrieved from www.parliament.uk/documents/commons-information-office/p01.pdf.

(2010b). *Some Traditions and Customs of the House.* (Factsheet G7, General Series). Retrieved from www.parliament.uk/documents/commons-information-office/g07.pdf.

House of Commons Procedure Committee (1995). Seventh Report of Session 1994–95, Prime Minister's Questions, *HC* 555.

(1991). Third Report of Session 1990–91, Parliamentary Questions, *HC* 178.

Irwin, H. (1988). Opportunities for backbenchers. In M. Ryle and P. G. Richards (Eds.), *The Commons under scrutiny* (pp. 76–98). London: Routledge.

Irwin, H., Kennon, A., Natzler, D. and Rogers, R. (1993). Evolving rules. In M. Franklin and P. Norton (Eds.), *Parliamentary questions* (pp. 23–72). Oxford, UK: Clarendon Press.

ITV. (2015, 14 August). Jeremy Corbyn promises 'new kind of politics' as he unveils 10-point policy plan. *ITV report.* Retrieved from www.itv.com/news/2015-08-14/jeremy-corbyn-promises-new-kind-of-politics-as-he-unveils-10-point-policy-plan/.

John, P., Bertelli, A., Jennings, W. and Bevan, S. (2013). *Policy agendas in British politics.* Basingstoke: Palgrave Macmillan.

Lee, J. R. (1977). Rallying around the flag: Foreign policy events and presidential popularity. *Presidential Studies Quarterly, 7,* 252–256.

Norton, P. (1993). Introduction: Parliament since 1960. In M. Franklin and P. Norton (Eds.), *Parliamentary questions* (pp. 1–22). Oxford, UK: Clarendon Press.

Rasiah, P. (2010). A framework for the systematic analysis of evasion in parliamentary discourse. *Journal of Pragmatics*, 42(3), 664–680.

Sedgemore, B. (1980). *The secret constitution*. London: Hodder and Stoughton.

Thatcher, M. (1993). *The Downing Street years*. London: HarperCollins.

Thomas, G. P. (2006). United Kingdom: The Prime Minister and Parliament. In N. D. J. Baldwin (Ed.), *Executive leadership and legislative assemblies* (pp. 4–37). London: Routledge.

Waddle, M. and Bull, P. (2020a). Curbing their antagonism: Topics associated with a reduction in personal attacks at Prime Minister's Questions. *Parliamentary Affairs*, 73(3), 543–564.

(2020b). 'You're important, Jeremy, but not that important': Personalised responses and equivocation in political interviews. *Journal of Social and Political Psychology*, 8(2), 560–581.

Waddle, M., Bull, P. and Böhnke, J. R. (2019). 'He is just the nowhere man of British politics': Personal attacks in Prime Minister's Questions. *Journal of Language and Social Psychology*, 38(1), 61–84.

Wilson, H. (1977). *The governance of Britain*. London: Sphere.

CHAPTER 5

Cognitive Complexity:
Sometimes a Boon and Sometimes a Danger to Democracy

Peter Suedfeld

Introduction: Cognitive Interactionism

The approach summarised in this chapter is what I have called 'cognitive interactionism' (Suedfeld, 1983). It takes the decision-making, perspective-taking, social perception and information-processing functions of human cognition as its main foci, and the interaction of those functions with the constraints, opportunities and other characteristics of the environment, as its core concern. This view complements, without trying to supplant, more traditional theories of political psychology such as depth psychology (which takes into account unconscious processes), identity politics or any kind of determinism – structural, neurological, genetic or historical.

Some cognitive interactionist research starts by positing and measuring stable individual differences – i.e. *traits* – in cognition (cognitive styles) and then identifying how people with different levels of these traits function under various politically relevant circumstances. Other researchers do not deny that cognitive styles may exist, but are more interested in *states* of complexity, patterns of how ideas, decisions, allegiances and behaviours emerge and change under different conditions, and in how these patterns can be used to understand and perhaps forecast political behaviours and events.

This chapter will look at both the trait and the state conceptions of the roles that cognitive complexity may play with regard to democracy.

Complexity of Thought as a Personality Variable

The trait approach to cognitive personality theory has succeeded in identifying a large number of fixed individual differences that govern people's cognitive processes (Suedfeld, 2000). Several of the theories were developed before the dominance of the cognitive approach to psychology that began in the 1950s, and have been recognised as belonging to it relatively recently (and sometimes controversially).

Authoritarianism as a Cognitive Style

A major example is the concept of authoritarian personality. In its original form (*The Authoritarian Personality*, Adorno et al., 1950), the researchers who developed the idea used interviews and questionnaires designed to identify traits that hypothetically made the person susceptible to the lure of autocratic, anti-democratic structures and forms of government. These traits included intolerance of ambiguity, adherence to the conventional mores of society and punitiveness toward those who transgressed those mores, suspiciousness of other people (especially members of minority groups), submissiveness to authority figures, aversion to introspection and attitudinal rigidity. Supposedly, these traits were fixed during early life, based to a great extent on parental behaviours toward the child. Adorno et al.'s explanations were mostly based in depth psychology, prominently including Freudian interpretations of child development. One of the lasting contributions of the book is the F-Scale (F for Fascism), still used in personality studies, although a number of alternative measures have been created to correct some of the flaws and fill in some of the gaps that later scholars perceived in the work (e.g. Christie and Jahoda, 1954; Stone, Lederer and Christie, 1993).

At a casual glance, there seems to be no unitary reason why all of the traits packaged under Adorno et al.'s authoritarianism construct should co-vary or be related to each other. Therefore, why is it legitimate to subsume them under one label? Why, for example, should a dislike of stories with ambiguous endings go hand-in-hand with hostility toward people who ignore parking regulations?

The answer to those questions relates the authoritarian personality to cognitive psychology. The relationship among the traits is that they share a bimodal comprehension and assessment of human attributes. In this sense, people are viewed as either 'we' or 'they', beliefs are either true or false, acts are either moral or immoral. Each pole of every bifurcated dimension is judged as either good or bad. Anything that introduces doubt into the judgement, such as ambiguity, the possible effect of introspection or membership of a group that may have different ideas, is bad. This view is a perfect prototype of what cognitive complexity theories view as a simple cognitive style.

Conceptual Complexity

Among cognitive personality variables studied in the wake of authoritarianism theory has been cognitive complexity, the major focus of this chapter. Complexity is an aspect of the prevalent way in which a person processes information and makes decisions. Different theories of cognitive complexity define it and measure it in a variety of ways (Goldstein and Blackman, 1978; Schroder and Suedfeld, 1971).

Many complexity theories deal with the structure of thought, not with its content. In other words, they analyse *how* one thinks, not *what* one thinks. Any belief, idea or opinion can be thought about, supported or opposed at any level of complexity and, conversely, any level of complexity can generate any given belief, idea or opinion.

An early formulation is the theory of stages of conceptual structure (Harvey, Hunt and Schroder, 1961): a developmental theory proposing four basic belief systems. It proposed that, depending on parental discipline and family structure, children can progress through four sequential stages.

System I: Reliable unilateral training. When parents unilaterally lay down rules of thought and conduct, and reliably reinforce compliance (and punish disobedience), the result is a pervasive tendency to be submissive to authority, rules and traditions.

System II: Unreliable unilateral training. Parents who teach unilateral rules, but frustrate the child because the rules are not reliably linked to outcomes, create rebellious people who are prone to disobey societal demands and expectations.

System III: Protective interdependent training. Families where rules are developed in interactions between the child and the parents, but where the parents intervene to protect the child from disappointment, frustration or harm when the rules do not work, produce people who are concerned with fitting into the group, being liked and conforming to the in-group's expectations and norms.

System IV: Informational interdependent training. Finally, interactive rule development that results in guidelines whose validity is confirmed by the child's direct experience of positive or negative outcomes (within the limits set by real-life dangers) leads to a personality structure that guides behaviour and thought according to information sought and obtained.

Conceptual complexity theory (Schroder, Driver and Streufert, 1967) is a refinement of conceptual structure theory. It abandons the idea of developmental stages, and looks at complexity as a dimension. The level underlying an individual's cognitive processes is a function of the person's levels of openness to information, flexibility in planning, tolerance of ambiguity and uncertainty, recognition of nuanced differences and possible relationships among stimuli (including, ideas, opinions and beliefs), sensitivity to environmental factors and ability to change one's plans and positions when appropriate. Two components are involved: differentiation, the ability to perceive more than one dimension or viewpoint when processing information about a stimulus, and integration, the ability to perceive relationships among the differentiated dimensions or points of view. Obviously, differentiation is a prerequisite for integration. The construct is moderately related to IQ, and is a theoretical cousin of such factors as authoritarianism, need for cognition, dogmatism and tolerance of uncertainty. It represents a junction between complexity theory and more traditional concepts of cognitive style.

Conceptual complexity can be measured by a variety of tests, one of the earliest being the semi-projective Paragraph Completion Test or PCT (Schroder et al., 1967). PCT scores range from 1 (no differentiation or integration) through 3 (differentiation without integration) and 5 (integration of differentiated elements) to 7 (integration within a higher-level conceptual schema). The scores of 2, 4 and 6 indicate that some signs of the next highest score are present, but they do not fully meet the criteria for that level.

Integrative Complexity

Integrative complexity, IC for short (Suedfeld, Tetlock and Streufert, 1992), is an offshoot of conceptual complexity theory and shares that theory's general definition of the components that comprise the complexity of thought. It also uses the same 1–7 scoring schema as the PCT. However, it differs from conceptual complexity both in theory and in methodology. Theoretically, the IC approach defines complexity as a mutable state, not a fixed trait; methodologically, it measures complexity in any sample of connected verbal communication, not a specific test such as the PCT; and it can use as its source of materials the spoken, written or electronically recorded utterances that people produce in the course of their ordinary, working or private lives rather than in a laboratory or interview setting. An added refinement is the distinction between elaborative and dialectical complexity, respectively the level exhibited when the text deals with a single dominant theme or point of view or whether it focuses on views or ideas that are in significant tension, such as opposition or dissonance (Conway et al., 2008), such as differing political standpoints.

IC theory focuses on the level of functional complexity – i.e. the level implied by specific behaviours and in specific situations. IC theory's domain is the dynamic relationship between stimuli, both external (environmental) and internal (organismic and psychological), and functional complexity. Although trait-like levels may be inferred from multi-situational stability and correlations between complexity scores and the results of personality testing (Coren and Suedfeld, 1995; Tetlock, Peterson and Berry, 1993), in IC the core concept is complexity as a variable *state*, not a fixed *trait*.

As mentioned above, IC can be measured in any meaningful text, rather than only in an established test or task. Following appropriate training in the use of a detailed manual, scorers abide by a range of instructions and examples, in order to minimise the likelihood of bias or other artifacts contaminating the results (Baker-Brown et al., 1992; Suedfeld, 2010). More recently, computer-based scoring systems have also been developed (Symposium, 2014). They include a programme called 'AutoIC' (Conway, Conway and Houck, 2020), which may solve the major problem in measuring IC: i.e. the need for lengthy training of scorers and the labour- and time-intensiveness of subsequent manual scoring.

Conceptual complexity has often been a selection or classification tool to study the constancy of cognitive behaviour, as shown by the person's complexity level. Integrative complexity tends to be applied to the study of how complexity levels change as a situation persists or varies, as well as the link between such temporary variations in IC and the resultant relevant behaviours. In political psychology, conceptual complexity research is often used in *profiling*; IC research is more likely to be *tracking*.

Profiling is usually multi-trait, measuring complexity among a constellation of traits, in recognition of the many personality characteristics that influence behaviour in most situations. For example, Hermann (e.g. 2003) used media interviews to analyse the leadership styles of major political figures. The traits measured include their belief that they can influence events, need for power, conceptual complexity, self-esteem, in-group favouritism, distrust of others and problem versus group-maintenance orientation. These traits are considered in different combinations, and the scores of the leader are compared with other leaders from similar backgrounds and in similar positions. The method is well illustrated in Hermann's (2003) chapters presenting a general overview of her method and the examples of Saddam Hussein and Bill Clinton. Such analyses are used to predict, for example, how a leader's personal values, childhood experiences or understanding of his/her nation's history might affect his/her responses to an international controversy. A famous example was the assessment provided by the late political psychologist, Jerrold Post, to President Carter, who applied Post's analyses in the negotiations leading to the Camp David accords between Israel and Egypt (Riedel, 2020).

IC has mostly been used as the single characteristic being scored, but it has occasionally been measured in conjunction with other variables, e.g. motive imagery and psychological distancing (Suedfeld, Morrison and Kuznar, 2020; Suedfeld, Tetlock and Jhangiani, 2007; Winter, 2007).

The Relationship of Cognitive Complexity to Democracy

The characteristics of highly complex functioning are almost a definition of the ways of thought required by a democratic system. They share many hallmarks: the ability to accept and understand the existence of dissenting views and values; to evaluate the legitimacy of those perspectives and react to them accordingly; to make fine distinctions among ideas and ideologies and to integrate them, or parts of them, into a new *Gestalt;* to be open to new information; to change plans and opinions when the circumstances dictate – regardless of ideology or egotism – and not to jump to conclusions. It seems to follow that low complexity must characterise undemocratic or anti-democratic politicians, political systems, organisations and populations. As we shall see, the evidence does not support such a generalised conclusion.

A Second Look

Adorno et al. recognised that, although their focus was on fascistic pre-dilections, authoritarianism can also occur on the political Left, and that it is also possible to be conservative but not authoritarian. Attempts have been made to develop measures more clearly related to specific political beliefs. A mislabeled offshoot, Right-Wing Authoritarianism (RWA; Altemeyer, 1981 and later), is based on three traits that actually are neither logically nor empirically tied to the political implications of the term, 'right-wing': submissiveness to established authority, adherence to social norms and punitive hostility toward those who dissent from either. These qualities are obviously found in leftist dictatorships and mass movements, just as in rightist ones, so 'RWA' would describe enthusiasts of either.

Although the existence of Left-wing Authoritarianism has been questioned, research closely focused on that construct has empirically confirmed the intuitive belief in its existence (Conway et al., 2017; Regt, Mortelmans and Smits, 2011). The relationship between political adherence and authoritarianism is problematic because scales must measure both the *content* of the belief system (e.g. Left to Right) and its *structural* aspect (e.g. authoritarian to democratic) (Conway, Conway and Houck, 2020). This distinction will become crucial in our consideration of integrative complexity.

The difference between complexity, a structural 'how we think' character-istic, and authoritarianism, a 'what we think' content variable, is pointed up in the negative correlation between Schroder et al.'s Paragraph Completion Test and Adorno et al.'s F-Scale: between −0.10 and −0.40, varying from study to study based on the participants, the time made available for the PCT and other extraneous factors. For the less politically biased, but equally content-oriented, measure of dogmatism (Rokeach, 1960), the correlations with the PCT are about the same, ranging from −0.20 to −0.40 (Schroder et al., 1967). Thus, the two variables have some, but not very much, overlap.

Complexity: Left, Right and Centre

It is often assumed that liberal ideologies and politicians are democratic and that conservative ones are autocratic. Consequently, there is an under-standable inference that higher complexity is the property of the Left. However, researchers comparing the complexity of leftists and rightists have not found a consistent difference between them.

For example, Thoemmes and Conway (2007) found both trait and state complexity in the first-term State of the Union messages of forty-one US presidents, with correlations between IC and personality measures, changes from the beginning of their first term to the end, as well as a variety of political environment factors. Intelligence, historical eminence, liberalism and party affiliation were not significantly correlated with com-plexity, although trends indicated higher complexity among liberals.

In the 2008 US presidential campaign, each party had three major contenders for the nomination. The collective mean ICs of their campaign speeches and statements were equal, with John Edwards (Democrat) having the highest score of the six men and Barack Obama (Democrat and eventual winner) the lowest (Cassel et al., 2007). This is only one example of the fact that higher IC is not necessarily conducive to electoral victory.

Suedfeld and Ahmadian (2018) measured IC in political texts dealing with the issue of immigration policy. The group of top-level European and North American leaders were chosen as a yoked pair from each country, one supporting relatively free entry to their land and the other demanding more restrictions. The two groups also differed in political party, most of the former belonging to mainstream left-of-centre parties and the latter to conservative ones. Contrary to expectations, the pairs did not differ significantly in IC.

Similar results were obtained among members of university political clubs. IC was higher among supporters of two pragmatic, middle-of-the-road parties than more ideologically Left- *or* Right-leaning parties

(Suedfeld et al., 1994). In the same way, a fierce political controversy over economic development of a natural environment produced higher IC in statements by a scientific committee judging the possible effects and a government group trying to mediate the conflict, than on the part of either pro-development industry personnel or anti-development environmental groups (Lavallee and Suedfeld, 1997). Tetlock, Armor and Peterson (1993) reported basically the same pattern: before the American Civil War, groups supporting a compromise on slavery (no new slave states, but continuing the status quo in those already in the Union) showed higher IC than either pro-slavery advocates or abolitionists.

The malleability of IC is supported by data showing differences as a function of topic domain. For example, Conway et al. (2016) found that, among college students and political candidates, higher IC was generally correlated with increasing topic importance and there were implications of the topic for each politically oriented group, with higher IC when a topic of importance to that particular group was involved. The same tendency has been found in studies of US Senators and both Canadian and British Members of Parliament, as well as individual politicians such as Sir Winston Churchill. Tetlock (1986) suggested that the moderate Left, to which most liberal legislators belong, is more likely to experience value conflict than the moderate Right or either extreme. When two or more of a person's highly valued principles conflict, complex thought is needed to diminish cognitive dissonance. This explains the skewed curvilinear relationship between political position and complexity. It is also a persuasive and empirically supported view of the extreme Left and Right as equally low in complexity. Their structural similarity may explain how extremists on either side can become enthusiasts of the opposite side's content when circumstances so dictate (Goodfellow, 1992; Koehler, 2020).

Complexity: Up and Down

IC can change in response to personal and environmental circumstances. For example, the finding that higher IC is exhibited by political incumbents than by challengers is quite consistent, despite some exceptions. It has been confirmed in studies of democratic election campaigns. Critics can afford to be unsubtle, admitting no virtue in the opponent's policies or their outcomes, while the defence must be more nuanced, explaining or excusing imperfect results and occasional outright failures while in power. Indicating a reduction in tension, there is a tendency for political winners to show a rise in IC after their victory, at least until the next election approaches.

The same tendency, for IC to drop as stress increases and to rise when stress is resolved, was found in General Robert E. Lee's life. Commanding the Army of Northern Virginia, Lee led a string of successful battles against larger forces, led by commanders whose IC was lower than his. Lee's IC dropped over the course of the war, as the Confederacy succumbed to the Union's superiority in manpower, logistics and funds, and when he faced a general whose IC was higher than his own (U. S. Grant). When Lee freed himself and his troops of further fruitless fighting, at Appomattox, there was an immediate jump in his IC. It remained high through the rest of his life (Suedfeld, Corteen and McCormick, 1986).

However, stress is not the only influence on IC levels. Among the leaders of eventually victorious revolutions, those whose rhetoric is low in IC during the combat phase but rises after they take power (e.g. Lenin, Cromwell) have more successful post-revolution careers than those who are either complex during the fighting (e.g. Alexander Hamilton) or fail to become more complex afterward (Trotsky, Guevara). The reason is probably the different requirements of the two positions: single-mindedness and implacability while fighting, but flexibility in negotiations, policies and political relationships as peacetime civil leaders (Suedfeld and Rank, 1976).

Last, it seems that the ability to resist 'disruptive stress' – which has the effect of reducing IC in the face of adversity or difficulty – may be connected to successful problem-solving. IC measurement of Andrei Gromyko, who managed to fill high-level Soviet diplomatic posts from 1939 to 1988 (Wallace and Suedfeld, 1988), showed him to be imperturbable in the face of both domestic and international crises. In fact, although his pre-crisis scores were about the same as those of his colleagues, they increased markedly during crises. Among sixteen important Soviet and American statesmen, Gromyko was the only one who did not show the usual IC drop under stress. A follow-up study (Suedfeld, 2014) showed an increase or no change in IC in response to stressful events among fourteen of twenty-one of history's outstanding political and/or military leaders, from Julius Caesar to Mao Zedong, an impressive exception to the usual reaction. 'Immunity' to disruptive stress may also occur at relatively low IC, as in the case of President Bill Clinton (Suedfeld, 1994).

IC and Political Events: A Brief Review

Although IC measurement has been used to study a wide range of topics, much of it has focused on political decisions. In this area, the importance of complexity as an expendable but limited resource becomes crucial.

Compared to simple thinking, complex thinking uses more resources. It takes more time, collects and considers more information, processes it more fully and carefully, and requires the generation and consideration of more alternatives and plans. Consequently, more cognitive resources and energy must be expended than in thinking at a simpler level. In political decisions, it may also expend more extrinsic resources such as the number and time of staff, gaining access to more information sources, cyber options, surveillance/intelligence sources, etc. However, I remind the reader that more complex thought or decision is not necessarily better – not in theory, practical application or morality. Different levels of complexity are appropriate for different situations.

Intrapersonal economy, i.e. expending the minimal level of time and energy needed to reach a goal, leads to the processing of information at the lowest level of IC that is feasible, has a high probability of success and is within the capacity of the individual. Psychological research has shown that there are conditions that narrow cognitive scope, including a wide range of stressors: danger, fatigue, illness, information overload, time pressure, the nearness of death, among many others. To the extent that these are present in a problem situation, they tend to decrease the level of complexity that is engaged by the solver. They also raise the probability of overlearned reactions being chosen, such as standard operating procedures or drilled movements: again, a low-complexity response – and one that in many emergencies is optimal (Suedfeld, 1992a).

Other factors, such as being accountable for one's actions and utterances, addressing a neutral or hostile audience, or having to reconcile conflict among important values, may have the opposite effect (Levi and Tetlock, 1980; Tetlock, 1983, 1986). A seldom-noted set of findings has pointed to a difference in the impact of different *areas* of stress: adverse personal events tend to be associated with increased IC, whereas professional or societal setbacks and dangers decrease it. This pattern, which may be related to the individual's perceived ability to affect the outcome of the problem, has been observed in eminent authors (Porter and Suedfeld, 1981), as well as famous people across different walks of life and historical eras (Suedfeld and Bluck, 1993; Suedfeld and Granatstein, 1995).

IC research began with a focus on political psychology, and the study of international crisis decision-making has been one of its continuing concerns. During major crises, any or all of the stressors mentioned above are likely to impinge on the problem-solving processes of national leaders. Suedfeld's (1992a) cognitive manager model likens the sequence of those processes to Selye's General Adaptation Syndrome (1956). When a problem first appears, there may be an immediate startle effect, with the leader or leadership group assessing the problem without subtle analysis (i.e. at a low level of complexity). Leaders consider whether it is important and urgent enough – within the context of the government's problem environment – to be dealt with immediately (Selye's stage of 'alarm').

If the answer is 'Yes', cognitive resources are dedicated to finding a solution (Selye's 'resistance' phase), in other words, to coping. The leaders must decide which of their resources should be devoted, how intensely and for how long, with IC rising synchronically with those decisions. The level of IC involved is a function of the feasibility a solution is understood to require and can be adjusted in response to feedback regarding progress toward an acceptable solution.

If no acceptable solution is found within the time and resources available, or if too many simultaneous problems requiring attention arise in the same time period, cognitive resources may be exhausted. If, consequently, none of the plans has worked satisfactorily, the leaders are left tired, frustrated and at an impasse (the stage of 'exhaustion'); IC drops and a solution is found that may involve giving up on the problem, or transferring it to another realm of discourse and another set of problem-solvers. The prototypical move at this stage of an international confrontation for a national leadership is to declare war and turn the matter over to the military; in a domestic confrontation, to turn it over to the internal security apparatus. Although the other major option in such a case is to concede or surrender, that is a solution that is found only in cases of extreme cognitive, emotional and usually material depletion.

We have to remember that the link between IC and democracy may or may not be causal, and that our argument that there is such a relationship must necessarily be indirect and inferential. Stress is known to narrow information search and attentional focus; it is also known to strengthen already dominant response tendencies. On the political level, for both leaders and followers, these changes imply decreased tolerance of criticism or opposition, reduced consideration of alternative policies, discomfort with delay and uncertainty, and stronger adherence to overlearned, traditional approaches – all antithetical to democracy. These phenomena can be related to a decrease in IC.

On the other hand, although stress may generally decrease IC, it may also motivate some leaders who are already high in trait complexity to consider new information, explore more options and plans and consult new sources of advice – potentially with highly successful outcomes. It could also motivate the electorate to consider and choose new leaders who have those tendencies. Such changes would be in the direction of higher IC.

The extant literature on this issue has favoured the hypothesis that stress will reduce the complexity of leaders' thinking. The best-documented topic in this context is the measurement of IC prior to and during war.

The association of IC with the large-scale threat and stress of national-level armed conflict has been studied extensively, with consistent results. Starting three to six months prior to the outbreak of war, leaders – heads of government or state, ministers of defence and foreign relations, diplomats and government spokespersons – show substantial decreases in complexity. This is true whether the war is the culmination of a cycle of increasing hostility and frustration (e.g. World War I), a major spike of open warfare in a long-duration intractable conflict (e.g. India and Pakistan) or a strategic surprise attack (e.g. Pearl Harbor). In the last category, only the eventual attacker shows the decrease in IC ahead of time, but, once the attack has occurred, both sides simplify to the same level. During crises that end without war (the Berlin Blockade, the Cuban Missile Crisis), IC mostly remains stable or even rises (reviewed in Suedfeld, 2010).

How Widespread Are IC Changes?

Relatively few studies have specifically addressed the issue of how international relations affect the IC of individuals who have no decision-making power and are not personally involved in the search for crisis resolution. However, there are some pieces of evidence that point the way.

Editorials published during the Cold War (1947–1982) in the leading newspapers of the United States of America, Canada and the USSR were sampled. The focus was on texts dealing with any of the other two nations or the People's Republic of China. Although *Pravda*, a Soviet government-controlled publication, was expected to conform to the party line, there was a question of whether independent and frequently critical newspapers (the New York *Times* and the Toronto *Globe and Mail*) would continue to exhibit such freedom during times of increased international friction (Suedfeld, 1992b). The IC of the editorials in all three newspapers was significantly higher during periods when bilateral events were more positive and relations presumably more relaxed. Both US and Canadian newspapers exhibited significantly higher IC than *Pravda*, but did not differ significantly from each other.

Another relevant study (Suedfeld, 1981) calculated IC levels in editorials of the *Bulletin of the Atomic Scientists,* as the magazine's famous 'Doomsday Clock' approached the fateful midnight point or retreated further from it, showing the editors' judgement of the danger of nuclear war. Editorials were categorised as reflecting high tension (clock hands at 11:55 or closer to midnight), medium tension (11:50–11:54) or low tension (10:49 or earlier). Mean IC scores on the seven-point scale were 1.62, 2.87 and 3.05 respectively. Importantly, the editorials being scored for IC rarely dealt with the situation that determined the setting of the clock hands: the levels of IC thus reflected the general effect of changing levels of stress on the writing of editorials, mostly by eminent scientists with significant degrees of autonomy from the government.

A related piece of research repeated the same stress-IC analysis in presidential addresses of the American Psychological Association (APA) (Suedfeld, 1985). All eighty-five published speeches from the beginning of the APA in 1894 to the last one before data collection was finished in 1981 were scored for IC. Compared with speeches given in the years before and after each major war involving the United States of America during that period (the Spanish–American War, the two World Wars and the Vietnam War), speeches by APA presidents who served during a war were significantly lower in IC than those before or after the war. The Korean War was excluded because it began chronologically too close to the end of World War II for the before-and-after comparisons to be made. To test the effect of other kinds of national stress, the addresses given during the years before and during ten major economic downturns were compared. Although IC was again lower during than before the event, this difference did not reach statistical significance.

As in the other studies in this section, it is clear that wars have the effect of reducing cognitive complexity not only among governmental decision-makers, but among the population – at least among a population of elite scientists.

There is another relevant category of research, which does not directly measure the effects of societal stress on cognitive complexity, but uses data from which some tentative inferences may be made. In general, proxy variables are used rather than direct measures of complexity, so a short summary of the reports will suffice.

Basically, these studies look for associations between adverse conditions in society, often loosely labelled 'threats' (as I use 'stressor', although, in my usage, not all stressors are threats), and some behaviours that the author considers to be a sign of growing authoritarianism. As discussed earlier, authoritarianism in its original formulation goes far beyond mere cognitive simplicity, although the implication is that high authoritarianism and low complexity go together. In what follows, measures (and sometimes just impressions) of authoritarianism are sometimes taken as a proxy for complexity. This strategy is used because relatively few such studies actually measure complexity; but the results should be considered with the caveat that the two variables are not identical.

Public IC in Stressful Times

In democratic states, it is likely (and desired) that the government's relations with other countries reflect the feelings of the people, both opinion leaders and the general public, who are not involved in the government. In both democratic and non-democratic systems, the government is likely to try to foster such agreement; in the former, if the attempt fails, the government is more likely to change its stance to accommodate the popular will. Such a change may happen in dictatorships as well, but is less likely to occur without eventual regime change.

In situations of nationwide stressors, such as hostile though non-violent confrontations with other countries, civil unrest, terrorism, natural or anthropogenic disasters, economic depressions, lethal epidemics and so on, leaders and citizens both are likely to manifest the same tendencies as in pre-war and war periods. That is, an early recognition of the crisis may increase general complexity, but prolonged and perhaps even increased suffering and danger are likely to lead to decisions indicating lower IC on the part of the government and the people alike. For government at that point, the tendency would be to dispense with democratic forms, especially those that may hamper the development and application of drastic measures to deal with the problems.

The people's responses may be characterised by either a more docile or even enthusiastic acceptance of infringements on civil and human rights (as is often the case during wartime) or, in at least part of the population, increasingly extreme, determined and possibly violent resistance up to and including revolution. Historical examples show a plethora of episodes in which nations under stress moved away from democratic laws, customs and traditions – justified by government as necessary to deal with the 'crisis' – which were accepted, sometimes reluctantly and sometimes enthusiastically, by the populace. The rise of dictatorships in the newly democratised nations of Western and Central Europe as the Great Depression destroyed their economies in the 1930s is only one historical example. The attraction of undemocratic organisations during stressful times is not limited to politics: for example, the conversion successes of authoritarian religious sects during the Great Depression in the United States of America has also been documented (Sales, 1972).

The 2020 worldwide pandemic occasioned autocratic rules promulgated by governments in complete disregard of legal, and often constitutional, civil liberties of the population. These included the regimentation of business openings and closures, private gatherings, religious services, political meetings, educational activities, recreational facilities, interpersonal distancing, etc. Even the deliberations of legislative and judicial bodies became subjected to interference, with heads of government and ruling parties making unilateral decisions rapidly and with minimal, if any, information search or consultation. The point is not whether these decisions were wise, appropriate or effective; I mention them as demonstrating the proliferation of low-complexity thinking under stress and pressure.

It would be facile, and unscientific in the absence of actual data, to cite events in specific nations as they have tried to deal with the COVID-19 pandemic and its assorted economic and social effects. Anecdotes are not data, as the cliché goes; but enough anecdotes illustrating the same points should be taken seriously enough to initiate a search for data, especially in polities where data-based decisions and conclusions are valued. News media around the world have documented dictatorial efforts of governments to enforce curfews, social distancing, the wearing of protective masks, vaccinations, prohibition or severe limiting of group events and even visits among family members; and the increasing amount and prominence of resistance against those efforts. In some jurisdictions, including the federal Parliament of Canada, legislative assemblies have reduced their meetings and debates, allowing the Executive to impose and enforce tax increases, business closures, travel restrictions, quarantine rules, etc. The responses of opposition parties and the citizenry have often been angry and rebellious. Governmental response has sometimes clearly reflected the view that legal niceties could be abandoned during the pandemic.[1] All of these are incursions upon democracy, and scholars interested in IC may well collect the documents related to them. At the same time, the violations of

---

[1] Here is an example: 'On April 3, the town of Lakewood [New Jersey, P. S.] broke up an Orthodox Jewish funeral for a local rabbi and charged 15 mourners with violating lockdown edicts. Pressed by Fox News Channel's Tucker Carlson to explain where the authority to abridge the right to worship could be found in the Constitution, the governor [Phil Murphy] explained that he "wasn't thinking of the Bill of Rights" when he issued the order' (Rothman, 2020).

democracy seem fairly limited (Joffee, 2020), and do not – at least, not as yet – justify 'the sky is falling' panic of some political commentators.

Complexity: Good or Bad

Most commentators and researchers tacitly assume that high complexity is preferable to low, but the basic theory explicitly rejects such assumptions: it insists that either high or low IC decisions can be appropriate under different circumstances. The same is true of democratic and undemocratic government actions. As one frequently cited example goes, 'When the sergeant yells, "Hit the ground!"', it is not a good time for collecting extensive information, considering different aspects of the situation and of possible responses and maintaining flexibility of decisions – in other words, a high-IC approach to the decision. Similarly, it may not be a good time for debate and democratic voting.

Occasions when rapid decisions are crucial are not the only ones in which low IC may be preferable to high. When faced with an implacable and dangerous enemy, open-mindedness, empathy and the search for compromise may be deadly. In the Munich negotiations of 1938, UK Prime Minister Neville Chamberlain's complexity was considerably higher than that of Adolf Hitler (Tetlock and Tyler, 1996). The agreement hammered out in conference seemed to be a compromise between Hitler's demands and the wish of Britain and France to maintain the peace while protecting Czech security (Czechoslovakia was not consulted). Chamberlain returned to England proclaiming that he had assured an honourable peace 'for our time'; Hitler started World War II about a year later. Chamberlain became the symbol of appeasement, and Churchill (whose rhetorical style was also lower in IC than Chamberlain's) became the heroic prime minister whose rhetoric inspired the Western defence of democracy against Nazism, and later against Stalinist Communism.

Tetlock and Tyler (1996) provide a succinct list of characteristics that reduce the advantages of high IC. Decision-makers functioning at high levels are more prone to the 'dilution effect', placing too much emphasis on unimportant and sometimes irrelevant factors; they are easily distracted; they try hard to avoid responsibility for decisions that could harm others, even when not making those decisions ends up harming more, perhaps many more, people (the Munich example is a prototype here); they are willing to compromise basic values and principles that should be defended at almost any cost. The defence of democracy may well be one of those.

IC Training for Democracy

If we consider IC a characteristic that changes in response to changes in the stimulus environment, we may think about how to modify it for various purposes. To begin with, we should consider the possibility that any change will be limited in scope. Suspending, for the moment, our insistence that any level of IC can be optimal, depending on the circumstances, we may posit that we can identify circumstances for the desirability of either the high or the low part of the complexity dimension. Historical cases of de-radicalisation illustrate the importance of cognition and the difference between the content and structure of thought. For example, attempts to change the *content* of hostile thinking could include ideological topics, religion, cultural influences, social connections, etc., while attempted change to the *structure* of thought concerns flexibility of thought, trade-offs between alternatives, perspective-taking and synthesis between recognised differenti-ations and higher-order concepts (Suedfeld et al., 1992).

This can be done indirectly, by manipulating the circumstances of the task performance. Knowing a list of stimulus factors that affect IC, researchers can change those factors to increase or decrease the probability of different levels of complexity in the response. For example, putting an experimental participant under stress (sleep or food deprivation, the cold pressor test, time pressure, etc) will in most cases result in relatively low IC in written materials; arousing value conflict or presenting highly complex 'model passages' will raise it. These are obvious and at this point not very interesting manipulations, regardless of how effective they may be.

Much more interesting have been programmes aimed at changing nega-tive intergroup attitudes by familiarising participants with the principles of high-IC cognition. We know that a negative correlation exists between IC and pro-violence orientations among radical and extremist groups (e.g. Conway et al., 2011; Suedfeld, Cross and Logan, 2013). The IC Thinking research group at Cambridge University used that fact to design programmes to reduce intergroup hostility among Christian sects and between Muslim youths and the wider British population in the UK (e.g. Boyd-MacMillan et al, 2016; Boyd-MacMillan, 2016). The IC-focused approach can be used to create openness to alternative viewpoints (e.g. Koehler, 2017; Savage and Liht, 2008), and thus to show the contending parties that their views of themselves and the world can be reconceptualised to enable cooperation or collaboration while holding on to their core values.

The interventions worked, and the researchers went on to develop multidimensional programmes with a major emphasis on the raising of participant IC. These are tailored to specific countries and groups in Europe and Africa (so far, some eighty projects in eight countries) and are designed to enable participants to choose to turn away from radical and violent movements. Collaboration with a Pakistan programme involved reintegrating former militants in their communities (Nemr and Savage, 2019). More recently, the Cambridge Partnership for Education, UK, has been developing educational materials under the aegis of UNICEF for children of migrants, refugees, asylum seekers, and displaced families in general. The result was the IC-ADAPT Consortium with members and consultants[2] from a number of countries, and the creation of a detailed and comprehensive plan, the 'Learning Passport', which includes IC-oriented material in its section on Social Emotional Learning (https://www .cambridge.org/partnership/learning-passport).

Conclusion

This chapter has traced the development of theory, research and applications connecting democracy and integrative complexity. Beginning with social psychological experiments, the research progressed to field studies and 'assessment at a distance' content analyses of texts, trying to maintain as much scientific rigour as possible while studying the behaviour of individuals in the course of their daily lives and thoughts. The research has supported the essential aspects of the theory, and has moved into the application of the work to the inculcation of positive social values and practices among individuals who were at risk of, or had actually been involved in, ideologically motivated antisocial actions.

Notes and Acknowledgements

Space limits dictated that many studies were referred to, but not individually cited; the author will supply such citations if requested: psuedfeld@psych.ubc.ca.

I thank the Social Sciences Research Council of Canada, the Strategic Multilayer Assessment programme administered by the University of Maryland and subsequently by Arizona State University, and the University of British Columbia for funding years of my work on integrative complexity. I am also grateful to many friends, colleagues and students for their part in building the IC structure. Philip E. Tetlock and Lucian G. Conway III deserve special mention, as does Phyllis J. Johnson for her perceptive critical reading and comments on many manuscripts.

---

[2] Full disclosure: I have acted as a consultant to the project.

REFERENCES

Adorno, T. W., Frenkel-Brunswik, E., Levinson, D. and Sanford, N. (1950). *The authoritarian personality*. New York: Harper and Bros.

Altemeyer, B. (1981). *Right-wing authoritarianism*. Winnipeg: University of Manitoba Press.

Baker-Brown, G., Ballard, E. J., Bluck, S., de Vries, B., Suedfeld, P. and Tetlock, P. E. (1992). The conceptual/integrative complexity scoring manual. In C. P. Smith (Ed.), *Motivation and personality: A handbook of thematic content analysis* (pp. 401–418). New York: Cambridge University Press.

Boyd-MacMillan, E. M. (2016). Increasing cognitive complexity and collaboration across communities: Being Muslim being Scottish. *Journal of Strategic Security*, 9(4), 53–78.

Boyd-MacMillan, E. M., Andrews Fearon, P., Ptolomey, A. M. and Mathieson, L. J. (2016). I SEE! Scotland: Tackling sectarianism and promoting community psychosocial health. *Journal of Strategic Security*, 9(4), 53–78.

Cassel, L., Cross, R., Ivanova, V., Jhangiani, R., Legkaia, K. and Suedfeld, P. (2007). Complexity and values of candidates. *Clio's Psyche*, 14(3), 45–47.

Christie, R. and Jahoda, M. (Eds.) (1954). *Studies in the scope and methods of 'The Authoritarian Personality'*. Glencoe, IL: Free Press.

Conway, L. G. III, Conway, K. R. and Houck, S. C. (2020). Validating automated integrative complexity: Natural language processing and the Donald Trump test. *Journal of Social and Political Psychology*, 8(2), 502–524.

Conway, L. G. III, Gornick, L. J., Houck, S. C., Anderson, C., Stockert, J., Sessoms, D. and McCue, K. (2016). Are conservatives really more simple-minded than liberals? The domain specificity of complex thinking. *Political Psychology*, 37(6), 777–798.

Conway, L. G. III, Gornick, L. J., Houck, S. C., Towgood, K. H. and Conway, K. R. (2011). The hidden implications of radical group rhetoric: Integrative complexity and terrorism. *Journal of Asymmetric Conflict*, 4(2), 155–165.

Conway, L. G. III, Houck, S. C., Gornick, L. J. and Repke, M. A. (2017). Finding the Loch Ness Monster: Left-Wing Authoritarianism in the United States. *Political Psychology*, 39(5), 1049–1067.

Conway, L. G. III, Thoemmes, F., Allison, A. M., Towgood, K. H., Wagner, M. J., Davey, K., Salcido, A., Stovall, A.N., Dodds, D.P., Bongard, K. and Conway, K. R. (2008). Two ways to be complex and why they matter: Implications for attitude strength and lying. *Journal of Personality and Social Psychology*, 95(5), 1029–1044.

Coren, S. C. and Suedfeld, P. (1995). Personality correlates of conceptual complexity. *Journal of Social Behavior and Personality*, 10(1), 229–242.

Goldstein, K. M. and Blackman, S. (1978). *Cognitive style: Five approaches and relevant research*. New York: Wiley.

Goodfellow, S. (1992). From Communism to Nazism: The transformation of Alsatian Communists. *Journal of Contemporary History*, 27(2), 231–258.

Harvey, O. J., Hunt, D. E. and Schroder, H. M. (1961). *Conceptual systems and personality organization.* New York: Wiley.

Hermann, M. G. (2003). Assessing leadership style: Trait analysis. In J. M. Post (Ed.), *The psychological assessment of political leaders, with profiles of Saddam Hussein and Bill Clinton* (pp. 178–212; separate chapters applying the method to the two leaders follow). Ann Arbor: University of Michigan Press.

Joffee, J. (2020, 13 May). The coronavirus isn't killing democracy. *Tablet,* accessed 17 June 2020 from www.tabletmag.com/sections/news/articles/coronavirus-not-killing-democracy.

Koehler, D. (2020). Switching sides: Exploring violent extremist intergroup migration across hostile ideologies. *Political Psychology,* 41(3), 499–515.

(2017). *Understanding deradicalization: Methods, tools, and programs for countering violent extremism.* Oxford, UK: Routledge.

Lavallee, L. and Suedfeld, P. (1997). Conflict in Clayoquot Sound: Using thematic content analysis to understand psychological aspects of environmental controversy. *Canadian Journal of Behavioural Science,* 29, 194–209.

Levi, A. and Tetlock, P. E. (1980). A cognitive analysis of Japan's 1941 decision for war. *Journal of Conflict Resolution,* 24(2), 195–211.

Nemr, C. and Savage, S. (2019). Integrative complexity interventions to prevent and counter violent extremism. Global Center on Cooperative Security. Accessed at: www.globalcenter.org/wp-content/uploads/2019/02/GCCS-PB-IC-Interventions-Prevent-Counter-Violent-Extremism-2019.pdf.

Porter, C. A. and Suedfeld, P. (1981). Integrative complexity in the correspondence of literary figures: Effects of personal and societal stress. *Journal of Personality and Social Psychology,* 40, 321–330.

Regt, S., Mortelmans, D. and Smits, T. (2011). Left-wing authoritarianism: Not a myth, but a worrisome reality: Evidence from 13 Eastern European countries. *Communist and Post-Communist Studies,* 44(4), 299–308.

Riedel, B. (2020, 7 December). Jerrold Post: One of the CIA's truly great innovators. Brookings, 7 December. Accessed at: www.brookings.edu/blog/order-from-chaos/2020/12/07/jerrold-post-one-of-the-cias-truly-great-innovators/.

Rokeach, M. (1960). *The open and closed mind.* New York: Basic Books.

Rothman, N. (2020). New Jersey's coronavirus response is no "model." Commentary, 6 August 2020. Accessed 12 August from www.commentarymagazine.com/noah-rothman/new-jerseys-coronavirus-response-is-no-model/.

Sales, S. M. (1972). Economic threat as a determinant of conversion in authoritarian and nonauthoritarian churches. *Journal of Personality and Social Psychology,* 23, 420–428.

Savage, S. and Liht, J. (2008). Mapping fundamentalisms: The psychology of religion as a sub-discipline in the understanding of religiously motivated violence. *Archiv für Religionspsychologie / Archive for the Psychology of Religion,* 3, 75–91.

Schroder, H. M., Driver, M. J. and Streufert, A. (1967). *Human information processing*. New York: Holt, Rinehart, and Winston.

Schroder, H. M. and Suedfeld, P. (Eds.) (1971). *Personality theory and information processing*. New York: Ronald.

Selye, H. (1956). *The stress of life*. New York: McGraw-Hill.

Stone, W. F., Lederer, G. and Christie, R. (Eds.) (1993). *Strength and weakness: The Authoritarian Personality today*. New York: Springer-Verlag.

Suedfeld, P. (2014). Political and military geniuses: Psychological profiles and responses to stress. In D. K. Simonton (Ed.), *The Wiley handbook of genius* (pp. 244–265). New York: Wiley.

(2010). The cognitive processing of politics and politicians: Archival studies of conceptual and integrative complexity. *Journal of Personality, 78*(6), 1669–1702.

(2000). Cognitive styles: Personality. In A. E. Kazdin (Ed. in Chief), *Encyclopedia of psychology* (Vol. 2, pp. 166–169). New York and Washington, DC: Oxford University Press and Amer. Psychological Assoc.

(1994). President Clinton's policy dilemmas: A cognitive analysis. *Political Psychology, 15*, 337–349.

(1992a). Cognitive managers and their critics. *Political Psychology, 13*(3), 435–453.

(1992b). Bilateral relations between countries and the complexity of newspaper editorials. *Political Psychology, 13*(4), 601–611.

(1985). APA presidential addresses: The relation of integrative complexity to historical professional, and personal factors. *Journal of Personality and Social Psychology, 49*(60), 1643–1651.

(1983). Authoritarian leadership: A cognitive-interactionist view. In J. Held (Ed.) *The cult of power: Dictators in the twentieth century* (pp. 1–22). Boulder, CO: East European Monographs.

(1981). Indices of world tension in *The Bulletin of the Atomic Scientists*. *Political Psychology, 2*(3/4), 114–123.

Suedfeld, P. and Ahmadian, S. (2018, July). *Implicit markers of attitudes toward asylum-seekers*. Presented at the annual meeting of the International Society of Political Psychology, San Antonio, TX.

Suedfeld, P. and Bluck, S. (1993). Changes in integrative complexity accompanying significant life events: Historical evidence. *Journal of Personality and Social Psychology, 64*, 124–130.

Suedfeld, P., Bluck, S., Loewen, L. and Elkins, D. J. (1994). Sociopolitical values and integrative complexity of members of student political groups. *Canadian Journal of Behavioural Science, 26*, 121–141.

Suedfeld, P., Corteen, R. S. and McCormick, C. (1986). The role of integrative complexity in military leadership: Robert E. Lee and his opponents. *Journal of Applied Social Psychology, 16*, 498–507.

Suedfeld, P., Cross, R. W. and Logan, C. (2013). Can thematic content analysis separate the pyramid of ideas from the pyramid of action? A comparison among different degrees of commitment to violence. In H. Cabayan, V. Sitterle and M. Yandura (Eds.), *Looking back, looking forward: Perspectives on terrorism and responses to it* (pp. 61–68). Washington, DC; Strategic Multilayer Assessment Occasional White Paper.

Suedfeld, P. and Granatstein, J. L. (1995). Leader complexity in personal and professional crises: Concurrent and retrospective information processing. *Political Psychology,* 16(3), 509–522.

Suedfeld, P., Morrison, B. H. and Kuznar, L. A. (2020). National interests and the meaning of 'America First'. In S. A. Renshon and P. Suedfeld (Eds.), *The Trump Doctrine and the emerging international system* (pp. 39–70). Cham, Switzerland: Palgrave Macmillan.

Suedfeld, P. and Rank, D. A. (1976). Revolutionary leaders: Long-term success as a function of changes in conceptual complexity. *Journal of Personality and Social Psychology,* 34, 169–178.

Suedfeld, P., Tetlock, P. E. and Jhangiani, R. (2007). The new psychology of alliances. In S. A. Renshon and P. Suedfeld (Eds.), *Understanding the Bush Doctrine: Psychology and strategy in an age of terrorism* (pp. 105–128). New York: Routledge.

Suedfeld, P., Tetlock, P. E. and Streufert, S. (1992). Conceptual/integrative complexity. In C. P. Smith (Ed.), *Motivation and personality: Handbook of thematic content analysis* (pp. 393–400). Cambridge, USA: Cambridge University Press.

Symposium on the scoring of integrative complexity. (2014). *Political Psychology,* 35(5), 597–659.

Tetlock, P. E. (1986). A value pluralism model of ideological reasoning. *Journal of Personality and Social Psychology,* 50(4), 819–827.

    (1983). Accountability and complexity of thought. *Journal of Personality and Social Psychology,* 45(1), 74–83.

Tetlock, P. E., Armor, D. and Peterson, R. S. (1993). The slavery debate in antebellum America: Cognitive style, value conflict, and the limits of compromise. *Journal of Personality and Social Psychology,* 66(1), 115–126.

Tetlock, P. E., Peterson, R. S. and Berry, J. S. (1993). Flattering and unflattering personality portraits of integratively simple and complex managers. *Journal of Personality and Social Psychology,* 64, 500–511.

Tetlock, P. E. and Tyler, A. (1996). Churchill's cognitive and rhetorical style: The debates over Nazi intentions and self-government for India. *Political Psychology,* 17(1), 149–170.

Thoemmes, F. J. and Conway, L. G. III. (2007). Integrative complexity of 41 U.S. presidents. *Political Psychology,* 28(2), 193–226.

Wallace, M. D. and Suedfeld, P. (1988). Leadership performance in crisis: The longevity – complexity link. *International Studies Quarterly,* 32, 439–451.

Winter, D. G. (2007). The role of motivation, responsibility, and integrative complexity in crisis escalation: Comparative studies of war and peace crises. *Journal of Personality and Social Psychology,* 92(5), 920–937.

CHAPTER 6

In 'A League of Their Own?'
Judgement and Decision-Making by Politicians and Non-Politicians

Barbara Vis and Sjoerd Stolwijk

Introduction

Are politicians – such as ministers, party leaders, Members of Parliament (MPs) and elected municipal council members – in 'a league of their own' in terms of how they take decisions and make judgements?[1] In other words, are there systematic differences between politicians' behaviour and that of the rest of us: a political elite-public gap? Making judgements and taking decisions are core tasks of elected politicians. Knowledge of the character of these decisions is important because politicians' decisions are often consequential, both for themselves (e.g. by influencing their career prospects) and for the wider public. For example, how governments assessed the risk of COVID-19 affected the stringency of the measures they took and the swiftness (or lack thereof) by which they took them (Hale et al., 2020). As we all experienced in 2020, these measures have had a major impact on how we work (and whether we still have work to begin with), our social lives and sometimes our own or loved ones' health. The assumption of an elite-public gap is prominent in much work in political science (see for a recent overview Kertzer, 2020). What is more, some political science theories presume that elite cognition is superior to that of the rest of us (Byman and Pollack, 2001). Interestingly, behavioural economists and psychologists are usually surprised by this presumption. For them, politicians are also humans, so why would their judgement and decision-making differ from that of 'the rest of us'? However, empirically, and with political elites defined broadly as politicians, military personnel or government bureaucrats, the findings on an elite-public gap are conflicting (see Kertzer, 2020) and there is no overriding consensus or clear majority of findings. Whereas some studies find mostly similarities between the

---

[1] With judgements being assessments of situations often preceding decision-making (Newell, Lagnado and Shanks, 2015, p.20).

behaviour of elites and the masses (Sheffer et al., 2018), i.e. no gap, other studies find mostly differences (e.g. Mintz, Redd and Vedlitz, 2006), i.e. a gap; yet other studies find something in between (e.g. Renshon, 2015).

In this chapter, we aim to contribute to this discussion by assessing whether politicians differ from non-politicians in their judgement and decision-making. We also examine whether there is a difference in the direction of the findings and in the strength of the effect. We leverage findings from an experiment that we have conducted previously using a sample of Dutch local politicians and a student sample, i.e. a paired experiment. The overall study is reported in two publications (Stolwijk and Vis, 2018, 2020).[2] Our findings will show that politicians largely make judgements and take decisions like the rest of us, i.e. that there is little evidence of an elite-public gap in this regard (cf. Kertzer's [2020] meta-analysis). However, our findings will also reveal that, under specific circumstances, politicians do differ in their judgement and decision-making. In the final section, we will discuss what all this means for a psychology of democracy, particularly for government of the people.

Existing Studies on (Non-Existing) Differences in Decision-Making between Politicians and Non-Politicians

Let us first briefly summarise the conflicting findings of existing studies on supposed differences between politicians and non-politicians in terms of judgement and decision-making. It is not our aim to be comprehensive here; for more extensive discussions, we refer readers to extant work (e.g. Linde and Vis, 2017; Sheffer, 2018; Sheffer et al., 2018; Vis, 2019).

Broadly speaking, existing work can be grouped into two categories. The first strand of studies stresses the distinctiveness of political elites, including elected politicians (the elite-public gap); the second strand highlights the similarities between political elites and 'the rest of us'. Work that stresses politicians' distinctiveness often focuses on their *experience* of making judgements and taking decisions, and on their *expertise*. For example, it is an empirical question whether experienced decision-makers behave more in line with the predictions of Expected Utility

---

[2] We pre-registered the design of the larger study at AsPredicted.org (https://aspredicted.org/pi28u .pdf); this chapter is part of this larger study. The pre-registration included the analyses on judgement by politicians, which are reported in the studies cited, as well as (some) predictions on the difference between politicians and students for which the results are reported in this chapter. This chapter also reports several exploratory results. Details on the preregistration plan and how we distributed the reporting across different publications are provided in Stolwijk and Vis (2020).

Theory (EUT) (Von Neumann and Morgenstern, 1944), the theory that underlies most rational choice approaches (e.g. Bueno de Mesquita et al., 2003). EUT's key axioms include transitivity, dominance and invariance. Transitivity implies that, if option A is preferred to option B, and B is preferred to C, then A should be preferred to C. Dominance posits that, if an option is better on at least one aspect, and at least as good on the other aspects, it will be preferred to lesser options. Invariance means that a preference order should remain the same irrespective of how options are presented. If experienced decision-makers behave more in line with EUT, this would be contrary to a string of findings about how 'the rest of us' take decisions (for overviews and discussions, see e.g. Gilovich, Griffin and Kahneman, 2002; Kahneman, 2011). There are studies showing that more experienced decision-makers' behaviour supports EUT's predictions (List, 2004), but there are also studies finding that this behaviour is not more in line with EUT (Fréchette, 2011). There may also be differences across politicians and non-politicians because of *selection effects*. As Linde and Vis (2017: 102) note, politicians 'are selected by themselves (Mattozzi and Merlo, 2008), their party (Rahat, 2007) and by the voters (Besley, 2005)'. As there are studies finding that politicians have different attitudes towards risk compared to the general population (Fatas, Neugebauer and Tamborero, 2007; Heß et al., 2013), 'this process could select (. . .) decision-makers who may be less likely to violate a normative decision-making theory such as expected utility theory' (Linde and Vis, 2017: 102). Also, there is a potentially contentious perspective, especially in International Relations, that views heads of state as 'Great' (Byman and Pollack, 2001; see Copeland, 2001) and stresses an elite-public gap.

The second stream of research finds that politicians and non-politicians are mostly similar in their judgement and decision-making, although these studies agree with the first stream that the context in which politicians operate differs from that of the mass public. Politicians, for instance, receive much larger quantities of information on a daily basis (Baumgartner and Jones, 2015; Walgrave et al., 2013) and the decisions they take typically have larger consequences. In addition, politicians as people use heuristics: cognitive rules of thumb that facilitate judgement and decision-making (see e.g. Gigerenzer and Selten, 2001; Gilovich et al., 2002), but may also lead to decision-making bias, i.e. deviations from the predictions of EUT. There is a difference in degree here: the bar for politicians to use heuristics is generally higher than it is for ordinary citizens (see Vis, 2019 for an overview), as determined by the complexity of a decision (which in theory should be higher for politicians). However, these studies suggest that there is no fundamental difference, i.e. no difference in kind (see for an overview e.g. Hallsworth et al., 2018).

Empirically, the second strand of work has received most support. For example, only six of the eighteen behavioural traits that could influence political decision-making, as surveyed by Hafner-Burton, Alex Hughes and Victor (2013), provided evidence of differences across experienced and inexperienced decision-makers. What is more, a meta-analysis on elite-public gaps by Kertzer (2020) found little evidence of an elite-public gap. Kertzer's analysis of published and unpublished work includes 162 paired treatments (i.e. 162 elite samples and 162 mass public/convenience samples) from 45 studies, covering 12 countries, which were reported over a 43-year period. Contrary to an elite-public gap, the findings for elites and the mass public were very similar: '(. . .) the treatment effects recovered in the elite samples (. . .) do not significantly differ in magnitude from those recovered from mass samples 88% of the time, and do not significantly differ in sign 98% of the time' (Kertzer, 2020, p.7). This was also the case for a study included in the meta-analysis conducted by one of this chapter's authors on whether politicians take risks like the rest of us (Linde and Vis, 2017). That study – which was an experiment with a sample of Dutch Members of Parliament (n = 46) and a student sample (n = 176) – showed that politicians displayed the 'reflection effect' like the rest of us, meaning their risk attitudes were influenced by whether the outcomes were framed as losses or as gains. It also showed that politicians were less susceptible to probability weighting (Vieider and Vis, 2019), which means that they were less suscep-tible to overweighing very small odds or underweighing very large ones, less likely than the rest of us to avoid treating probabilities linearly and partic-ularly sensitive to the possibility of a sure outcome. In general, individual studies from Kertzer's meta-analysis that did find significant elite-public differences were typically about attitudes and not about judgement and decision-making, on which we focus here. Importantly, these differences in attitudes proved to be mostly the result of compositional differences: elites were typically older, more highly educated and more often male. This means that, if there is, or actually seems to be, an elite-public gap, this is often due to these compositional differences and not – or at least not only – due to differences in domain-specific expertise and experience.

Leveraging Findings from a Previous Paired Experiment

In this section, we will leverage findings from a paired experiment of politicians' and non-politicians' use of heuristics that we conducted previously (Stolwijk and Vis, 2018, 2020). The study used students as the mass public/convenience sample. Since the original experiments on which we built also relied on student samples (Kahneman and Frederick, 2002; Kahneman and Tversky, 1972; Simonson and Tversky, 1992; Tversky and Simonson, 1993), using the same demographic group enabled us to compare our findings directly to those of the original tests. However, since education is one variable often argued to reduce heuristic use (Kahneman and Frederick, 2002), a sample of highly educated students predisposed us against demonstrating the use of heuristics in this sample. At the same time, politicians are also generally highly educated (Bovens and Wille, 2017), so that means that these two samples differ little in terms of education. They can, of course, differ in experience and expertise in decision-making.

Our study's research question was whether politicians use the representativeness and/or availability heuristic when making judgements. These are so-called general purpose heuristics from Kahneman and Tversky's heuristics and biases tradition (Kahneman and Frederick, 2002; see Kelman, 2011). People use the *representativeness heuristic* when they 'bypass more detailed processing of the likelihood of the event in question, but instead focus on what (stereotypical) category it appears to fit and the associations they have about that category. Simply put: If it looks like a duck, it probably is a duck' (Stolwijk, 2019, p. 1). People use the *availability heuristic* if they 'assess the frequency of a class or the probability of an event by the ease with which instances or occurrences can be brought to mind' (Tversky and Kahneman, 1974, p. 1127).

In this chapter, we will not discuss in detail how we went about testing whether politicians used these heuristics in their judgement and decision-making (for that, we refer readers to Stolwijk and Vis, 2018, 2020). We will examine whether politicians differ from non-politicians in their judgement and decision-making – which is a question that has received much less attention in our other publications. To answer this question, it is important to describe the general approach of our previous work. We followed most of the existing work, as well as Tversky and Kahneman's own approach, which inferred politicians' use of heuristics 'by measuring the biases that their use is supposed to evoke' (Bellur and Sundar, 2014, p.121). In the case of representativeness heuristics, these biases are termed 'conjunction error' and 'scope neglect'. People make a conjunction error when they consider the conjunction A *and* B (e.g. working at a bank *and* being active in the feminist movement) more likely than, for example A (working at a bank). In this instance, A alone is – logically speaking at least – as large, and probably larger, than the conjunction of A *and*

Table 6.1. *Hypotheses for testing use of the representativeness heuristic.*[1]

H1   *Conjunction error I: The Linda/Vera problem:*[2] When given a stereotypical feminist description of Linda, participants will generally judge the conjunction ('She is a bank employee and is active in the feminist movement') more likely than one or both of its parts ('She is a bank employee' or 'She is active in the feminist movement').

H2   *Conjunction error II: The 'making the headlines' scenario:* Participants will judge it more likely that a terrorist attack will lead to their municipality making the headlines of all major newspapers, compared to making those headlines in general (since making the headlines is supposedly hard, but becomes very likely after such an attack, even though such an attack is very unlikely).

H3   *Conjunction error III: Earthquake scenario:* Participants will judge the likelihood of an earthquake in Groningen to be higher than of a natural disaster in the eastern half of the Netherlands (this is based on the supposition that Groningen is associated with earthquakes, but, although Groningen is geographically in the east of the Netherlands, the east is less associated with natural disasters).

H4   *Scope neglect I: Nuisance scenario (importance):* Participants will generally consider it equally important to deal with twenty-three people who cause a nuisance as with fifty-three (supposedly since people judge the issue relative to their feelings towards nuisance rather than to the scope of the problem).

H5   *Scope neglect II: Nuisance scenario (total budget):* Participants will generally allocate an equal budget to deal with twenty-three people who cause a nuisance as they would to deal with fifty-three (again supposedly since people judge the issue relative to their feelings towards nuisance rather than towards the scope of the problem).

[1] Please note that some of the hypotheses have been slightly reworded with a view to readability of this chapter, but they are in line with the pre-registered hypotheses (see footnote 2 for more information about the pre-registration).
[2] To avoid participants thinking about a famous Dutch person named 'Linda', we used the name 'Vera' instead. In writing this chapter, we revert to the name 'Linda' because this is the name used in the seminal studies (see e.g. Kahneman (2011) for a discussion).

B (Tversky and Kahneman, 1983). Scope neglect is people's tendency to neglect the representativeness of an event; in this case, of working at a bank. The use of representative heuristics by politicians and students is tested by five hypotheses (see Table 6.1).

In the case of the availability heuristic, a well-established bias is the 'asymmetric dominance effect' (Tversky and Simonson, 1993). People display this effect when their preference among alternatives is influenced by the addition of an irrelevant alternative, i.e. one that is less attractive than at least one of the existing choice options. An example here comes from a study by Simonson and Tversky (1992), in which an ordinary pen (z) was added as the additional option in the choice between a branded pen (y) and money (x). Since an ordinary pen (z) is very likely less attractive than a branded one (y), this should not affect the choice between y and x

(the money). However, it does: it makes option y – the branded pen – appear more attractive. Additionally, we examined whether the availability of costs and the scope of a problem (its severity) influenced judgements (which it should not, according to Rational Choice Theory) (Stolwijk and Vis, 2018). The use of availability heuristics by politicians and students is tested by three hypotheses (see Table 6.4). Finally, we examined the reflection effect – the tendency of people to be risk-seeking for gains and risk averse to losses (Kahneman and Tversky, 1979), mainly to test whether, based on our samples, we could identify well-known effects. The reflection effect hypothesis is presented in Table 6.5.

Data

Before turning to the findings, let us briefly discuss the data from our study. Our politician-participants were a sample of elected local politicians from twenty-seven larger Dutch municipalities (sample frame: 1,063, complete responses: 211). This sample is representative of the full population of Dutch elected council members in terms of age, gender and party membership, but somewhat more highly educated: almost 90 per cent self-report holding an applied higher college or university degree compared to 67 per cent on average for the full population (Ministerie van Binnelandse Zaken en Koninkrijksrelaties, 2016).[3] Randomisation tests showed that gender, age, municipality, party and education level were not significantly different between the different conditions (see Stolwijk and Vis, 2020). The non-politician participants were students from three large research-intensive Dutch universities (260 responses from a total sample frame of 1,295).

Results

In this chapter's analyses, we compare: (1) whether politicians made different judgements in the various scenarios we provided to them compared to non-politicians; (2) whether politicians responded differently compared with non-politicians in the various conditions; and (3) whether such differences can be explained by: (a) compositional differences of the characteristics of politicians compared to the population at large; (b) experience with political judgement; or (c) expertise in the area of the judgement in question. Compositional differences might reflect differences between ordinary citizens and those motivated to run for office, or biases in the selection process for which individuals achieve office, for example

---

[3] Note that the sample of politicians is hereby very similar to the student sample, which consists entirely of people who follow education at university level.

biases in the electoral chances of different candidates due to (elements of) the electoral system or due to voter biases. There may also be differences across politicians and non-politicians because of *selection effects* (as discussed above in the section titled 'Existing Studies'). We tested such compositional differences in terms of age, education, gender, news consumption (as a proxy for political interest), ideology (political Right/ Left orientation) and ability (maths skill). Experience is tested by comparing the judgements of politicians varying in tenure of office. Expertise is tested by comparing the judgements of politicians who are spokespersons on the judgement area in question or not.

Representativeness Heuristics

As we explained above, we tested participants' use of the representative heuristic by examining whether they displayed the key biases related to this heuristic: the conjunction error and scope neglect. We included three scenarios for the former and two for the latter. Table 6.1 displays the five hypotheses related to these scenarios (for more extensive descriptions, we refer the reader to Stolwijk and Vis (2020)).

Conjunction Error I: The Linda/Vera Problem (H1)

We found that both politicians and non-politicians made the conjunction error – so there was no difference in the direction of the findings. However, a t-test showed that the non-politicians were more likely to commit the conjunction error, but this result was only marginally significant (single tailed). We found no effect of control variables (gender, education, maths skill, political experience, Right-Left self-placement). When adding controls, the difference between politicians and non-politicians remained. We were unable to test the effect of age on the difference between politicians and non-politicians, since age was nearly collinear (all students are from [approximately] the same cohort, thus do not vary in age, and are generally [much] younger than the politicians). However, we were able to test the effect of age within the sample of politicians and found that it did not influence politicians' judgements. This implies that it is not the reason for the difference between politicians and non-politicians (otherwise younger politicians would be more like the non-politician student sample). Finally, Left-Right orientation had no effect among the non-politicians, but it did influence the rate of the conjunction error among politicians. The results of logistic regressions (see Table 6.2) show that Left-wing politicians are less likely to make the conjunction error in the Linda scenario than Right-wing politicians (63 per cent of Left-wing politicians committed the error versus 85 per cent of Right-wing politicians in our sample). Since the conjunction error involves stereotypes, this might

Table 6.2. *Logistic regressions predicting expectation order for Left-wing and Right-wing politicians in the Linda/Vera scenario.*

	Made the conjunction error	Ranks the conjunction ('A and B') as more probable for Linda compared to her being active in the feminist movement ('B')	Ranks the conjunction ('A and B') as more probable for Linda compared to her being active in the feminist movement ('B')	Ranks the conjunction ('A and B') as more probable for Linda compared to her being a bank teller ('A')	Ranks the conjunction ('A and B') as more probable for Linda compared to her being a bank teller ('A')
Left-wing	$-.83^*$ (.33)	$-.41$ (.30)		$-.26$ (.30)	
Right-wing	1.05^* (.41)		$.63^*$ (.32)		$.15$ (.32)
Constant	1.34^{***} (.24)	$-.15$ (.19)	$-.53^{**}$ (.18)	$.11$ (.19)	$-.05$ (.18)

Note: N (Politicians) = 186; * $p<.05$; ** $p<.01$; *** $p<.001$; 'A' = active in the feminist movement; 'B' = being a bank teller; 'A and B' = a bank teller active in the feminist movement.

suggest that some Left-wing politicians have applied positive discrimination (favouring the opposite of the prejudice in their judgement). However, Left-wing politicians were not more likely to opt for a reverse stereotypical ordering (and Right-wing politicians were *more,* rather than less, likely to do so: 32 per cent of Right-wing politicians made this error versus 16 per cent of Left-wing politicians in our sample). Equally, Right-wing politicians were not more likely to opt for a stereotypical ordering (and Left-wing politicians were not less likely to do so: 32 per cent of Right-wing politicians made this error versus 26 per cent of Left-wing politicians in our sample).[4] These results appear to contradict each other: Right-wing politicians were more likely to choose the reverse stereotypical ordering, but Left-wing politicians were less likely to make the conjunction error. The mixed findings mean the inferences are difficult to interpret and suggest that further research is needed.

Conjunction Error II: 'Making the Headlines' Scenario (H2)
In the 'making the headlines' scenario, neither the politicians nor the non-politicians judged it more likely that a terrorist attack would lead to their municipality making the headlines of all major newspapers, compared to making those headlines in general. However, we found that politicians judged it more likely that their municipality would make the headlines in general than non-politicians would judge Apeldoorn to do (the municipality we asked them to think about). What is more, the non-politicians judged it likelier that Apeldoorn would make the headlines due to a terrorist attack than politicians judged their municipality to make the headlines due to a terrorist attack (see Figure 6.1).

Control variables did not explain the difference in the strength of the effect between the politicians and non-politicians. This suggests that the politicians were influenced by the availability heuristic referencing their municipality (as the questions were directed at their municipality), but questions to non-politicians were directed to consider Apeldoorn. However, Apeldoorn is more related to terror than other municipalities, because of a terrorist attack there about a decade before, implying that its cognitive

---

[4] From the six different orderings participants could propose, several listed feminist higher than bank employee, and vice versa. All of these are accounted for in the logistic regressions in Table 6.2. One even listed feminist as more likely than bank employee (stereotypical), while also listing feminist bank employee as more likely than feminist (anti-stereotypical). To avoid confusing readers with overlapping percentages, we only present percentages here for the quintessential stereotypical ordering (most likely a feminist, than a feminist bank employee, then a bank employee) and its reverse (most likely a bank employee, than a feminist bank employee, then a feminist). Note that both of these are examples of the conjunction fallacy, since they list the conjunction (feminist bank employee) as more likely than at least one of its constituents (i.e. either feminist (reverse stereotype) or bank employee (stereotype).

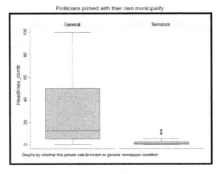

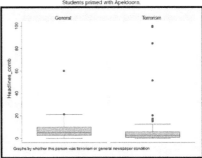

Figure 6.1   'Making the headlines' scenario comparing politicians' and students' ratings of probability.

Note: The y axis displays the participant's judged probability that their municipality would make it to the headlines. The x axis indicates whether the participant was in the general condition (figures on the left-hand side of each paired box plot) or in the terrorism condition (figure on the right-hand side of each paired box plot).

availability was stronger than that of politicians' own municipalities. It is notable that the non-politicians did not deviate from politicians in their baseline assessment of the likelihood across conditions, which would have suggested an effect of proximity of the city of interest (since the students did not live in Apeldoorn, while the politicians were asked about their own city). Rather, on average, they gave a lower probability in the general condition (6.8 per cent for non-politicians versus 28.4 per cent for politicians) and a higher probability in the terrorism conditions (8.0 per cent for non-politicians versus 1.5 per cent for politicians), suggesting that the terrorism association overrode the availability of politicians' 'own' municipality.

Conjunction Error III: The Earthquake Scenario (H3)
In the earthquake scenario, both politicians and non-politicians judged it more likely that an earthquake will hit Groningen than that a natural disaster

will hit the east of the Netherlands, thereby making a conjunction error. Politicians estimated both the likelihood of an earthquake and the likelihood of a natural disaster lower than non-politicians (pooled over conditions 5.3 per cent [politicians] versus 5.9 per cent [non-politicians]), but the difference between estimates for the earthquake or natural disaster were similar among politicians and non-politicians. Again, there are no differences in the direction of the findings, but some difference in the strength of the effect. The control variables did not influence the absence of a difference between politicians and non-politicians and we may conclude from this that politicians seem to judge the odds of danger to be smaller. They did so in this scenario as well as in the terrorism condition (see 'Making the headlines' scenario).

Scope Neglect I: Nuisance Scenario (Importance) (H4)
In the first of two 'scope neglect' scenarios, we found that politicians judged the issue of dealing with people who cause a nuisance more important than non-politicians, regardless of the condition. In contrast to the politicians, the non-politicians on average judged the problem of fifty-three people who cause a nuisance to be slightly more important than the problem caused by twenty-three (4.20 vs 4.40 on a 1–6 scale; t = 1.68, p = 0.05, n[non-politicians] = 263).

The difference between the politicians and non-politicians is significant: politicians are less sensitive to the difference between twenty-three versus fifty-three people who cause a nuisance in assessing the importance of the issue than are non-politicians. In this scenario, Left-Right political orientation influences judgement of importance, but the difference between politicians and non-politicians in this Left-Right orientation does not (fully) explain the difference in judged importance between them. The other control variables had no effect.

Scope Neglect II: Nuisance Scenario (Total Budget) (H5)
In the second 'scope neglect' scenario, we found that the non-politicians took the difference between twenty-three and fifty-three nuisance makers into account, i.e. not neglecting scope, contrasting with politicians. This happened even though both non-politicians and politicians confirmed in additional answers that they believed that the budget should be different for twenty-three compared to fifty-three people who make a nuisance. In line with their judgement that the issue is more important, politicians also allocated a higher budget on average than did the non-politicians[5] and had

---

[5] After controlling for perceived importance of the issue, the difference between politicians and non-politicians in allocated budget is no longer significant.

Table 6.3. *Similarities and differences in the use by politicians and non-politicians of representativeness heuristics.*

	Test	Direction of the effect was the same for politicians and non-politicians?	Strength of the effect was the same for politicians and non-politicians?
H1	Conjunction error I: The Linda problem	√	X The non-politicians were more likely to commit the conjunction error.
H2	Conjunction error II: The making the headlines scenario	√	X Non-politicians judged it more likely that Apeldoorn would make the headlines due to a terrorist attack than did politicians of their municipality.
H3	Conjunction error III: The earthquake scenario	√	X Politicians estimated the likelihood of a natural disaster and an earthquake lower than the non-politicians.
H4	Scope neglect I: Nuisance scenario (importance)	X The politicians neglected scope, whereas the non-politicians did not.	*N.A.*
H5	Scope neglect II: Nuisance scenario (total budget)	X The politicians neglected scope, whereas the non-politicians did not.	*N.A.*

a higher proportion of extreme answers among them. The control variables, such as Left-Right orientation, had no effect on the allocated budget. From this finding, we may conclude that politicians are more likely to use heuristics in their judgement of a scenario like this one as it is more like their day-to-day decisions (compared to the Linda/Vera problem). Table 6.3 summarises the similarities and differences in the findings for politicians and non-politicians for the representativeness heuristic.

The difference we find between the politician and student samples for H4 and H5 might be explained by issue saliency. The task of assigning a budget for such an issue might have been more difficult for non-politicians who have less experience in doing so, prompting them to think harder about it and so triggering System 2 (Evans and Stanovich, 2013; Kahneman, 2011), that is, effortful, logical 'slow' thinking. Conversely, for politicians this may be more of a routine task suited for System 1, that is, automatic, stereotypic and 'fast' thinking (see Hafner-Burton et al., 2013 for more arguments why elites might rely more rather than less on heuristics). While the direction of the effect in H3 was the same for the politician and non-politician samples, we found that politicians were less likely to display the bias related to the heuristic in the 'making the headlines' scenario.

Availability Heuristic Scenarios

Three scenarios examined the biases related to the availability heuristic: the asymmetric dominance effect, cost availability and scope availability. Table 6.4 displays the hypotheses related to these scenarios; for more extensive discussions, we refer the reader to Stolwijk and Vis (2018).

Asymmetric Dominance Effect (H6)

Neither the politicians nor the non-politicians increased their preference for the 'broad' option y (employing both city council watchmen and neighbourhood volunteers to deal with the nuisance issue relative to the preference for extra police) over extra police (option x) when offered the

Table 6.4. Hypotheses on the availability heuristic.[1]

H6	*Asymmetric dominance hypothesis.* When asked how they would deal with the nuisance problem referred to above, participants will be more likely to prefer policy option y over option x when these are contrasted with option z (which is supposedly similar but inferior to option y), i.e. the premise is the presence of option z makes option y look more favourable.
H7	*Cost availability hypothesis.* Participants will be more likely to prefer policy option y as a policy response to the nuisance problem when first asked about the amount of budget allocated, compared to when the budget questions follow the policy question (supposedly because the budget question raises cost concerns and policy option y is supposed to be cheaper than option x).
H8	*Scope availability hypothesis.* Participants will generally allocate a larger budget to deal with fifty-three people who cause a nuisance than in dealing with twenty-three such people if they are asked about the budget per person first, than if they are asked about the total budget right away (supposedly because asking about the budget per person highlights the relevance of scope, i.e. the number of people causing a nuisance).

[1]Please note that some of the hypotheses have been slightly reworded with a view to readability of this chapter, but they are in line with the pre-registered hypotheses (see footnote 2 for more information about the pre-registration)'.

additional option z (only employ city council watchmen), which means that neither displayed the asymmetric dominance effect. The politicians and non-politicians also did not differ in their overall preference for the broad option. Either this test did not (or was not sensitive enough to) capture the asymmetric dominance effect, or this effect does not apply to the choice between these policy options.

Cost Availability (H7)

Neither the politicians nor the non-politicians appeared to be influenced by the enhanced availability of a policy's financial consequence – by asking about it first – in determining their preference for a specific policy option. Actually, they more often preferred the costly option of extra police, and less often the 'broad' option to deal with troublemakers when they were asked initially about how much budget they wanted to allocate – compared with before they were asked about the budget to be allocated, i.e. the percentage of politicians preferring extra police after being asked about the budget allocation was higher (28 per cent) than before being asked about the budget (19 per cent), which was a similar outcome for non-politicians: 32 per cent preferred extra police after being asked about the budget versus seventeen per cent before being asked about the budget allocation ($p < .01$). This means that neither group displayed the cost availability heuristic.

Scope Availability (H8)

Neither in the case of politicians nor of non-politicians did we find an interaction effect in the budget allocation to twenty-three versus fifty-three troublemakers and whether they were first asked to allocate a budget per troublemaker or not. This means that neither displayed the scope availability heuristic. Rather, non-politicians allocated a higher budget to both twenty-three and fifty-three troublemakers after being asked about the budget allocation per troublemaker, compared to beforehand.

Summing up this scenario: it appears that the per-person budget question alerted the non-politicians to the costs involved by giving them more time to think about the cost needed to tackle the larger problem of fifty-three versus twenty-three nuisance makers. Perhaps the difficulty of reasoning from a per-person budget to a budget for twenty-three/fifty-three triggered heuristic processing, because the costs of dealing with more 'nuisance causers' do not increase linearly, as funding is needed to pay at least one person to deal with it regardless of group size. Among politicians, the answers to the budget allocated to deal with the issue per person depended

on whether the preceding description listed twenty-three or fifty-three troublemakers, but this was not the case among non-politicians. This suggests that
the question was easier for politicians to address – and they were already
thinking of their total budget for the issue – while the non-politicians were still
contemplating the size of a reasonable budget to allocate.

Reflection Effect (H9)

The reflection effect hypothesis states that participants will generally
prefer the certainty of an amount when choosing between gains, while
preferring the lottery when choosing between losses. This is indeed what
we found. Facing negative prospects, the politicians (see top panel in
Figure 6.2) preferred the risky choice less often than did the non-
politicians (see bottom panel in Figure 6.2), while they preferred the risky
choice more often than did the non-politicians facing positive prospects.
So, both politicians and non-politicians showed evidence of the reflection
effect, but the politicians were less sensitive to it than were the students.

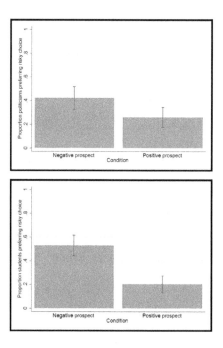

Figure 6.2   Reflection effect findings (politicians – top panel; non-politicians –
bottom panel).

Table 6.5. *Similarities and differences between politicians and non-politicians in displaying the biases related to the availability heuristic and the reflection effect.*

	Test	Direction of the effect was the same for politicians and non-politicians?	Strength of the effect was the same for politicians and non-politicians?
H6	Asymmetric dominance effect	√	√
H7	Cost availability	√	X Differences were significant for non-politicians, but not for politicians.
H8	Scope availability	√	X Students allocated a higher budget to both twenty-three and fifty-three troublemakers after being asked about the per troublemaker budget (compared to being asked beforehand).
H9	Reflection effect	√	X Politicians were somewhat less sensitive to the framing in terms of gains and losses (increasing their preference for the risky option by only seventeen percentage points when framed as a loss rather than a gain, compared to a thirty-three percentage points increase in this preference among non-politicians).

Table 6.5 summarises the similarities and differences in the findings for politicians and non-politicians for the availability heuristic and the reflection effect.

Additional Analyses

In Stolwijk and Vis (2020), we conducted an additional analysis to examine whether politicians with different levels of political experience – measured by length of time serving as a local council member – were sensitive to displaying the biases related to the representativeness heuristic.

We did so by interacting the treatments in the various scenarios with political experience. We found no significant interaction effects for any of the scenarios. This should not be interpreted as strong evidence that political experience has no effect, since the many missing values on this variable make the sample size for these analyses rather small. By means of similar analyses, we also examined the effect of expertise – measured by being a spokesperson on an area related to the troublemaker scenario, i.e. order/security/safety [*veiligheid*] or use/management of public spaces [*openbare orde*]. Again, we found no significant interaction effects between political expertise and the treatments in the various scenarios. These findings suggest that neither experience nor expertise appears to explain the difference between politicians and non-politicians.

Discussion

We end this chapter with a methodological comment. To enable the accumulation of findings and to assess their stability across contexts, it is valuable to use the same or at least similar scenarios as earlier studies. However, using the same scenario on samples of politicians and non-politicians can be challenging if it is abstract and thus detached from the judgements and decisions politicians actually make. We experienced this in our study on the use of the availability heuristic by Dutch local politicians (Stolwijk and Vis, 2018). Originally, we wanted to include two abstract, seminal scenarios on the availability heuristic – a so-called word frequency test (Tversky and Kahneman, 1973) and a maths problem test (Tversky and Kahneman, 1974) – and pre-registered hypotheses to this end,[2] however, ultimately it was not possible to include these two seminal scenarios in testing the availability heuristic in this experiment. In Online Appendix A, which is available at https://www.barbaravis.nl/publications/, we discuss these scenarios in more detail. In this appendix, we also explain how new insights emerged during the pre-testing phase that made clear that including these scenarios in our survey experiment would jeopardize the rest of our study.

What do our findings mean for a psychology of democracy, particularly for government of the people? Similar to earlier findings and meta-analyses by Hafner-Burton et al. (2013) and Kertzer (2020), our results show no systematic difference between elites and non-elites. As such, this contradicts the notion that selection makes politicians different as a decision-making group from non-politicians. We also found little evidence to support the two other mechanisms that might produce differences: political experience and expertise, which means that, overall, there is little ground to suggest that politicians are in 'a league of their own'.

However, there are also some differences that may have consequences for the functioning of representative democracy and for policy-making. Politicians are no worse, but also no better, than non-politicians in avoiding decision-making biases. This suggests that expertise and experience, while relevant for other parts of the policy- and decision-making process (like negotiation skills, or suggesting alternative policy options, etc), did not play a part in these scenarios. Moreover, in the scenario where experience and expertise could be expected to yield the largest benefit – the complex and rather tedious task of assigning a budget – politicians actually performed worse than non-politicians, at least from a policy-seeking perspective in which funding reflects the political priorities of a politician rather than the wording of an issue. As Hafner-Burton et al. (2013) argued, the benefits of experience and expertise in decision-making are very domain specific. Perhaps the best political decisions are ill-served by the accumulation of expertise, due to the many areas for which politicians are responsible. This would be an interesting avenue for further research.

Acknowledgements

An earlier version of this chapter was presented at the NIG Annual Work Conference, 2019. We thank all participants for their helpful comments and suggestions. The chapter draws on research done by the authors in the context of a VIDI grant from the Netherlands Organisation for Scientific Research (grant nr. 452-11-005).

REFERENCES

Baumgartner, F. R. and Jones, B. D. (2015). *The politics of information: Problem definition and the course of public policy in America*. Chicago and London: The University of Chicago Press.

Bellur, S. and Sundar, S. S. (2014). How can we tell when a heuristic has been used? Design and analysis strategies for capturing the operation of heuristics. *Communication Methods and Measures*, 8(2), 116–137.

Besley, T. (2005). Political selection. *Journal of Economic Perspectives*, 19(3), 43–60.

Bovens, M. and Wille, A. (2017). *Diploma democracy: The rise of political meritocracy*. Oxford, UK: Oxford University Press.

Bueno de Mesquita, B., Smith, A., Siverson, R. M. and Morrow, J. D. (2003). *The logic of political survival*. Cambridge, MA: MIT Press.

Byman, D. L. and Pollack, K. M. (2001). Let us now praise great men: Bringing the statesman back in. *International Security*, 25(4), 107–146.

Copeland, D. C. (2001). Theory and history in the study of major war. *Security Studies*, 10(4), 212–239.

Evans, J. S. B. T. and Stanovich, K. E. (2013). Dual-process theories of higher cognition: Advancing the debate. *Perspectives on Psychological Science*, 8(3), 223–241.

Fatas, E., Neugebauer, T. and Tamborero, P. (2007). How politicians make decisions: A political choice experiment. *Journal of Economics*, 92(2), 167–196.

Fréchette, G. R. (20011). *Laboratory experiments: Professionals versus student.* Available at SSRN: https://ssrn.com/abstract=1939219 or http://dx.doi .org/10.2139/ssrn.1939219

Gigerenzer, G. and Selten, R. (Eds.) (2001). *Bounded rationality: The adaptive toolbox.* Cambridge, MA and London, UK: The MIT Press.

Gilovich, T., Griffin, D. and Kahneman, D. (Eds.) (2002). *Heuristics and biases: The psychology of intuitive judgment.* New York: Cambridge University Press.

Hafner-Burton, E. M., Alex Hughes, D. and Victor, D. G. (2013). The cognitive revolution and the political psychology of elite decision making. *Perspectives on Politics*, 11(2), 368–386. https://doi.org/10.1017/S1537592713001084

Hale, T., Webster, S., Petherick, A., Phillips, T. and Kira, B. (2020). Oxford COVID-19 government response tracker. *Blavatnik School of Government.* Available at: www.bsg.ox.ac.uk/research/research-projects/covid-19-govern ment-response-tracker.

Hallsworth, M., Egan, M., Rutter, J. and McCrae, J. (2018). *Behavioural government: Using behavioural science to improve how governments make decisions.* London: The Behavioural Insights Team.

Heß, M., Scheve, C. von, Schupp, J. and Wagner, G. G. (2013). Members of German federal parliament more risk-loving than general population. SOEP Papers 546. Accessed at: www.diw.de/documents/publikationen/73/diw_01 .c.418993.de/diw_sp0546.pdf.

Kahneman, D. (2011). *Thinking, fast and slow.* London: Penguin Books.

Kahneman, D. and Frederick, S. (2002). Representativeness revisited: Attribute substitution in intuitive judgment. In T. Gilovich, D. Griffin, and D. Kahneman (Eds.), *Heuristics and biases: The psychology of intuitive judgment* (pp. 49–81). New York: Cambridge University Press.

Kahneman, D. and Tversky, A. (1979). Prospect theory: An analysis of decision under risk. *Econometrica*, 47(2), 263–193.

(1972). Subjective probability: A judgment of representativeness. *Cognitive Psychology*, 3(3), 430–454.

Kelman, M. (2011). *The heuristics debate.* Oxford, UK: Oxford University Press.

Kertzer, J. D. (2020). Re-assessing elite-public gaps in political behavior. *American Journal of Political Science,* https://doi.org/10.1111/ajps.12583

Linde, J. and Vis, B. (2017). Do politicians take risks like the rest of us? An experimental test of prospect theory under MPs. *Political Psychology*, 38(1), 101–117.

List, J. A. (2004). Neoclassical theory versus prospect theory: Evidence from the marketplace. *Econometrica*, 72(2), 615–625. https://doi.org/10.1111/j.1468-0262.2004.00502.x

Mattozzi, A. and Merlo, A. (2008). Political careers or career politicians? *Journal of Public Economics*, 92(3–4), 597–608.

Ministerie van Binnenlandse Zaken en Koninkrijksrelaties (2016). *Staat van het Bestuur*. Available at: https://kennisopenbaarbestuur.nl/media/254488/staat-van-het-bestuur-2016-webrichtlijnenproof.pdf.

Mintz, A., Redd, S. B. and Vedlitz, A. (2006). Can we generalize from student experiments to the real world in political science, military affairs, and international relations? *Journal of Conflict Resolution*, 50(5), 757–776.

Newell, B. R., Lagnado, D. A. and Shanks, D. R. (2015). *Straight choices: The psychology of decision making* (2nd ed.). Hove and New York: Psychology Press.

Rahat, G. (2007). Candidate selection: The choice before the choice. *Journal of Democracy*, 18(1), 157–170.

Renshon, J. (2015). Losing face and sinking costs: Experimental evidence on the judgment of political and military leaders. *International Organization*, 69(3), 659–695.

Sheffer, L. (2018). *Behavioural foundations of elite politics: How individual-level characteristics shape the decision making of elected politicians*. PhD Dissertation: University of Toronto.

Sheffer, L., Loewen, P. J., Soroka, S., Walgrave, S. and Shaefer, T. (2018). Nonrepresentative representatives: An experimental study of the decision making of elected politicians. *American Political Science Review*, 112(2), 302–321.

Simonson, I. and Tversky, A. (1992). Choice in context: Tradeoff contrast and extremeness aversion. *Journal of Marketing Research*, 29(3), 231–295.

Stolwijk, S. (2019). The representativeness heuristic in political decision making. In D. P. Redlawsk, C. Erisen, E. Hennes, Z. Oxley, D. Schreiber and B. Vis (Eds.), *The Oxford research encyclopedia of politics*. Available at: https://oxfordre.com/politics/browse?page=60&pageSize=20&sort=authorsort&subSite=politics.

Stolwijk, S. and Vis, B. (2020). Politicians, the representativeness heuristic and decision-making Biases. *Political Behavior*. https://doi.org/10.1007/s11109-020-09594-6

(2018). Political decision making and the availability heuristic. *Paper prepared for the seventy-sixth Annual MPSA Conference, Chicago, USA, 5–8 April*.

Tversky, A. and Kahneman, D. (1983). Extensional versus intuitive reasoning: The conjunction fallacy in probability judgment. *Psychological Review*, 90(4), 293–315.

(1974). Judgment under uncertainty: Heuristics and biases. *Science*, 185(4157), 1124–1131.

(1973). Availability: A heuristic for judging frequency and probability. *Cognitive Psychology*, 5(2), 207–232.

Tversky, A. and Simonson, I. (1993). Context-dependent preferences. *Management Science*, 39(10), 1179–1189.

Vieider, F. and Vis, B. (2019). Prospect theory in political decision making. In D. Redlawsk, C. Erisen, E. Hennes, Z. Oxley, D. Schreiber and B. Vis (Eds.),

Oxford research encyclopedia of politics. Available at: https://oxfordre.com/politics/browse?page=60&pageSize=20&sort=authorsort&subSite=politics.

Vis, B. (2019). Heuristics and political elites' judgment and decision making. *Political Studies Review*, 17(1), 41–52.

Von Neumann, J. and Morgenstern, O. (1944). *Theory of games and economic behavior*. Princeton, NJ: Princeton University Press.

Walgrave, S., Epping, L. and Sevenan, J. (2013). *Het Informatiemenu van politici en hun medewerkers: Resultaten van Interviews met Federale Parlementsleden, Ministers, Partijvoorzitters en hun Persoonlijke Medewerkers*. Antwerp: University of Antwerp.

CHAPTER 7

The Mental Well-Being of Politicians

Ashley Weinberg

Why should we care about the mental health of politicians? Would we worry for their sake or for ours? After all, what happens if they are not able to perform their function in taking key decisions on behalf of a whole nation? The answer is potentially straightforward. If they are not appropriately supported to act on behalf of others and their health is breaking down, then there needs to be a safety net – not only for them, but for all of us. Without support for politicians' positive mental health, their ability to safeguard effectively the democratic system or to conduct due processes may be compromised, as might a job-holder's performance in any other type of work. In most occupations, from running a nuclear power plant to teaching in a classroom, one would expect systems designed to protect those doing the job and thereby the communities they serve. Without this clear support in politics, the losers are, not only the individual politicians concerned, but democracy and the people it serves.

However, it is important to bear in mind that every one of us is subject to variation in our psychological health over time. This can be dependent on a host of factors, including, but not limited to: the impact of events in our lives – including at work and in our relationships – our own health histories, as well as those of our families and loved ones, and the access we have to sources of emotional support in everyday life and in times of particular need. Politicians are no different from anyone else in this regard. In considering the importance of mental health in politics, this chapter seeks to dispel the stigma that is readily invoked by some for political gain and, instead, to highlight the benefits of enlightened attention to daily challenges posed to mental health in the lives of so many – including those who take decisions on behalf of entire peoples.

The Case of Politics

It is likely that many regard national politicians as a privileged occupa-tional group with access to wealth and resources not commonly available to others; as such, politicians are not generally considered by the public to be deserving of any particularly sympathy. However, the premise of shared responsibility for exercising power – which is the apparent context in a democracy – points to a similar need for healthy working for those in political office as it does for the people they represent. Public furore over exploitation and gain by some corrupt politicians – a worldwide theme with recent examples from most continents – is clearly justified. Equally, levels of positive concern about health should apply to politicians just as much as to other citizens of a nation. General disregard for such matters is likely to be to the detriment of the many rather than simply to individual sufferers. For example, in practical terms, will policies pursued in times of crisis meet the public need or, instead, represent lunges from one policy disaster to another in the context of multiple pressures adversely affecting those taking decisions – without available support for maintaining their well-being? This raises important questions in any system of government and, in particular, in democracies where transparency of process is a reasonable expectation – and especially in emergency situations (see also Chapter 5 by Peter Suedfeld).

What is the worst that could happen if an individual elected to represent others became unwell? Naturally, there should be concern for the welfare of the politician as a human being. In addition, there might also be delays for those waiting on their availability and decisions at constituency level, although politicians' support teams are generally capable of facilitating solutions. Within parliament, it is possible that a politician's ill health may prevent participation in voting and debates until they are well enough. At the highest political level, if the leader of a country becomes unwell, there may be a deputy or high-ranking minister who can take over. However, the chances of the leader being unable to function as expected and taking decisions that may have a disastrous impact on the wider nation is unlikely, isn't it? After all, the resilience demanded in achieving high office would surely select those who are most likely to withstand its brickbats. Yet, when Russian President Boris Yeltsin – whose enjoyment of alcohol was well known – fell asleep for hours at Dublin airport on a state visit to Ireland, or when a beleaguered US President Bill Clinton ordered the bombing of targets in the Sudan after his own indictment for lying about an extra-marital affair, were issues of impaired well-being involved?

There are numerous examples of politicians worldwide – whether members or leaders of a national parliament – who have experienced episodes of poor psychological health. Some of these have become evident in the most tragic of circumstances, such as following suicide or, more rarely, in public openness about diagnosis of a mental-health condition. From an historical perspective, many are aware of the struggles with depression of ultimately successful politicians such as Abraham Lincoln and Winston Churchill. Freeman (1991) has highlighted many rulers and leaders whose health conditions coincided with poor decisions linked to disastrous policies. However, the examples of Norway's prime minister, Kjell Magne Bondevik, Canadian government minister, Seamus O'Regan, and Australian minster for trade, Andrew Robb, stand out, not least for their openness, but for what happened subsequently. Having recognised his symptoms of depression, Bondevik took a leave of absence to receive treatment and, months later, returned to the political fray, running again for the highest office. He won and, in so doing, demonstrated the equal capacity for recovery from psychological ill health that so many experience. Vitally, his example created a healthier environment in Norwegian society for anyone experiencing such a common mental-health condition to share their experiences, seek support and carry on with their lives. Similarly, O'Regan's openness about his experience of depression and seeking an alcohol-free lifestyle did not prejudice his appointment to a number of ministerial roles in the Canadian government and Andrew Robb's book about battling depression predated his promotion to government in Australia. Such examples emphasise that it is not essentially the existence of a mental-health challenge, but the way in which it is addressed and supported by individuals, families and work colleagues, that determines the outcomes.

Prevalence and Stigma

It is important to consider what is meant by good and poor psychological well-being and to highlight the inappropriate role of stigma when considering these issues. 'There is no health without mental health' has been a popular phrase used in promoting awareness of the need for care and support of psychological well-being worldwide (World Health Organization, 2018). However, since the global economic crisis of 2008 and the start of the COVID-19 pandemic in 2020, the issue of mental health has assumed even greater significance for global economies as well as for public health. Increasingly, organisations have realised the huge financial costs of poor mental health manifest in sickness absence, presenteeism (trying to work while ill) and turnover (Hassard et al., 2018). Across the world – and before the global COVID-19 pandemic – governments have been keener to acknowledge the importance of mental-health challenges for citizens, families and communities; for example, Kenya held its first national conference on mental health to combat suicide and drug abuse (Kenyan Ministry of Health, 2019), while New Zealand allocated record financial resources in its first 'well-being budget' (Sutherland, 2019). The global pandemic has further underlined the need for action to address the challenges for mental health, following on from the World Health Organization's (WHO) seven-year plan (2013–2020) to stimulate psychological health initiatives worldwide.

The knowledge that mental-health conditions represent one of the biggest challenges identified by WHO (2020) is a clear indication of the seriousness with which psychological well-being should be considered. The equivalence between what are defined in many parts of the world as physical- versus mental-health conditions has been historically denied, so it is positive to see that the most common diagnoses of depression and anxiety are beginning to receive the coverage and attention they deserve. However, these are among a range of conditions that affect psychological functioning, either temporarily, periodically or chronically. Additionally, there are categories of mental-health condition that traditionally have been less readily recognised, such as personality disorders, partly because of the continuum of expression of our personality along which all of us are situated. Nonetheless, these are officially determined by clinical diagnoses (DSM-5), although the role of these within politics – including narcissistic personality disorder and its component attributes – has yet to receive systematic consideration (Fazekas and Hatemi, 2020). However, notable 'at a distance' attempts to identify grandiose narcissism in US presidents suggests a greater prevalence in the individuals achieving the office when compared with the general population (Watts et al, 2013).

So, what is the prevalence of diagnoses of psychological ill health among politicians? Given the continuing stigma with which mental-health conditions can be viewed – often by those with less understanding of what is entailed in how these are caused and manifest – perhaps it is not surprising that knowledge of who suffers with what is relatively unshared and may be a carefully guarded personal secret by politicians. The right for the individual to exercise their choice over whether to share such information is obvious. However, one of the demands of many jobs when joining an organisation includes an occupational health assessment, in order to determine whether the employee is well enough – physically and psychologically – to begin work. In the workplace, the importance of this is clear, not only for the functioning of organisations, but in their ability to appropriately exercise a duty of care to employees where this is enshrined in law.

In other words, safeguards can exist for employees and the organisations they represent, although the application of these may differ between contexts. In politics, it is not clear who are the employers and, therefore, a duty of care for politicians 'employed' by their political party or indeed by the people is not routinely recorded in legislation or policy. This anomaly creates challenges, not only for individuals, but potentially for the electorates they represent.

It is important to make clear that a pre-existing health condition should not preclude an individual from a job, particularly where it does not impact on their functioning or, indeed, is monitored and controlled via ongoing support. Equally, it is wrong to discriminate against individuals because of past experience of a mental-health problem. For example, depression is common in the wider population and, through individual experiences of this, many people learn and develop psychological coping strategies that not only enhance their future functioning, but also mean they and those around them are able to identify and address issues that may yet arise – and, potentially, in a way that is more adaptive for future coping than afforded to those who have not (yet) experienced a depressive episode.

The scope for wider recognition – and parity in attitude to physical health – of mental well-being is clear, even though the historical stigma has been considerable. In surveys of UK MPs (APPG on Mental Health, 2008; Poulter et al., 2019), 45–48 per cent felt they would not be comfortable discussing a mental-health issue with parliamentary colleagues. A 2012 UK parliamentary debate that saw a number of MPs participating in a discussion on mental health stands out, as some took the opportunity to describe their own experiences (Hansard, 2012), even though this was not anticipated. The positive impact of such actions, not only raises awareness, but also helps in addressing issues of stigma and promoting acceptance that our psychological well-being is important, is subject to ill health and can be considered positively in any context. Furthermore, for those encountering poor mental health, it carries implications for how we may address a need for support or intervention where it arises, whether inside or outside of politics.

Experiences of Psychological Well-Being and Ill Health in Everyday Politics

Before considering what poor psychological health looks like, it is also important to contemplate ideals for our mental well-being. The direction in which effects are witnessed is significant too – whether it is from the job to the job-holder and/or from the job-holder to the job (Burns,

Butterworth and Anstey, 2016). Either or both ways, there is broad agreement that a sense of control is predictive of positive mental health and, in addition, occupational psychologists have identified a range of subjective experiences favourable for well-being. These include aspirations to engage with our surroundings and with others, a sense of competence and self-belief in what we do, as well as a range of positive emotions (van Horn et al., 2004; Warr, 1989).

Enhanced opportunities to experience these components of psychological well-being can be brought about in conjunction with working, including the structure, purpose, identity and social contact that performing a job can involve (Jahoda, 1982). Accordingly, studies over many decades have shown the consistently negative impact of unemployment on mental health (Paul and Moser, 2009). However, the availability (or not) of positive experiences in a job environment carries considerable implications for employee well-being and, increasingly, the shortcomings of 'poor quality' jobs are recognised, as well as the role of 'stressors' – or sources of pressure – which take a negative toll on the psychological health of the job-holder (Butterworth et al., 2013). Research in occupational psychology since the 1970s has underlined such effects and, in turn, highlighted the need for well-designed jobs that offer the opportunities to maintain or build on factors that underpin well-being (British Psychological Society, 2017).

Despite the potential for variability, certain aspects of a work environment do routinely impact in a negative manner on the majority of employees. For example, lack of control and high workload are well-known sources of pressure on job-holders in many occupational settings (Karasek and Theorell, 1990). Naturally – and perhaps with some good fortune – employees may craft their own ways of dealing with such stressors (Wrzesniewski and Dutton, 2001) or accordingly gravitate and adapt to types of work and job situation that suit them. Yet, exposure to negative job conditions is a possibility in any context, and may proliferate in the context of unfortunate events. This is no different for politicians. Although described as 'a way of life', because of its personal – and time-consuming – nature, a job in national politics is clearly one of choice for most involved and attained after surmounting considerable challenges in candidate selection, campaigning, getting elected and staying in office. Nevertheless, the aspect of choice does not guarantee positive work experiences and, indeed, there is a clear expectation in politics that challenge is endemic to the role, whether as part of contributing to change or, indeed, maintaining a status quo. Combined with the commitments as a Member of Parliament of time, energy, personal and professional resources, it is understandable that surviving the workplace is a priority to the individuals who serve (as is the case in other types of work).

Within this psychological context of ambitious motivation confronted by unending uncertainty and unstinting demands, the occupational equation appears not too dissimilar to that described as a high job strain environment (Karasek, 1979), characterised by low levels of control and high workload. Surveys show almost half of MPs work more than seventy hours per week, with a similar proportion working fifty-five to seventy hours weekly (Weinberg, 2012). However, the requirement to perform in the full glare of public scrutiny, handling matters of national and local contention while continuing to function as a human being with family or other responsibilities, elevates further the potential sources of strain. However, the importance of resources at the job-holder's disposal should not be ignored (Demerouti et al., 2001), nor should it be forgotten that any given job may be experienced differently by one individual to another (e.g. Caplan et al., 1975). Access to the social, political and other capital available to politicians may offer moderating influences on the experiences of doing the job, which even give it the hint of glamour and celebrity apparent to the casual observer.

Yet, when viewed close up, what is the job like? Interviews with UK MPs have certainly highlighted benefits of privilege and opportunities, and of an interesting and stimulating career path, with the potential to choose subjects in which to specialise. However, accounts also indicate experiences of sleep loss, weight gain, stress and depression, with marital break-ups among a range of costs paid by MPs and their families. These are co-existing with long working hours, considerable travel requirements, conflicting daily demands on time and constant pressures to cut short any given activity (Weinberg and Weinberg, 2019). Such findings are not unusual or indeed a surprise to politicians as survey data obtained over decades have yielded consistent patterns (Weinberg, 2012) and found echoes in testaments to 'ruined marriages' and 'exhausted irrationality' (Jopling Report, 1992). Indeed, alarming proportions of MPs continue to rate as 'moderate' to 'severe' the negative impact of long working hours on their health (44 per cent), on work performance (36 per cent) and on family relationships (57 per cent)(Weinberg, 2015). Such figures are also reflected in self-reported effects of long hours on health and job functioning in other legislative contexts, including Malawi (55 and 63 per cent respectively; Malenga, 2016) and the Scottish parliament and Welsh Senedd (61 and 69 per cent respectively; Weinberg, 2012).

To some, the symptoms of the problems facing politicians may seem – on the surface – to belong to the individuals concerned. Yet, until and unless one contemplates the difficulties such factors create for effective performance in the job of representing others, their communities and ultimately their nations, there is a risk of overlooking how well democracy is working – or whether it is being allowed to work at all well. The notion that a fixed proportion of politicians – as with any other occupational group – will usually experience poor psychological health is outdated and unsupported by contemporary observation of events and studies. This is evident in reports that detail the increasing rates of suicide in populations during economic recession and hardship (World Health Organization, 2011) to research showing the psychologically debilitating impact of negative events on otherwise resilient national politicians (Weinberg, 2015). Prevalence of symptoms of mental ill health – including feeling unhappy, experiencing worry, finding it difficult to make decisions or physical manifestations of these in poor diet and sleep loss – have been recorded in eighteen up to 34 per cent of UK (Poulter et al., 2019; Weinberg and Cooper, 2003; Weinberg, Cooper and Weinberg, 1999) and Australian national politicians (Weinberg, 2012). These match or exceed comparable population samples (Poulter et al., 2019) as well as providing a broader context to the anecdotal evidence of autobiographies, such as those by Canadian political party leader, Michael Ignatieff (2013) and Australian government minister, Andrew Robb (2011). However, the doubling of the percentage of a cohort of UK politicians experiencing severe psychological strain following negative work events (Weinberg, 2015), or indeed the spike in negative symptoms in association with changing exposure to challenging job conditions across whole cities (Burns et al., 2016), illustrates both the potential negative psychological impact of some work factors, as well as the susceptibility of much wider populations.

The mental toll of conducting the job at a time when colleagues are killed is not hard to imagine and, in politics, has tragic precedent in nations around the world, including in the UK and Ghana respectively, with the murders of serving politicians, Jo Cox MP, Sir David Amess MP and the Honourable Ekow Quansah Hayford. A survey completed by 102 New Zealand MPs revealed that half had been threatened physically, with 15 per cent becoming victims of an actual attack (Every-Palmer, Barry-Walsh and Pathé, 2015). Half of respondents believed their attackers were not themselves experiencing severe forms of mental health disorder and it is clearly important to consider, not only safeguards for MPs as a matter of routine, but also the potential contributions of political instability and online harassment to the increased likelihood of assault on politicians.

Aside from such contending with extreme behaviours, the psychological challenge of actually carrying out the job of MP in the context of national economic and political crises has, in itself, been associated with raised prevalence of symptoms of psychological ill health among national politicians in Malawi, where in one survey, 95 per cent of respondents agreed with the need for counselling services for MPs (Malenga, 2019).

In summary, it is evident that – as humans – we are universally disposed to experience mental health, which can alter over time and across job and other situations, and that exposure to circumstances stretching us beyond our individual coping capacities and resources will take a toll. While these may differ between individuals, this is not a cause for complacency about how our political workplaces are shaped or endured. Without due care to these environments and working arrangements, the risks to fully functioning democracies mount, as the act of effective representation becomes too difficult to maintain and individuals elected to carry them out are hampered by unreasonable and harmful expectations and unwieldy work environments not of their own design.

Well-Being, Political Performance and the Role of Parliament

So, how does mental health suffer and what could be the impact on political job performance? Quite simply, one would expect the same symptoms in politics as in another work (or non-work) role. Surveys such as the General Health Questionnaire (Goldberg and Williams, 1988) and the Patient Health Questionnaire (PHQ-9) assess psychological ill health as indicated by a range of key symptoms evident in physiological (e.g. sleep problems and tiredness), cognitive (e.g. difficulties in concentrating or remembering) and emotional responses (e.g. feeling happy, unhappy or depressed) to pressure. These apply equally to politicians as to anyone else and affect job-related behaviours, including those relevant to political functioning, such as making decisions and problem-solving. Again, it is worth emphasising that symptoms of poor mental well-being are subject to change over time and, where these are evident, can impair usual functioning and, if persisting – usually beyond a fortnight, may indicate the presence of an episode of ill health (Royal College of Psychiatrists, 2020). These may improve without assistance or, indeed, they may benefit from access to appropriate informal or formal support, which enlightened workplaces have been increasingly seeking to offer (SHRM, 2019).

Levels of recognition of the importance of mental health and of the risks posed by the strains of political work are increasing. The UK Parliament began offering counselling services to MPs following the parliamentary debate on mental-health services in 2012 and acknowledgement of the difficulties in accessing this for well-known individuals alongside their constituents. There have been calls for counselling to be made available to politicians in parliamentary settings worldwide (e.g. Ghana News, 2017; Weinberg, 2012), as well as a growing interest apparent to the author in consideration of the working conditions of politicians by parliaments around the world, including Malawi and Canada. There are also initiatives that seek to engage politicians in supporting positive mental health through mindfulness, which have gained in popularity in parliamentary as well as other workplace settings (Mindful Nation Report, 2015), with over 200 UK MPs and twice that number of their staff receiving relevant training.

Indeed, the positive reception to discussing mental health among MPs and political staff in the UK Parliament – in debates, Prime Minister's Questions and the launch of All-Party Parliamentary Groups in Mindfulness and Psychology – suggests a culture change within political organisations is both necessary and welcome. When Kevan Jones MP contributed his own experiences to the 2012 parliamentary debate on mental health, it seemed the logical next step. Other politicians present shared their experiences and a cross-party campaign followed, leading to the establishment of psychological counselling support for UK MPs. However, after a subsequent spate of General Elections, a majority of MPs surveyed did not know how to access this valuable service (Poulter et al., 2019). Growing interest around the world suggests other countries are poised to consider similar interventions, however, the politics of well-being can make it hard for politicians to ask for, or indeed suggest, specialist support that may actually be denied to electors due to resource issues. Nevertheless, the provision of occupational health support – which can include mental health provision – would be consistent with measures taken by many organisations in other types of job. Equally, in the face of online hostility already reported, it is conceivable that many MPs and their partners and families may need psychological support to ensure they are able to cope. In other words, what has become a recognised danger in doing the job should be met with all possible means to combat it, i.e. not only appropriate levels of security, but also provision of suitable mental-health support.

Sources of Pressure on Politicians Worldwide

In considering the impact of doing the job on the mental state and functioning of national politicians, it is clear there is a range of factors that give rise to psychological pressure. The attempt to organise these into a framework that helps to shape future research also reflects the need for further studies into the mental health of politicians. Indeed, in claiming that 'The health of democracy may, to an extent, depend on the mental health and psychological wellbeing of those we elect to represent and take decisions on our behalf' (Flinders et al., 2020), it is clear the importance of this field should not be underestimated. Even the briefest of considerations of the violence endured by politicians, both threatened and physical, underlines the turbulent environment within which their work is conducted and demands urgent attention. In addition, routine exposure to negative factors within the job constitutes a steadier, but nonetheless debilitating, influence on well-being. While occupational psychologists have highlighted common sources of such pressure in the psycho-social aspects of working per se, it seems sensible to consider these in the context of political work in order to identify opportunities for progress: both by preventing problems and by designing interventions that seek to remedy unhealthy work practices. As highlighted earlier, the significance of taking such steps is not purely for the individualised gain of politicians and their employees, but carries far wider implications. How (well) can democracy function if its decision-makers and representatives are beset by aspects of their work environment that prevent them from performing as expected? Viewed in this way, interests in improving political workplaces are also those which seek to promote more effective democracy.

Of course, the nature of democracy, with its balancing acts between frequently opposing ideological viewpoints, may not create an easy environment for altering factors such as working conditions, particularly where improvements may be perceived to favour one political group over another. However, the aim of redesigning the way the job is done should be more overarching than overt political concerns, particularly where it underpins effective democratic functioning and regardless of who is in power. The UK Westminster Parliament provides an interesting example, not least as it took over a decade at the turn of the Millennium to modernise its debating hours, which had been designed over a century earlier. Indeed, the fabric of the building is so old it is decaying at such a rate that future relocation has been planned while rebuilding is underway! The precedent of all-night debates, with votes taking place at unsociable weekday hours, had been long-established and – with it – tacit acceptance that MPs' personal lives would suffer as additionally they continued to squeeze constituency work into their weekends. However, a lobby for reform gathered pace at a time when the number of women MPs entering

Parliament was increasing and more family-friendly policies were finally being favoured by workplace organisations. Nevertheless, proposals to change parliamentary debating hours became a battle between those wishing to reform MPs' working hours and the 'traditionalists'. Over two decades, compromises evolved as UK MPs have demarcated a weekday for constituency work as well as earlier daytime debates to permit more manageable working hours and family lives. Nevertheless, for those with constituencies more than 150 miles from Parliament, this has proved of limited help during the week and, indeed, symptoms of psychological strain were significantly greater among MPs juggling this particular work-life situation (Weinberg, 2015).

The issue of time and its implications for the design and conduct of the job of MP is a challenge wherever it is conducted. From the UK to Malawi to Australia, surveys of national politicians reveal similar themes. There are positive comments about working with others, representing the people and issues that are important to so many, as well as the opportunities to work at the heart of things and make a difference. Understandably, there are challenges – some of which are particular to enacting political roles – whether representing constituents or party, negotiating with the infrastructure of parliament or handling issues of national or local importance. In standing for election, it would be interesting to know how many politicians anticipate the time they will yet spend travelling (to and from their constituency), away from their families and loved ones, sitting in debates, reading papers to prepare for upcoming events, championing and scrutinising legislation, combating unfriendly media or realising the limitations of their role in helping others or saying 'No'. This potential gap in expectations is manifest in different ways and numerous MPs have shared the pathos invoked by passing time away from what mattered to them as private individuals, rather than as career politicians: 'Politics consumes your life and you lose close friends from earlier days', wrote one Australian MP, while others reflected on, 'too many competing demands on time – constant guilt about what I'm *not* doing' and 'insufficient time to spend on self-renewal'.

Concerns expressed by MPs in Malawi and the UK have indicated pressures created by the lack of resources on their capacity to do the job and the lack of understanding by the public about what the job entails or what MPs can achieve. As such, calls for civic education and for greater support for their constituency-based work are common to both (Malenga, 2016; Weinberg, 2012). The pressure to bow to public expectations by over-promising and then later struggling with the consequences of under-delivering are evident at both personal and professional levels: 'There is this belief that as an MP you have solutions to economic woes affecting family, friends and constituents', wrote one MP in Malawi. Another MP dealing with 'requests for condolences, coffins and school fees', complained, 'if [the constituent is] not assisted it's taken as if the MP is failing to deliver the services to the constituency' (Malenga, 2016). Meanwhile, some UK MPs have found they are being considered as a reserve maintenance service, receiving requests to clean gutters or reduce the number of geese in the local park! (BPS, 2020).

In considering such studies of the psychological health of politicians, which draw on data provided by MPs from three nations across as many continents, consistent themes of a job with long working hours and unstinting demands are clear, as are the difficulties MPs experience at the interface between home and work lives. Arguably, this provides an added dimension that is not directly part of many job roles. The ubiquity of new technology means political news is everywhere and may require the attention of politicians at any time of any day. It is also worth noting that, for local politicians, the clash of life's 'spheres' is just as marked and equally demands the development of a range of coping strategies (Emery, Meier and Mortelmans, 2018) to contend with the 'greedy' nature of the role. Through interviews with Belgian councillors, it emerged that the political role exerts strong borders likely to impinge on the sphere of family life (Emery et al., 2018), which may say as much about the choices made by politicians who are local or national as it does about their capacity to juggle life's priorities.

This brief overview of themes emerging from research with politicians around the globe indicates some of the factors that democratically elected representatives face. While it is likely their ability to serve constituents may vary with individual priorities and the local political terrain, their requirement to do so is unquestioned and the verdict inevitable with the next election.

A Framework of Stressors Facing Politicians

In seeking to translate this array of images into a continuous vista of the job-related challenges facing MPs, a framework of sources of pressure (henceforth referred to as stressors) has been proposed. As with the structure of this book, it borrows from Bronfenbrenner's (1979) ecological approach, in this case to aid consideration of the types of influence on politicians' well-being from factors operating at the macro- (societal), meso- (institutional) and micro- (individual) levels of their working lives (Flinders et al., 2020).The framework appears to suppose commonalities in politicians' experiences, but these are intended as indicative rather than prescriptive and invite the reader to test out the nine factors.

Table 7.1 includes a brief description of the stressors within each level of politicians' experience and highlights studies that have examined them (see also chapters indicated in this book for the broader context). However, this is not intended to be an exhaustive list of research and indicates gaps that are in the process of being addressed or remain unaddressed. There remains considerable scope to add to this body of knowledge and to the framework, particularly from an international dimension.

Sources of pressure – mainly at the micro-level – have already been considered in this chapter to some extent and are also reflected in other chapters of the book as indicated. The subsections that follow consider each stressor in turn and, where available, include reference to recent testing of the framework by psychologists and political scientists using qualitative techniques.

Macro-Level Stressors

Macro-level issues relate to the broader societal and cultural context in which political work is conducted. Naturally, these are beyond the scope of influence of one politician or indeed the body politic, yet the repercussions for how this occupational group is perceived are considerable. These incorporate both myths and reality, historical and current, and are never far from immediate reach in a 24/7 news media context. Idealised *expectations* of politicians may well fit with the needs of an era, but – as such – cannot ever be properly fulfilled given the vagaries of capacity to deliver, let alone any wavering in politicians' commitment. The 'gap' in expectations is often a 'trap' (Flinders and Kelso, 2011) into which politicians fall, particularly in seeking office. This breeds a *distrust* manifest in anything ranging from scepticism to ire among the public, for some of whom social media provides a readily accessible means of verbal attack and actual threat. However, the issue of trust is not simply about relationships with the general public, as one MP realised, 'there were very few people in Parliament, where I really felt I could trust them. Even in my party' (BPS, 2020). For whichever audience, navigating the political tightrope can be unforgiving: 'the difficulty of a reputation is that you can build it up over years, but you can lose it in five minutes' (BPS, 2020).

One aspect of the job that an MP may influence is the capacity to invest their own emotional labour in how they present themselves to the watching world. In the context of a political party or situation that may require a

Table 7.1. *Key stressors facing politicians (from Flinders et al., 2020).*

	Stressor	Meaning	Relevant research studies
1. Macro-level (cultural)	1.1 *Expectations*	High expectations, but limited resources and capacity to deliver.	Pending
	1.2 *Distrust*	Intense scrutiny of politicians with focus on sensationalism and negativity; public accountability can include blame and threat.	Pending
	1.3 *Political labour*	Political labour reflects dissonance between personal and politically required views – potential for personal and professional costs.	Weinberg, J. 2020
2. Meso-level (institutional)	2.1 *Organisational Culture*	Majoritarian politics is competitive; lack of clarity around organisational procedures in parliament, e.g., induction.	Cooper-Thomas and Silvester, 2014; Kwiatkowski, 2012
	2.2 *Leadership*	The impact of leadership style and of responsibility for appropriate handling of crises and daily demands.	Lilienfeld et al., 2012; Owen and Davidson, 2009; **See Nair – Chapter 9; Eidenfalk and Woodcock – Chapter 12; Caprara – Chapter 14**
	2.3 *Temporal*	Electoral cycles mean limited time to enact change; impact of job loss and an uncertain future after politics.	Roberts, 2017; Theakston, 2012; Weinberg, 2007; **See Roberts – Chapter 13**
3. Micro-level (individual)	3.1 *Lifestyle*	All-encompassing, featuring long working hours. The psychological strain of political life is often felt in family life and relationships.	Weinberg et al, 1999; Weinberg and Cooper, 2003; Weinberg, 2015
	3.2 *Control*	Limited influence over many job-related factors, lack of control over events.	Weinberg, 2015
	3.3 *Skills*	Availability of appropriate training and support to strengthen competence, although reluctance to prescribe a 'right way' to be a politician.	Hartley, 2012; Silvester & Dykes, 2007; Silvester, Wyatt and Randall, 2013

message at odds with their own, this is described as *'political labour'*. Recognising that 60 per cent of politicians believe their work addresses emotionally charged issues, a similar proportion 'feel that they are regularly required to be "artificially" or "professionally" friendly' (Weinberg, 2020). Similarly, a 'sophisticated approach to the provision of information and use of language' (Flinders et al., 2020) that helps the politician to 'steer a course between saving your own integrity, and not falling out and being side-lined and alienated by the parties is very difficult' (BPS, 2020). Perhaps it is not surprising that this type of 'surface acting' (Hochschild, 1983) predicts burnout in politicians, (Weinberg, 2020), i.e. a serious negative impact on psychological well-being linked with job-related emotional exhaustion.

Meso-Level Stressors

These emanate from within the political context, system and institutions in which politicians operate. As such, sources of pressure at the meso-level can be linked with behaviours and norms often moulded by custom, tradition and precedent, all of which are combined within *organisational culture*. For example, absence of effective induction or lack of clarity over organisational processes in parliaments are frequently observed by new MPs around the world (e.g. the UK and New Zealand, Cooper-Thomas and Silvester, 2014): 'The lack of support compared to a traditional organisation where you'd have an HR function and a line management function is very amorphous', (BPS, 2020). Exposure of harassment and bullying in the UK Parliament (Cox, 2018) has further underlined the potentially toxic working conditions where power dynamics are abused – which we also know is not limited to political work. Understandably, the slowness of the organisation to address these destructive problems has come under increasing criticism.

Leadership styles are eye-catching in politics the world over and set the tone, not only for working conditions, but also for approaches to decision-making at the highest level. However, politicians occupy leadership roles whether in the highest office or not, by virtue of the status of their job within communities and running parliamentary and constituency offices: 'You are a line manager for a number of staff, and you have a duty of care to those staff as well' (BPS, 2020).

With any leadership scenario comes competition from rivals, as well as responsibility for handling crisis situations. Limitations on time and electoral cycles (the *temporal* stressor) mean the clock is always ticking on a period in office. In itself this stimulates a level of uncertainty about the future of any political job and, while this may be exacerbated by slender voting majorities or simply by uncontrollable events, it may prove a motivation that eventually cannot ultimately be satisfied; as one member of an MP's team noted: 'Those of us who work for MPs with marginal constituencies are permanently on the edge of our seats'.

Micro-Level Stressors

Much of the focus of this chapter has been on the politician as a working person in a specific and potentially extraordinary context. Examples from both quantitative and qualitative findings illustrate the power and meaning of these to individuals who pursue a career in politics. The challenges to a healthy *lifestyle* lie, not only in functioning effectively throughout extended working hours, but also the cumulative impact of these and of the incessant demands on personal and family relationships: 'When I first got to parliament, I remember thinking, "who has done this timetable?"' (BPS, 2020). It is not surprising that *control* – or lack of it – is an issue for MPs' mental well-being, as it is for everyone. Aside from its role in daily psychological functioning, the perceptions held by a politician are often mismatched between the job-holder and the electorate. Again, quotes featured earlier in the chapter from politicians around the world attest to this and continue to uphold an early finding in research with MPs – 80 per cent score lower in perceived levels of control than the general population! (Weinberg, Cooper and Weinberg, 1999).

The impact of change on MPs has confirmed a phenomenon recognised more widely in the occupational psychology literature. When UK MPs were consulted over potential reforms to their debating hours in Parliament – which also meant changing the shape of their working week – voting on these provided an opportunity to participate and thereby to exercise a level of control. While a proportion of MPs were unhappy about the finalised arrangements, this was reflected in increased symptoms of poor psychological health for a proportion, but these were half the rates produced following the revelation of the UK 2009 expenses scandal, over which MPs had no control at all – as media revealed their details and exposed the wrongdoing of some and the working processes of all (Weinberg, 2015). In other words, for many politicians, the lack of control was the difference between successful coping or not.

Skills training for politicians is a potentially contentious topic as it suggests a 'right way to be a politician', but the opportunities for personal development in a political career can be elusive and may favour certain sections of the population, in part dependent on their social capital. On arriving in parliament, induction may be lacking and no clear route to success is apparent until MPs have gained experience, by which time it may be too late for career success (Kwiatkowski, 2012). Nonetheless, it is clear that certain skillsets lead to more favourable political outcomes, including election performance (Silvester and Dykes, 2007). This is not to deny the existence of numerous programmes around the world (e.g. Hartley, 2012) that offer opportunities to receive coaching and mentoring, which in turn depend on finding time to fit these into already packed work schedules. However, the perennial challenge remains for a politician, who may enter the field with a background in a different career (or perhaps only within politics) and find themselves rising to be minister in charge of an area of government for which they have no prior relevant experience.

It is hoped that the Key Stressors' Framework outlined here, based on existing empirical research by range of sources, will yield further studies into the factors that influence the psychological functioning of politicians. One of the first studies to test the framework employed interviews with both MPs and their staff by the British Psychological Society (BPS, 2020) and found they 'may be experiencing none to all nine stressors at any one point, or over a sustained period. They may ebb and flow based on events, or they may be constant'. This suggests promise for this model and other studies are emerging that will hopefully engage elected representatives across the world. Whether a politician experiences these challenges or not, it has been noted that, 'In terms of an adequately functioning democracy, [these] create a serious challenge for achievable representation of the people' (BPS, 2020).

Too Hot to Handle?

This chapter has mainly focused on the challenges, with brief reference to perceived benefits of performing the job of national politician. However, as attempts to reform parliamentary working conditions have shown and was confirmed in an interview for this chapter by the author with one of the UK's most senior politicians, 'There is no one way to be an MP'. Indeed, individual approaches and coping strategies are a common theme – such as 'finding your own level' – which emerges in discussing the job with those who have 'survived' in it for many years, whether as a backbencher or a minister. In conversation with MPs, a high level of commitment to public service is often apparent, but rarely acknowledged in the flurry of media coverage, so it is not surprising that some politicians buffer themselves from the contents of social media or choose to specialise in particular causes, rather than forge a route to the top of government. Hearing politicians from different parts of the political spectrum talk about the value they place on inclusion of those marginalised in society is perhaps a discovery that would surprise the general public. This includes politicians who are clear about their own good fortune and those who confide that, after leaving Parliament, e.g., 'I would carry on working, even if unpaid, doing the kinds of things that one does as MP [in the community]'.

Social aspects of work are clearly valued by MPs, as they are in other occupations. This is particularly relevant to getting things decided or changed. Hence the resistance to electronic voting in some parliaments, where the physical act of walking through the lobby to vote provides an opportunity to discuss things with a government minister that otherwise could take weeks or months to set up. The restrictions on meeting during the COVID-19 pandemic exposed the limitations of technology for holding parliamentary debates, however, there are also logistical benefits with regard to voting. This aspect highlights the challenge of designing a political workplace that suits all and indicates the need to open discussions about how this could look as one key to addressing sources of pressure. Equally, dealing with routine organisational issues is not something that is considered 'doing politics', yet 'your day to day, your office, is the most important thing. So, you have to get that right, but no one thinks about it. You've got a function and you can't function without that support' (BPS, 2020). Hence the call by Dame Laura Cox (2018) and the British Psychological Society (2020) for parliamentary training that supports appropriate behaviours between all those working in political teams, whether as MPs or in supporting roles.

Time is the precious commodity that limits everyone and achieving a balance in terms of the pace of an MP's work is a major challenge. Those who have served in the role for many years recognise their ability to take more control of their time – which they acknowledge is an advantage of being in this type of leadership role. For whether politicians serve on the backbenches or as ministers, each has also the opportunity to influence developments on behalf of their constituents, who themselves may have been given the rough end of the system and waited years for some form of justice. When a politician can help achieve this, 'that's leadership' stated one MP.

Politics – like so many occupations – is about people and, yet, in the 'behind the scenes' work of preparing and supporting effective representation, loneliness can be a frequent issue (BPS, 2020). The support of family and friends is a central focus of coping for many MPs and usually induction to the job – as far as this exists – does not include them. Yet, as a politician, 'You put yourself out there to be judged' and this carries implications for how the individual MP is viewed, as well as for their loved ones. It would make sense to see organisationally sponsored processes for newcomers to the job that also support family members and recognise the potential toll on their lives.

Change for the Better?

That the job of an elected representative should be made possible – or not made impossible – by its design and the level of support for job-holders in carrying it out deserves urgent consideration. Such scrutiny would benefit from involvement of stakeholders who are politicians and electors, as well as parliaments, political parties and the media. Based on the research literature and interviews with politicians reviewed in this chapter, it is apparent that a number of changes could help improve political work and, hopefully, the efficacy of democracy. These include civic education that supports realistic and informed expectations of elected representatives; effective induction procedures, appropriate training and mental health support for politicians, their families and parliamentary staff; as well as structural efforts to ensure that every citizen has the opportunity to run for democratic office, thus helping to (re)build public trust in political processes and institutions, which physical and socially determined distances have too often eroded.

An approach that is more oriented to an enlightened human resources approach may not resonate with older-fashioned notions that the job of MP can be created along the way. Nevertheless, the introduction of induction sessions in parliaments around the world is an acknowledgement of such needs, although the identity of the guardians of the 'duty of care' for elected representatives remains undefined. In one sense, it is the responsibility of all – as democracy serves the people – to campaign for a resolution to this dilemma. In another sense, it is likely the organisation (i.e. parliament itself) will need to define a clear grasp of its own procedures and how these can be used to support the legitimate needs, behaviour and functioning of MPs and parliamentary staff. 'Getting by' is not likely to be considered good enough in facilitating the effectiveness of the decision-making bodies that govern the lives of all. As John Stuart Mill observed (see Chapter 1), in a democracy, society, maturity and

responsibility flow from the capacity to reflect upon issues, yet the pres-
surised environment of modern politics appears to prevent this vital
purpose. So, in answer to the question, 'Why should we consider the
mental health of politicians?' perhaps it is sufficient to reply, 'The health of
democracy may, to an extent, depend on the mental health and psychological wellbeing of those we elect to represent and take decisions on our
behalf' (Flinders et al., 2020). It is in keeping with the concept of
democracy that the solutions may depend on the ability of politicians
and the public to give priority to psychological well-being in all our
working lives and to ensure that parliament is an exemplar for all
workplaces.

Acknowledgements

I would like to thank, and am indebted to, all my research colleagues and
politicians who have contributed to the research featured here, including
those who allowed me to interview them for this chapter. I am particularly
indebted to Macjellings Malenga (Parliament of Malawi), Sir Peter
Bottomley MP ('Father of the House of Commons' in the UK) and the
Rt Honourable Kevan Jones MP.

REFERENCES

All-Party Parliamentary Group (APPG) on Mental Health (2008). Mental health
    in Parliament. Report by the APPG on Mental Health.
British Psychological Society (BPS) (2020). Cognitive strain in Parliament: How
    can we reduce psychological stressors to improve policy-making? By
    Baldwin, A., Pinto, C., Perriard-Abdoh, S and Weinberg, A. Available at:
    www.bps.org.uk/sites/www.bps.org.uk/files/Policy/Policy%20-%20Files/
    Cognitive%20strain%20in%20Parliament.pdf.
    (2017). Psychology at Work: Improving wellbeing and productivity in the work-
    place. By Weinberg, A. and Doyle, N. Available at: www.bps.org.uk/news-and-
    policy/psychology-work-improving-wellbeing-and-productivity-workplace.
Bronfenbrenner, U. (1979). *The ecology of human development: Experiments by
    nature and design.* Mass: Harvard University Press.
Burns, R. A., Butterworth, P. and Anstey, K. J. (2016). An examination of the
    long-term impact of job strain on mental health and wellbeing over a 12-year
    period. *Social Psychiatry and Psychiatric Epidemiology: The International
    Journal for Research in Social and Genetic Epidemiology and Mental Health
    Services,* 51(5), 725–733.
Butterworth, P., Leach, L. S., McManus, S. and Stansfeld, S. A. (2013). Common
    mental disorders, unemployment and psychosocial job quality: Is a poor job
    better than no job at all? *Psychological Medicine,* 43(8), 1763–1772.

Caplan, R. D., Cobb, S., French Jr, J. R. P., Harrison, R. V. and Pinneau Jr., S. R. (1975). *Job demands and work health. U.S. Department of Health, Education, and Welfare, NIOSH Publication No. 75–160*. Washington, DC: US Government Printing Office.

Cooper-Thomas, H. and Silvester, J. (2014). Ideas and advice to accelerate the transition for new MPs entering New Zealand's House of Representatives. Available at: https://margf2011.files.wordpress.com/2014/09/report-to-support-new-mp-adjustment-final.pdf.

Cox, L. (2018). The bullying and harassment of House of Commons staff. Independent inquiry report. Available from: www.parliament.uk/globalassets/documents/conduct-in-parliament/dame-laura-cox-independent-inquiry-report.pdf.

Demerouti, E., Bakker, A. B., Nachreiner, F. and Schaufeli, W. B. (2001). The job demands – resources model of burnout. *Journal of Applied Psychology*, 86, 499–512.

Emery, L., Meier, P. and Mortelmans, D. (2018). Juggling three life spheres: Reconciling work, family and politics. *Community, Work & Family*, 21(2), 226–242.

Every-Palmer, S., Barry-Walsh, J. and Pathé, M. (2015). Harassment, stalking, threats and attacks targeting New Zealand politicians: A mental health issue. *Australia and New Zealand Journal of Psychiatry*, 49(7), 634–641.

Fazekas, Z. and Hatemi, P. K. (2020) Narcissism in political participation. *Journal of Personality and Social Psychology*. doi.org/10.1177/0146167220919212

Flinders, M. and Kelso, A. (2011), Mind the gap: Political analysis, public expectations and the parliamentary decline thesis. *The British Journal of Politics & International Relations*, 13, 249–268.

Flinders, M., Weinberg, A., Weinberg, J., Geddes, M. and Kwiatkowski, R. (2020). Governing under pressure? The mental wellbeing of politicians. *Parliamentary Affairs*, 73(2), 253–273.

Freeman, H. (1991). The human brain and political behaviour. *British Journal of Psychiatry*, 159, 19–32.

Ghana News (2017). MP wants counseling office for parliamentarians. 17 March. Available at: http://3news.com/mp-wants-counseling-office-for-parliamentarians/.

Goldberg, D. and Williams, D. (1988). *General Health Questionnaire*. Windsor: NFER-Nelson.

Hansard (2012). Mental health. Available at: https://hansard.parliament.uk/Commons/2012-06-14/debates/12061445000002/MentalHealth.

Hartley, J. (2012). Political leadership and its development. In A. Weinberg (Ed.), *The psychology of politicians* (pp. 97–120). Cambridge, UK: Cambridge University Press.

Hassard, J., Teoh, K. R. H., Visockaite, G., Dewe, P. and Cox, T. (2018). The cost of work-related stress to society. *Journal of Occupational Health Psychology*, 23(1), 1–17.

Hochschild, A. (1983). *The managed heart: The commercialization of human feeling*. Berkeley, CA: University of California Press.

Ignatieff, M. (2013). *Fire and ashes: Success and failure in politics*. Cambridge, MA: Harvard University Press.

Jahoda, M. (1982). *Employment and unemployment: A social-psychological analysis*. Cambridge, UK: Cambridge University Press.

Jopling Report (1992). *Report from the Select Committee on sittings of the House*, vol.1. London: HMSO.

Karasek, R. A. (1979). Job demands, job decision latitude and mental strain: Implications for job redesign. *Administrative Science Quarterly*, 24, 285–308.

Karasek, R. A. and Theorell, T. (1990). *Healthy work: Stress, productivity and the reconstruction of working life*. New York: Basic Books.

Kenyan Ministry for Health (2019). Kenya launches Quality Rights Initiative to promote mental health care. Available at: www.health.go.ke/kenya-launches-qualityrights-initiative-to-promote-mental-health-care/.

Kwiatkowski, R. (2012). Politicians and power: MPs in the UK Parliament. In A. Weinberg (Ed.), *The psychology of politicians* (pp. 39–58). Cambridge, UK: Cambridge University Press.

Lilienfeld, S., Waldman, I., Landfield, K., Watts, A., Rubenzer, S. and Faschingbauer, T. (2012). 'Fearless dominance and the US presidency, *Journal of Personality and Social Psychology*, 103(3), 489–505.

Malenga, M. (2019). The work-life balance of an MP in Malawi. *The Work-Life Balance Bulletin*, 3(1). Leicester: BPS Division of Occupational Psychology.

Malenga, M. (2016). An exploration of occupational stress among Members of Parliament: A case of parliamentarians in Malawi. Unpublished thesis, Africa University of Guidance, Counselling and Youth Development.

Mill. J. S. (1859/1983) *On liberty (Reprinted)*. Middlesex: Penguin.

Mindful Nation (2015). Mindful Nation UK. Report by the Mindfulness All-Party Parliamentary Group. Available at: www.themindfulnessinitiative.org/mindful-nation-report.

Owen, D. and Davidson, J. (2009). Hubris Syndrome. *Brain*, 132, 1396–1406.

Paul, K. I. and Moser, K. (2009). Unemployment impairs mental health: Meta-analyses. *Journal of Vocational Behavior*, 74(3), 264–282.

Poulter, D., Votruba, N., Bakolis, I., Debell, F., Das-Munshi, J. and Thornicroft, G. (2019). Mental health of UK Members of Parliament in the House of Commons: A cross-sectional survey. *BMJ Open* 2019;9:e027892. doi: 10.1136/bmjopen-2018-027892

Robb, A. (2011). *Black dog daze: Public life, private demons*. Melbourne University Press.

Roberts, J. (2017). *Losing political office*. Basingstoke: Palgrave Macmillan.

Royal College of Psychiatrists (2020). Depression in adults. Available at: www.rcpsych.ac.uk/mental-health/problems-disorders/depression.

Silvester, J. and Dykes, C. (2007). Selecting political candidates: A longitudinal study of assessment centre performance and political success in the 2005 UK

General Election. *Journal of Occupational and Organizational Psychology*, 80 (1), pp. 11–25.

Silvester, J., Wyatt, M. and Randall, R. (2013). Politician personality, Machiavellianism, and political skill as predictors of performance ratings in political roles. *Journal of Occupational and Organizational Psychology*, 87(2), pp. 258–279.

Society for Human Resource Management (SHRM) (2019). Underused EAPs are a missed opportunity to help workers. Available at: www.shrm.org/resource sandtools/hr-topics/benefits/pages/under-used-eaps-are-a-missed-opportunity.aspx.

Sutherland, D. (2019). Mental health wins record funding in New Zealand's first 'well-being budget'. Available at: https://theconversation.com/mental-health-wins-record-funding-in-new-zealands-first-well-being-budget-118047.

Theakston, K. (2012). Life after political death, *Representation*, 48(2), 139–149.

van Horn, J. E., Taris, T., Schaufeli, W. B. and Schreurs, P. J. G. (2004). The structure of occupational well-being: A study among Dutch teachers. *Journal of Occupational and Organizational Psychology*, 77(3), 365–375.

Warr, P. (1989). *Work, unemployment and mental health*. Oxford, UK: Clarendon Press.

Watts, A. L., Lilienfeld, S. O., Smith, S. F., Miller, D. J., Campbell, W. K., Waldman, I. D., Rubenzer, S. J. and Faschingbauer, T. J., (2013). The double-edged sword of grandiose narcissism: Implications for successful and unsuccessful leadership among US Presidents. Psychological Science, 24(12), 2379–2389.

Weinberg, A. (2015). A longitudinal study of the impact of changes in the job and the expenses scandal on UK national politicians' experiences of work, stress and the home-work interface. *Parliamentary Affairs*, 68(2), 248–271.

(2012). Should the job of national politician carry a government health warning? The impact of psychological strain on politicians. In A. Weinberg, A. (Ed.), *The psychology of politicians*, pp. 123–142. Cambridge, UK: Cambridge University Press.

(2007). Your destiny in their hands: Job loss and success in Members of Parliament. *British Psychological Society annual conference, York. Proceedings of the BPS*, 15(2), 135.

Weinberg, A. and Cooper, C. L. (2003). Stress among national politicians elected to Parliament for the first time. *Stress and Health*, 19, 111–117.

Weinberg, A., Cooper, C. L. and Weinberg, A. (1999). Workload, stress and family life in British Members of Parliament and the psychological impact of reforms to their working hours. *Stress Medicine*, 15, 79–87.

Weinberg, J. (2020). Emotional labour and occupational wellbeing in political office. *The British Journal of Politics and International Relations*, https://doi.org/10.1177/1369148120959044

Weinberg, J. and Weinberg, A. (2019). *The mental health of politicians: Testing the parameters (poster presentation)*. Annual conference of International Society for Political Psychology, Berlin.

World Health Organization (2020). Global challenge for movement on mental health kicks off as lack of investment in mental health leaves millions without access to services. Available at: www.who.int/news/item/07-10-2020-global-challenge-for-movement-on-mental-health-kicks-off-as-lack-of-investment-in-mental-health-leaves-millions-without-access-to-services.

(2018). Mental health: Strengthening our response. Available at: www.who.int/en/news-room/fact-sheets/detail/mental-health-strengthening-our-response.

(2011). Impact of economic crises on mental health. Available at: www.euro.who.int/__data/assets/pdf_file/0008/134999/e94837.pdf.

Wrzesniewski, A. and Dutton, J. E. (2001). Crafting a job: Revisioning employees as active crafters of their work. *Academy of Management Review*, 25, 179–201.

PART II

By the People

CHAPTER 8

Trust in Political Institutions and Support for Authoritarianism
Latin American Students – Does Civic Knowledge Make a Difference?

Daniel Miranda, Juan Carlos Castillo, Catalina Miranda and José Daniel Conejeros

Introduction

Institutional trust is a central aspect of the functioning of democracies as well as of their legitimacy (Lipset, 1959; Uslaner, 2018; Zmerli and van der Meer, 2017). Latin America has traditionally shown one of the lowest levels of trust worldwide (Catterberg and Moreno, 2006), most commonly associated with its history of authoritarian governments (Bargsted, Somma and Castillo, 2017). Several Latin American countries experienced military dictatorships during the 1970s and 1980s, usually characterised by human rights violations and political corruption. Although, nowadays, most of these countries have democratic systems, the cultural legacy of authoritarianism persists (Hite and Cesarini, 2004), as reflected in political practices that follow particular interests instead of collective demands. Such a scenario puts at risk the legitimacy of democracy in Latin America, particularly at times of economic crisis, such as the one faced due to the COVID-19 pandemic.

One of the aspects to take into account when evaluating both trust in institutions and authoritarianism is the role of political knowledge. In an ideal sense, civic-political knowledge is considered the 'mother' of trust (Galston, 2001, 2007), based on the simple assumption that it is undoubtedly difficult to trust in something that one does not know. In international studies evaluating civic-political knowledge, Latin American countries tend to obtain lower levels of achievement than more economically developed countries (Schulz et al., 2018), although most countries in Latin America count on civic education programmes monitored by international organisations like UNESCO (Cox, 2010). This raises concerns in the Latin American context as civic-political knowledge has proven to play a role in different areas of citizenship, including institutional trust, participation, tolerance and authoritarian beliefs (Castillo et al., 2014; Miranda,

Castillo and Cumsille, 2018; Sandoval-Hernandez et al., 2019). However, it is still not clear how political knowledge at school age could affect democratic attitudes in a region characterised by weak democratic foundations: is political knowledge at school age a predictor of greater political trust and less authoritarianism in contexts where political institutions are weak and delegitimised as in Latin America? In this chapter, we develop the main arguments in light of previous evidence on political trust and authoritarianism, as well as their link with political knowledge.

Institutional Trust

Institutional trust commands a vast research agenda in the social sciences (see Zmerli and Meer, 2017) and is generally understood as an evaluation of civic and political institutions (van der Meer and Hakhverdian, 2016). Such an evaluation is based on the performance of these institutions (Offe, 1999; Segovia et al., 2008) in a given context (Hardin, 2001). Thus, trust in political institutions such as a parliament or political parties can be understood as the evaluation that citizens make of the functioning of these in a particular scenario.

Although trust in the institution is observed as a contextualised issue, there is evidence that indicates political distrust as a global problem. Schyns and Koop (2009) show that, in six countries (Denmark, Netherlands, Spain, Portugal, Poland and Slovenia) from distinct regions across Europe, there is political distrust, despite their different contexts. In France and Germany, there is a general distrust and disconnect between citizens and the political elite (Dageförde and Schindler, 2018). Also, in the United States of America, there are high public levels of political distrust and scepticism in governments (Gershtenson and Plane, 2015).

Political distrust is clearly a global problem, but, as the context in which the development of institutional trust occurs is relevant for the acquisition of related attitudes, it is important to take into account the particularities of the evolution of democracy in Latin America. The history of democratic institutions in the region has suffered from a series of contradictions, marked by an alternation between authoritarianism, democracy and semi-democracy (Bargsted et al., 2017).

The seven countries covered in this chapter all had military dictatorships between the 1930s–1970s, with large heterogeneity in the process of democratic recovery (Kirsten, 2020). The social and political context among these countries varies significantly and, for each one, it illuminates the relevance of studying the development of political trust and authoritarian attitudes. All of these, to some extent, have presented periods of political conflict and dictatorship in past decades and, in some cases, up to the present. For instance, Guatemala only achieved peace in 1995 after thirty years of armed conflict and several periods of dictatorship. The Dominican Republic alternated between dictatorships and political instability between the 1930s and the mid-1990s. Paraguay is recognised for having had the longest dictatorship in the region, between 1954 and 1989. For its part, Peru, between the years 1968 and 1990, coexisted with dictatorships and armed conflicts with terrorism, the most visible being the '*Sendero Luminoso*' terrorist group. The case of Chile did not escape this pattern. Between the years 1973 and 1989, a civil-military dictatorship was established whose echoes are heard to this day. Colombia did not go through the dictatorships of the 1970s and 1980s, but it has had to live with decades of conflict arising from the presence of guerrillas and drug trafficking. Of this group of countries, Mexico is a potential exception. Since the Mexican Revolution, a democratic election system was established, although with almost no renewal of the governing coalitions until the 2000s. However, it does not escape the general difficulties of the region, such as high levels of inequality or the presence of corruption at different levels.

All these countries have entered a period of consolidation of their democracies during the 1990s and 2000s, significantly improving indicators of civil liberties or representativeness of governments (de Viteri Vázquez and Bjørnskov, 2020), although far from the levels obtained by consolidated democracies. Despite institutional development efforts, these and other countries in the region indicated consistently high levels of institutional corruption over fifty years, with the exception of Chile, which showed some improvements after 1989 (de Viteri Vázquez and Bjørnskov, 2020). This phenomenon can be seen in the recurring political scandals linked to institutional corruption. Economic crises and corruption throughout Latin America have certainly complicated these political scenarios, bearing witness to low and declining levels of trust in institutions, particularly in the government and political parties (Latinobarometro, 2018). Finally – and without going into considerable detail – recent institutional crises in the last decade (2010–20) have produced serious threats to democracy in Venezuela, Brazil, Peru, Bolivia and Chile – just to mention the most prominent. In these contexts, young people have developed their beliefs, attitudes and knowledge about democracy and its principles. Given these contexts, the importance of studying these topics in the region is further underlined.

Besides political history, institutional trust is affected by a series of contextual and individual characteristics. At a contextual level, aspects of society such as economic performance, wealth distribution and/or political change have shown evidence of affecting levels of trust (Citrin and Stoker, 2018; Martini and Quaranta, 2020). At the individual level, a number of factors have been taken into account in several studies, such as genetics, personality, socio-economic characteristics, awareness of corruptibility (Carrasco et al., 2019) and/or the perceived effectiveness of institutions (Lauglo, 2013). Among these, education has proven to be one of the most consistent predictors of political trust, as the more educated citizens are, the greater their abilities to evaluate the functioning of institutions (Lipset, 1960; van der Meer and Hakhverdian, 2016). Based on these antecedents, our first hypothesis is that students with higher levels of civic knowledge will exhibit greater support for political institutions.

Authoritarianism

The concept of authoritarianism, widely used in social psychology, consists of an ideological orientation to support strong authority and punish normative deviation (Altemeyer, 1996). Three central dimensions of authoritarianism have been proposed (Duckitt, 2015): authoritarian submission, which describes the degree of submission to the established authority; authoritarian aggression, which is understood as an aggressive attitude against groups or people sanctioned by those perceived to be in authority; and conventionalism, which describes the degree of adherence to conventions, traditions and social norms (Altemeyer, 1996; Funke, 2005). Citizens carry out authoritarian practices when they support traditional values endorsed by the authorities and show aggression towards minority groups (Ching et al., 2020). Sochos (2019) also indicates that individuals express authoritarian attitudes before an experience or threat to their collective identity and/or bonds with social groups.

A high proportion of Latin American citizens present some support for authoritarianism. A typical approach that captures this trend is derived from levels of agreement with the following phrases: (a) democracy is preferable to any other form of government; (b) in some circumstances, an authoritarian government is preferable to a democratic one; or (c) people like me do not care more about a democratic government than an authoritarian one. Both non-democratic options (b and c) are supported by up 43 per cent of people in Latin America, who do not decisively support democracy as the best form of government (Latinobarometro, 2018). Along the same lines, studies of school-age populations have also shown evidence of supporting authoritarian practices (Schulz et al., 2018). More than 60 per cent of young students in Latin America would rate their complete or limited agreement with justifying dictatorship if it brought order, safety and/or economic benefits (Sandoval-Hernandez et al., 2019). Therefore, it is suggested that some support for authoritarian practices has become part of the political culture in Latin America (Almond and Verba, 1989).

As authoritarianism is seen as a major threat to democracy (Dewey, 1989), countries have made various efforts to expand democratic ideals through citizenship training within the school system (Cox and Castillo, 2015). In this sense, the assumption is that higher levels of political knowledge, improved through better citizenship education, should lead to less prevalence of authoritarian ideas (Schulz et al., 2018). Nevertheless, the impact of citizenship education on lessening authoritarianism is still an under-researched area.

The Role of Civic Knowledge

Civic knowledge can be defined as the capacity for, and proficiency of, knowledge about various domains such as civic-social systems, civic principles, participation procedures and civic identities (Schulz et al., 2018). This definition has great similarities with two concepts widely used in the political literature: political knowledge, referring to information that citizens handle about the political system, and political sophistication, a more complex approach to expertise on political issues. Beyond conceptual specificities, each recognises the role that civic knowledge plays in a better understanding of various relevant attitudes and behaviours within a democratic framework (Rapeli, 2013).

Regarding the link between civic knowledge and political attitudes (such as institutional trust and authoritarianism), previous literature generally states that those with higher levels of knowledge will have a greater attachment to public life (Galston, 2001, 2007). The literature systematically shows that people with higher levels of civic knowledge tend to engage politically differently than those with lower levels of knowledge (Rapeli, 2013). For instance, they develop higher levels of political tolerance (Miranda et al., 2018), they present higher levels of political participation (Castillo et al., 2014, 2015) and have lower levels of authoritarianism (Sandoval-Hernandez et al., 2019). Thus, it is expected that higher levels of civic knowledge are associated with greater institutional trust (H1) and lower levels of authoritarianism (H2). However, comparative studies of populations of fourteen-year-old students show mixed evidence for H1. From the International Association for the Evaluation of Educational Achievement (IEA) Civic Education Study 1999 (Schulz and Sibberns, 2004), International Civic and Citizenship Education Study (ICCS) 2019 (Schulz, Ainley and Fraillon, 2011) and ICCS 2016 (Köhler et al., 2018), it is possible to observe that, in developed countries with low corruption rates, the association between civic knowledge and institutional trust is positive, while, in countries with less development and high corruption, higher levels of civic knowledge are associated with lower institutional trust (Sandoval-Hernandez et al., 2019; Torney-Purta, Richardson and Barber, 2004). Therefore, although we follow a more intuitive hypothesis regarding the role of knowledge in trust, this is probably affected by some of the historical and contextual factors mentioned above.

Methods

Data Collection

The data analysed in this research correspond to the ICCS. This study is carried out by the IEA and has been conducted three times: CIVED 1999; ICCS 2009 and ICCS 2016. Its purpose is to investigate how educational systems prepare young people to assume their roles as citizens. The ICCS results have contributed to the debate about delivering civic and citizenship education in schools around the world. For this particular study, we use data from ICCS 2009 and 2016 for seven Latin American countries: Chile, Colombia, the Dominican Republic, Mexico, Guatemala, Paraguay and Peru. The first four countries participated in the two waves, whereas Guatemala and Paraguay took part only in 2009 and Peru only in 2016.

The ICCS 2009–2016 Latin America dataset encompasses a nationally representative sample of eighth-grade students who, on average, are approximately thirteen to fourteen years old, reaching a total of 29,896 observations in 2009 and 25,319 in 2016. Students were selected through stratified random sampling in two stages. In the first stage, a minimum of 150 schools per country was selected, and at least one class per school was chosen at random, including as participants all the students of that class (Schulz, Ainley, and Fraillon, 2011). In Latin America, a class refers to a group of students from a specific grade or academic level that attend most classes together. The sample sizes of students and schools for each country and year are summarised below (see Table 8.1).

Table 8.1. *Samples of students participating in the International Civic and Citizenship Education Study per country, per year.*

Country	Year	School	Students	Woman (%)	Age (mean)
Chile	2009	177	5,173	0.51	14.18
Chile	2016	178	5,081	0.49	14.17
Colombia	2009	196	6,200	0.54	14.38
Colombia	2016	150	5,609	0.52	14.59
Dominican Republic	2009	145	4,569	0.55	14.86
Dominican Republic	2016	141	3,937	0.51	14.19
Mexico	2009	215	6,565	0.52	14.08
Mexico	2016	213	5,526	0.50	14.03
Guatemala	2009	145	3,998	0.49	15.52
Paraguay	2009	149	3,391	0.52	14.82
Peru	2016	206	5,166	0.48	14.03

The ICCS comprises a test of civic knowledge assessing students' civic knowledge and citizen reasoning. Knowledge refers to information learned and used by students to make sense of their civic worlds, while citizen reasoning is how students use said civic and citizen information to reach conclusions in a real context. At the same time, it also includes a questionnaire measuring students' perceptions, attitudes and background on issues related to citizenship, participation in school and school climate, among other variables. Finally, it utilises a series of instruments to capture relevant information on teacher perceptions of citizenship education in their school: the organisation and culture in their school and classrooms and their teaching backgrounds. In addition, information is provided by principals regarding the characteristics of the school, the culture and the school climate, and the provision of civic and citizenship education curricula (Schulz et al., 2011).

Variables

Dependent Variables
The first dependent variable of this study is political trust, an index built upon four indicators from the ICCS questionnaire. Based on the question *'How much do you trust each of the following groups, institutions or sources of information?'* Students rated their level of trust using the following responses: *'completely', 'somewhat', 'a little', 'not at all'* for the following institutions: (1) National Government, (2) National Parliament, (3) political parties and (4) courts of justice.

The second dependent variable is support for authoritarianism. Starting with the question '*How much do you agree or disagree with the following statements about the government and its power?*' A scale of three indicators is constructed that serves to identify the extent to which students support undemocratic practices: (1) 'Concentration of power in one person guarantees order', (2) 'Dictatorships are justified when they bring order and safety' and (3) 'Dictatorships are justified when they bring economic benefits'. Students rated their level of agreement as '*strongly agree*', '*agree*', '*disagree*', '*strongly disagree*' for each of these statements.

Both political trust and authoritarianism indices were estimated using confirmatory factor analyses, which show adequate fit ($\chi 2 = 2099.19$, p < 0.001; CFI = 0.977; TLI = 0.962; RMSEA = 0.057). Once estimated, each of the latent measures was rescaled to a mean of fifty and a standard deviation of ten for ease of interpretation.

Independent Variables
The main independent variable in this study was the civic knowledge score achieved in the ICCS. The civic knowledge test consists of a set of seventy-nine items applied and organised into seven different booklets with four content domains: civic society and systems, civic principles, civic participation and civic identities. Each of these domains is made up of a set of sub-domains incorporating aspects and key concepts.[1] Students responded in a booklet containing three kinds of questions: multiple-choice, true/false and open-ended response.

To elicit levels of civic knowledge, an Item Response Theory (IRT) model was used to estimate five plausible values as a score. This kind of model makes it possible to use all the information available from the students' tests and questionnaires to obtain precise estimates when it comes to measuring cognitive abilities that cannot be directly observed. The average score of civic knowledge in the ICCS test for 2009 was 500 points with a standard deviation of 100 and an empirical range of 380–576 points for the thirty-eight countries evaluated, while the average score of

---

[1] 'Society and civic systems' consist of knowledge about the roles, rights, responsibilities and opportunities of citizens; state institutions that are in charge of governance and enforce laws; and the civil institutions that mediate the relationship between citizens and state institutions. 'Civic principles' correspond to knowledge in the sub-domains of equity, freedom and social cohesion. 'Civic participation' is relative to knowledge about decision-making at the governmental and voting level; the ability to debate and develop proposals; and community participation. 'Civic identities' evaluate civic self-image as an individual experience in each of their civic communities and the sense of connection to those communities.

Table 8.2. *Independent variable: civic knowledge score.*

Country	ICCS 2009	ICCS 2016	Diff.
Chile	483 (3.5)	482 (3.1)	−1 (5.6)
Colombia	462 (2.9)	482 (3.4)	20 (5.5)
Dominican Republic	380 (2.4)	381 (3.0)	1 (5.0)
Mexico	452 (2.8)	467 (2.5)	15 (4.9)
Guatemala	435 (3.8)	–	–
Paraguay	424 (3.4)	–	–
Peru	–	438 (3.5)	–

Notes: Statistically significant differences ($p < 0.05$) () Standard errors appear in parentheses.

the countries for the ICCS test 2016 was 517 with a standard deviation of 101 points and a range between 381 and 586. Also, performance levels are presented in ICCS that seek to provide a substantive description of the scores obtained. There are four levels (A–D) that are structured hierarchically so that, at a higher level of performance, it is understood that students have more complex knowledge and citizenship skills.[2] The scores for each Latin American country participating in ICCS in 2009 and 2016 are summarised in Table 8.2. In general, the results of the knowledge test for each Latin American country are below the international average.

The rest of the independent variables fulfil the objective of controlling the statistical association between support for authoritarianism, trust in political institutions and civic knowledge. In this sense, a proxy variable is used to assess the student's socio-economic and cultural background based on the highest educational level reached by his/her father or

---

[2] Scores at 'Low level D' are considered those below 311 points, reflecting a lack of knowledge and skills measured in ICCS. In 'Level D' (311–394 points), students recognise explicit examples that represent the basic characteristics of a democracy, for example, they can identify the relationship between the secret ballot and the freedom of the voters. In 'Level C' (395–478), the students show familiarity with the ideas of equity, social cohesion and freedom as principles of democracy and relate them to everyday-life situations. For example, they relate freedom of the press to the accuracy of the information provided by the media. In 'Level B' (479–562 points), students demonstrate familiarity with the general concept of representative democracy as a political system and can, for example, identify that informed voters are capable of making better decisions when voting in an election. In that sense, they recognise the ways in which laws and institutions can be used to protect and promote the principles and values of a society. Finally, at 'Level A' (higher than 563 points), students are able to relate the processes of political and social organisation and influence and the legal and institutional mechanisms designed to control them; for example, students would be able to identify the possible strategic objectives of an ethical consumption programme or evaluate a policy according to ideas of equality and inclusion (Description based on national report of ICCS 2016, from the Chilean Agency for Quality Education).

Table 8.3. *Descriptive statistics for control variables as a function of country and year.*

Country 2009	Education		Books		Pol. discussion		Gender	
	M	SD	M	SD	M	SD	M	SD
Chile	2.41	1.08	1.76	1.14	49.53	9.92	0.51	0.50
Colombia	2.16	1.53	1.44	1.09	50.87	10.04	0.54	0.50
Dominican Republic	2.08	1.25	1.05	1.08	51.91	10.29	0.55	0.50
Mexico	1.31	1.52	1.26	1.10	53.16	9.97	0.49	0.50
Guatemala	1.91	1.43	1.43	1.13	47.62	9.64	0.52	0.50
Paraguay	1.76	1.47	1.10	1.11	51.60	9.81	0.52	0.50
Country 2016								
Chile	2.61	1.10	1.49	1.14	49.72	9.45	0.49	0.50
Colombia	2.30	1.42	1.05	1.02	50.59	9.24	0.52	0.50
Dominican Republic	2.24	1.25	0.91	0.97	52.39	10.20	0.51	0.50
Mexico	1.99	1.39	1.08	1.08	48.87	9.08	0.50	0.50
Guatemala	2.43	1.31	1.40	1.04	53.68	8.95	0.48	0.50

Note: M and SD represent mean and standard deviation, respectively.

mother[3] as well as by the number of books at home.[4] Additionally, we included the student's gender[5] and the level of political discussion the student conducts with friends and family outside the classroom.[6]

Analytical Strategy

We began the analyses exploring the differences within countries over time (2009–2016) in both dependent variables (institutional trust and authoritarianism). Next, the model estimation was performed on a multi-level framework in order to account for the variance at the school level for both institutional trust and authoritarianism. First, we estimated a null model (without predictors) that provided a variance decomposition at the individual and school levels, to identify the proportion of variance of the dependent variables explained by the characteristics of the school.

[3] Students rated the level of parents' education using: 0 = *did not complete eighth grade*, 1 = *completed eighth grade*, 2 = *high school*, 3 = *vocational or technical career* and 4 = *career at university or postgraduate*.

[4] Students rated the number of books at home using: 0 = *none or very few (0–10 books)*, 1 = *enough to fill one shelf (11–25 books)*, 2 = *enough to fill one bookcase (26–100 books)*, 3 = *enough to fill two bookcases (101–200 books)* and 4 = *enough to fill three or more bookcases (more than 200 books)*.

[5] 0 = *Boy* and 1 = *Girl*

[6] IRT WLE (weighted likelihood estimation) scores with mean of 50 and standard deviation of 10 within each participating country

Second, we estimated a model adding the main predictor, civic knowledge, to assess its association with institutional trust and authoritarianism. For a better understanding of regression coefficients, we divided the scale by 100, so that 300 points would be represented by '3' and 700 points would be represented by '7'. The next model included the control variables for testing the stability of civic knowledge effect beyond individual socio-economic variables. Finally, the fourth model included the fixed effects of country and time in order to test the stability of civic knowledge between countries across time.

Results

Descriptive Results

Figure 8.1 shows an item-by-item comparison of the political trust items between countries. First, it can be observed that, in all the countries studied, political parties receive the lowest trust levels whereas the government obtains the highest. Second, considering the general trend between countries, it appears that the Dominican Republic and Paraguay are the countries with the highest average trust, whereas Peru and Guatemala show the lowest levels. Although it is difficult to make a connection between this pattern of results and the countries' political events, it is striking that the three countries with the lowest levels of trust had major corruption scandals during 2015 (ICCS-2016 assessment period). In Guatemala, President Otto Peréz Molina resigned in connection with corruption scandals; in Peru, President Ollanta Humala had to face several accusations and was eventually linked to one of the largest corruption scandals in the region, the 'Odebrecht' case. Furthermore, Chile, although considered the country with the 'best' corruption indices in the region, saw widely reported revelations during 2014 and 2015 about illegal financing of politics known as 'Pentagate'.

Third, we also observe some difference in the variability of trust in different institutions within countries, which tends to co-vary with the average trust levels: the higher the average, the more the variability. Finally, it is noteworthy that young people tend to show higher levels of trust in all the institutions evaluated when compared to adult population surveys (Bargsted et al., 2017). The 2018 Latinobarometer, which is applied to an adult representative sample in several countries in Latin America, reported that only 21 per cent of the adult respondents trust in their parliament and 13 per cent trust in the political parties: both below or considerably lower than the results from ICCS.

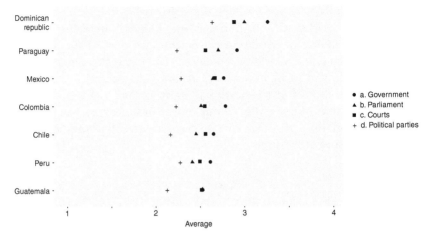

Figure 8.1   Institutional trust in Latin America by country.

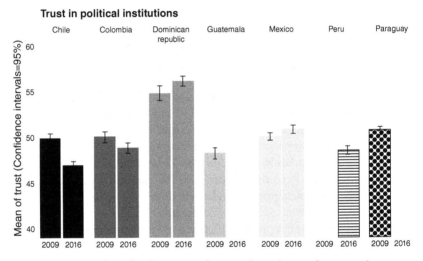

Figure 8.2   The scale of institutional trust in Latin America by country/year.

With regard to institutional trust (see Figure 8.2), the Dominican Republic and Paraguay recorded the highest levels of trust (above the scaled average of fifty considering confidence intervals). As far as changes over time are concerned, Mexico slightly increased its trust levels whereas Colombia and particularly Chile showed a decrease, which coincides with

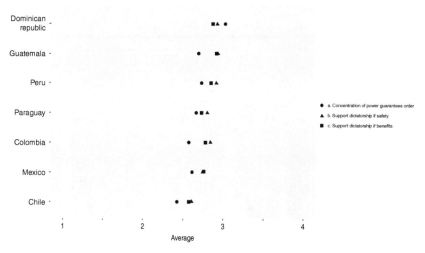

Figure 8.3   Support for authoritarianism in Latin America by country.

the decline in institutional trust observed in the last decade in Chile, not only in political institutions, but also in those in charge of public order (Morales Quiroga, 2020).

Moving on to our second variable of interest, Figure 8.3 shows an item-by-item comparison of support for authoritarian practices between countries. Interestingly, the average levels for the three evaluated authoritarian practices are above the midpoint of the scale. In other words, there is support for the concentration of power and dictatorships if this brings order, economic benefits and security. This aspect has been widely discussed as a warning about the persistence of authoritarian beliefs in Latin America (Sandoval-Hernandez et al., 2019; Schulz et al., 2018). The samples from the Dominican Republic, Guatemala and Peru show the strongest tendency towards authoritarianism, while Colombia, Mexico and Chile show the weakest among this group of countries. Regarding the clustering of averages between the three evaluated statements, the closeness is somewhat surprising: although the three items evaluate aspects clearly linked to authoritarianism, it is quite different to support the concentration of power than to support a dictatorship in an explicit way, therefore a clearer differentiation between each would be expected. Only Guatemala and Colombia show some dispersion of the mean scores, but this is no greater than a half-point on the scale.

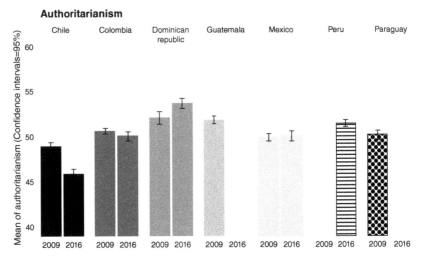

Figure 8.4   The scale of support for authoritarianism in Latin America by country/year.

With regard to changes (or stability) over time in levels of authoritarianism between 2009 and 2016 (see Figure 8.4), the Dominican Republic, Guatemala, Peru and Paraguay display higher levels of support for authoritarian practices (above the scaled average = fifty, considering confidence intervals); Mexico and Colombia are observed close to the average and Chile presents the lowest level of authoritarianism (below the scaled average = fifity). Considering differences between 2009 and 2016, the Dominican Republic and Mexico show increased levels whereas Chile shows the largest decrease.

Regarding the role that civic knowledge plays in supporting authoritarian practices and levels of trust (see Table 8.4), we observe that, at higher levels of civic knowledge, levels of support for authoritarian practices decrease (average $r = -0.350$), as do levels of trust (average $r = -0.254$). Additionally, it is possible to observe that higher support for authoritarianism is positively correlated with trust in civic-political institutions (average $r = 0.388$), which is somewhat counter-intuitive in light of the theoretical assumptions presented above.

Regression Models

The previous descriptive results depict the puzzling role of civic knowledge regarding trust in institutions and authoritarianism. In order to advance

Table 8.4. *Correlations between trust in civic institutions, support for authoritarianism and civic knowledge.*

	Civic knowledge with institutional trust	Civic knowledge with authoritarianism	Institutional trust with authoritarianism
Chile	−0.140 ***	−0.336 ***	0.365 ***
Colombia	−0.187 ***	−0.318 ***	0.362 ***
Dominican Republic	−0.271 ***	−0.337 ***	0.389 ***
Guatemala	−0.280 ***	−0.304 ***	0.389 ***
Mexico	−0.192 ***	−0.313 ***	0.397 ***
Peru	−0.278 ***	−0.266 ***	0.380 ***
Paraguay	−0.267 ***	−0.350 ***	0.369 ***
Full sample	−0.254 ***	−0.350 ***	0.388 ***

understanding of these associations, we estimated a series of multi-level regression models. In turn, we present below the results for institutional trust as the dependent variable (see Table 8.6) and then for authoritarianism.

In Table 8.5, Model 0 is a null model (without predictors) allowing estimation of the proportion of the variance of institutional trust associated with school level, which in this case is 12 per cent. This proportion is a little high, considering previous evidence on attitudinal outcomes in educational studies. In Model 1, we observe that higher levels of civic knowledge are associated with lower levels of institutional trust. This means that students who perform less well on the knowledge test (e.g. 300 points) obtain 54.24 points on average in political trust (α:*62.01* + (β:−*2.59*3*)), whereas those with high performance (e.g. 700 points) obtain 43.88 points (α:*62.01* + (β:−*2.59*7*)), which is below the scale average. Model 2 enters a series of statistical controls. The result indicates that having more books at home and being a girl decreases institutional trust, while talking about social and political issues with family and friends increases it. Finally, Model 3 enters the fixed effects of the country and year of the study (coded as dummy variables) to control for differences between countries and between the year of study. The result shows that the observed effects remain similar when controlled by country and year.

Table 8.6 presents the results for authoritarianism, following the same logic presented in Table 8.5 for institutional trust. In this case, the null model (Model 0) shows that over 11 per cent of the variance in authoritarianism is associated with school level, meaning that a small part of the variance could be linked to school characteristics. Model 1 enters civic knowledge as the main predictor. The result indicates that, at higher levels of civic knowledge, lower

Table 8.5. *Regression models: the association between trust in civic institutions and civic knowledge in Latin America.*

	M0: Null		M1: Trust		M2: Trust		M3: Trust	
Predictors	Estimates	p	Estimates	p	Estimates	p	Estimates	p
(Intercept)	50.26	<0.001	62.01	<0.001	56.31	<0.001	54.65	<0.001
civic_know100			−2.59	<0.001	−2.54	<0.001	−2.36	<0.001
parental_education					0.11	0.001	0.05	0.124
books_at_home					−0.17	<0.001	−0.13	0.002
gender					−1.24	<0.001	−1.31	<0.001
political_discussion					0.12	<0.001	0.12	<0.001
time [2016]							−0.42	0.008
Country [Colombia]							0.79	<0.001
Country [Dominicana]							4.72	<0.001
Country [Guatemala]							−1.72	<0.001
Country [Mexico]							1.69	<0.001
Country [Peru]							0.99	0.002
Country [Paraguay]							−1.04	<0.001
Random Effects								
σ^2	88.34		85.67		83.97		83.95	
τ_{00}	12.16 $_{idsch}$		8.25 $_{idsch}$		7.97 $_{idsch}$		4.88 $_{idsch}$	
ICC	0.12		0.09		0.09		0.05	
N	1911 $_{idsch}$		1911 $_{idsch}$		1911 $_{idsch}$		1911 $_{idsch}$	
Observations	48861		48861		47757		47757	
Marginal R^2 / Conditional R^2	0.000 / 0.121		0.053 / 0.136		0.070 / 0.151		0.108 / 0.157	

Note: σ^2: within variance component; τ_{00}: between variance component; ICC: intraclass correlation; N: number of schools; Observations: number of students; Marginal R^2: explained variance by fixed parameters; Conditional R^2: explained variance by fixed and random parameters.

Table 8.6. *Regression models: the association between support for authoritarianism and civic knowledge in Latin America.*

Predictors	M0: Null		M1: Authoritarianism		M2: Authoritarianism		M3: Authoritarianism	
	Estimates	p	Estimates	p	Estimates	p	Estimates	p
(Intercept)	50.21	<0.001	67.36	<0.001	65.74	<0.001	63.82	<0.001
civic_know100			−3.77	<0.001	−3.72	<0.001	−3.63	<0.001
parental_education					−0.13	<0.001	−0.13	<0.001
books_at_home					−0.20	<0.001	−0.18	<0.001
gender					−0.19	0.029	−0.29	.018
political_discussion					0.04	<0.001	0.04	<0.001
time [2016]							−0.46	0.002
Country [Colombia]							2.89	<0.001
Country [Dominicana]							2.25	<0.001
Country [Guatemala]							2.58	<0.001
Country [Mexico]							2.00	<0.001
Country [Peru]							1.12	<0.001
Country [Paraguay]							2.88	<0.001
Random Effects								
σ^2	88.76		82.67		82.51		82.53	
τ_{00}	11.45 $_{idsch}$		5.22 $_{idsch}$		4.89 $_{idsch}$		3.78 $_{idsch}$	
ICC	0.11		0.06		0.06		0.04	
N	1911 $_{idsch}$		1911 $_{idsch}$		1911 $_{idsch}$		1911 $_{idsch}$	
Observations	48861		48861		47757		47757	
Marginal R² / Conditional R²	0.000 / 0.114		0.112 / 0.165		0.118 / 0.168		0.134 / 0.172	

Note: σ^2: within variance component; τ_{00}: between variance component; ICC: Intraclass correlation; N: number of schools; Observations: number of students; Marginal R²: explained variance by fixed parameters; Conditional R²: explained variance by fixed and random parameters.

189

levels of support for authoritarian practices are observed. This translates into the finding that young people who perform poorly on the knowledge test (e.g. 300 points) obtain 56.05 points on the scale of support for authoritarian practices (α:67.36 + (β:-3.77^*3)), which is half of one standard deviation above the scale average. In contrast, young people who obtain a high performance in the knowledge test (e.g. 700 points) obtain on average 40.97 points on authoritarianism (α:67.36 + (β:-3.77^*7)), which is closer to one standard deviation below the scale average. Once again, Model 2 enters a series of statistical controls. The result indicates that living in homes with parents with higher levels of educational attainment, having more books at home and being a girl decrease support for authoritarian practices. Furthermore, it indicates that the effect of civic knowledge remains stable even after controlling for this set of variables. Finally, as before, Model 3 enters the fixed effects of the country and year of the study (coded as dummy variables) to control for differences between countries and the year of study.

Discussion and Conclusions

The present chapter was aimed at evaluating the effect of civic knowledge on two central aspects of democratic legitimacy in Latin American school students: institutional trust and authoritarian attitudes. Regarding institutional trust, there are two main results to highlight. First, students show higher average institutional trust levels than are observed in the adult population, raising the question of whether this younger generation is more trusting than their adult counterparts and/or whether trust levels decrease when becoming adults. Second, certain consistencies are observed in both the young and adult populations; for example, that certain institutions (such as political parties) are the worst evaluated. Third, Chile and Colombia show significant decreases in trust in civic institutions, while findings for Mexico and the Dominican Republic remain stable and even increase in levels of trust over time. Therefore, across the region, trust levels are far from being stable and appear to follow a different pattern from that observed in the adult population. These age group differences could be due to multiple factors, such as experiences with institutions, generational differences or exposure to political crises in the region. However, assessing these possibilities is the subject of future research.

When considering the different authoritarian practices evaluated, most students tended to support some of them consistently, with a striking level of stability. Except for Chile, which shows significant decreases, in most of the countries observed, young people maintained and even increased levels of support for authoritarianism over time, which again points in the direction of a deeply authoritarian culture across Latin America.

Regarding the central question of the chapter, it is possible to affirm that having higher levels of civic knowledge has a paradoxical effect. On the one hand, school-age students with higher levels of civic knowledge show less support for the authoritarian practices of governments, since they seem to understand better that such practices are inconsistent with democratic life. However, on the other hand, those same students who are better versed in civic knowledge show less trust in the institutions that comprise the political system. Thus, greater civic knowledge improves one source of democratic legitimacy (less authoritarianism), but, at the same time, erodes another (less trust in institutions).

There is a series of implications for civic education in Latin America from the results presented here. It would be naive to expect that increased civic knowledge would automatically have a positive impact on democratic attitudes. Enhanced civic knowledge could lead to more scepticism and a more critical perspective on citizenship, affecting confidence in political institutions in contexts where they are characterised by low efficiency and/ or corruption. In this sense, low trust is not always a synonym for weak democratic attitudes, but could be actually the opposite. Furthermore, it is worth asking how what is observed here has played a role in the COVID-19 pandemic, where levels of public information and trust and the role of authority are at the centre of the management of the crisis. Therefore, it would be wrong to simply evaluate the impact of civic knowledge by the levels of trust in political institutions.

Funding

This paper was supported by the National Agency of Research and Development through the grants ANID/FONDECYT N°1181239, ANID/FONDECYT N°11190508 and the Center of Social Conflict and Cohesion Studies – COES ANID/FONDAP N°15130009.

REFERENCES

Almond, G. A. and Verba, S. (1989). *The civic culture: Political attitudes and democracy in five nations*. Newbury Park, CA: SAGE.

Altemeyer, B. (1996). *The authoritarian specter*. (First edition). Cambridge, MA: Harvard University Press.

Bargsted, M., Somma, N. and Castillo, J. C. (2017). Dynamics of political trust in Latin America. In S. Zmerli and T. W. G. van der Meer (Eds.), *Handbook on political trust* (pp. 395–417). etc. Cheltenham, UK; Northampton, MA: Edward Elgar Publishing Ltd.

Carrasco, D., Banerjee, R., Treviño, E. and Villalobos, C. (2019). Civic knowledge and open classroom discussion: Explaining tolerance of corruption among 8th-grade students in Latin America. *Educational Psychology*, 40(2), 186–206.

Castillo, J. C., Miranda, D., Bonhomme, M., Cox, C. and Bascopé, M. (2015). Mitigating the political participation gap from the school: The roles of civic knowledge and classroom climate. *Journal of Youth Studies*, 18(1), 16–35.

(2014). Social inequality and changes in students' expected political participation in Chile. *Education, Citizenship and Social Justice*, 9(2), 140–156.

Catterberg, G. and Moreno, A. (2006). The individual bases of political trust: Trends in new and established democracies. *International Journal of Public Opinion Research*, 18(1), 31–48.

Ching, B. H.-H., Xu, J. T., Chen, T. T. and Kong, K. H. C. (2020). Gender essentialism, authoritarianism, social dominance orientation, and filial piety as predictors for transprejudice in Chinese people. *Sex Roles*, 83(1), 426–441 doi:10.1007/s11199-020-01123-3

Citrin, J. and Stoker, L. (2018). Political trust in a cynical age. *Annual Review of Political Science*, 21(1), 49–70. https://doi.org/10.1146/annurev-polisci-050316-092550

Cox, C. (2010). Informe de Referente Regional 2010. Oportunidades de aprendizaje escolar de la ciudadanía en América Latina: currículos comparados. Sistema Regional de Evaluación y Desarrollo de Competencias Ciudadanas (SREDECC), Banco Interamericano de Desarrollo. Bogotá: CERLALC

Cox, C. and Castillo, J. C. (Eds.). (2015). *Aprendizaje de la ciudadanía: Contextos, experiencias y resultados* (First). Santiago, Chile: Ediciones UC.

Dageförde, M. and Schindler, D. (2018). 'Oh, that is a big word'. MPs' and citizens' perspectives on parliamentary representation. In W. Paterson and T. Saalfeld (Eds), *Political Representation in France and Germany: Attitudes and Activities of Citizens and MPs.* (pp. 197–226). Switzerland, Palgrave Macmillan.

de Viteri Vázquez, A. S. and Bjørnskov, C. (2020). Constitutional power concentration and corruption: Evidence from Latin America and the Caribbean, *Constitutional Political Economy, Springer*, 31(4), 509–536.

Dewey, J. (1989). *Freedom and culture.* New York: Prometheus.

Duckitt, J. (2015). Authoritarian personality. In J. D. Wright (editor-in-chief), *International encyclopedia of the social and behavioral sciences* 2nd edition (Vol. 2) (pp. 255–261). Oxford, NY: Elsevier.

Funke, F. (2005). The dimensionality of right-wing authoritarianism: Lessons from the dilemma between theory and measurement. *Political Psychology*, 26 (2), 195–218. https://doi.org/10.1111/j.1467-9221.2005.00415.x

Galston, W. A. (2007). Civic knowledge, civic education, and civic engagement: A summary of recent research. *International Journal of Public Administration*, 30(6–7), 623–642. https://doi.org/10.1080/01900690701215888

(2001). Political knowledge, political engagement, and civic education. *Annual Review of Political Science*, 4(1), 217–234. https://doi.org/10.1146/annurev .polisci.4.1.217

Gershtenson, J. and Plane, D. L. (2015). In government we distrust: Citizen skepticism and democracy in the United States. *The Forum*, 13(3). doi:10.1515/for-2015-0029

Hardin, R. (2001). Norms of cooperativeness and networks of trust, (with Karen S. Cook). In M. Hechter and K-D. Opp (Eds.), *Social norms* (pp. 327–347). New York: Russell Sage Foundation.

Hite, K. and Cesarini, P. (2004) (Eds.). *Authoritarian legacies and democracy in Latin America and Southern Europe*. Notre Dame: University of Notre Dame Press.

Kirsten, W. (2020). Cold War archives and democratic aspirations in Latin America. In S. L. Mizruchi (Ed), *Cold War archives and democratic aspirations in Latin America* (pp. 149–170). Switzerland, Palgrave Macmillan.

Köhler, H., Weber, S., Brese, F., Schulz, W. and Carstens, R. (2018). ICCS 2016 User Guide for the International Database: IEA International Civic and Citizenship Education Study 2016 Latin American Report. *International Association for the Evaluation of Educational Achievement*.

Latinobarometro. (2018). *Informe 2018*. Santiago, Chile: Corporación Latinobarometro.

Lauglo, J. (2013). Do more knowledgeable adolescents have more rationally based civic attitudes? Analysis of 38 countries. *Educational Psychology*, 33(3), 262–282. https://doi.org/10.1080/01443410.2 013.772773

Lipset, S. M. (1960). *Political man: The social bases of politics*. Garden City, NY: Doubleday.

(1959). Some social requisites of democracy: Economic development and political legitimacy. *The American Political Science Review*, 53(1), 69–105. https://doi.org/10.2307/1951731

Martini, S. and Quaranta, M. (2020). Political Support in Flux. In S. Martini and M. Quaranta (Eds.), *Citizens and Democracy in Europe: Contexts, Changes and Political Support* (pp. 1–20). Switzerland, Palgrave Macmillan. Available at: https://link.springer.com/content/pdf/bfm%3A978-3-030-21633-7%2F1.pdf.

Miranda, D., Castillo, J. C. and Cumsille, P. (2018). The political socialization of attitudes toward equal rights from a comparative perspective. In A. Sandoval-Hernández, M. Isac and D. Miranda (Eds), Teaching tolerance in a globalized world. *IEA Research for Education*. (A series of in-depth analyses based on data of the International Association for the Evaluation of Educational Achievement (IEA)), vol 4. Springer, Cham. https://doi.org/ 10.1007/978-3-319-78692-6_7

Morales Quiroga, M. (2020). Estallido social en Chile 2019: participación, representación, confianza institucional y escándalos públicos. *Análisis Político*, 33(98), 3–25. https://doi.org/10.15446/anpol.v33n98.89407

Offe, C. (1999). How can we trust our fellow citizens? In M. E. Warren (Ed.), *Democracy and Trust* (pp. 42–87). Cambridge, UK: Cambridge University Press. https://doi.org/10.1017/CBO9780511659959.003

Rapeli, L. (2013). *The conception of citizen knowledge in democratic theory*. Basingstoke: Palgrave Macmillan.

Sandoval-Hernandez, A., Miranda, D., Treviño, E. and Schmelkes, S. (2019). *Is democracy overrated? Latin American students' support for dictatorships. IEA Compass: Briefs in education. Number 7*. Amsterdam: International Association for the Evaluation of Educational Achievement.

Schulz, W., Ainley, J., Cox, C. and Friedman, T. (2018). *Young People's Views of Government, Peaceful Coexistence, and Diversity in Five Latin American Countries: IEA International Civic and Citizenship Education Study 2016 Latin American Report*. https://doi.org/10.1007/978-3-319-95393-9

Schulz, W., Ainley, J. and Fraillon, J. (2011). ICCS 2009 Technical Report. *International Association for the Evaluation of Educational Achievement*.

Schulz, W. and Sibberns, H. (2004). IEA Civic Education Study Technical Report. *International Association for the Evaluation of Educational Achievement*.

Schyns, P. and Koop, C. (2009). Political distrust and social capital in Europe and the USA. *Social Indicators Research*, 96(1), 145–167. doi:10.1007/s11205-009-9471-4

Segovia, C., Haye, A., González, R., Manzi, J. and Carvacho, H. (2008). Confianza en instituciones políticas en Chile: Un modelo de los componentes centrales de juicios de confianza. *Revista de Ciencia Política (Santiago)*, 28(2), 39–60. https://doi.org/10.4067/S0718–090X2008000200002

Sochos, A. (2019). Authoritarianism, trauma, and insecure bonds during the Greek economic crisis. *Current Psychology*. doi:10.1007/s12144-018-0111-5

Torney-Purta, J., Richardson, W. K. and Barber, C. H. (2004). Trust in Government-Related Institutions and Civic Engagement among Adolescents: Analysis of Five Countries from the IEA Civic Education Study. CIRCLE Working Paper 17. *Center for Information and Research on Civic Learning and Engagement*.

Uslaner, E. M. (2018). *The Oxford handbook of social and political trust*. Oxford, NY: Oxford University Press.

van der Meer, T. and Hakhverdian, A. (2016). Political Trust as the Evaluation of Process and Performance: A Cross-National Study of 42 European Countries: *Political Studies*. https://doi.org/10.1177/0032321715607514

Zmerli, S. and van der Meer, T. W. G. (2017). *Handbook on political trust*. Cheltenham, UK; Northampton, MA: Edward Elgar Publishing Ltd.

CHAPTER 9

New Technology, Language and Gesture in Contemporary Indian Political Discourse

Rukmini Bhaya Nair

'There's no art to find the mind's construction in the face', wrote Shakespeare in the seventeenth century. Scholars at the turn of the twenty-first century (Ekman, 2003a) might disagree. They would suggest that our facial expressions and body language afford valuable glimpses into our thought processes. This silent but inalienable presence of the non-verbal alongside speech is particularly relevant to an analysis of political discourse. Politicians overtly engage in the art of persuasion; it is, therefore, not unreasonable to look for corroborating evidence that their rhetoric is trustworthy. Is what they say what they really think? It is here that attention to gesture may prove rewarding.

As long ago as 1872, Charles Darwin argued in his pioneering work *The Expression of Emotions in Man and the Animals* that, given the hypothesis of a common 'origin of the species', certain basic emotions (fear, surprise, etc.) would have similar physical expressions in terms of non-verbal gestures across species as well as human cultures. In pursuit of this hypothesis, he sent a questionnaire to over thirty countries, including India, to document as many as sixteen gestures across cultures. The technologies Darwin employed were simple: pen and paper, sketches and notes, augmented by the relatively new art of photography. At the time, little was known either about the structure of the brain or about genetics; but Darwin used a broad spectrum of expertise to support his ideas. He consulted leading medical specialists on movements of the facial muscles as well as on nervous disorders; he used photographs of famous actors' performances of emotions such as sadness and scorn; and he tracked children from infancy to young adulthood as they developed their emotional repertoires. In effect, Darwin sought to show, through a 'mixed methods' approach, that a mature ability to communicate one's own emotions was also to be able to interactively control and guide the feelings of other members of the species, surely a relevant observation for those who wish to understand the psychological import of political action.

At least three strands of Darwin's research: the physiological, the performative and the psychological have since advanced greatly. Pavlov (1927), Skinner (1947) and Penfield's (1961) early experiments on human and animal behaviour, linking physical reflexes with mental states, are much cited. Although such studies have since been critically reviewed, they laid important foundations for current debate. Meanwhile, philosophers of language (Austin, 1962; Nussbaum, 2013; Searle, 1969) have theorised the performative, intentional and affective aspects of linguistic speech acts with some sophistication, while studies in the cognitive sciences have taken Darwin's insights on gesture in exciting new directions (Church, Alibali and Kelly, 2017; Corballis, 2002; Goldin-Meadow, 2003). Simultaneously, the interplay between the mechanics of ordinary conversation and 'people's technologies', such as tape recorders and, now, mobile phones, has given researchers a reliable set of non-invasive tools for the micro-analysis of speech (Levinson, 1983; Fetzer and Weizman, 2018; Nair, 2002, 2020a; Sacks, Schegloff and Jefferson, 1974). As well, in the popular domain, a burgeoning global industry is devoted to decoding telltale non-verbal signs of emotional attitude, especially in the public sphere (Mehrabian, 1981; Morris, 2013).

Given all this frenetic activity in the field of language and gesture studies, it is noteworthy that no research-based studies of politicians or other public figures have been undertaken in the Indian context. This absence is particularly striking given that India is the world's largest democracy, with as much lively diversity in its styles of political campaigning as in its linguistic and cultural structures. The present chapter attempts to fill this lacuna.

The span of time considered in the analysis is the four-year period dating from mid-2013 before the present Prime Minister of India, Narendra Modi, came to power with an absolute majority, to mid-2017, just before he was elected to a second term in 2018 with similar jaw-dropping electoral success. My suggestion is that this short period was pivotal in modern Indian politics because a primary tool of human communication, namely language, came to be conjoined with a dazzling set of new technologies. Together, they amplified the effect of a leader's words through dynamic visual means (videos, holograms, 24/7 online channels in multiple languages) as well as an incredibly fast diffusion of social media memes. Thus, India's young and cell-phone savvy millennials became a decisive factor in populist political reckonings at the exact conjunction when perhaps the most media savvy of India's politicians readied himself for office.

In the first section of the chapter, I present results from a study of Modi's speeches and gestures in the years and months before his momentous victory in the Indian General Elections of 2014. In the second section, I suggest that Prime Minister Modi's radical takeover of the Indian political scene after 2014 has not only affected his own political prospects, it has also had a significant effect on a younger generation of Indian leaders and, especially, Rahul Gandhi, leader of the opposition Indian National Congress (INC). It has forced Gandhi and others to define their own styles of technologically mediated leadership, with quite interesting consequences. In the final section, I end by offering researchers a putative general framework for the study of political gestures as they influence both national narratives and the personal stances of individual politicians.

Personal Power: Integrating the Verbal and Non-Verbal in a Mediated Political Sphere

In 2013–2014, one candidate stood out among many hopefuls vying to be declared the prime-ministerial choice of the leading opposition party, the Bharatiya Janata Party (henceforth BJP). This was the chief minister of Gujarat state, Narendra Modi. It was widely observed at the time that Modi seemed to have a particular ability to make himself the cynosure of all eyes. He offered almost a textbook example of how verbal and non-verbal language can combine to propel some personalities to the centre stage in the hurly-burly of a pre-election year when conflicting narratives compete for attention. Several reasons were adduced for this: the general political climate of disenchantment, the crises of leadership in the BJP, as well the media focus on, and amplification of, Modi's 'dominance'. However, the media had to have something to amplify in the first place.

Bearing in mind the evolutionary 'Darwinian' background mentioned earlier, my research into how Modi became so prominent in national politics in such short order involved three main hypotheses:

First, that the 'polarising' rhetoric so often associated with Modi (and, inter alia, several other populist leaders across the world today) would be related to patterns in his language output, since language is the main medium the human species uses to structure their world.

Second, that significantly more 'fight' gestures would be observable in Modi's communications during public appearances. This is based on the premise that socially tense situations in this political world are likely to arouse the embodied fight-or-flight reactions that have evolved over millions of years in human communication. Such tense situations would aptly describe the circumstances surrounding a politician like Modi, an avowed 'Hindu nationalist' who was widely criticised for being complicit in the grave violence inflicted on the Muslim minority by Hindu mobs and state police during the infamous 'Gujarat riots' of 2002. In the Indian context, Modi has seldom been categorised as anything other than a bold and controversial politician whose actions cause noticeable perturbations in the political arena.

Third, the performative dimensions of both language and gesture used by politicians were likely to be enhanced given the demands of the political arena, providing an opportunity to observe the relationship between thoughts and emotions and their on-record public expressions that Darwin considered so critical to the evolution of human societies.

The initial study examined the rise to power of one of India's most-watched politicians along three axes – the linguistic, the gestural and the performative.

The Linguistic Axis in Indian Political Discourse

This part of our exploratory research concerns our **first hypothesis** outlined above relating to expected patterns of linguistic polarisation in Modi's discourse. Sixty-eight speeches from Modi's official website were downloaded in May 2013 and a simple analysis undertaken of the main themes related to key political domains, using a three-step approach. First, my team and I located 'topic clusters' in our database of Modi speeches; second, our team of more than fifteen research assistants selected words they agreed were important in any Indian national contest ('poor', 'development', 'industry', etc.) from the clusters found, to which we added some common emotion-laden terms; third, we conducted contrastive counts of the chosen words in our dataset and computed the results.

Perhaps the single most striking discovery was that the word 'Hindu' did not even occur once in all the 200 or so pages of text analysed. This was quite significant in the Indian political context because one intuitively expected 'Hindu' to be a prominent word in Modi's vocabulary given his election campaign on a 'Hindutva' (pro-Hindu) platform. That the word Hindu simply did not occur in the sample of Modi's speeches examined was most surprising and led us to search for the word 'Muslim', which was politically opposed to it; as it turned out, we found relatively few instances of this religious deictic (see Figure 9.3) as well. In contrast, the word 'development', which presumably applied to Muslims as well as Hindus, occurred 534 times (see Figure 9.1). As the curious case of the missing word 'Hindu' was further investigated, we began to see that some nuance was needed in our **first hypothesis**, even as we expected strong contrasts to appear in the discourse of a politician who adopted an overtly 'polarising' stance in his public appearances. For example, on a much-debated occasion in 2011, Modi publicly refused to wear a skull-cap offered to him by a Sufi Muslim religious leader. One interpretation of this finding is that a word like 'Hindu' did not need explicit mention in his discourse because it represented what linguists would call the 'unmarked' instance: 'Hindu' is understood by default to indicate the religious affiliation of Modi's addressees at large. However, the difficulties of finding clinching evidence for such an 'absence' are notorious, so this conjecture would certainly need to be confirmed or disconfirmed in further research.

Figure 9.1   Frequency of keywords used in political speeches by Modi during his last year before becoming Prime Minister of India.

At the same time, it should be noted that we did indeed identify a number of regularities in the speeches analysed that appeared to provide strong support for our **first hypothesis**, namely, that very sharp 'black and white' semantic emphases and contrasts would be found in Modi's speeches. Furthermore, such linguistic evidence, in tandem with his gestural repertoire examined in relation to our **second hypothesis**, would clearly differentiate him from other politicians on the national stage in terms of the emotional appeal that constitutes the theme of our **third hypothesis**.

Emerging from our word counts of Modi's speeches was, at the very least, a strong pattern of contrasts. As Figure 9.1 demonstrates, one in every pair of vocabulary items outperforms its counterpart by a statistically significant margin: for example, industry/business versus labour; political power versus money; youth versus age; poor versus rich; and technology versus the social sciences. Modi's much-remarked orientation towards a constituency of technologically driven, globally aspiring youth is apparent in the frequency of use of these items. The old are relatively marginalised; however, the poor and 'village' India make a strong showing (see Figure 9.2), as do women, who overall are referenced far more frequently than men (58.8 per cent versus 41.2 per cent respectively).

Why are women so frequently referenced in Modi's speeches? The replies to this question are various and range from ascriptions of personal motivations – he left a young wife behind at home when he was about eighteen and never acknowledged her existence until he had to file his nomination papers for his prime-ministerial election – to political calculations: he is aware that women across the county form huge voting blocks and that winning their support and confidence can decisively affect

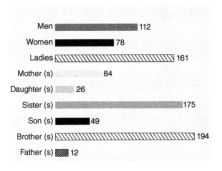

Figure 9.2   Frequency of use of terms referring to gender.

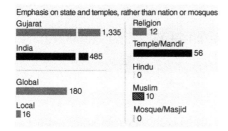

Figure 9.3   Frequency of references to state/nation and religious affiliation.

electoral results. What is to be noted in terms of discourse semantics, however, is that women in these speeches are usually addressed in a folksy relational manner (sisters, mothers, daughters) that references trust-inducing idioms of kinship, except for the ubiquitous use of the term 'ladies', which appears to be a polite, if slightly awkward, way of referring to urban working women, who constitute a relatively new and unfamiliar cohort in the social hierarchy but who tend to exercise their vote and so are electorally quite critical.

In terms of kinship, references to men and brothers outnumber those to women and sisters, while sons are mentioned almost twice as often as daughters. This is significant because figures show that 'son preference' is a common phenomenon in India and is, in many cases, accompanied by the cruelty of female foeticide and severe neglect of young girls, with male births outnumbering those of girls in almost all of India's states. In terms of our **first hypothesis** concerning language polarisation, Modi's political speeches seem to subtly acknowledge these deep psychosocial fissures while overtly using the comforting language of kinship.

Other observations arising from these frequency counts concern the social linkages made between region, nation and faith. Here, we notice that 'Gujarat' occurs far more frequently than 'India' in Modi's speeches. This is not in itself that revelatory since many of these speeches were delivered to Gujarati audiences, but it does indicate that, in this period, 'India' for Modi was refracted through the lens of his own state of Gujarat.

Indeed, several speeches ended with the ringing call 'Jai Gujarat' (Victory for Gujarat!), as exemplified in Modi's long speech at the laying of a foundation stone for a 'Gandhi temple' on 1 May 2010:

> Today is May first, opening of 'The Golden Jubilee' of Gujarat state. We are beginning. . . with a firm resolve to illuminate our state with plenty of ambitious projects in the coming year. This is an occasion to remember the

great revolutionary, respected Bapu. Let's bow down to the statue of
Induchacha and pay homage to martyrs and honour their families. When
we think of nationhood over politics, only then one can think of constructing the Mahatma-temple. Politics is an activity of parties, whereas nationhood is an activity of nation. This is an occasion of national pride and
national interest, which is greater than politics and can reach the top
of Everest.

In this rousing populist speech, Gandhi, a man of mass movements in the
streets, appears ironically confined within a 'Mahatma Mandir' ('Temple
of a Great Soul'). 'Hindu' might be a missing term, but there are a
significant number of references to temples and *mandir*s, though none at
all to mosques. This strong contrast seems to suggest that, while Hindus'
rights to their places of worship can be openly acknowledged, in such
political speeches Muslim places of worship may verbally, and thus con-
ceptually, be erased from public consciousness without consequence. It is
generally acknowledged that Modi and his party, the BJP, have traditionally not made much effort to woo the Muslim vote, preferring to focus on
their large Hindu base during elections.

Noticeably, too, the theme of 'national pride' (implicitly associated in
BJP discourse with the 'Hindu' nature of India's polity) is emphasised
throughout the speech. Evidence surfaces here for a subtle verbal strategy
that Modi adopts in his references to revered past leaders in national
politics – most of whom belonged to the rival Congress Party. Modi has
to claim this lineage of the 'other' while at the same time enhancing his
own pre-eminence and unique oppositional role in current India politics.
How does he achieve this double goal? The way in which he frames the
role of Mahatma Gandhi in the speech extract above is illustrative.
Gandhi, from Modi's own home state of Gujarat, is acknowledged to be
the tallest leader the Congress Party and India have ever had. In the
ubiquitous kinship terminology mentioned earlier, Gandhi is widely
known as 'Bapu' or 'Father of the Nation'. The rhetorical route that
Modi chooses is to try and contain or diminish this formidable reputation.
For instance, when he talks here about a 'national pride' that leads to
'Mount Everest', the human figure of Gandhi is dwarfed by the natural
splendour of this highest of Himalyan peaks long associated with India.
Such a focus on pride or *asmita*, a word and concept Indians recognise as
an intrinsic part of Modi's vocabulary, also obscures the crucial fact that
Gandhi himself emphasised the virtue of national 'tolerance' far more than
that of national 'pride'. Gandhi repeatedly advocated for Hindu-Muslim
amity in his classic speeches. Modi efficiently counters this aspect of the

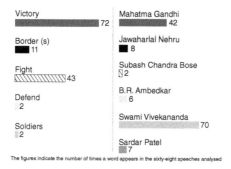

The figures indicate the number of times a word appears in the sixty-eight speeches analysed

Figure 9.4   Frequency of reference to historic Indian politicians in Modi's speeches.

'Gandhi challenge' by metaphorically placing him, as already mentioned, within the confines of a temple on the occasion of this speech. Thus is the 'great revolutionary' Gandhi tamed by the great rhetorician Modi. Another strategy Modi has constantly used to reduce the past reputation of the Congress Party is to claim the rare nationalist leader who had no links to the Congress as his most crucial political ancestor. This is apparent in Figure 9.4, where the 'Hindu' religious guru, Swami Vivekananda, garners by far the most mentions in Modi's speeches.

Correlating this pattern of Gandhi references with other patterns in Modi's text, we also found the crucial Gandhian virtue of tolerance to be, by far, the lowest on the roster of positive emotional attitudes (e.g. happiness, hope) alluded to.

Among the 'negative' emotions mentioned by Modi, 'anger' and 'fear' were the most frequent, contrasting with the frequency of references to 'shame' and 'guilt' (see Figure 9.5). 'Peace' often figured as an ideal, but so did 'victory' and 'fight', which link to the importance of fight-or-flight gestures in the political arena.

Overall, from an analysis of the basic language data, I argue in favour of our **first hypothesis** that the persistent patterns of word-contrasts found in Modi's speeches both reflect and reinforce the perception of 'polarisation' so widely associated with his discourse. His verbal decisiveness supports public perceptions of Modi as a sublimely focused leader with a singularly prophetic vision about the direction in which his country is headed. At the same time, his strong verbal choices perhaps indicate a personality unwilling or unable to engage in nuanced dialogue and debate, consistent with a limited and unipolar view of the world. Some corroboration is offered by Modi's behaviour of walking out of interviews he considers too probing.

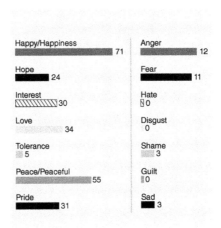

Figure 9.5   Frequency of emotions mentioned in the text of the prime minister's speeches.

Similarly, he never meets with reporters at large, as nearly all his prime-ministerial predecessors had; and seldom, if ever, does he grant one-on-one interviews. Instead, he prefers to do scheduled and widely advertised radio sessions every month called 'Mann ki Baat' ('Matters of the Mind'), along the lines of Roosevelt's 'fireside chats', in which he interacts with school-children and other volunteers – although questions asked on these occasions, if any, are always anodyne. Finally, he frequently makes solo addresses to the nation on topics ranging from National Security to COVID-19 safety measures. This distanced, yet intimate, style of communication adds to the impression that Modi is a leader whose stature is both unquestioned and unquestionable, indicative of a remote and superior visionary whose view of the world is singularly free of everyday bias. In a traditional, 'developing' society where so many are engaged in a daily struggle for survival, such 'strong' leadership appears reassuringly worthy of trust, and can only be opposed by a 'Westernised', 'English-speaking', 'urban' elite who are, in the popular mind, alienated from the lives of the poor and ordinary people for whose interests Modi projects himself as sole custodian.

In terms of the **first hypothesis**, it may be contended that a long-standing psychosocial, linguistically underwritten and powerful divide between rich and poor, between 'elite' and 'common' folk, is astutely deployed by Modi to enhance his own populist appeal. Modi, of course, is well aware that the total vote-count of these elites in national elections is negligible, and so makes little attempt to placate them. On the contrary, his strategy is to portray the elites as servitors of a dynastic, corrupt and passé Congress Party who have no inkling of the emotions and aspirations that drive the 'new India' he leads.

The Gestural System in the Indian Political Sphere

In the long history of human communication, gesture is likely to have preceded spoken language by at least 50,000 years (Graddol, 2004). When language developed, the basic non-verbal system continued to support talk (Goldin-Meadow, 2003), often revealing the instinctive fight-or-flight or other emotional reactions that our more 'intentional' spoken words might or might not (See Noroozi et al., 2018 for a wide-ranging summary of gestural research in the machine/AI (artificial intelligence)-dominated world of today; see also Pascalis et al., 2011 for a similar research of 'face processing' and facial expressions). Contemporary research, in short, emphasises that language and gesture are evolutionarily, developmentally and socio-culturally connected (Cartmill, Beilock and Goldin-Meadow, 2012; Sterelny, 2012). The third element in this triad is emotion, which can range from abstract, high-level feelings such as altruism to 'moral emotions' such as shame and guilt to 'basic' feelings like 'happiness' or 'anger'. It has been conjectured that this wide palette of emotion can drive social action, well beyond primal kinship networks. For example, Tomasello et al. (2012) propose an 'interdependence hypothesis' of a chief difference between the great apes and humans in which humans developed cooperative methods of sharing – including the sharing of knowledge – and that such behaviour 'inevitably' led in time to altruism and thought for others beyond one's immediate circle of kin. This evolutionary thesis has implications for political behaviour pertaining to the relationship between a leader and voters. Modi may, as we have observed, use the traditional and time-honoured vocabulary of family kinship, but the rhetoric he has used appears to have a much wider 'altruistic' appeal in current national populist politics. It is this complex set of relationships between language, gestures, feelings and worldview that Darwin placed on the research agenda of psychobiology more than a century ago. It has also turned out, since Darwin's time, that our brains pay vastly more attention to some parts of our bodies (notably, hands, mouth and eyes, as in Penfield's (1961) early but uncontested studies) than to others, whether we are consciously aware of these effects or not. Thus, current research has produced a slew of neurobiological studies on the links between language, gesture and emotion that are beyond the scope of this chapter, but that still

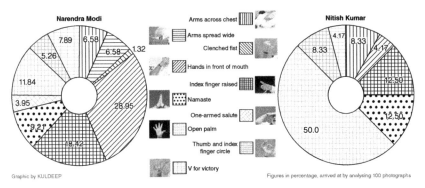

Figure 9.6   A comparison of the use of hands and fingers in gestures, illustrating the contrasting fight-or-flight communicative styles of Modi and Kumar.

Note: Of the ten gestures above, the following five are considered aggressive 'fight' gestures: the clenched fist, index finger raised, arms spread wide, the one-armed 'militaristic' salute and the 'V' for victory; while the arms across chest, hands in front of mouth, the Namaste, the thumb and index finger circle and the open palm are taken to be friendly or defensive.

It should be noted, however, that cultural interpretations are also critical here.

contribute to its very foundations (see, for example, De Stefani and De Marco, 2019). In this section, I explore the variations in communicative gestures of two Indian populist politicians. This was undertaken by first downloading 100 photographs, on the same day in May 2013, of Prime Minister Narendra Modi and Nitish Kumar – a charismatic politician from Bihar to whom Modi is often compared as both have held Chief Ministerships. Based on these downloads, an initial categorisation of facial expressions and hand gestures revealed obvious differences between Modi and Kumar's physical stances and their putative displays of possible political stress. In terms of facial expressions, Modi's serious demeanour contrasted starkly with Kumar's. His repertoire of gestures was also remarkably more versatile (see Figure 9.6).

About 50 per cent of Kumar's gestures consisted of the open palm gesture, generally associated with a 'nothing-to-hide' or 'wait' message; while Modi uses this gesture only about 12 per cent of the time. In contrast, nearly 50 per cent of Modi's gestures consist of just two note-worthy indicators: first, the highly assertive upraised finger, routinely interpreted as a domineering fight gesture, and second, the ambiguous 'self-touch' hand-on-face-or-mouth gesture. The latter signal is the most frequently represented among Modi's hand movements and is variously associated with thoughtfulness and on-the-spot decision-making, or a lack of self-confidence and commitment and sometimes deception. The relationship between hand-and-mouth gestures and evolutionary cues has been explicitly made in research; *The Nonverbal Dictionary of Gestures, Signs and Body Language* (Givens and Whyte, 2020) takes this point further by making a direct connection with displays of political 'stress', arguing that 'self-touch cues reflect the arousal level of our sympathetic nervous system's fight-or-flight response. We unconsciously touch our bodies when emotions run high to comfort, relieve, or release stress. Lips are favourite places for fingertips to land and deliver reassuring body contact'.

The 'social tension' indicated in our **second hypothesis** is thus very much in evidence in the photographs analysed. While, in many respects, Modi conveys the impression of firmly standing his ground and holding his torso and body rock solid (Noroozi et al., 2018), these body stances appear in stark contrast to his expressive 'hands-on' talk that can be more or less arranged in a graded series of responses from fight to flight.

Thus, plausible primary evidence for the classic fight-or-flight responses was discovered in this initial comparative analysis of Modi's body language with Kumar's, but the main focus of our research was to account for Modi's across-the-board public appeal. The next set of tests was designed to figure out whether Indian audiences clearly perceived these as cues. Accordingly, a series of 'implicit association tests' was conducted online using a multiple-choice format. These related to (a) syllables; (b) words (see Figure 9.7); (c) sentences; (d) speech acts; (e) emoticons (see Figure 9.7) and f) matching

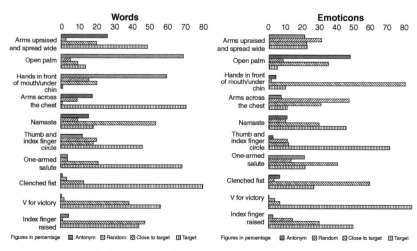

Figure 9.7   Voters' identification of words and emoticons as indicating 'fight' or 'flight'.

various gestures to the politicians who respondents thought were most likely to use them.

The basic demographic data on 100 participant volunteers in these tests shows them to be part of that educated, technologically attuned and young demographic that psephology has shown constitute an important segment of Modi-voters. These online experiments yield significant results from a statistical point of view, showing that our respondents were, by and large, enormously skilled at identifying fight (aggressive) or flight (defensive) gestures, even though they did not know the purpose of our tests and so did not have any inkling about the 'correct' answers. The findings illustrate identification of the words and emoticons as cues of fight or flight and, therefore, suggest that politicians' use of these has the capacity to influence audience perceptions of their character. In each of these randomly presented implicit association tests, the experimental procedure involved participants choosing one out of four choices (target, close to target, random, antonymous) that coders had previously agreed most matched either a fight or a flight gesture. There was a notable exception in the results: i.e. the 'open palm' identified both in the literature and by coders as non-aggressive was mostly seen as a 'fight' gesture by our respondents. We can only speculate about the cause for this, but post-test informal conversations in our group indicated that this gesture, identified with the now near universal traffic light 'Stop' sign, could perhaps be interpreted in the political context as 'Stop, I've had enough. Now listen to what I have to say!' In this sense, the 'open palm' might well be interpreted as tending towards an aggressive 'fight' stance. However, such ambiguity was relatively rare and our study found clear evidence that Modi's gestures, in particular, were judged by respondents as heavily skewed towards an unambiguous 'fight' schema.

As our respondents clearly recognised 'fight' gestures, overwhelmingly choosing 'target' or 'close to target' word-to-image matches when presented with verbal or even 'emoticon' multiple-choices, two further tests explicitly asked participants to associate the 'fight' and 'flight' gestures in 100 test stimuli from photos and videos of contemporary political figures (see Figure 9.8a). First, these associations were to be made with four well-known political figures who were all chief ministers in 2013: Narendra Modi from Gujarat (BJP); Digvijay Singh of Madhya Pradesh from the Congress Party (INC); Nitish Kumar of Bihar from the Janata Dal United (JDU); Naveen Patnaik of Orissa from the Biju Janata Dal (BJD). We chose these particular political stalwarts because of their similar political profile to Modi: they were male, in their 60s and all had been voted in for

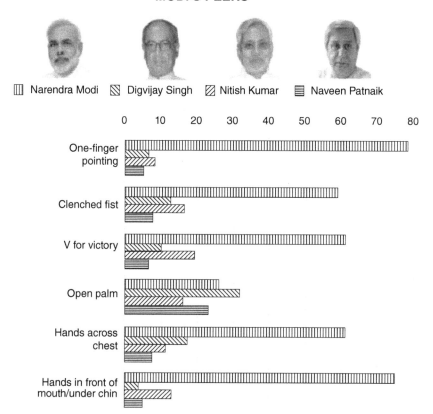

Figure 9.8a   Voters' identification (in per cent) of the gestures used by present key political figures.

at least two terms. Second, we asked respondents to associate these same gestures with four historical leaders of India (Subhash Chandra Bose, Jawaharlal Nehru, Sardar Patel and, of course, Mahatma Gandhi), since one of Modi's conundrums has always been to establish a lineage for himself that would enhance his prestige as a strong pan-Indian leader (see Figure 9.8b).

The first of these bar graphs demonstrates that respondents associated the first three 'fight' gestures (finger pointing, clenched fist and 'V' for victory) with Modi more than any other politician. Interestingly, the ambiguous 'hands in front of mouth' gesture is also attributed to him,

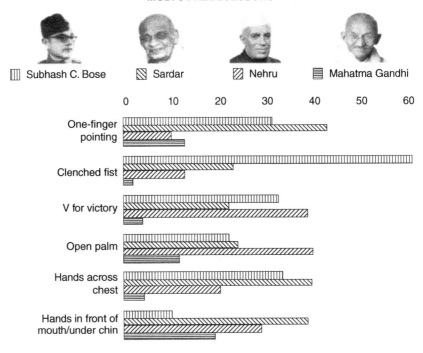

Figure 9.8b   Voters' identification (in per cent) of the gestures used by past key political figures.

although it should be noted that some participants recognised Modi in a couple of photographs since his face was partly visible. Regardless of categorisation as a 'fight' signal or 'flight' (for example, a defensive arms across chest), it appears that participants paid far more attention to Modi's body language than to any other current politician, even though this data collection was prior to his election as Prime Minister.

In relation to our **second hypothesis**, our supposition was that few of the gestures used by contemporary politicians would be found during the Gandhi-Nehru era (circa 1930–1970), as the INC was then unchallenged and the strong influences of regional states evident in today's 'federalist' politics were absent. This paucity of political peer rivalry would lessen the need for displaying 'fight' gestures. Notably, in all cases, past and present, a narrative of 'strong' (fight) versus 'weak' (flight) gestures appeared associated with national leaders. This lends some credence to the basic hypothesis that language and gesture powerfully intertwine to inform our political allegiances, or, to put it more bluntly, how we vote.

The Performative Dimension in the Indian Political Arena

This last part of my first section returns to the **third hypothesis** that the performative dimensions of both language and gesture are enhanced in the political arena, more so than ever in the present era of 'amplifying' technologies. This point also relates to the **second hypothesis**, which predicts that any political 'action' must be inherently stressful since a political actor is always under surveillance, his 'image' being online and on-screen 24/7. Modi himself has expressed strong views on the matter: 'I have not spent a single minute on my image... I am dedicated to Gujarat. I never talk about my image' (interview with Karan Thapar, 2012). Now, the second and third of these declarations may well be true, but the first is more problematic. Modi is on record as having designed his own self-identifying brand of garment, the extremely popular 'Modi Kurta', with workmanlike cut-off sleeves, which surely took more than a minute. His choice of the symbolic nationalist colours saffron (traditionally associated with Hinduism in India) and white, with only a hint of green (associated with Islam), is also evident from his photographs, while his penchant for flamboyant turbans would not escape being dubbed as showy plumage displays (see Savalli, 1995) by some evolutionary biologists (see Nakahashi, 2017, on arguably parallel preferences among humans).

Like Sergius, the mock soldier hero of George Bernard Shaw's *Arms and the Man*, Modi's language explored in our **first hypothesis** can border deliciously on the melodramatic: 'Look at the written evidence. Has anything been proven against me? Hang me if you find such evidence!' More than a hint of a 'fight' reaction is evidenced in such violent imagery. Shaw's play ridicules Sergius for folding his arms in the 'defensive' manner noted in our study and endlessly repeating the stock phrase, 'I never apologise'.

One last experiment related to putative 'performance stress' in Modi's interviews. Body language research suggests that the left and right side of our faces can show different intensities and types of emotion (see Dopson et al., 1984; Ekman, 2003b; Mandal and Singh, 1990; Matsumoto and Hwang, 2018). When President Bill Clinton was questioned about Monica Lewinsky, the two sides of his face, experts alleged, showed very different emotions. Such 'tests' are not admissible as legal evidence, but they may tell gripping Rashomon tales. In moments of stress, these two parts can apparently produce increasingly divergent narratives. The power of the proscenium play and the key constellations in Modi's semantic universe thus interestingly come together in a 'face-reading' exercise.

This study used five micro-expressions from Modi's television interviews during which he was questioned over the major anti-Muslim carnage in Gujarat in 2002, when he was Chief Minister. Respondents were asked to identify separated 'half-face' expressions shown by Modi. Some respondents did complain that the test did not 'make any sense' since they were only shown a randomised half-face, but even they identified anger as the dominant emotion on the 'truthful' left side of Modi's face while 'happiness' and 'surprise' were the emotions identified on the socialised right side. This difference has the potential to lend support to the **third hypothesis** (Figure 9.9).

Furthermore, this finding appears to correspond to the word counts tested for the **first hypothesis** – where 'anger' was also the most mentioned emotion – and with the predominance of perceived 'fight' gestures predicted by the **second hypothesis**. Thus, all three hypotheses seem to mesh, as current research suggests (see Jablonka, Ginsburg and Dor, 2012) when we consider these putative stressful moments in Modi's riveting political performances.

Of course, the results of these initial studies of Modi's embodied gestures and public language rely on a level of interpretation. Fine-grained grammatical analyses were made difficult since the speeches on Modi's website had already been translated into English from Hindi or Gujarati. Modi's talk abounds with wordplay ('life/file'), acronyms (STCs standing for 'Superior Technology Centres'), one-liners, jokes and anecdotes. Little of this language prestidigitation is captured in our analyses. Like a professional magician, Modi is ever ready to ally with virtual technology to create stage effects in which 'doubt is out' and underline that his is the sole presence to be trusted when it comes to voicing the nation's interests. I end this section with a gesture in the direction of a striking visual appurtenance widely noticed in Modi's pre-2013 political campaign. This was the advent of the 'Modi Mask', when huge crowds of Modi supporters attended his rallies wearing paper masks that superimposed Modi's face on their own. The simple message: 'Modi possesses the political power to turn everyone into Modi. His face is our face.' In this metamorphosis, the mundane 'ordinariness' of the common man (*aam aadmi*) instantly partook of the magical extraordinariness of a Modi (*khaas aadmi*).

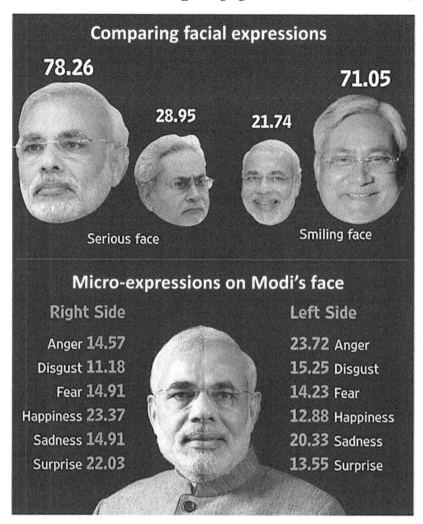

Figure 9.9   What the visage says: emotions on display by Modi and Kumar.

Public Endeavour: Projecting Ordinariness and Extraordinariness in a Polarised Political Context

This section focuses on the post-2014 phase in Indian politics during which Modi has been a dominant presence. It observes the effects of his rhetorical style on a newer generation of political combatants who must also now contend with the populist merging of the ordinary with the extraordinary.

Theory and Praxis

Ordinariness was a central theme in ethnomethodological analyses of language in the 1970s. Such research 'uncoupled' conversation from its context insofar as it relied on tape recordings as a primary source of data. Transcripts from tapes engendered analytic procedures whereby the mechanics of everyday conversational turn taking could be studied independent of the face-to-face circumstances in which they occurred. In other words, not only did the ethnomethodological techniques of Conversational Analysis (CA) rely on a machine (the tape recorder), it presented conversation itself as a machine with technical parts that could be separately dismantled and studied with precision, without necessary reference to the messy 'intentionality' of speakers so crucial to other streams of 'ordinary language philosophy' such as Austin and Searle's Speech-act Theory (Nair, 2002, 2019, 2021). We might also recall that 'tapes' emerged as a political keyword from 1972 onwards, when the Watergate scandal broke in the United States of America. Tape recordings became a prime investigative tool of that era, greatly influencing both the socio-political sphere and academic research. The ethnomethodologist, Harvey Sacks' excitement in 1968 at the tape-recorder initiating a new observational methodology to study 'talk' is palpable:

> The tape-recorded materials constituted a good enough record of what happened. Other things, to be sure, happened, but at least what was on the tape had happened. It was not from any large interest in language or from some theoretical formulation of what should be studied that I had started with tape-recorded conversations, but simply because I could get my hands on it and I could study it again and again. . . So the work I am doing is about. . . the details of talk. In some sense, it is about how conversation works. (1984)

Nearly half a century later, Fetzer and Weizman (2017, 2018) point out that media discourses today allow for another sort of 'uncoupling of space and time and thus communication with distant others'. They add that 'unlike face-to-face interaction', this enables the 'construction of ordinariness' as 'a public endeavour. . . which is generally produced and interpreted in accordance with institutional and genre-specific constraints'.

Once again, we have an important tool that can literally be held in the palms of our hands. Mobile technology puts the ability to record scenarios, gestures and other accompaniments of 'talk' directly into the hands of ordinary people, thus reducing the distance between public and private power. This has had, as we shall observe, an important effect of styles of political outreach in India. In addition, e-technologies have created a range of instant tools such as calculations of word count, graphic presentations in the form of pie charts and so forth that enable researchers to extend, as I see it, one of Harvey Sacks' primary insights, namely, that machines allow us to look at ourselves as producers of what he called a 'simplest systematics of (interactional) regularities' (Sacks et al., 1974).

In this section, I will suggest that there is a similar systematic set of 'gestural regularities' accompanying the production of speech and political speech in particular. To the extent that conversation is a mechanical self-organising system, so is the body. Furthermore, because we can so easily lift videos and stills of politicians and public personalities from our computer screens, a further, radical stage in the project of technically recording interaction – especially as it relates to what the ethno-methodologists called 'doing being ordinary', has been enabled. So how does this work in the actual political domain?

Narrative, Biography and Dynasty

Using basic e-tools (videos, online still photos, extracts from speeches and interviews), this part of the chapter argues, on the basis of 'ordinary' political activity, that an ethnomethodological analysis can significantly contribute to an understanding of the co-construction of national narratives as a 'public endeavour'. In the larger, ongoing study on which this section of the chapter is based, I selected four younger politicians from northern India. Here, the focus is on just two of them, both from Uttar Pradesh, which is by far India's largest state (with a population of 205 million), each very much in the public eye and each belonging to India's leading national parties in opposition. They are contrasting in their respective backgrounds: Rahul Gandhi of the INC – who is the scion of a high-ranking political 'dynasty' – and Yogi Adityanath of the BJP – who has 'risen from below'.

Rahul Gandhi was born in 1970. His great-grandfather (Jawaharlal Nehru), his grandmother (Indira Gandhi) and father (Rajiv Gandhi) were all prime ministers of India, the latter two dying by assassination. Rahul was present at both funerals in full public gaze. His mother, Sonia Gandhi, is an Indian citizen who is Italian by birth, making him vulnerable to the charge of not being authentically Indian. His nickname in the popular press is 'Pappu', meaning 'Baby' – a dynastic slur. In contrast, Modi's nickname is 'Feku', implying a wily faker or pretender (see Nair, 2003 on ordinariness and narrative aesthetics; 2018, on 'pretending').

Yogi Adityanath was born in 1972. Adiyanath's father was a forest ranger in Uttarakhand and he was second of seven siblings, 'renouncing' his family at the age of twenty-one, as did Modi at a similar age. He was the founder of the Hindu Yuva Vahini, a militant youth organisation, and part of the movement that pulled down a sixteenth-century mosque in Ayodhya in 1992, an event that resulted in widespread violence and national trauma as well as the meteoric rise of the BJP as a national party. He is the current Chief Minister of Uttar Pradesh and has been a Member of Parliament for five consecutive terms since 1998.

My hypothesis, based on the data presented below, is that Gandhi and Adityanath, both younger than Modi by approximately two decades, have developed diametrically opposed political styles in the new age of mobile politics. While Gandhi persistently strives to play down his lineage by 'doing being ordinary' in the classic ethnomethodological sense, Adityanath follows the supreme leader of his party, Modi, by what I shall call 'doing being extraordinary'. This second paired term is a conceptual addition of sorts to the ethnomethodological arsenal. To explain this difference further, I draw on William Labov's (1972) and Harvey Sacks' works on everyday conversational narratives.

Labov, who studied 'danger of death' narratives by African-American youth in New York, maintains: 'We find that most narratives are so designed as to emphasise the strange and unusual character of the situation'. On the other hand, Sacks' analysis of 'danger of death' earthquake narratives in California, remarks: 'It seems plain enough that people monitor the scenes they are in for their storyable characteristics. And yet the awesome overwhelming fact is that they come away with no storyable characteristics'. Sacks reveals the ways in which tellers strive to achieve 'the nothing-happened sense of really catastrophic events', i.e. their 'ordinariness'. He is struck by the 'overwhelming banality of the stories we encounter'.

At first, Sacks' observations seem to conflict sharply with Labov's claim that a narrative is 'tellable' or reportable if it is constructed out of unusual materials. Yet, disasters, classic 'tellables' in Labov's sense – as Sacks remarks – are merely 'things in the world'. Despite their immense potential as reportable events, these stories have to be worked on, fashioned into what he calls 'something for us'; something that engages a teller's particular audience. In effect, reportable story material has to be rendered 'ordinary' ('it could happen to you, this is your story'). Conversely, ordinary story material has to be made reportable if it is not to be criticised as pointless ('why are you telling me this?'). My data suggests that political narratives have to walk a thin line between being 'tellable' in that they concern matters of public interest and, at the same time, 'banal' in that they must present well-worn themes that are all too familiar (corruption, economic issues, state/regional versus national interests, etc.). So, how do politicians address the daily imperative of making their stories 'something for us'?

In the Indian context at least, 'ordinariness construction' seems greatly to depend on whether the politicians in question are – or are perceived to be – 'one of us' or 'not one of us'. Hence, 'dynastic heirs' such as Rahul Gandhi seem to want to project an embodied ordinariness in dress, behaviour, speech and gesture, while the onus on 'ordinary', non-dynastic politicians is to embody a parallel extraordinariness. It is no surprise, then, that the 'taking down' of INC dynasts and the inherited privilege of princelings has been a rhetorical constant in BJP speeches. This is often dubbed the fight between '*Vansh*' and '*Vikas*', or 'Dynasty versus Development'. The following reports are typical.

> Dynasty and democracy cannot go together. Very simple. . . it weakens our system. Dynasty in democracy is nasty (Vice President of India M. Venkaiah Naidu) (Press Trust of India, 2017).

> Terming Rahul Gandhi a 'failed dynast', the BJP hit back at his criticism of Prime Minister Modi and the government, with the Minister of Information and Broadcasting Smriti Irani saying he had chosen to air his views in the US as no one was listening to him in India. (*The Economic Times*, 2017).

Gestures and Language in Everyday Politics

With the background outlined above in mind, three visual features are especially foregrounded in our data: first, Gandhi (INC) and his cousin, Varun Gandhi (BJP), although belonging to warring political parties, invariably dress down, with a preference for homespun black and white clothing; second, their joint-palm Namaste, essential parts of 'opening' and 'closing' interactional sequences in Indian politics, are modestly held close to their bodies; third, their families, especially their mothers, are often part of their public photographic record.

In contrast, politicians like Yogi Adityanath and Navjot Singh Sidhu tend to dress in eye-catching saffrons and blues; their Namaste is directed outward from the body or up in front of the face; and their families hardly

ever feature in their public appearances. Rahul Gandhi's and Yogi
Adityanath's hand gestures arguably reinforce these impressions of under-
played modesty versus overstated flamboyance in dress and stance.

The analysis of the three most common gestures Gandhi used
(expressed as a percentage of gestures used) is based on sixty-two photographs taken while he delivered a single public speech:

> **Both hands together/clasped:** This gesture is supposed to show a state
> of mind that seeks to reduce or contain conflict in a potentially tense
> social situation (24 per cent).
>
> **Hand purse:** In the 'hand purse', the tips of all five digits are brought
> together until they touch in a tight circle, like the mouth of a string-
> closed purse. This is usually used to emphasise a particular point and
> to weigh an argument (19 per cent).
>
> **Palm back:** This reflects an attempt to embrace an idea, often abstract,
> to encompass the concept under discussion, or to pull the other
> person metaphorically closer to the speaker (18 per cent).

None of these three gestures, which together make up 61 per cent of
Gandhi's gestural repertoire, are deemed to be aggressive. They certainly
do not belong to the 'fight' end of the gestural system.

Adityanath's gestural stances once again show a predominance of three
gestures. However, his favourite gestures are strikingly different from
Gandhi's. In his case, we have the following: **Raised forefinger** (49 per cent);
Palm front (20 per cent); and **Tight Fist** (20 per cent). These gestures, which
together make up 89 per cent of Adityanath's repertoire, are visibly more
belligerent, emphasising his fighting Hindu nationalist stance.

A similar pattern of contrast is apparent when we look at the pattern of
the top ten words used in Rahul Gandhi's speeches featured on the INC
site versus Yogi Adityanath's (Mr Gandhi first):

> system, go, people, party, country, question, want, thing, Congress, power
>
> Uttar Pradesh, country, Gorakhpur, house, develop, year, people, said,
> Prime Minister, govern.

The word 'country', so important to nationalist discourse, appears in the
speeches of both young politicians, but it is obvious that Rahul Gandhi's
canvas is far less 'localised'. Statistically, Gandhi's preference is for abstract
nouns, such as 'people', whereas Yogi Adityanath deliberately roots himself
in the Uttar Pradesh 'Hindu Heartland' of Gorakhpur. Perhaps the most
striking feature that differentiates Rahul Gandhi's public persona from

both Modi's and Adityanath's is his propensity for one-on-one conversations rather than speeches. Indeed, he has been subject to much criticism for choosing to be a 'television anchor' during the COVID-19 crisis by actually interviewing scientists and eminent public figures on the subject, rather than making his own public statements. This move is seen as odd for a leading politician and a self-inflicted diminishment of his political stature; it is also in stark contrast to Modi, who hardly ever grants interviews and certainly would never interview others.

Such a politically marked penchant for projecting 'ordinariness' was apparent even in Gandhi's earliest interviews, where he distinctly wants to change places with his interviewer:

RG. *The real question is what I am doing sitting here... you are a journalist, when you were small you must have said to yourself I want to do something, you decided to become a journalist at some point, why did you do that?*
INTERVIEWER: *You are asking me the question.*
RG: *Yes, I am asking you a question, it is a conversation.*

Here, we observe a clear conversational move by Gandhi aimed at reducing the status difference between him and the interviewer. His use of conversational hedges such as 'I mean', preceding his hesitant assertions that he has no special status as a witness, also appears to reduce his authority. In terms of content, Rahul Gandhi, when interviewed, unlike Modi or Adityanath, stresses his and others' emotional vulnerability. The following three themes are emphasised:

1. His feeling that family tragedy has beset him throughout, causing great suffering but, at the same time, bestowing on him the virtues of endurance and emotional understanding: *'All I saw when I was small after my grandmother died was my father in constant combat with the system in India and then I saw him die actually. In my life I have seen my grandmother die, I have seen my father die, I have seen my grandmother go to jail and I have actually been through a tremendous amount of pain as a child. When these things happen to you, what I had to be scared of I lost, [so] there is absolutely nothing I am scared of. I have an aim, I have a clear aim in my mind and the aim is that I do not like what I see in Indian politics, it is something that is inside my heart'.*

2. His solidarity with the poor, which places him among the common people and strengthens his own and his party's identification with the victimised, including women and unemployed youth: *'Our party believes that women should be empowered, democracy should go to every house'.*

3. His desire to stay out of the limelight and be an ordinary party worker, without capitalising on his pedigree: *'[I] have done a little media interaction... [the] bulk of my focus has been on internal party work and that's where I have been concentrating, that is where most of my energy was going'.*

Rahul Gandhi's interviews share these features in common with his 'high-born' cousin, Varun Gandhi from the opposing BJP. Their narratives stress a shared family inheritance where the 'right to ordinariness' has been cruelly denied. The irony of being dynasts in both Rahul and Varun Gandhi's cases is that they embody 'tellability', yet are condemned to conveying the 'banality' of their narratives. Both have struggled to create national narratives of ordinariness using a simple menu of words, gesture and dress to counteract the story of their privileged birth. Each asserts repeatedly that it is precisely his privilege that drives him to serve the most ordinary of people; each points out that he is the innocent victim of generations of tragedy. It is exactly this 'subject positioning', however, that seems to inhibit their growth as political beings. Despite their appeals to 'democracy', the strategies they use to downplay themselves are seen by the public to be intrinsically undemocratic, owing to the familial narrative of their birth. They are thus never freed to be 'extraordinary'. As a result, the Indian public appears to show little empathy for them, often categor-ising them as 'weak' and 'unworthy' of the positions they occupy. In short, Rahul Gandhi, like his cousin Varun, seems caught in an inescapable rhetorical double-bind defined by the narrative of his high birth.

On the other hand, Yogi Adityanath, who rose 'from below', cannot, it appears, afford to be 'banal' at any cost. Like Modi, he is eye-catching in dress and gesture, 'fearlessly' disruptive and often politically incorrect in his speeches, for example (*Hindustan Times*, 2017):

1. *I will not stop till I turn UP and India into a Hindu Rashtra.* (Etah, UP in 2005)
2. *On 'Love Jihad': If one Hindu girl is converted, we will convert 100 Muslim girls.* (See above)
3. *Mother Teresa was part of a conspiracy to evangelise India. Hindus were converted in the name of doing service.* (Basti, UP in July, 2016)

Unlike the 'dynasts' Rahul and Varun Gandhi, Yogi Adityanath and Navjot Singh Sidhu stay in the news by being perennially provocative in their words and flamboyant in their gestures. Yet, despite the outrageous-ness of the things they say – in a manner sometimes reminiscent of Donald

Trump or Boris Johnson – a seemingly indulgent public has repeatedly returned them to power. Adityanath has made a career out of being virulently 'anti-Muslim', but has been 'rewarded' by being made the Chief Minister of UP, India's most politically powerful state. As the head of a leading 'math' or Hindu temple organisation, he has enormous independent influence – and knows it. Likewise, as an international level cricketer, Sidhu has huge media and crowd appeal of which he is also aware. He has moved in and out of both the BJP and the Congress, seeking major political advantage, yet is embraced by both parties. Both these politicians stress their local rather than national moorings and their uniqueness as religious and sports leaders in their own right. The 'entitled' Rahul or Varun Gandhi cannot ever hope to enter this gladiatorial space.

Towards a Typology of Gesture Based on Political Displays

On the basis of the data presented above on political appearances, there appears enough empirical support to postulate a 'simplest systematics of gesture' here, following on from previous work on a 'simplest systematics of talk' by Sacks, Schegloff and Jefferson (1974). To reiterate, in their classic paper, the main focus was on analysing the finely coordinated turn-taking in interactions among 'ordinary' people observable in private tape recordings. In the present research, the focus of analysis was, rather, on observing the fine-tuned coordination of gesture with speech in the talk interactions of 'extraordinary' people (politicians) on the basis of public video recordings. In this respect, it was the internalised 'cognitive' coordination of talk and gesture in a single individual as oriented toward the audience that was of central concern.

Given the rubric above, some points are shared in all human social interactions (see Table 9.1, points numbered 1, 2, 6, 8, 9 and 10), but the current study of Indian political behaviour found some evidence for the following (as indicated on the right-hand side of Table 9.1):

Gesture preference: There is a clear preference for just three–four gestures out of a range of thirteen gestures examined for each of the young politicians in our study, comprising 50–60 per cent of their gestures. Such a preference for two or three favourite 'fight' gestures was found in the study of Modi as well as in relation to the **second hypothesis** (see Table 9.1; points 3, 4, 5, 7 and 14).

Gesture type: There is a clear difference in the type of gestures used by politicians with a political pedigree (Rahul and Varun Gandhi), in

Table 9.1. *A 'simplest systematics' framework for ordinary interactional gestures.*

Sacks, Schegloff & Jefferson (1974): systematics of speech	Nair, 2017: systematics of gesture
1. Speaker change recurs or, at least, occurs.	1. Gesture change recurs or, at least, occurs.
2. Overwhelmingly, one party talks at a time.	2. Overwhelmingly, one gesture occurs at a time.
3. Occurrences of more than one speaker at a time are common but brief.	3. Gestures almost always accompany speech and only occur briefly, if at all, in isolation.
4. Transitions (from one turn to the next) with no gap and no overlap are common. Together with transitions characterised by a slight gap or slight overlap, they make up the vast majority of transitions.	4. Typically, gestures show a 'preference' for one hand over the other (right versus left).
5. Turn order is not fixed, but varies.	5. Among individuals, a clear preference for three or four types of gestures and facial expressions over available others can be detected.
6. Turn size is not fixed, but varies.	
7. Length of conversation is not specified in advance.	6. Transitions from one gesture to another are common and vary across a specified range of facial and hand gestures. These can be coded and make up the vast majority of transitions.
8. What parties say is not specified in advance.	
9. Relative distribution of time is not specified in advance.	7. Gestures unrelated to speech occur, e.g. brushing away a fly.
10. Number of parties can vary.	8. Gestures have a fixed duration.
11. Talk can be continuous or discontinuous.	9. Gesture orders are not fixed but vary.
12. Turn allocation techniques are obviously used.	10. Gestures' numbers are not fixed but vary.
13. A current speaker may select a next speaker (as when s/he addresses a question to another party), or parties may self-select, in starting to talk.	11. Gestures' speeds are not fixed but vary often according to the speaker's affect.
14. Various 'turn construction units' are employed; e.g. turns can be projectedly one word long, or they can be sentential in length.	12. The gestures parties use are not specified in advance but can partially be predicted from the genre of discourse.
15. Repair mechanisms exist for dealing with turn-taking errors and violations, e.g., if two parties find themselves talking at the same time, one will stop prematurely, thus repairing the trouble.	13. There is a coordinated match between the genre of speech/discourse, the words chosen and the accompanying facial and hand gestures.
	14. Various 'gesture construction units' are used.
	15. Repair mechanisms exist to correct mismatches in coordination between speech and gesture.

contrast to politicians with a non-political background (Yogi Adityanath and Navjot Sidhu). The former use gesture types that are markedly non-aggressive while the latter use highly aggressive 'fight' gestures. This seems to lead to a public inference that the former are politically 'ordinary' and only privileged by birth (see Table 9.1, points 11 and 12). This also relates to the **second hypothesis.**

Gesture culture: There is clear evidence that there are/could be gestures in political space that are culturally specific/unique, e.g., the 'Namaste' (see point 14).

Gesture style: Some individuals may display a stance not in the common repertoire of political gestures: for example, Rahul Gandhi's 'handclasp' gesture is rare and appears special to him (see points 5 and 11).

Gesture and speech coordination: In contrast to the deliberate, eye-catching gestures of Modi and Adityanath, the 'dynastic' cousins Rahul and Varun Gandhi were judged to be uncoordinated in their use of gestures and speech, leading also to the inference that they were politically unschooled and 'ordinary'. This point relates to the **first** and **third hypotheses** concerning impressions left on the public mind of the strongly polarising effect of performances by more aggressive leaders (see points 13 and 15).

In consonance with Fetzer and Weizman (2017), this research supports the idea that there is now another 'uncoupling of space and time' that enables the 'construction of ordinariness' as 'a public endeavour' (p. 88). The lens I have looked through in this chapter is political discourse as it is assimilated by large local and national publics through the new media, where 'mass technologies' such as smart phones and other recording devices have put the ability to record scenarios, gestures and other accompaniments directly into the hands of ordinary people. Such developments seem to have significantly reduced the distance between public and private power, ordinariness and extraordinariness, and, ultimately, between self and other in ways that cannot but have long term effects on the democratisation, not excluding the divisive polarisation, of political space.

Going back to Shakespeare at the end of this chapter, we may recall that, in A Midsummer Night's Dream – set in the city of Athens, the classical seat of Western democracy, the fairy Puck boasts that he can 'put a girdle round the earth in forty minutes'. It was, however, well understood by the audience of that age that space and time could never in fact be 'coupled' in the absurd way Puck suggested, except through magical means. Today, the inconspicuous handheld technology of the mobile phone has ensured that, what was once pure make-believe, is now part of our everyday lived reality. It is almost as if humankind has grown an extra limb in the past couple of decades – not quite Puck's fairy wings perhaps, yet still an appendage that most, especially the young of the species, find increasingly hard to survive without. Becoming stressed when mobiles, storehouses of memory, secrets and knowledge, as well as powerhouses of communication, are even temporarily lost or damaged now seems a generic cross-cultural experience – as Darwin might perhaps have suggested.

A main function of this 'additional limb' appears to be that it informs our perceptions of intimacy, distance and group belonging, e.g., which leaders we implicitly 'follow' and those from whom we must morally and affectively distance ourselves. It is not uncommon, for instance, for our personal mobile phones to ring and for us to hear the voice of Prime Minister Modi himself performing such familiar speech acts as greeting, advising, promising, directing and reassuring, once again cognitively reducing the perceived distance between his elevated stature and our ordinary selves. Like the wearing of Modi Masks at physical mass rallies – somewhat similar to Trump's 'Make America Great Again' hats – these virtual gestures convey closely shared affects that could well influence political voting behaviour, depending on which leader and which party is most effective at such distance-erasing mass communication (see Verma and Barthwal, 2020; Nair, 2020b). Interestingly, Modi and Trump appeared together at major 'friendly' venues in both democracies: notably at the 'Howdy Modi' mega-event at the NRG Stadium in Houston, Texas, in September 2019; and the similar 'Namaste Trump' rally held at the Montera Stadium in Modi's home base of Ahmedabad, Gujarat, in February 2020. After this latter event, President Trump commented on his return to the United States of America that he would 'never be excited again about a crowd after going to India' and witnessing the huge crowd sizes that his counterpart, Prime Minister Modi, a 'great guy, loved by the people of India', could summon up.

The phrase 'social distancing' became an essential part of the vocabulary of global culture during the COVID-19 pandemic, while academic studies of embodied proxemics date back to Hall (1966). Yet, the regulation of what one might call 'virtual distancing' via 'viral' mobile-phone usage is, surprisingly, a less remarked on phenomenon – although its cognitive influence could be enormous. In its radical resetting of hitherto well-established boundaries between ephemeral speech and authoritative writing (see Biber, 1988; Nair, 2008, 2015) via forms like the tweet and SMS; between the sensory modalities of hearing, touch and sight; between far flung geographical locations; and, most importantly for the purposes of this chapter, between politicians and their 'followers' – who can monitor and record, as well as assess and discuss, leaders' activities almost as soon as these events unfold – the mobile phone as an all-purpose technological device is unparalleled in human history. In this chapter, I have specifically suggested that the mobile phone can be a research tool in the hands of ordinary citizens, thereby, not only reducing the distance between politicians and their publics, but also between academic ivory towers and the 'unruly' world that lies without.

Acknowledgements

I must record my great debt to Dr Snehlata Jaswal, experimental psychologist and colleague, a conversation with whom initiated this research, as well as to Anita Fetzer and Elda Weizman for inviting me to be on the International Pragmatics Association (IPrA) panel on 'Ordinariness and the Media' at the biannual International Conference in Belfast hosted by Ulster University in July 2017. Discussions with Amit Bhaya, Professor of Electrical Engineering at the Federal University of Rio de Janeiro, on the intricate interconnections between technological and sociopolitical changes on a mass scale proved highly rewarding.

I am very grateful to my wonderfully enthusiastic undergraduate students Ashish Ranjan, Adarsh Prasad, Ashutosh Chugh and Anshul Toshniwal, not to mention my ever-reliable research assistants Sakshi Oberoi and Chandrika Panday. My graduate and undergraduate students helped selflessly in the framing, distribution and collation of our online questionnaires and databases. They are: Shuvi, Sakshi, Nikunj, Mahashu, Piyush, Annie, Srividya, Nivida, Sanchita, Dipti, Shweta, Priyanka, Sugandh Ashraf, Ayurdhi and Vasundhara, all essential contributors to this cooperative project. Finally, I thank Satish Padmanabhan and *Outlook* magazine for publishing an early version of this chapter, for their kind support and for the use of their professional graphics.

REFERENCES

Austin, J. L. (1962). *How to do things with words.* Oxford, UK: Oxford University Press.
Biber, D. (1988). *Variations across speech and writing.* Cambridge, UK: Cambridge University Press.
Church, R. B., Alibali, M. W. and Kelly, S. D. (Eds.). (2017). *Why gesture? How the hands function in speaking, thinking and communicating.* Philadelphia, PA: John Benjamins. https://doi.org/10.1075/gs.7

Corballis, M. (2002). *From hand to mouth*. Princeton: Princeton University Press.

Cartmill, E. A., Beilock, S. and Goldin-Meadow, S. A (2012). Word in the hand: Action, gesture, and mental representation in human evolutions. *Philosophical Transaction of the Royal Society, Series B*, 367, 129–143.

Darwin, C. (1872). *The expression of the emotions in man and animals*. London: J. Murray.

De Stefani, E. and De Marco, D. (2019). Language, gesture, and emotional communication: An embodied view of social interaction. Frontiers in Psychology, 10, 2063.

Dopson, W. G., Beckwith, B. E., Tucker, D. M. and Bullard-Bates, P. C. (1984). Asymmetry of facial expression in spontaneous emotion. *Cortex*, 20(2), 243–251.

Ekman, P. (2003a). *Emotions revealed: Understanding faces and feelings*. London: Weidenfeld and Nicholson.

(2003b) Darwin, deception, and facial expression. *Annals of the New York Academy of Sciences,* 1000, 205–221.

Fetzer, A. and Weizman, E. (2018). 'What I would say to John and everyone like John is. . .': The construction of ordinariness through quotations in mediated political discourse. *Discourse & Society,* 29(5), 495–513. https://doi.org/10.1177/0957926518770259

Fetzer, A, and Weizman, E. (2017). Panel on 'Ordinariness and the Media' at the International Pragmatics Association (IPrA) Conference, hosted by Ulster University, Belfast.

Givens, D. B. and Whyte, J. (2020). *The nonverbal dictionary of gestures, signs and body gestures cues*. Spokane, Washington, DC: Center for Nonverbal Studies Press.

Goldin-Meadow, S. (2003). *Hearing gesture: How our hands help us think*. Cambridge, MA.: Harvard University Press.

Graddol, D. (2004). The future of language. *Science, Special Issue: Evolution of Language*, 303, 1329–1331.

Hall, E. T. (1966). *The hidden dimension*. New York: Anchor Books.

Hindustan Times (2017). From love jihad, conversion to SRK: 10 controversial comments by UP's new CM Yogi Adityanath. 6 April.

Jablonka, E., Ginsburg, S. and Dor, D. (2012). The co-evolution of language and emotions. *Philosophical Transactions of The Royal Society B Biological Sciences*, 367(1599), 2152–2159.

Labov, W. (1972). *Language in the inner city: Studies in the black English vernacular*. Philadelphia: Pennsylvania University Press.

Levinson, S. C. (1983). *Pragmatics*. Cambridge, UK: Cambridge University Press.

Mandal, M. K. and Singh, S. K. (1990). Lateral asymmetry in identification and expression of facial emotions. *Cognition and Emotion*, 4, 61–70.

Matsumoto, D. and Hwang, H. C. (2018). Microexpressions Differentiate Truths from Lies about Future Malicious Intent. *Frontiers in Psychology*, December. https://doi.org/10.3389/fpsyg.2018.02545

McNeill, J. (2002). *Language and gesture*. Cambridge, UK: Cambridge University Press.

Mehrabian, A. (1981). *Silent messages: Implicit communication of emotions and attitudes* (2nd ed.). Belmont, California: Wadsworth.

Morris, D. (2013). *People watching: The Desmond Morris guide to body language* (Revised Edition). London: Vintage.

Nair, R. B. (2021). Language: Editor in Chief? Seminar, Special issue on 'Editing history', 743, 81–88. Available at: india-seminar.com/2021/743/743_rukmini_bhaya_nair.htm

(2020a). Figuring it out: Old modes and new codes for multimodality, technology and creative performativity in 21st century India. In L. Hidalgo Downing and B. Kraljevic Mujic (Eds.), *Performing Metaphorical Creativity* (pp. 311–342). Amsterdam: John Benjamins.

(2020b). *Keywords for India: A conceptual lexicon for the 21st century* (Ed. with P. deSouza) London: Bloomsbury Academic.

(2019). Epithymetics: The psychology of desire. In G. Misra (Ed.), *Annual review of Indian psychology: Vol 1. Cognitive and affective processes* (pp. 204–270). Oxford and New Delhi: Oxford University Press, supported by the Indian Council of Social Sciences Research (ICSSR).

(2018). Intending to mean, pretending to be: Reflections on the limits on genre. In R. Page, B. Busse and N. Nørgaard (Eds.), *Rethinking language, text and context: Interdisciplinary research in stylistics in honour of Michael Toolan* (pp. 147–163). New York: Routledge, https://doi.org/10.4324/9781351183222

(2017). Famous politicians, infamous progeny: Being ordinary onscreen when you are a dynastic heir apparent in the Indian context, Conference Paper (unpublished) at Panel 'Constructing Ordinariness across Media Genres', fifteenth International Pragmatics Conference, Belfast, July.

(2015). Virtue, virtuosity and the virtual: Experiments in the contemporary Indian English novel. In U. Anjaria (Ed.), *The history of the Indian novel in English*. Cambridge, UK: Cambridge University Press.

(2008). Language and youth culture. In Kachru, B. B., Kachru, Y. and Sridhar, S. N. (Eds.) *Language in South Asia*. Cambridge, UK: Cambridge University Press.

(2003). The Aesthetics of the ordinary: Evoking narrative wonder within the linear grammar of modernity. In *Evam: Forum on Indian Representations* 2, Vols. 1 & 2, January, pp. 266–288.

(2002). *Narrative gravity: Conversation, cognition, culture*. New Delhi and Oxford: Oxford University Press.

Nakahashi, W. (2017). Cultural sexual selection in monogamous human populations. *Royal Society Open Science*. Available at: https://doi.org/10.1098/rsos.160946

Noroozi, F., Kaminska, D., Corneanu, C., Sapinski, T., Escalera, S. and Anbarjafari, G. (2018). Survey on Emotional Body Gesture Recognition'.

In IEEE Transactions on Affective Computing, doi: 10.1109/TAFFC.2018.2874986

Nussbaum, M. (2013). *Political Emotions.* Massachusetts: Harvard University Press.

Pascalis, O., de Martin de Viviés, X., Anzures, G., Quinn, P. C., Slater, A. M., Tanaka, J. W. and Lee, K. (2011). Development of face processing. *Wiley Interdisciplinary Reviews. Cognitive science,* 2(6), 666–675.

Pavlov, I. P. (1927). *Conditioned reflexes: An investigation of the physiological activity of the cerebral cortex.* Translated and Edited by G. V. Anrep. London: Oxford University Press.

Penfield W. (1961). Activation of the record of human experience: Summary of the Lister oration delivered at the Royal College of Surgeons of England on 27th April 1961. *Annals of the Royal College of Surgeons of England,* 29(2), 77–84.

Press Trust of India (2017). Dynasty in democracy is 'nasty': Venkaiah Naidu. 15 September. Accessed at: www.hindustantimes.com/india-news/dynasty-in-democracy-is-nasty-venkaiah-naidu/story-n7Ab7JnfHNm9aVEpfpjerM.html.

Sacks, H., Schegloff, E. and Jefferson, G. (1974). A simplest systematics for the organization of turn-taking for conversation. *Language,* 50(4), 696–735. doi:10.2307/412243

Sacks, H. (1984). Notes on methodology. In J. Maxwell Atkinson and J. Heritage (Eds.), *Structures of social action: Studies of conversation analysis,* (pp. 21–27). Cambridge, UK: Cambridge University Press.

Savalli, U. M. (1995). The evolution of bird coloration and plumage elaboration: A review of hypotheses. *Current Ornithology,* 141–190.

Searle, J. R. (1969) *Speech acts: An essay in the philosophy of language,* Cambridge, UK: Cambridge University Press.

Skinner, B. F. (1947). 'Superstition' in the pigeon. *Journal of Experimental Psychology,* 38, 168–172.

Sterelny, K. (2012). Language, gesture, skill: The co-evolutionary foundations of language. *Philosophical Transactions of the Royal Society B – Biological Sciences.* Available at: https://royalsocietypublishing.org/doi/full/10.1098/rstb.2012.0116

The Economic Times (2017). Rahul Gandhi is a failed politician: Smriti Irani. 13 September. Accessed at: https://economictimes.indiatimes.com/news/politics-and-nation/rahul-gandhi-is-a-failed-politician-smriti-irani/articleshow/60475468.cms?from=mdr.

Tomasello, M., Melis, A. P., Tennie, C., Wyman, E. and Herrmann, E. (2012). Two key steps in the evolution of human cooperation: The Interdependence Hypothesis. *Current Anthropology,* 53(6), 673–692.

Verma, R. and Barthwal, A. (2020). The singular appeal of Narendra Modi explained in six charts. *Mint,* 9th November. Available at: www.livemint.com/news/india/the-singular-appeal-of-narendra-modi-explained-in-six-charts-11604678665561.html. Retrieved 15 November 2020.

CHAPTER 10

Fact or Fiction
Influences on Voter Decision-Making in a Disinformation Environment

David P. Redlawsk, Kyle Mattes and Karol Solís Menco

> For a long time I have not said what I believed, nor do I ever believe
> what I say, and if indeed sometimes I do happen to tell the truth,
> I hide it among so many lies that it is hard to find.
>
> (Niccolo Machiavelli[1])

It can be disturbing whenever political actors take Machiavelli's quote to heart. In today's political environment, this seems to happen regularly. False information abounds; for example, leading up to the 2016 US presidential election, approximately 25 per cent of Americans viewed political news from factually challenged websites (Guess, Nyhan and Reifler, 2017). Perhaps worse, evidence shows that false political news spreads more quickly and more broadly than true information (Vosoughi, Roy and Aral, 2018).

Disinformation is easier to transmit than in the recent past. Voters need not sit back and wait for information to be fed to them, as was the case in the twentieth century broadcast age (Lau et al., 2017), with its focus on mass media: radio, television and traditional print newspapers (Young, 2011). This dynamic has been disrupted by the advent of the Internet era that began in the late twentieth century. Now, voters can and do actively learn about campaigns online and use the information to compare candidates. In doing so, they select the information they wish to see, ultimately leading to concerns about information bubbles and confirmation bias (Redlawsk, Civettini and Emmerson, 2010; Thibodeau et al., 2013; Wason, 1960; Weeks, 2015). Such voters are also prime targets for misinformation.

Concerns about the impact of disinformation, or 'fake news', on voters' preferences and election outcomes are common around the world. This has inspired a considerable amount of research covering a variety of

---

[1] Machiavelli: The Chief Works and Others. 1989. Vol 2, trans. Alan Gilbert. Durham, N.C.: Duke University Press.

countries and elections. For instance, Fraccaroli, Cantarella and Volpe (2019) measure the causal effect of the spread of misinformation on electoral outcomes in the 2018 Italian General Elections. Ema Kušen, and Mark Strembeck (2018) provide a sentiment analysis of the Twitter discussion during the 2016 Austrian presidential elections; one of their main findings was that the followers of the winning candidate substantially engaged in the spread of misinformation.

The best vehicle for misinformation is often a negative campaign. Even though voters prefer positive campaigning (e.g. Lipsitz et al., 2005), negativity is more engaging. To a certain extent, people appear to be 'hardwired' to process and weigh negative information more heavily than positive information (Holbrook et al., 2001; Lau, 1985). This so-called automatic vigilance effect implies that people tend to direct attention toward events that they perceive may have undesirable consequences, so information delivered with a negative content and tone has the power to grab attention easily (Kahneman and Tversky, 1984). The brain's response to negativity is stronger, and negative information is easier to recall and more memorable than positive information (Cacioppo and Gardner, 1999).

Pratto and John (1991) explain that there are good evolutionary reasons for this asymmetry in people's reactions to negative stimuli, as the events that represent a danger to the individual often require an immediate response and the costs of failing to respond (potentially death) are much worse than the costs of an inappropriate response (delaying some positive outcome). Therefore, there is an adaptive and survival advantage for those individuals capable of identifying and responding faster to undesirable stimuli; effectively, we are 'wired' to notice the negative, which perhaps makes negative advertising more effective than positive advertisements.

Negativity in the context of politics is not intrinsically bad, nor are voters necessarily against its use (Mattes and Redlawsk, 2014). Studies show that, while negativity factors into voters' decisions (Fiorina and Shepsle, 1989; Holbrook et al., 2001; Kernell, 1977; Lau, 1985), there is no 'by–default' effect of 'going negative' (Lau et al., 1999; with Lee and Rovner, 2007). The impact of negativity on candidate evaluations is predominantly contextual and election specific.

Nonetheless, even for those who believe negativity has its place, it is difficult to make a case in support of disinformation campaigns, whether negative or not, since they undermine electoral accountability. Fortunately, US-based voters who seek the truth have a readily available resource: external fact-checkers such as Politifact and the *Washington Post*. Non-US fact-checkers have also arisen; for example, FactCheckEU fact-checked the May 2019 EU elections. External fact-checking 'consists of publishing an evidence-based analysis of the accuracy of a political claim, news report, or other public text' (Graves and Amazeen, 2019). The role of fact-checks is to try to set the record straight.

How much, if at all, do fact-check results affect voting decisions? There is some evidence that fact-checks affect voter behaviour and attitudes. They have been shown to affect readers' factual beliefs (Pingree, Brossard and McLeod, 2014), and readers of fact-checks have more knowledge of certain observable characteristics (Gottfried et al., 2013; Nyhan and Reifler, 2015). According to Gottfried et al. (2013), consumers of fact-checking sites tend to be consumers of a greater amount of news media, and in their study 'had more basic campaign knowledge, were more educated, identified as less conservative, identified less as Hispanic or Black, and were younger' (p. 1564). They also knew more about candidates' stands on issues or about general background facts of the election than those who do not consume fact-checking sites.

Citizens will heed factual information, even when such information challenges their partisan and ideological commitments (Wood and Porter, 2019), however, they must perceive the fact-checker as competent and credible (Amazeen, 2015). This latter point can be a serious limitation. Decision-makers, usually elected officials, perceive biased advisers as more informative sources (Calvert, 1985). Similarly, voters are more willing to consider fact-checks in the first place when they believe that their interests and the source's interests align (Berinsky, 2017; Swire et al., 2017).

Fact-checkers undoubtedly have a difficult wall to climb to get the right type of attention. False facts are resilient in the minds of voters, and misinformation is difficult to correct (Thorson, 2015). Even with new factual information, partisans engage in motivated reasoning – the tendency to hold on to existing evaluations even when challenged – so they have a tendency to reject inconvenient truths (Redlawsk, 2002; Redlawsk et al., 2010; Taber and Lodge, 2006). Thus, despite its potential, and some evidence that the process sometimes works, fact-checking may fail to reduce misperceptions, especially among those who are most predisposed to believe false information (Lewandowsky et al., 2012; Nyhan and Reifler, 2012). Even worse, some studies find a backfire effect (Nyhan and Reifler, 2010; Nyhan, Reifler and Ubel, 2013), in which counter-attitudinal material actually enhances misperceptions. Thus, as Jarman (2016) argues, fact-check analysis may be unlikely to result in significant attitude change.

Why these contradictory results? A methodological limitation of many fact-check studies is that they require participants to read fact-checking messages they would otherwise not choose to consume. The literature on political polarisation and selective exposure casts doubt on the assumption that partisans seek out content that challenges their views; fact-check results are shared within social networks selectively, so fact-checks that confirm existing beliefs are more likely encountered in the real world (Shin and Thorson, 2017). Conceivably, even just one favourable fact-check could assuage a candidate's more entrenched supporters.

We addressed this source of contradiction here by examining the role of negativity and fact-checking in the context of a primary election where study participants were allowed to choose both the information they received and whether to view a fact-check on that information. Using a controlled experiment, we simulated a presidential primary where, before voting, voters learned about candidates whose statements might be true or false. Apart from the disinformation environment, the key difference from other studies is participants' ability to make choices that reflect what information is salient for them, much like they would in the real world. This allows us to ask, when provided with the opportunity to pick and choose what to learn, what would voters prefer to learn? What information matters to voters, and to what degree are they interested in investigating whether that information is accurate?

Data and Methods

Research Design

We make use of Lau and Redlawsk's (2006) Dynamic Process Tracing Environment (DPTE, www.processtracing.org; Andersen, Redlawsk and Lau, 2019) to deploy an online experiment designed to learn how voters react to negativity and fact-checks. Following a brief questionnaire designed to capture political attitudes and demographic information, participants saw a hypothetical presidential primary campaign in which two candidates competed to win their party's nomination for a forthcoming general election. Participants could choose between voting in the Republican or Democratic primary. Available candidate information was created by the researchers to be typical of candidates within a participant's party. Our goal was to make the candidates in the primary seem realistic across a range of issues and personal characteristics. Candidates were all male, white and of a similar age, in order to minimise the impacts of any of these potential confounding variables. The campaign was designed to pit a candidate choosing a positive strategy against a candidate using a negative campaign.

Each of the 276 participants was presented with a total of twenty-five separate screens, one at a time, with 'headlines' from which they could choose to learn something about the candidates. Screens showed either two, four or six competing headlines depending on the screen, evenly divided between the two candidates. By the end of the campaign, participants learned twenty-five pieces of information, one per screen, across both candidates in whatever proportion a participant selected. The headline could suggest an issue position (e.g. 'Judson's Position on Social Security Reform'), personal information ('Judson Attacks Opponent's Lack of Experience') or a generic political statement ('Judson: I will restore the American Dream'). Participants clicked on one of the headlines, which then revealed detailed information about the headline they had chosen.

In addition, every fifth screen presented a set of 'distractor' headlines to provide some relief from a constant barrage of screens pitting positive and negative statements against each other (please see below). Distractors were headlines like 'Charles Judson Attends Farmers' Market' and, as with generic items, they were not subject to being fact-checked.

The headline screens were presented in a fixed sequence, representing five different rhetorical comparisons often made by candidates using Mattes and Redlawsk's (2014) typology: 1) a candidate directly attacks the opponent, 2) the candidates express disagreement, 3) a candidate states that his position/trait is better than the other's, 4) a candidate calls the opponent inconsistent and 5) a candidate 'talks about' his opponent. More detail on the specific items used can be found in Mattes and Redlawsk (2020). For the analysis reported here, the rhetorical approaches are combined rather than analysed individually.

There were five information screens presented for each of the five rhetorical approaches. Within each rhetorical approach, headlines were presented in the following sequence:

> Screen 1: One previously unseen issue topic (two headlines, one for each candidate)
> Screen 2: Two previously unseen issue topics (four headlines, two for each candidate)
> Screen 3: One previously unseen distractor topic (two headlines, one for each candidate)
> Screen 4: One previously unseen personal topic, and the previously seen issue topic NOT selected on screen 2, for a total of two topics (four headlines, two for each candidate)
> Screen 5: One previously unseen generic topic, and the remaining previously seen topic NOT selected from screens 2 and 4, for a total of two topics (four headlines, two for each candidate).

Within an issue, personal or generic topic, the headlines were always presented as competing, with one candidate taking a positive position and the other a negative (or comparative) position. For example, there would

Figure 10.1   Item detail for 'Price Attacks Opponent on Abortion' (Democratic Primary).

be a choice between the headlines 'Thompson's Position on Abortion' and 'Price Attacks Opponent on Abortion'. Participants had a choice of selecting information on twenty out of the twenty-five screens (i.e. all but the distractor screens) between one or more positive statements by one candidate and one or more negative statements by the other.

When participants clicked on a headline to open it, a new screen appeared with a short statement about the issue, personal, generic or distractor item (Figure 10.1). A 'Close' button was available to click when the participant had finished reading the item. Upon closing the detailed information screen, a new screen appeared asking if the participant wished to 'keep' the item to review it immediately before voting.

In the study instructions, participants were told that, across the entire campaign, they could only 'keep' up to six items for review prior to the vote. The system updated the number of 'keeps' already chosen and reported this total when asking if the participant wished to keep the current item. If the participant had already chosen to keep six items, the 'keep' question was no longer presented. In the analysis below, we use the 'keep' choices of participants to provide an unobtrusive measure of information importance or salience. A system programming error allowed

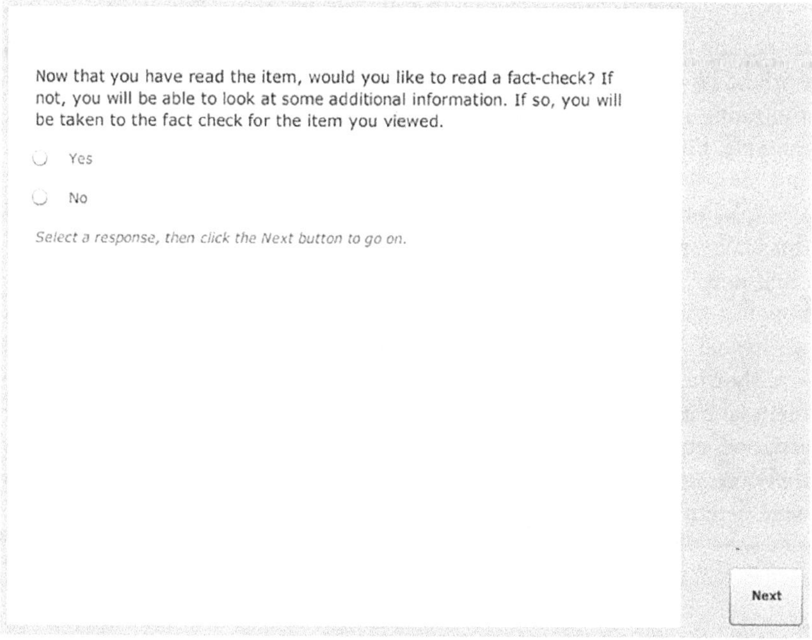

Now that you have read the item, would you like to read a fact-check? If not, you will be able to look at some additional information. If so, you will be taken to the fact check for the item you viewed.

○ Yes

○ No

Select a response, then click the Next button to go on.

Next

Figure 10.2   Fact-check request.

a total of 21 out of the 272 participants that completed the study to keep seven items instead of six. To adjust for this, we dropped the last item kept by those participants, thus including the six items that participants decided to keep having known the expected limit from the beginning.

Following the 'keep' decision, participants were given the opportunity to view a 'fact-check' of the information they had just read, though only for issue and personal items (Figure 10.2). Distractor items could not be fact-checked, nor could generic statements, since the latter were simply broad statements lacking any details (e.g. 'If I'm so fortunate as to be elected, I will immediately start working on fixing things'). The fact-checks were designed for the purpose of the study and were short and simple statements about whether what the candidate expressed was true or false. While all participants had to view distractor items, choosing a generic item was optional. The actual maximum number of fact-checks available to a participant ranged from fifteen (if all five generic topics had been chosen) to twenty (if no generic topics had been chosen). There were no other limits to requesting fact-checks, although it is possible a participant's desire to shorten the experiment could have been an incentive to avoid the fact-checking options.

Participants could not determine the result of the fact-check without requesting it. By design, each contained limited information: a source and a verdict. To increase the impact of our fact-check results, we used the names and rating systems of real organisations who provide fact-check ratings. For example, PolitiFact is known to rate a campaign statement as 'Pants on Fire!' and the *Washington Post* would similarly assign four 'Pinocchios'. For example, one of our possible fact-check results read: 'Politifact examined this claim and has determined that it is completely inaccurate. They have rated it as "Pants on Fire!"' We varied the intensity of the verdict to reflect how fact-checkers use distinctions such as 'somewhat false'. In our analysis, we treated any verdict labelling a candidate's statement true (e.g. 'true' or 'mostly true') as confirming and any verdict labelling the candidate's statement false as disconfirming. The fact-check results presented were randomly assigned, equally likely to either confirm or disconfirm the items to which they were attached. Participants were not made aware that fact-check results were determined by random assignment.

Experimental Procedure

A total of 276 participants, 58.6 per cent male with a mean age of 34, were recruited through Amazon's Mechanical Turk Service and completed the study.[2] Participants were required to be US citizens and of eighteen years of age or older. After participants clicked on the task request, they were directed to the DPTE study page where consent was obtained.

Then, participants were shown some basic instructions and asked to choose a party primary in which to participate; 64.5 per cent chose the Democratic primary, while 35.5 per cent chose the Republican primary. The study followed with a questionnaire designed to elicit basic demographic and attitudinal data, including political interest, ideology, partisanship, approval of President Obama, and 2012 and 2016 presidential vote preferences. Participants were then instructed about how the campaign would proceed, including an explanation of the 'keep' and 'fact-check' process. They were given basic biographical information about the fictitious candidates, including their pictures; the pictures also appeared with the headlines to help participants remember which candidate was which.

---

[2] Mattes and Redlawsk (2020) provide additional detail on the study design and participants. Much of the data and methods sections of this chapter are derived from this article. (The study can be examined online from the perspective of a participant at http://bit.ly/2vqvZyS. A browser with the latest version of Flash installed is required and pop-up blockers need to be turned off.)

After exposure to the campaign material, participants were shown the headlines corresponding to the information they had chosen to keep for review. Participants had up to one minute to re-familiarise themselves with the information, by clicking on any headlines to get the statements they wished to review. A countdown clock on the screen displayed the remaining time, and a participant could move on to the vote whenever ready, even before the time expired. If no items had been selected to keep, this section of the study was skipped.

Next, participants were required to vote for one of the candidates, as they could not abstain. Immediately afterwards, they answered an open-ended question about the reason for their vote choice and gave each candidate a favourability rating using a 0–100 'feeling' thermometer scale. Following this, participants were asked to judge how 'negative' each candidate's campaign was on a 1–10 scale and respond to four emotion questions for each candidate. The questions asked whether the candidate, 'because of the kind of person he is or because of something he did, made the participant feel' anger, anxiety, contempt and enthusiasm; the emotions were presented in random order. Finally, participants completed another short questionnaire asking key questions about candidate competence, negative campaigning, trust in media and the types of candidate statements voters found most useful. They were then debriefed, and the study ended. On average, participants required 28.5 minutes to complete the study and were paid $3 for their time.

Results

We found that, in our campaign environment, participants preferred positive information to negative, but ultimately considered negative information to be more salient. They were quite interested in fact-checking, especially for any type of information salient to them. When voting, respondents penalised candidates who were relentlessly negative and/or were frequently found (via fact-checks) to have made false statements.

Use of the Keep and Fact-Check Options

As explained above, the 'keep' option is our measure of topic salience for each individual voter. As such, these 'keep' decisions inform our discussion about what is relevant for voters and how the presentation of information impacts voters' decisions. This, of course, assumes that our respondents chose to keep anything at all. This action was not mandatory and might have been viewed as an impediment to completing the study quickly; or perhaps the campaign information we provided was simply not interesting enough to keep!

In general, the 'keep' option was frequently used by participants, with only 12.7 per cent of 276 participants deciding not to take this option. Thus, 87.3 per cent kept at least one item and, on average, participants kept 4.65 items. In fact, the majority (64 per cent) fully utilised the option, keeping the maximum number of items allowed. This is an indicator that, not only were the instructions presented in a clear way, but that participants in the experiment were engaged and active. MTurk respondents have every incentive to minimise the time they take to complete a study, since they get paid on completion and may aim to do as many as possible in a given time. Thus, it is all the more remarkable that they chose to take an action that was guaranteed to lengthen the time of the study, given that it would result in reviewing items before voting.

We did not find any statistical difference between the number of items kept between the Democratic (4.62) and Republican (4.67) primaries. We interpret this as an indicator that validates our research design. Notably it demonstrates that we were able to create items for the Democratic primary that were of as much interest as the ones created for the Republican primary and vice versa.

We also found that participants were very interested in requesting fact-checks despite the limited information they received from them. On average, when available, fact-checks were viewed 54.2 per cent of the time. Democrats asked for fact-checks 57.8 per cent of the time, while Republicans asked for them 47.8 per cent of the time. It may be worth emphasising that there was no requirement to view a fact-check, and even viewing one would lengthen the time the study took the participant to complete. Thus, we believe the incentive structure was set up to minimise fact-check requests; that they were requested more than half the time appears significant to us.

Voters' Interest in Negativity

We expected that participants would more often choose to view positive headlines when given a choice between positive and negative information. However, because negative information has a tendency to grab attention and is weighted more heavily in evaluations, we anticipated that negative information, when chosen, would be perceived as more salient to the vote decision. Thus, we expected negative information would be more likely to be kept for later review.

Our first analyses support this expectation. While all participants encountered an equal number of positive and negative headlines, positive headlines were chosen 61.2 per cent of the time, significantly different from chance (binomial test, p < 0.001). After reading the information behind the headline, the respondents were in the end more likely to keep negative information for later review – 35.4 per cent of negative information viewed was kept, as opposed to 28.9 per cent of positive information (z = 4.27, p < 0.001).

In the 38.8 per cent of the cases when voters chose to view a negative campaign message, they more often chose the candidate they voted for attacking the opponent. Participants selected attacks by their preferred candidate (53.6 per cent) significantly more than attacks by the other candidate (46.4 per cent; binomial test, p = 0.0013). Though, the fact that, in our experiment, voters selected attacks from both candidates may show initial 'openness' to receiving potentially disconfirming information.

When Do Voters Look for Fact-Checks?

We expected information considered more salient (i.e. kept) items to be more likely to generate a fact-check request. After all, why fact-check something you care little about? Our results support this: 68.7 per cent of salient items were fact-checked compared to 48.5 per cent on the less salient ones (z = 11.31, $p <$ 0.001). Second, if negativity looms larger than positivity in voters' attention, we would expect them to dedicate more time to evaluating the veracity of these statements. Our next test examined whether salient negative information is considered less believable than salient positive information. We find that to be the case, as participants were more likely to ask for fact-checks for salient (kept) negative rather than positive information (72.8 per cent versus 66.0 per cent; z = 2.47, p = 0.013). For information *not* kept, participants requested fact-checks for 56.8 per cent of negative information and 44.0 per cent of positive information (z = 5.73; p < 0.001).

At the same time, participants requested fact-checks less often for information provided by their preferred (i.e. voted for) candidate as compared to the other candidate (52.1 per cent to 57.0 per cent; z = 3.34; $p <$ 0.001). The most fact-checked statements were negative statements by the other candidate (64.2 per cent), followed by negative statements by the preferred candidate (58.4 per cent), positive statements by the other candidate (52.4 per cent) and positive statements by the preferred candidate (48.5 per cent).

Voting Decisions: The Price of Going Negative

In order to test the effect of negativity in our campaigns, one candidate was always more negative than the other, i.e. his campaign had a greater percentage

Table 10.1. *Self-reported reasons for vote choice.*

	First reason listed (in percentages)
Political Issues	54.35
Honesty	18.19
Competence	6.58
Negativity	6.24
Shared Values	2.93
Other	11.70

of negative headlines (60–40 per cent). In our disinformation environment, where fact-checked statements had a 50 per cent chance of a false verdict, we expected negativity to be viewed more harshly than usual (Mattes and Redlawsk, 2014). In fact, in both the Republican and Democratic primaries, the more negative candidate received a lower percentage of the vote (43.6 per cent) than the more positive candidate (56.7 per cent).

Furthermore, voters clearly recognised which candidate was the more negative. In the Republican primary, the more negative candidate averaged 5.3 on the ten-point negativity scale compared to 4.3 for the more positive candidate. On the side of the Democrats, the negative candidate averaged 5.7 versus 4.7 for the positive candidate. In both cases, we find a significant full point difference ($t = 4.75$, $p < 0.001$ for the Democrats; $t = 3.40$; $p = 0.001$ for the Republicans), with voters correctly believing the more positive candidate to have been more positive.

At the end of our experiment, we also provided participants with the opportunity to express, through an open-ended question, the main reasons for their vote decision. We coded six different categories for the responses, as shown in Table 10.1, which we list alongside the percentage of respondents for whom it was their first reason given:

1. The candidate's issue proposals or ideology (Political Issues)
2. The candidate was clear, honest or trustworthy (Honesty)
3. The candidate's qualifications and preparation for the job (Competence)
4. Dislike the negativity of the opponent's campaign (Negativity)
5. Respondent shared the values of the candidate chosen (Shared Values)
6. Any other reason (Other)

A noteworthy finding is that there was a small subset of participants (15 per cent) who genuinely disliked negativity: 6.2 per cent listed it as their first reason along with another 8.8 per cent who mentioned negativity as a reason (but not first). This is not to say that they preferred zero negativity;

65 per cent of this group chose positive headlines, which was similar to all other voters, 63 per cent of whom chose positive headlines. More likely, they took issue with the allocation between positive and negative advertisements. Their voting behaviour was strikingly consistent with their stated preference: thirty-five out of the forty-one (85 per cent, $z = 4.19$, $p < 0.001$) who mentioned dislike of negativity as a reason for their vote choice voted for the less negative candidate. On the other hand, those who did not mention negativity were not significantly more likely to vote for either candidate. Furthermore, in both elections, the more positive candidate won the majority of votes, so one could argue that our anti-negativity voters were swing voters. Negativity was the only category of voting reason that predicted voting outcomes.

In examining how participants responded emotionally to the candidates, we find some evidence that negativity can suppress enthusiasm, but not as much the other emotions. In Republican primaries, participants reported that the candidate who issued more negative statements made them feel less enthusiastic than the more positive candidate (41.8 per cent–51.0 per cent), though this difference was not statistically significant ($z = 1.29$, $p = 0.197$). The same pattern exists in the Democratic primaries, but to an even greater degree; just 35.6 per cent felt enthusiasm for the more negative candidate compared to 51.6 per cent for the less negative one ($z = 3.05$, $p = 0.002$).

Negative emotions mirror this for Republicans. When candidates choose to be negative – and, in half the cases due to the study design, were found to be lying – negative emotions among voters are increased. Anger (37.8 per cent felt angry about the more negative candidate, versus 25.6 per cent about the less negative candidate), anxiety (38.8 per cent versus 32.7 per cent) and contempt (32.7 per cent versus 21.4 per cent) all show this pattern too, though only anger ($z = 1.84$; $p = 0.065$) and contempt ($z = 1.77$; $p = 0.077$) differences approached statistical significance.

The results for Democrats are less clear, and none are significant: reports of anger (30.3 per cent versus 27 per cent) and contempt (30.3 per cent versus 25.9 per cent) produced similar results, with small decreases in negative emotions for the less negative candidate. Anxiety is an exception, as Democrats felt less anxiety in relation to the more negative candidate than the less negative one (38.8 per cent versus 42.1 per cent).

Voting Decisions: Multivariate Analysis

We turn now to factors affecting vote choice. Our primary focus is the effect of fact-checking on voter decisions. To examine this, we conducted a series of subject-level logistic regressions with the vote decision (0 = candidate 0;

1 = candidate 1) as the dependent variable. A participant must have requested at least one fact-check for each candidate to be included in this subject-level regression.

Because the true/false verdict for fact-checks was randomised, many respondents would 'learn' that one candidate was a bigger liar than the other. To measure this disparity, we created an independent variable for the difference in the proportion of false/discrediting fact-checks between candidates – specifically, the proportion of false fact-checks a given respondent viewed for candidate 1 minus the proportion of false fact-checks that same respondent viewed for candidate 0. Thus, a negative coefficient would indicate that people were inclined to vote against the bigger liar. To capture other factors affecting vote choice, we included independent variables for the difference in a participant's feeling thermometer scores and the difference in the number of kept (salient) items for each candidate. Results are shown in Table 10.2. For Model 1, we combined results from the two primaries. This limited our ability to use other independent variables in the model, because there is no clear comparison between 'candidate 1' in the Democratic primary and 'candidate 1' in the Republican primary. For instance, suppose we find that women favoured candidate 1 in one primary and candidate 0 in the other: since the 0/1 distinction is arbitrary, whether they cancel each other out (or do not) is effectively meaningless.

In Model 1, we find that fact-check results make a significant contribution to voting decisions. As the percentage difference in disconfirming fact-checks increases, the candidate shown to be lying more often is less likely to receive the vote. We also find that the difference in feeling thermometer scores and the difference in kept items positively affect the chances of a candidate receiving the vote.

We next separate results by party primary (Models 2 and 3) so that we can control for differences using a more comprehensive set of independent variables. In both primaries, the verification of fact-checks influence a person's vote; as the difference between proportions of disconfirming fact-checks widened between the candidates, the dishonest candidate was less likely to be chosen. Figure 10.3 (Republicans) and Figure 10.4 (Democrats) show the average marginal effect on the probability of voting for a candidate, varying the difference in honesty (i.e. percentage of false/discredited fact-checks) between the two candidates.

Otherwise, no variable is a significant contributor to vote decisions in *both* primaries, though we suspect that the variable representing the difference in items kept would become significant in the Republican primary (as it is in the Democratic) with a larger sample size.

Table 10.2. *Explaining vote decisions, logistic regression (standard errors in parentheses).*

	Model 1: Pooled	Model 2: Republican primary	Model 3: Democratic primary
Difference in proportion of disconfirming fact-checks	−1.23*** (0.43)	−3.03*** (1.03)	−1.14** (0.57)
Difference in feeling thermometer scores	0.02** (0.01)	0.04*** (0.02)	0.01 (0.01)
Difference in number of kept items	0.21*** (0.07)	0.21 (0.14)	0.26*** (0.09)
Age		−0.01 (0.04)	−0.01 (0.02)
Education		−0.20 (0.42)	0.07 (0.25)
Gender		−2.28*** (0.83)	0.34 (0.39)
Income		−0.53* (0.30)	0.04 (0.16)
Ideology		−0.19 (0.42)	−0.06 (0.24)
Political interest		−0.69 (0.47)	0.28 (0.26)
Candidate differences helpful		−0.40 (0.39)	0.12 (0.26)
Media should point out lies		0.19 (0.73)	−0.01 (0.39)
Trust media to report lies		0.02 (0.85)	0.13 (0.45)
Constant	−0.06 (0.22)	5.23 (3.68)	−1.06 (2.03)

Table 10.2. (cont.)

	Model 1: Pooled	Model 2: Republican primary	Model 3: Democratic primary
N	216	72	144
Pseudo R^2	0.08	0.30	0.08

* p < 0.1 ** p < 0.05 *** p < 0.01

Notes: Education level is on an increasing five-point scale (no high school degree, high school degree, some college, bachelor's degree, advanced degree) that we treated as continuous. Gender is 0 for male and 1 for female. Self-reported income levels are bracketed into five categories, with the bottom four maximised at 20k, 50k, 75k and 150k. Ideology is a five-point scale ranging from very conservative [1] to very liberal [5]. Political interest is measured with a four-point scale from 'not at all interested' [1] to 'very interested' [4]. 'Candidate differences helpful' refers to the question: 'How helpful do you find campaign ads that talk about the differences between the candidates' positions on the issues?' This is measured on a four-point scale ranging from 'not at all helpful' [1] to 'very helpful' [4]. For 'media should point out lies', we asked which statement they agreed with more 'if a candidate tells a lie in an ad': 'other candidates should point it out in their ads' [0], or 'other candidates should leave it to the media to point out' [1]. For 'trust media to report lies', we asked if they agreed more that 'I cannot rely on the media to tell me about a candidate's lie' [0], or 'the media can be trusted to report when candidates lie' [1].

Discussion

In our experimental design, we presented our fact-checks in real time, while eliminating confounding factors by controlling the stimuli presented to our respondents. As we did not require our participants to view the fact-checks, we believe our findings conform with how fact-checks are encountered in reality. By allowing voters to choose the information they wanted to learn about the candidates, we gave them a similar power to decide which information is truly significant to them, and we report evidence that campaigns providing useful information about policy preferences grab voters' attention. The Internet, of course, greatly enhances the ability of voters to decide what they want to learn and what they do not (Lau et al., 2017). We find that having this choice matters.

For the effect of negativity in a disinformation environment we have several findings. On the one hand, we found confirmatory evidence that voters are not particularly enthusiastic about negative campaigns and, if they can select the information to which they will expose themselves, they seem to prefer to look for positive information. However, the

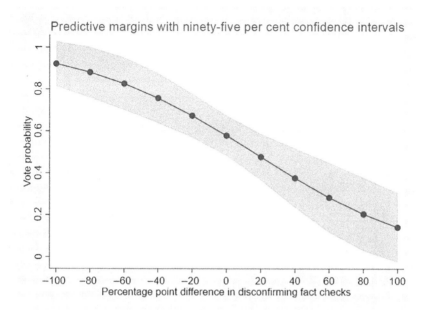

Figure 10.3   Vote probability and discredited fact-checks, Republican primary.
Notes: the x axis shows the difference between the percentage of false/discrediting fact-checks that a given individual would 'learn' about candidate 1 and the percentage of false/discrediting fact-checks that a given individual would 'learn' about the opponent (candidate 0). For example, suppose an individual receives three out of four (75 per cent) false fact-checks for candidate 1's statements, and one out of three (33 per cent) false for candidate 0's statements. This would give a value of forty-two for the difference.

attention-grabbing power of negative social information operates as expected as indicated by the choices made to keep and fact-check information, and it confirms that information that is offered to voters through negative campaigns is more salient, grabbing more attention even as voters prefer to avoid it. That is to say, a negative campaign can, and will, resonate more than a positive campaign, even if voters receive less negative information.

But, is that the *desired* attention? That is a different question. The new information age has also provided voters with the opportunity to test the veracity of information provided by candidates at the speed of a click. In our disinformation environment, we found evidence that sheds positive light on efforts to test the veracity of information provided by political candidates during electoral times. When voters are offered the option to check the veracity of information, they voluntarily fact-check it at a high

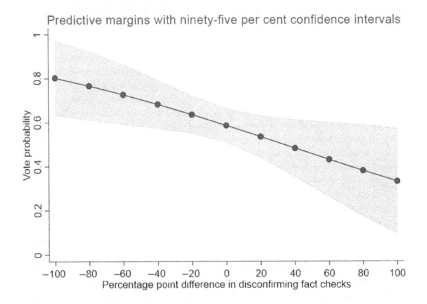

Figure 10.4   Vote probability and discredited fact-checks, Democratic primary.
See notes for Figure 10.3.

rate, especially if the information provided is negative. Before 'going negative', candidates might consider that the greater attention resulting from the use of negativity comes at the risk of a candidate's statements being challenged more often. Certainly, that is the case in our study, where negative campaign statements are fact-checked at a higher rate than positive ones, especially when information is salient to voters.

We know, however, that our experiment offered a dynamic environment in which fact-checking was amenable and low cost. However, it still required an additional effort that would-be voters chose independently to make. For future research, it would be desirable to provide more detailed and extensive fact-checking content as an additional step to better understand these dynamics.

What happens if voters find out that a candidate persistently lies? There is still a gap in the literature on how voters' learning about candidates' potential dishonesty can affect voting behaviour – whether they change their vote and if the effects are mitigated when a voter has a pre-established preference, as motivated reasoning would suggest. In our experiment, liars were punished at the ballot, especially as the honesty gap between the candidates widened. Yet, motivated biases were also evident. Voters were most likely to request negative information from the candidate they supported (i.e. voted for), which of course attacked the unsupported candidate. Also, voters were always more dubious about the opposing candidate's statements, fact-checking them at a higher rate, whether the statements were negative or positive.

Democracies are assumed to provide voters with the *right* to choose candidates in open and competitive elections. More so, we are now witnesses to, and participants in, an era during which voters have the ability to choose information in a digital world that is as open and as competitive as it has ever been. Thus, the question seems quite simple: if voters can choose what they learn to inform their voting decisions, what would they choose and how do they process that information? However, the answer is embedded with complexity, especially because the quality of the information available ranges from reliable to suspect to purposefully false. Furthermore, some political elites appear to have embraced disinformation and, wherever this occurs, there are likely implications for democracy. We believe that the study reported here offers initial important findings about choice in a disinformation environment and leaves fertile ground for future research.

REFERENCES

Amazeen, M. A. (2015). Revisiting the epistemology of fact-checking. *Critical Review*, 27(1), 1–22.

Andersen, D. J., Redlawsk, D. P. and Lau, R. R. (2019). The Dynamic Process Tracing Environment (DPTE) as a tool for studying political communication. *Political Communication*, 36(2), 303–314, doi: 10.1080/10584609.2019.1579771

Berinsky, A. J. (2017). Rumors and health care reform: Experiments in political misinformation. *British Journal of Political Science*, 47(2), 241–262.

Cacioppo, J. and Gardner, W. (1999). Emotion. *Annual Reviews of Psychology*, 50, 191–214.

Calvert, R. L. (1985). The value of biased information: A Rational Choice Model of political advice. *The Journal of Politics*, 47(2), 530–555.

Fiorina, M. and Shepsle, K. (1989). Is negative voting an artifact? *American Journal of Political Science*, 33(2), 423–439.

Fraccaroli, N., Cantarella, M. and Volpe, R. (2019). Does fake news affect voting behaviour? *SSRN Electronic Journal.* doi:10.2139/ssrn.3402913.

Gottfried, J. A., Hardy, B. W., Winneg, K. M. and Jamieson, K. H. (2013). Did fact-checking matter in the 2012 presidential campaign? *American Behavioral Scientist*, 57(11), 1558–1567.

Graves, L. and Amazeen, M. A. (2019). Fact-checking as idea and practice in journalism. In Nussbaum, J. (Ed.) *Oxford research encyclopedia of communication.* Oxford, UK: Oxford University Press.

Guess, A., Nyhan, B. and Reifler, J. (2017). *Selective exposure to misinformation: Evidence from the consumption of fake news during the 2016 US presidential campaign.* European Research Council. www.dartmouth.edu/~nyhan/fake-news-2016.pdf.

Holbrook, A. L., Krosnick, J. A., Visser, Gardner, W. L. and Cacioppo, J. T. (2001). Attitudes toward presidential candidates and political parties: Initial optimism, inertial first impressions, and a focus on flaws. *American Journal of Political Science*, 45(4), 930–950.

Jarman, J. W. (2016). Influence of political affiliation and criticism on the effectiveness of political fact-checking. *Communication Research Reports*, 33(1), 9–15.

Kahneman, D. and Tversky, A. (1984). Choices, values, and frames. *American Psychologist*, 39, 341–350.

Kernell, S. (1977). Presidential popularity and negative voting: An alternative explanation of the midterm Congressional decline of the president's party, *American Political Science Review*, 71(1), 44–66.

Kušen, E. and Strembeck, M. (2018). Politics, sentiments, and misinformation: An analysis of the Twitter discussion on the 2016 Austrian Presidential Elections. *Online Social Networks and Media*, 5. doi:10.1016/j.osnem.2017.12.002

Lau, R. R. (1985). Two explanations for negativity effects in political behavior. *American Journal of Political Science*, 29(1), 119–138.

Lau, R. R., Lee, S., Heldman and C. Babbit, P. (1999). The effects of negative political advertisements: A meta-analytical assessment. *American Political Science Review*, 93(4), 851–876.

Lau, R. R. and Redlawsk, D. P. (2006). *How voters decide: Information processing during election campaigns. Cambridge studies in public opinion and political psychology.* Cambridge, UK: Cambridge University Press.

Lau, R. R., Lee, S. and Rovner, I. B. (2007). The effects of negative political advertisements: A meta-analytical reassessment. *The Journal of Politics*, 69(Nov), 1176–1209.

Lau, R. R., Andersen, D. J., Ditonto, T. M., Kleinberg, M. S. and Redlawsk, D. P. (2017). Effect of media environment, diversity, and advertising tone on information search, selective exposure, and affective polarization. *Political Behavior*, 39(1), 231–255. doi:10.1007/s11109-016-9354-8

Lewandowsky, S., Ecker, U. K. H., Seifert, C. M., Schwarz, N. and Cook, J. (2012). Misinformation and its correction: Continued influence and successful debiasing. [eng]. *Psychological Science in the Public Interest: A Journal of the American Psychological Society*, 13(3), 106–131.

Lipsitz, K., Trost, C., Grossmann, M. and Sides, J. (2005). What voters want from political campaign communication. *Political Communication*, 22(3), 337–354.

Mattes, K. and Redlawsk, D. P. (2020). Voluntary exposure to fact-checks. *Journalism and Mass Communication Quarterly.* doi:10.1177/1077699020923603

(2014). *The positive case for negative campaigning.* Chicago: The University of Chicago Press.

Nyhan, B. and Reifler, J. (2015). The effect of fact-checking on elites: A field experiment on U.S. State Legislators. *American Journal of Political Science*, 59(3), 628–640.

(2012). Misinformation and fact-checking. Research Findings from Social Science. Media Policy Initiative, New America Foundation.

(2010). When corrections fail: The persistence of political misperceptions. *Political Behavior*, 32(2), 303–330.

Nyhan, B., Reifler, J. and Ubel, P. A. (2013). The hazards of correcting myths about health care reform. [eng]. *Medical care*, 51(2), 127–132.

Pingree, R. J., Brossard, D. and McLeod, D. M. (2014). Effects of journalistic adjudication on factual beliefs, news evaluations, information seeking, and epistemic political efficacy. *Mass Communication and Society*, 17(5), 615–638.

Pratto, F. and John, O. P. (1991). Automatic vigilance: The attention-grabbing power of negative social information. *Journal of Personality and Social Psychology*, 61(3), 380–391.

Redlawsk, D. P. (2002). Hot cognition or cool consideration?: Testing the effects of motivated reasoning on political decision making. *The Journal of Politics*, 64(4), 1021–1044.

Redlawsk, D. P., Civettini, A. J. W. and Emmerson, K. M. (2010). The affective tipping point: Do motivated reasoners ever 'Get it'? *Political Psychology*, 31(4), 563–593.

Shin, J. and Thorson, K. (2017). Partisan selective sharing: The biased diffusion of fact-checking messages on social media. *Journal of Communication*, 67(2), 233–255.

Swire, B., Berinsky, A. J., Lewandowsky, S. and Ecker, U. K. H. (2017). Processing political misinformation: Comprehending the Trump phenomenon. *Royal Society Open Science*, 4(3), 160802. doi:10.1098/rsos.160802

Taber, C. S. and Lodge, M. (2006). Motivated skepticism in the evaluation of political beliefs. *American Journal of Political Science*, 50(3), 755–769.

Thibodeau, P., Peebles, M. M., Grodner, D. J. and Durgin, F. H. (2013). The wished-for always wins until the winner was inevitable all along: Motivated reasoning and belief bias regulate emotion during elections, *Political Psychology*, 36(4), 431–448.

Thorson, E. (2015). Belief echoes: The persistent effects of corrected misinformation. *Political Communication*, 33(3), 460–480.

Vosoughi, S., Roy, D. and Aral, S. (2018). The spread of true and false news online. *Science*, 359(6380), 1146–1151.

Wason, P. C. (1960). On the failure to eliminate hypotheses in a conceptual task. *Quarterly Journal of Experimental Psychology*, 12, 12.

Weeks, B. E. (2015). Emotions, partisanship, and misperceptions: How anger and anxiety moderate the effect of partisan bias on susceptibility to political misinformation. *Journal of Communication*, 65(4), 699–719.

Wood, T. and Porter, E. (2019). The elusive backfire effect: Mass attitudes' steadfast factual adherence. *Political Behavior*, 41, 135–163.

Young, S. (2011). Television studies after TV: Understanding television in the post-broadcast era. *Continuum*, 25(1), 125–129, doi:10.1080/10304312.2010.506950

Dissecting the Psychology of a Voter
A Citizen-Centric Approach in Studying Electoral Experience and Behaviour

Sarah Harrison

A Paradox of Democracy Research

If, in the famous words of Lincoln's Gettysburg address (1863), democracy is the 'government of the people, by the people, for the people', then one of the greatest paradoxes of research on democracy must be that it overwhelmingly focuses on institutions, and conversely tends to assume that the people will just 'fall into place', following the intended logic of institutional designs like obedient or predictable peons in a game that escapes them.

Even the few approaches that have been described as psychological have frequently assumed an institution-centric approach: Duverger's (1951) 'psychological effect' is based on an electoral system and Campbell et al. (1960)'s model of identity is centred upon political parties. In recent years, research in the field of electoral psychology, for example, has challenged the assumption of this centrality of institutions rather than citizens' psychology in behavioural research (see for example Harrison, 2020, Bruter and Harrison, 2020a). These new approaches in behavioural research have highlighted the underlying assumptions of institution-centric approaches to question how models of democratic behaviour change when we relax them.

This chapter highlights some of the key paradoxes highlighted when research tries to move from an institution-centric to a voter-centric model of the psychology of elections, underlining some of the conceptual realities that this change of viewpoint uncovers, as well as some of the most counter-intuitive empirical findings that are thus revealed.

Some Untold Institution-centric Assumptions

Throughout the past seventy years, alongside research on political institutions and public policy, the study of political behaviour – and, notably, electoral behaviour – has been at the heart of political science research, merging a number of critical perspectives such as political sociology, political economy, political psychology and historical perspectives on context to understand the behaviour of individuals and polities alike.

On the face of it, this collective effort seemed to replace citizens as part of the global political picture and consider their role within democracies. The emergence of political behaviour as a major field of study has, however, followed a specific logic. After much attention had been devoted to the structures of power (institutions) and their outputs (public policy), political scientists wanted to assess the extent to which the democratic will of citizens would influence them. In other words, in terms of disciplinary genealogy, the study of political behaviour was perceived as relevant, not in its own right, but because of what it would tell us about the functioning and effects of institutions.

This has had a very direct impact on the types of questions that political behaviouralists wished to explore, chief of which was understanding why individuals or nations vote for a specific party or candidate. Of course, from a strictly institutionalist perspective, that question is critical. If parties on the Left and Right-wing of the ideological spectrum (or moderate and extremist ones) govern differently and produce different policies, then understanding what will lead to the victory of one or the other will be of the highest importance. Similarly, the question of what will lead a citizen to participate or not in the election can also explain which parties will be most favoured by participatory trends or, indeed, whether democratic institutions are legitimate and representative of the people. However, there is little reason to assume that who wins or loses an election – or indeed whether turnout is high or low – are the most important aspects of an election from the point of view of a voter him/herself. Indeed, looking at other aspects of psychology research, Bruter and Harrison (2020) claim that the questions of whether elections make citizens happy, emotional or more likely to live together and tolerate each other may all be far more meaningful to them than the question of whether candidate x or y has won the election.

The institutional focus of behaviour research has other more specific or peripheral effects. For instance, research on electoral cycles (e.g. Lewis-Beck, 1990), including on first- and second-order elections (Reif and Schmitt, 1980), have all assumed that institutions define cycles. In one case, the proximity to the election affects the behaviour of politicians and voters alike, while, in the other, the institutional stakes determine the nature of election cycles and of which elections voters will use in what specific way. It is, of course, always possible that voters' psychological perceptions would mirror and espouse institutional logics, but, equally, it is quite conceivable that voters may be able to load electoral affairs with their own perceptions and emotions beyond (and sometimes against) institutional intentions. For instance, Harrison (2020b) and Bruter and Harrison (2020) both claim that, in a way, the UK referendum on EU membership of June 2016 has not been a second-order election as would be expected from Reif and Schmitt (1980), but it has started its own new electoral cycle that, rather than ending with the next General Election, has encompassed the 2017 and 2019 General Elections in the same country as well as local and European elections in between.

Those two examples are interesting in their implications, namely that, while institutions can have intentions when it comes to defining democracy, voters – individually and collectively – do not systematically play along the lines defined for them by institutional designers. Instead, they may inhabit and interpret democratic processes to ascribe to them their own meanings, narratives and consequences, including away from their original top-down intentions.

In terms of the psychology of democracy, the direct consequence of this is that, the moment we relax the assumption that behavioural practice mirrors institutional intentions, possibilities become far more complex and the relationship between institutional design and electoral psychology is no longer as passive and predictable, but, instead, considered an interface, which, in our research we conceive as 'electoral ergonomics' (Bruter and Harrison, 2017).

Voter-centric Concepts, the Psychology of Democracy and the Integration of the Articulation between the Individual and Societal Dimensions of the Vote

Electoral ergonomics is thus the first of a number of concepts that our research has shown is needed to move to a more voter-centric understanding of electoral behaviour because it switches from an assumption that institutions simply 'define' or constrain political behaviour (top-down approach) to the alternative of an interface vision, i.e. that different institutional arrangements will trigger different psychological mechanisms (personality traits, memories, identity components, emotions, etc) in ways that are not entirely predictable or intended by institutions themselves (i.e. an interplay approach).

The introduction of the concept of electoral ergonomics has several key analytical implications.

The first of these is that, by relaxing the assumption that the 'intended' institutional logic of elections will naturally be embraced by voters, we paradoxically allow institutional designs to be more important. In other words, once we stop assuming that citizens' perceptions of election cycles will necessarily mirror the cycles intended by institutions – which will start with an election campaign and end on election night – we can understand how different aspects of institutional design will lead voters to perceive that the actual vote successfully brings an election cycle to a close and bring a sense of electoral resolution.

The second major implication is that, if we stop assuming that institutions solely perform their intended democratic articulation between individual preferences and aggregate verdicts (in other words, that they are the arbiters of democracy), individuals become capable of integrating some elements (whether real or imagined) of the societal dimension of elections within their own individual electoral experience and behaviour. In other words, next to the mechanical aggregation operated by democratic institutions that (wrongly) assume a complete independence, spontaneity and informational equality between all individual votes, individuals are viewed as capable of operating their own psychological and intellectual connections regarding the relationship between their own electoral experience and that of the rest of society. This includes not only ways to estimate how one's vote will gain or lose some of its power depending on the behaviour of other citizens, but also a mirror conception of how the alignment between our electoral preferences and experiences will either integrate us within, or alienate us from, the whole or parts of the society and groups within which we operate.

Thus, beyond electoral ergonomics mentioned above, a second concept also outlined in our research is that of 'empathic displacement' (Bruter and Harrison, 2020). The idea is that the relationship between the individual and the collective is not simply organised by institutional design as the aggregation of individual preferences. Instead, we suggest that, as part of their individual political behaviour, citizens comprehend and can project (often subconsciously) how the rest of the polity will behave or is behaving. In this way, citizens derive a sense of their own place within the polity, often perceiving their own efforts as likely to be all the more impactful as they are coupled with the symbiotic action of others like them (projected efficacy). On the contrary, this projection could also result in them interpreting a mismatch between their own feelings, attitudes or behavioural choices and those they ascribe to others in a community as a source of alienation and marginalisation. Note that this empathic displacement encompasses processes, such as strategic voting, which have been amply noted by the literature (Alvarez and Nagler, 2000; Blais et al., 2001). However, here again, while strategic voting is institution-centric – assuming that the reason why voters would not cast a ballot for their sincere preference must be to achieve a certain electoral outcome – empathic displacement allows for other motivations justifying a deviation from preference-based voting.

Conversely, projected efficacy is important in that, by capturing a sense of agency based on 'other people like me' acting together, it actively shifts conceptions of the collective back into the voter's mind, enabling individuals to consider the articulation between individual and societal dynamics as part of their own psychological dynamics rather than assuming that such projection – or consolidation – can only be institutional and objective.

While projected efficacy can be construed as one of the 'positive' concepts derived from the departure from institution-centric electoral analysis and the psychological capacity to configure their own electoral experience and preference within the societal reality of the election, other concepts are needed that cover more negative implications of the same. This is the case of electoral hostility (Bruter and Harrison, 2020) as well as, to a certain extent, the concept of democratic frustration (Harrison, 2020a, 2020b).

The concept of electoral hostility pertains to the negative emotions that some citizens develop towards others because of the way that they vote. While it can resemble the expression of affective polarisation (Huddy, Bankert and Davies, 2018; Iyengar and Westwood, 2015; Mason, 2015), the concept stems from a different analytical model that suggests that those negative emotions do not result from radicalising partisanship but, rather, from the extension of anti-politicians and anti-institution cynicism to also affect attitudes towards voters themselves. As a result, unlike the affective polarisation model, which increases with levels of partisan identity, electoral hostility can affect those who do not have strong partisan preferences and even those who do not vote and those who claim they do not care in the least about elections. Indeed, their electoral hostility is more likely to be based in the sense of alienation that stems from empathic displacement and the perception of an unresolvable gap between the electoral preferences and experience of the individual and those which (s)he ascribes to part or all of the rest of the electoral population. This can, in effect, be directed towards voters from one, several or all political parties and regardless of the identification of the electorally hostile individual with any party or partisan community. By contrast, the concept of democratic frustration relates to a different form of gap and alienation.

The shift towards more voter-centric models requires new concepts grounded in psychological models. How votes aggregate is suddenly no replacement for how voters believe their behaviour will interact with that of others and institutional cycles are no longer a replacement for the question of when voters believe that an electoral sequence is ending or finishing. Equally, the fact that an election took place and led to some institutionally-acknowledged winners and losers does not preclude the fact that citizens – both individually and collectively – may or may not feel that the election has brought them democratic closure (what we capture with yet another concept, which is electoral resolution). Furthermore, not only are most of those new concepts adding a subjective and psychological reality to objective processes and measurements, but they also tend to reassert the fact that most democratic perceptions, attitudes and behaviours are likely to be partly or wholly subconscious rather than solely conscious.

The Question of Electoral Identity

Perhaps the most extreme example of the need for new voter-focused electoral psychological concepts – where previous existing alternatives have been paradoxically institution-centric – pertains to the identity of voters.

One of the most influential models of electoral behaviour, the 'Michigan model' developed by Campbell et al. (1960) relied on the notion that citizens' identity is defined by their partisanship. In other words, part of citizens' identity would be based on their sense of affiliation with political parties and, in turn, this identification with political parties is what would define the consistency and coherence of their electoral (and more broadly political) behaviour and attitudes over time.

In many ways, this model is perhaps counter-intuitive. Identity research in Europe (e.g. Bruter, 2005) has highlighted multiple spontaneous references in how citizens perceive and define their own identity from parenthood to religion and from locality and Europeanness all the way to gender and race, profession and self-perceived psychological traits; but party references are certainly not such a feature. Moreover, how can partisanship even be conceivable as a standard source of identity in political systems where most parties and coalitions restructure regularly such as in Israel or Italy in recent decades? Finally, is it convincing that a voter could only be consistent in their behaviour where their votes are regularly cast for the same party election after election?

Many citizens may rationalise responses to survey questions about how they voted and those related to partisan identification, thus limiting their contribution in explanatory models. As a result, significant parts of the political behaviour literature have deserted the partisan identity framework in recent decades and, therefore, have thrown the identity baby out with the partisan bathwater. Are the two necessarily linked? Again, in our work (Bruter and Harrison, 2020), we suggest, instead, that there is a place for identity in the democratic behaviour of citizens, but that this identity is unlikely to be related to partisanship, as the coherence of voters over time can be expressed in many alternative ways to a constancy in partisan choice.

Thus, for instance, we give the example of a perpetually dissatisfied voter who may always cast a vote against the current government party, whichever it may be. This would lead to permanent changes in partisan expression, but an absolute consistency in behaviour – which would be an effort and desire to unseat and punish whoever is in power at any given point in time. In fact, the 'proof' that this attitude would be coherent is that, in many systems, on such a basis, the choice of this voter would be every bit as predictable as that of a voter with a high level of partisan identity under the Michigan model of the vote. Conversely, a revolutionary voter may consistently choose to support whichever radical party is offering to throw out the existing order without much regard for the specific identity or other ideological DNA of that party. There again, changes in partisan choice across elections could be fully compatible with immense coherence.

As a result, we propose instead a model of electoral identity that is not based on something 'external' and institutional (a party), but rather on an element of self-perception and self-definition, and specifically the way in which a citizens sees his/her own role as a voter and their function within democracy. To do so, we use a model that compares elections to the final of the FA Cup or the US Superbowl and where the political parties or candidates running for elections represent the teams aiming to win the tournament (Bruter and Harrison, 2017, 2020; Harrison, 2020a). In that context, we suggest that voters could see themselves either as referees – who are there to adjudicate, almost 'objectively', between the different contenders – or as supporters – who are, instead, focused on cheering in favour of one of the teams.

At first, this model of electoral identity reintegrates the notion of identity in democratic politics using a reference point, which is voter-centric rather than institution-centric. Beyond that, however, it represents an entire overhaul of the concept of the vote, which the political behaviour literature has assumed historically to be a measure of pure preference. Instead, by arguing that citizens inhabit and enact a given role when they are in the polling booth, the Bruter and Harrison (2020) model suggests that the vote is precisely, not simply, the expression of a preference. Indeed, just as a teacher who in grading an essay aims to give it the grade it deserves, regardless of whether they 'like' a student or not, because it is their job, the voter may end up casting the vote that they believe to be the right choice according to their enacted role, regardless of whether it might be discrepant with their more individualised preferences.

If voters are indeed in the position to try and 'do the right thing', it is the entire foundation of electoral analysis that is being questioned and potentially replaced by an alternative psychological model. This, instead, focuses on a matrix of self-perceptions, function and arbitration between desires and perceived duties, selfishness and dedication to others (notably future generations), and adjudication between short- and long-term goals.

This hiatus also appears in concepts such as democratic frustration (Harrison, 2020a) and electoral hostility (Bruter, 2019). Those two concepts represent different negative realities that are a direct function of the psychology of voters. They are particularly relevant here because they bring new light to phenomena that had been largely interpreted in purely institutionalist terms as though they were unrelated to electoral psychology.

When it comes to democratic frustration, while the existing literature has comprehensively discussed the potential sources of citizen dissatisfaction with democratic practice and processes, I argue that citizens become frustrated when a perceived democratic delivery deficit interacts with a strong democratic expectation or desire (Harrison, 2020a). By measuring expectations and delivery deficit separately, frustration can be mapped vis-à-vis alternative concepts such as apathy, criticality and cynicism, and is more widespread as an expectation–deficit combination than other alternative concepts. Moreover, a more detailed insight into the structure of the concept has revealed that democratic frustration comprises three dimensions: ideological, institutional and political. In behavioural terms, ideological frustration may lead to abstention (a form of withdrawal), institutional frustration may result in peaceful demonstrations, radical voting or envisaging leaving one's country (an expression of anger), while political and institutional frustrations may combine to lead citizens to take part in violent demonstrations or even join a revolution (a form of aggression). These reactions and expressions mirror the psychological model of frustration and are assumed to have vastly divergent consequences for democratic systems.

While also negatively connoted, the concept of electoral hostility is no longer based on a mismatch between citizens' expectations and those of their political system, but between citizens' expectations and those of fellow voters themselves. The notion of electoral hostility encapsulates a growing tendency of people who do not care about politics or elections – and who are not partisan – who have started to resent voters of a given party. Analytically, we do not look at electoral hostility as a step beyond partisan polarisation, but rather as a step beyond the increasing cynicism of citizens towards their politicians and institutions. At the same time, this can also lead to increasing cynicism towards fellow voters. Bruter and Harrison (2020) develop this model and describe the stages that it can assume as consecutive emotional steps from citizens experiencing 'mild' forms of hostility (such as a sense of misunderstanding or frustration) progressing to expressions of contempt, disgust and, ultimately, enmity.

Ultimately, this electoral hostility is, however, a direct by-product of our electoral identity, as it is our understanding of the role and function of a voter, which will filter our potential resentment towards other voters who do not match those expectations. Thus, electoral identity appears to be the most illustrative concept that embodies this tension and duality. The concept underlines the need to reintegrate electoral psychology in our understanding of democratic practice. It also allows us to question the assumption that institutions should determine how representative democracy should function: as an exercise in the aggregation of individual preferences. If we follow the logic of electoral identity, voters are far from being careless and selfish; instead, they are responsible, effective and complex citizens.

Empirical Findings from Electoral Psychology Research

Let us start with one empirical aspect of this new approach. This chapter has highlighted the concept of empathic displacement, which suggests that, in fact, rather than acting as stand-alone actors, individuals effectively take into account their projection of the societal dimension of electoral behaviour (i.e. what other people are doing at the same time as them) when developing their own electoral attitudes and behaviours. Indeed, citizens tend to think a lot about the way others are acting in the election, rather than simply focusing on their own behaviour. Perhaps even more importantly, however, our findings reveal that this tendency to projection and empathic displacement increases significantly throughout the campaign cycle, reaching its peak at the time citizens cast their vote. In other words, the electoral decision-making process initially starts as more individualistic, but progressively integrates the complexity of expectations about others' behaviour so that the individuality of the vote is increasingly ascribed within a projected societal reality (see Figure 11.1).

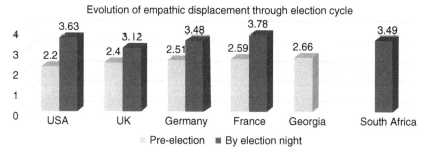

Figure 11.1 Empathic displacement and the articulation between individual and societal dimensions over the campaign cycle across six democracies.

Notes for Figure 1: - Indicates no data available (survey not run on election night in Georgia or pre-election in South Africa). Scale scored 0–7; figures shown are means. Data appears in Michael Bruter and Sarah Harrison (2020) Inside the mind of a voter: a new approach to electoral psychology: Princeton University Press. Appendices for data in book are available for viewing at www.epob.org.

The dynamic logic is exactly similar in the context of projected efficacy. As a reminder, most people are aware that it is somewhat unlikely that their individual vote alone could sway the result of an election. Projected efficacy significantly exceeds traditional (individual or internal) efficacy (see Table 11.1). In other words, if citizens often believe that their vote can make a difference, they also consider that difference to be much less to start with, than the difference effected as part of the collective decisions of 'people like them'.

Furthermore, as citizens increasingly integrate their expectations and uncertainties as to how the rest of the country will resolve the very same electoral dilemma with which they may be faced, they may also consider the power of their own electoral action in the context of synergies with that of other citizens who are either in a similar situation to theirs or simply like-minded. While traditional measures of external efficacy also increase throughout the same electoral period, this is far less so than for projected efficacy. In other words, the gap between the perceived efficacy one associates with our own electoral capacity and the efficacy projected through the concept of 'other people like me' mobilises in similar ways (or resolves our own hesitations in similar ways) and increases over time, with the dominance of projected efficacy becoming more evident. Thus, as the election period progresses, psychologically, citizens increasingly connect their own individual behaviour to its societal dimension, both in terms of their consciousness of their own preferences and its identity implications and in terms of the societal levers that can give them personal

Table 11.1. *Efficacy and projected efficacy over the campaign cycle across six democracies.*

	Efficacy Pre-Election	Efficacy Post-Election	Projected Efficacy Pre-Election	Projected Efficacy Post-Election
US	4.46 (2.14)	5.05 (2.11)	4.87 (2.06)	5.61 (1.77)
UK	3.84 (2.25)	4.14 (2.19)	4.49 (2.21)	5.09 (1.96)
Germany	3.55 (2.24)	4.35 (2.08)	4.30 (2.25)	4.88 (1.93)
France	4.95 (2.02)	5.07 (2.0)	4.62 (2.06)	5.25 (1.91)
Georgia	5.66 (1.83)		5.86 (1.76)	
South Africa		5.00 (2.29)		5.27 (2.17)

Notes for Table 1: - Indicates no data available (survey not run on election night in Georgia or pre-election in South Africa). Scale scored 0–7; figures shown are means. Data appears in Michael Bruter and Sarah Harrison (2020) Inside the mind of a voter: a new approach to electoral psychology: Princeton University Press. Appendices for data in book are available for viewing at www.epob.org.

power through inscribing their choice within the broader action of those they consider most similar to them.

Finally, we have tracked the levels of electoral hostility and democratic frustration of citizens – both concepts discussed earlier in this chapter – in both the UK and the USA using several new empirical instruments. In Spring 2020, the Electoral Psychology Observatory conducted a series of surveys as part of the Electoral Hostility Barometer.[1] The first survey was conducted six months prior to the November 2020 US presidential election to gauge the atmosphere of the election campaign (see Figure 11.2) and to understand how people are perceiving and relating to one another (see Figure 11.3). Our findings revealed that the atmosphere surrounding the election was described in particularly negative terms and that citizens were often directing their discouragement towards other voters. We found that many Americans harbour negative feelings towards 'opposite' voters. Just under half (47 per cent) admit they feel a sense of frustration, two-fifths (42 per cent) express distrust and more than a third (38 per cent) even feel disgust for those who vote for a different

[1] The Electoral Psychology Observatory (EPO), based at the London School of Economics and Political Science (LSE), and Insight Agency Opinium have launched a new 'Election Hostility Barometer' for US electoral politics. The new barometer will track the negative feelings American people hold toward those who vote differently from them, and wider feelings about the political climate. For results and more information, please visit www.epob.org. The sample size was 2,003 nationally representative US adults and fieldwork was conducted from 30 April to 4 May 2020.

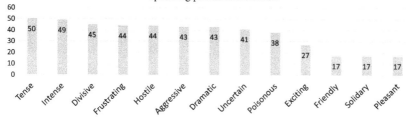

Percentage who selected that the following characterised the atmosphere of the upcoming presidential election

Figure 11.2   Characterisation of the atmosphere of the US 2020 presidential election.

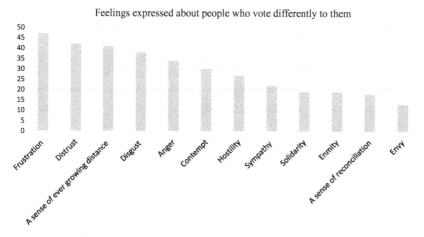

Feelings expressed about people who vote differently to them

Figure 11.3   How citizens felt about people voting differently to them in the lead-up to the US 2020 presidential election.
Notes Figures 11.2 and 11.3: Data from the Election Hostility Barometer. The sample size was 2,003 nationally representative US adults and fieldwork was conducted from 30 April to 4 May 2020. For results and more information, please visit www.epob.org.

political party. Nearly half (47 per cent) occasionally or frequently experience angry reactions from people who vote differently to them, while 42 per cent have occasionally or frequently experienced insults and, for almost a quarter (23 per cent) of the population, this even amounts to threats (a proportion that increases to 70 per cent if we include those who have experienced being insulted albeit rarely).

Expression of negative feelings towards politicians and representatives is nothing new, but, in recent years, it is often voters themselves who have become the target of others' hostility. Many even feel that things are going from bad to worse in terms of hostility between voters, with 41 per cent perceiving a sense of ever-growing distance from those who vote differently from themselves. Meanwhile, only 19 per cent say they feel a sense of solidarity with opposite voters and 18 per cent a sense of reconciliation.

Is the Proof in the Pudding? Psychology of Democracy and Emotionality of the Vote: The Case of First-Time Voters

Throughout this chapter, I have suggested why we need to better understand electoral psychology in order to frame the psychology of democracy by highlighting structural issues with existing models used to understand elections and electoral behaviour, conceptual gaps and empirical indications, but readers may still wonder why it all even matters. In this concluding section, I would like to suggest that it matters because elections are a lot more emotional to citizens than the literature often suspects and particularly so for young people invited to vote for the first time in their lives. If elections matter so much to young people as to make them emotional and even to make them cry, then it would seem very counterproductive to ignore the importance of electoral psychology. From that point of view, the findings we have uncovered in Bruter and Harrison (2017, 2020) leave no doubt as to how emotional elections are – both for those who realise it and for those who see themselves as flawlessly detached and rational or, indeed, interested – and how acute that emotionality is among first-time voters in particular.

Let us start with a single data point. Twenty-eight per cent of UK citizens claimed to have 'tears in their eyes' during EU Referendum night on 23 June 2016. Among those aged 18–24, that proportion increased to 39 per cent. However, it is not only negative emotions that are much stronger among first-time voters, but positive ones as well. In Germany, 64.3 per cent of first-time voters claimed to be excited as they voted, compared with only 31.7 per cent among those who were voting for at least the third time. In the UK, 52.1 per cent of first-time voters claimed to be happy as they voted while only 37.7 per cent of those voting for at least the third time did so and, in the USA, 61.6 per cent of those voting for the first or second time reported feeling emotional compared with 50.8 per cent for more experienced voters.

In many ways, these findings encapsulate everything that this chapter has tried to highlight. In other words, these reflect the fact that there is a significant aspect of democratic elections that has been largely overlooked and comes as a scientific and analytical disruptor of many of the existing models that we use to understand the foundation of democracy. This is what electoral psychology addresses – a sense that elections mean more to citizens than institutions ever intended, and more than they realise themselves as individuals. It is a conceptual and analytical gap whereby researchers in this field have missed the categories that correspond to citizens' critical appropriation of democracy and the interface between institutional design and intention on the one hand and voters' own psychology on the other hand. This underlines the notion that democracy shapes our identities as human beings and citizens, but not in the institution-centric partisan basis that has often been assumed, rather as a reflective definition of how democratic citizenship defines our role, functions, rights and duties on those occasions when our political systems and communities so obviously entrust us with a mission, i.e. during elections.

Democracy cannot have it both ways. Claiming that it is a system of government 'of the people, by the people, for the people' (Lincoln, 1863) necessarily implies that the people will need to be at the heart of democracy, not necessarily in the way the system wants them to, but rather with as much flexibility as their personality, memory, emotions and identity will be able to squeeze out of a fabric designed in the interest of the institutional system. This is what electoral psychology reflects on, and what it analyses, so that ultimately, citizens are logically understood as the rightful and effective owners of systems that have been adamant in claiming to have been established and organised in their names.

REFERENCES

Alvarez, R. M. and Nagler, J. (2000). A new approach for modelling strategic voting in multiparty elections. *British Journal of Political Science*, 30(1), 57–75.

Blais, A., Nadeau, R., Gidengil, E. and Nevitte, N. (2001). Measuring strategic voting in multiparty plurality elections. *Electoral Studies*, 20(3), 343–352.

Bruter, M. (2005). *Citizens of Europe?: The emergence of a mass European identity*. UK: Palgrave Macmillan.

(2019). Electoral ergonomics: Three empirical examples of the interface between electoral psychology and design. *Societies*, 9(4), 82.

Bruter, M. and Harrison, S. (2020). *Inside the mind of a voter: A new approach to electoral psychology*. Princeton, NJ: Princeton University Press.

(2017). Understanding the emotional act of voting. *Nature Human Behaviour*, 1(1), 1–3.

Duverger, M. (1951). *Les partis politiques*. Paris: Armand Colin.

Campbell, A., Converse, P. E., Miller, W. E. and Stokes, D. E. (1960). *The American voter*. Ann Arbor, MI: University of Michigan Press.

Harrison, S. (2020a). What is electoral psychology? Scope, concepts, and meth-
    odological challenges for studying conscious and subconscious patterns of
    electoral behavior, experience, and ergonomics. *Societies*, 10(1), 19.

    (2020b). Democratic frustration: Concept, dimensions and behavioural conse-
    quences. *Societies*, 10(1), 19.

Huddy, L., Bankert, A. and Davies, C. (2018). Expressive versus instrumental
    partisanship in multiparty European systems. *Political Psychology*, 39,
    173–199.

Iyengar, S. and Westwood, S. J. (2015). Fear and loathing across party lines: New
    evidence on group polarization. *American Journal of Political Science*, 59(3),
    690–707.

Lewis-Beck, M. S. (1990). *Economics and elections: The major Western democracies.*
    Ann Arbor, MI: University of Michigan Press.

Mason, L. (2015). 'I disrespectfully agree': The differential effects of partisan
    sorting on social and issue polarization. *American Journal of Political Science*,
    59(1), 128–145.

Reif, K. and Schmitt, H. (1980). Nine second-order national elections –
    A conceptual framework for the analysis of European Election results.
    European Journal of Political Research, 8(1), 3–44.

CHAPTER 12

Building Trust through a Revolving Door of Leaders: The Poisoned Chalice

Joakim Eidenfalk and Stuart Woodcock

Introduction

Leadership in liberal democracies has come under growing pressure during increasingly tumultuous times. While countries such as Germany in the early twenty-first century can point to stable political leadership, a growing number of liberal democracies have experienced unstable leadership, such as Spain, Greece and Italy. The reasons for this are varied. However, today's globalised world, with its fast paced twenty-four-hour news cycle, the constant polling and scrutiny, contributes to the erosion of stable leadership (Badie, 2013; Foa and Mounk, 2016; Lees-Marshment, 2012; Weller, 2014). Mistakes can, therefore, be costly and affect the leader's ability to remain in charge (Steketee, 2015). Furthermore, the 'presidentialisation' of politics means electoral fortunes are increasingly linked to the leader (Webb, Poguntke and Kolodny, 2012).

Australia belonged for a long time in the stable leadership category, with only four prime ministers between 1975 and 2007. However, in the early twenty-first century, the leadership position in the two main Australian political parties has resembled more of a revolving door, with the Australian Labor Party (ALP) going through a staggering nine leaders in twenty-one years (1997–2018) and the Liberal Party electing six different leaders during the same time period. Such instability adds further pressure on political leaders and on how they can ensure continuity of their leadership. A key to doing so is to build, or in some cases rebuild, trust with his or her colleagues, and equally importantly to build trust with the public. Failure to do so may result in failed outcomes of proposed policy goals and/or potential long-term consequences of immediate events or unstable leadership. For example, in a democratic environment, failing to build trust with the public could have a huge impact for the leadership, even leading to the loss of government. Building and rebuilding trust is, therefore, crucial for any political leader.

Table 12.1. *The changing of the Australian prime minister via the revolving door.*

Prime minister	Party	In	Out	Time in office
Scott Morrison	Liberal Party	August 2018	–	–
Malcolm Turnbull	Liberal Party	September 2015	August 2018	2 Years, 11 Months
Tony Abbott	Liberal Party	September 2013	September 2015	2 Years
Kevin Rudd	Labor Party	June 2013	September 2013	0 Years, 3 months
Julia Gillard	Labor Party	June 2010	June 2013	3 Years

This chapter will investigate three Australian prime ministers and their attempt to re/build trust through their actions regarding two long-term policy issues, asylum-seekers and climate change, as well as an immediate major event for each occurring during their respective prime ministership (Table 12.1).

The Changing of the Guard: A Poisoned Chalice

The two main policy case studies in this paper – asylum-seekers and climate change – were impacted directly by this revolving door of new leaders. Each new prime minister had to consider, not only the previous government's approach to these areas, but also – in many cases – the policies or views of the predecessors they had just ousted.

A rising number of asylum-seekers arriving by boat caused concern for the Howard government (1996–2007) during the late 1990s and early 2000s. Numbers reached 3,721 in 1999, a further 2,939 in 2000 and continued in 2001 with 1,600 arriving by mid-year. In an effort to deter further arrivals, the government introduced temporary protection visas. When the ship MV *Tampa* sought permission to offload a further 433 asylum-seekers it had picked up in Indonesian waters in August 2001, the Howard government drew a line in the sand, the ship was boarded and the asylum-seekers detained. Prime Minister Howard declared they would not be allowed to reach Australia and went on to create the 'Pacific Solution', which included housing them in Papua New Guinea (PNG) and in Nauru (Gyngell, 2017).

When the Rudd government entered the scene, it aimed swiftly to portray a more humanitarian image than the previous government and shut down the offshore centres on Nauru and PNG, as well as scrapping the temporary protection visas. This approach appeared to backfire on them when boats started to arrive in greater numbers again, reaching 60 boats with 2,767 asylum-seekers in 2009. This issue was once again at the centre of Australian politics (Gyngell, 2017).

The Howard government had also been reluctant to take strong measures on combatting climate change. It had signed the Kyoto Protocol in 1998, but never ratified the agreement. Kevin Rudd and his ALP declared climate change to be 'the great moral challenge of our generation' and, as one of the first acts of the new government, ratified the Kyoto Protocol in 2007 (Gyngell, 2017). In 2009, Rudd pushed further on stronger climate change policies and was involved in in-depth negotiations with Opposition Leader (OL) Malcolm Turnbull to set up a Carbon Pollution Reduction Scheme (Rudd, 2018). However, a revolt in his own parliamentary party against this deal saw Tony Abbott oust Turnbull by one vote in a ballot of members in December 2009 (Talberg, 2016). Abbott was a strong opponent of any measures that would, in his view, affect the economy and this, in combination with the issue over asylum-seekers and declining opinion polls, was an important reason for the eventual ousting of Rudd as leader of the ALP and as prime minister by Julia Gillard. In June 2010, Gillard became the new prime minister (Gyngell, 2017).

Climate change and asylum-seekers can therefore be viewed as two of the main policy areas that had an important role in several leaders losing their jobs and preparing the ground for a very chaotic decade in Australian politics.

Long-Term Domestic and Foreign Policy Issues

Asylum-Seekers

The Gillard government faced a growing backlash to the increasing number of asylum-seekers arriving by boat. In 2011–2012, a record 7,373 asylum-seekers arrived and sought refugee status, peaking in 2012–2013 with a staggering 18,365 refugee applications from 'boat people' (Phillips, 2015). The Gillard government received strong criticism for what was perceived as a security failure in protecting its borders (Davies, 2017). The OL (Abbott) was strongly against the government's approach and argued for a tougher stance, promising to turn boats around (Walsh, 2014). The failure to stop the large numbers of asylum-seekers arriving was considered an important reason why Gillard was ousted as leader of the ALP (and, consequently, prime minister) by Rudd in June 2013 (Evans and McCaffrie, 2014), who in turn moved to reopen the detention centres in PNG and Nauru (Beeson, 2014). However, this was not enough to stop the Abbott-led opposition winning the election in September 2013 (Evans and McCaffrie, 2014).

Perceived success in 'stopping the boats' was vital for the Abbott government, having built its election campaign on the perceived failures of the Rudd and Gillard governments in this area (Beeson, 2014). Abbott advocated a return to the Howard government's approach and, therefore, immediately introduced strict border security measures. Operation Sovereign Border (OSB) aimed to stop boat arrivals and deprive people-smugglers of their business model. It was successful in stopping boats coming to Australia (McCaffrie, 2016), however, the OSB was highly secretive, with little information on what the operation actually contained in terms of turning back boats, how many boats arrived, etc. (Beeson, 2014).

When Malcolm Turnbull ousted Tony Abbott as Liberal Party leader and prime minister in September 2015, it was with a promise of a 'different style of leadership' compared to Abbott's, including fewer slogans, fewer polarised views and a generally more positive approach as leader (Linnane, 2015). The Turnbull government continued with the same policies as the Abbott government, with no major changes needed due to a sharp reduction in boat arrivals. The focus instead turned more directly to the detention centres, in particular when Papua New Guinea's High Court ruled that the detention centre on Manus Island had to close. Furthermore, accusations of poor conditions for asylum-seekers in the centres continued to plague the Turnbull government. However, the policies towards asylum-seekers by the Abbott and Turnbull governments were seen as successful in achieving their original aim of stopping asylum-seekers reaching Australia by boat, with 49 per cent in support of the policies versus 41 per cent against in a 2016 nationwide ABC poll (McCaffrie, 2016).

Climate Change

In 2009, the Rudd government (2007–2010) planned to set up a Carbon Pollution Reduction Scheme (CPRS) and was negotiating with OL Malcolm Turnbull. However, a revolt within Turnbull's party led to his removal and the new leader, Tony Abbott, refused to support the scheme. This, in turn, added to multiple factors that caused Julia Gillard to challenge for the leadership of the Australian Labor Party in June 2010, ousting Kevin Rudd as leader and as prime minister (Gyngell, 2017).

Climate-change policy became a poisoned chalice for several leaders during this time and continued to be a tricky arena to act in.

The Gillard government (2010–2013) established a carbon tax to tackle climate change, but was hurt politically by it, since Gillard had previously declared, 'there will be no carbon tax under the government I lead' (Macintosh and Denniss, 2014, p. 196). OL Abbott relentlessly campaigned against it with slogans such as 'axe the tax', referring to it as 'a great big new tax on everything' (Talberg, 2016, p. 145). The campaign was ruthlessly effective and, in combination with the perceived failure of the carbon tax (as continuously described to the public by Abbott), it was now Gillard's turn to be ousted by Rudd in 2013, who thus returned as prime minister a second time for a brief period, until losing the election to Tony Abbott's coalition-government in September 2013. Climate change was again a vital clue to understanding the frequent changes in leadership and in government (Beeson, 2014).

Tony Abbott had a less concerned view of climate change compared to Rudd and Gillard, stating that it was, 'not the only or even the most important problem the world faces' (Talberg, 2016, p. 147) and referred to climate science as 'absolute crap' (Wile, 2013). He set out immediately to remove the carbon tax and instead promote his Direct Action Plan that focused on 'incentivise[d] emissions reduction activity in Australia', while at the same time withdrawing funding from several climate change research programmes (Talberg, 2016, pp. 150–151). However, the Abbott government in August 2015 promised to sign up to the Paris Agreement with a reduction of emissions by 26–28 per cent on 2005-emissions levels by 2030 (Elliott, 2017).

Malcolm Turnbull maintained most of the climate change policies he inherited from the Abbott government and refrained from criticising Abbott's handling of this area – no doubt remembering the reason for his ousting back in 2009 and not wanting to antagonise an important group of Members of Parliament (MPs) within his own coalition (Linnane, 2015). Turnbull continued the Abbott government's reduction target of 26–28 per cent, but with only minor progress on climate change policy overall (Linnane, 2015).

Eventually, in 2018, Turnbull was ousted in a leadership challenge brought on by Peter Dutton, but ironically won by Scott Morrison, when Turnbull conceded defeat.

Short-Term Domestic and Foreign Policy Issues

Each of the key prime ministers over the past decade (2010–2019) had, in addition to the two case studies above, to contend with an event that required special attention and involved the building and/or rebuilding of trust with the public. During Gillard's tenure as prime minister (2010–2013), it was how Australia would approach the deteriorating situation and increasing violence in Libya as part of the Arab Spring in 2011; for Abbott (2013–2015), it was the shooting down of the passenger aeroplane, Malaysia Airlines Flight MH17, killing thirty-eight Australians; and, for Turnbull (2015–2018), it was the election of Donald Trump as President of the United States of America, Australia's key ally.

In the early days of the Arab Spring, violence erupted in Libya and became an armed uprising against long-time leader Colonel Gaddafi. Australia had historically been involved in military interventions in Afghanistan and Iraq and the Gillard government were contemplating how to respond to this crisis. Gillard did not have, by her own admission, a keen interest in foreign policy and, after ousting Rudd for the leadership, he was given the Foreign Affairs portfolio. Rudd became one of the leading voices internationally for a no-fly zone over Libya (Sheridan, 2011). However, in the end, Gillard was not willing to commit Australia to any military participation in impending international action.

During Abbott's term of office, he was confronted with a tragedy on a massive scale when Flight MH17 was shot down over Ukraine, killing 298 people, including 38 Australians. The government aimed to get quick answers to what had happened and to find out who was responsible for the tragedy, and Abbott himself became a strong advocate for justice for the victims (Gyngell, 2017).

Finally, the election of President Trump caused challenges for Turnbull during his prime ministership when the new president issued policies that did not necessarily align with Australia's policy platform. In addition, Turnbull's first phone call with President Trump was widely reported as a bit of a disaster (Harris Rimmer, 2019). Given that the United States of America is Australia's most important ally, it was up to Turnbull to build trust, not only with the President himself, but also with the Australian public.

In order to deal successfully with the abovementioned issues, it was important for a leader to understand and communicate their perception of the causes for these ongoing issues and immediate events. Furthermore, they also needed to (re)build trust with their colleagues and with the public in order to address and work towards resolving these key issues, both in the short and the long term (resulting, not only in required outcomes, but also re-election). Failing to build or rebuild trust would likely result in failed outcomes of the proposed policy goals (with regards to long-term issues such as asylum-seekers and climate change) and potential long-term consequences of immediate events (such as the individual cases mentioned above). For example, failing to have built trust with US President Trump and his administration could have a huge impact for years to come, given that US support has been a fundamental pillar of Australian foreign policy since World War II. Building and rebuilding trust is, therefore, crucial for any political leader.

Trust

According to Carlin (2014), trust involves, 'becoming vulnerable to another group or institution [*or party*], with the capacity to harm or betray one' (p. 64). Untrusting, or distrusting, on the other hand is the refusal to do so. According to researchers (Carlin, 2014; Kim et al., 2006; Tomlinson and Mayer, 2009), there are three main dimensions to trust: integrity, competence/ability and benevolence/responsiveness. Perceived integrity relates to values to which the party adheres and which the trustor[1] finds acceptable. If the party betrays integrity, then it will likely be because it did not adhere to the trustor's interests, as well as breaking promises and/or becoming corrupt (Carlin, 2014). Perceived competence/ability relates to effective decision-making as well as skills that contribute to the trustor's interests and well-being. If the trustor believes that a party is incompetent, then (s)he is more likely to distrust, viewing the party as without the ability to make effective decisions (Carlin, 2014). Perceived benevolence/responsiveness relates to the trustor's belief that the party will do positive things for him/her. If the trustor believes that the party is unresponsive to their interests and concerns, they will lose trust in that party (Tomlinson and Mayer, 2009).

Furthermore, trust can be portrayed at two different levels. On one level, trust can be referred to as 'macro-level' or 'organisational' trust where such issues have been established from the perspective of trustors becoming distrustful or trustful of the government/party due to dis/satisfaction with the government's/party's policies (Blind, 2010; Eidenfalk and Woodcock, 2019). On the second level, trust can be referred to as 'micro-level' or 'individual' trust where it is based on individual leaders. It involves trustors having a person-oriented perspective on the party leader (Blind, 2010; Eidenfalk and Woodcock, 2019).

---

[1] A person, group or organisation that places trust in another.

'I Can't be Trusted. Trust Me': Trust in Australian Politics
Public trust in Australian politicians has been in decline for a long time, potentially undermining and threatening the democratic process. Evans, Halupka and Stoker (2019) point to the growing trust deficit in that 48 per cent of Australians distrust MPs and only 21 per cent say they trust MPs 'a little bit' or 'very much'. Key features of trust-building, such as honesty and integrity among politicians, are viewed as inadequate by an incredible 89 per cent of Australians. Furthermore, only around 30 per cent claim trust in the federal government, which compares poorly with European countries like Sweden and the Netherlands, who score around 70 per cent (Evans et al., 2019). On the other hand, only 17 per cent of Americans display trust in government (Pew Research Center, 2019). Leaders such as former Prime Minister Malcolm Turnbull were seen as 'inauthentic' by the public, illustrating the difficulty facing politicians in building trust (McCaffrie, 2019, p. 361)

Methods

The selection of three prime ministers for this study was based on several reasons. Each was in office consecutively between 2010 and 2018, with the exception of a brief three-month appearance by Kevin Rudd in 2013. The three prime ministers provide a good mix of circumstances, as two of them (Gillard and Turnbull) had ousted their own party leader to become prime minister, while one (Abbott) became prime minister by winning an election. In addition, one was from the ALP (Gillard) and two from the Liberal Party (Abbott and Turnbull). Furthermore, the two ongoing policy issues discussed above were prominent throughout all three prime ministerships, thereby providing a consistent comparative study.

The case studies were chosen to contrast ongoing issues with a more immediate issue, and how the prime minister responded and attempted to re/build trust for each type of issue. The ongoing issues chosen were asylum-seekers and climate change, since these policy areas were prominent throughout the time period of the three prime ministers. Moreover, a prominent and potentially challenging event that occurred suddenly in each prime ministership was identified.

The material for analysis came from press conferences held by the three leaders during the first six months of the respective leader's prime ministership or six months after the immediate major event happening. After Miles, Huberman, and Saldaña (2014), the authors took a recursive analytical approach to data coding: this entailed synthesising, coding and categorising a large amount of data in light of the theorising of re/building of trust. Both authors independently analysed each prime minister's press conferences and shared those preliminary insights and modified accordingly. This also occurred while simultaneously considering the nature of trust in its three dimensions of integrity, competence/ability and benevolence/responsiveness (Carlin, 2014; Kim et al., 2006; Tomlinson and Mayer, 2009). The authors sought to explore (re)building trust in more detail, as manifest in prime ministers' beliefs and responses to key issues during their leadership.

Findings: Prime Ministers' Beliefs and Responses to Key Issues during their Leadership

In this section, we outline how and in what ways the prime ministers responded, or planned to respond, to the long-term key issues around asylum-seekers and climate change, as well as key issues that occurred during their prime ministership.

Julia Gillard

Gillard's building of trust in regard to asylum-seekers focused on integrity and competence. She identified *integrity* as a key part of her policy, stating:

> This is our sanctuary; this is our home. Protecting the Australian way, I think that's about protecting values like we've all got care and concern for innocent children and we want to extend to them our best.

She also attacked the integrity of the Opposition's policies, stating:

> Mr Abbott's slogan of 'Turn the boats around' – ... is just a slogan because what actually happens at sea is that boats are scuttled and the choice you face is whether you let people drown, children drown, or you go and rescue them with all of the risk that entails to defence force and border protection command personnel.

Furthermore, Gillard attempted to highlight her government's *competence*, invoking some inventive statistical descriptions:

> A little-known statistic though Laurie is we intercept 98 per cent of boats. Under the Howard Government 1 in 10 reached the mainland.

She further assured the public that:

> We've got more assets patrolling our borders than ever before, but I want to make sure we're doing everything effective in this area.

Finally, she emphasised her conversations with world leaders:

> - ... I reported to the Australian people on my discussions with the Prime Minister of New Zealand and the President of East Timor. What I indicated then is that we would engage in further dialogue.

Moreover, she briefly referred to her government's *responsiveness*, stating:

> - Of course, I obviously believe that as Prime Minister it is the role of the Government to do everything we can to best manage our borders.

Gillard's building of trust regarding climate change focused mainly on *integrity* and to a lesser extent on competence and responsiveness. In particular, she emphasised, in her view, OL Abbott's lack of integrity:

> Mr Abbott backed action on climate change, particularly the Carbon Pollution Reduction Scheme in the last parliament, and then when he saw it in his political interest, he trashed that and he walked away from the agreement.

Gillard also attempted to contrast herself with Abbott and stress her own integrity in regard to dealing with climate change:

> Now I believe we should have a price on carbon, and I will be prepared to argue for a price on carbon... so that we get to that lasting and deep community consensus, but we're not there yet.

Gillard listed her government's achievements and future aims to highlight her government's *competence*:

> We have provided record support for renewable energy. We are working on energy efficiency for individual homes and businesses. We made some key election commitments in this area which we will deliver, like investing a billion dollars to bring, through new energy lines, the energy of the future into the national electricity grid.

Finally, she illustrated her *responsiveness* by being clear about her view and approach towards dealing with climate change:

> I believe climate change is real. I believe that it is caused by human activity. I believe that we have got to therefore change the way we do things and that this nation will in the future need a price on carbon.

Gillard's building of trust with regard to Libya focused mainly on competence and to a lesser extent on integrity and responsiveness. In regard to
integrity, Gillard focused on the deteriorating situation in Libya, stating:

> Both the Foreign Minister and I have been very clear about what we view as
> absolutely revolting and repugnant, the violence that we're seeing against
> the people of Libya. It's truly disgusting. We are calling on Colonel
> Gaddafi to cease this violence and to go.

And on a micro-level:

> I am deeply concerned about that deteriorating situation; no one wants
> to see the kind of violence that we're seeing in Libya continue.

Gillard thus showed integrity on behalf of the government, but also on an
individual level. This dual mindset was even more apparent with regard to
competence, for which she provided several reassuring comments on
behalf of the government, such as:

> For the Australians who are there, we are providing them with consular
> assistance. We are looking at evacuation options, not only by air but
> potentially by sea.

As well as on a micro-level:

> I called then for the United Nations Security Council to consider a no-
> fly zone. I've repeated that at every occasion I've ever been asked
> about this issue.

With regard to responsiveness, Gillard was keen to show that her government had responded quickly to the violence in Libya:

> The Australian Government was among the first to call for decisive action
> by the international community, including a UN-mandated no-fly zone.

She was equally keen to show her government's response to Australians
affected by the crisis:

> As Prime Minister, I've got a duty of care to our consular staff and like
> other nations I formed the view that it was not safe to have them stay
> in Tripoli, so we have got them out.

The main theme across the three areas with regard to trust-building is
slightly more varied in comparison to the other leaders, but her focus on
competence appears to stand out. Displaying a sense of competence by her

and her government seems important, while also pointing to the lack of integrity of OL Tony Abbott.

Tony Abbott

Abbott's building of trust in regard to asylum-seekers focused on competence and responsiveness, but with no reference to integrity. **Competence** was illustrated through the reduction of arriving boats:

> There is still a long, long way to go but in the first two months of the new government we had a 75 per cent reduction on the last two months of the old government; and in the month of October there was a 90 per cent reduction on the peak month of July under the former government. So, while the boats certainly haven't stopped, they are, on the evidence, at least stopping.

Meanwhile, Abbott kept on assuring the public of its **responsiveness**, stating:

> But Lisa, stop the boats we will, and the people smugglers are on notice: their game is up, it's all over for them.

Abbott's building of trust in relation to climate change focused on competence and responsiveness. Negative responsiveness came about in terms of climate change, and positive responsiveness came in terms of the economy. Abbott made only one comment in regard to **integrity**:

> So, look, climate change is real as I've often said and we should take strong action against it, but these fires are certainly not a function of climate change, they're just a function of life in Australia...

With regard to **competence**,

> So, we'll have direct action measures – you are all very familiar with them – that we are confident will bring about a five per cent reduction in our emissions by 2020.

And furthermore:

> We are investing some $2.5 billion on direct action programmes to reduce our emissions to meet our emissions reduction target.

Abbott's **responsiveness** was negative in nature, in two ways, focusing on repealing the previous government's climate change policy and stopping contributions to the climate finance fund:

I'll be saying when I introduce the carbon tax repeal bill: this is my bill to reduce your bills; this is my bill to reduce everyone else's bills; this is my bill to reduce the bill that you and your listeners pay, Alan, every time your power bill comes through.

And:

One of the things that's on the agenda is a climate finance fund and we're not going to be making any contributions to that.

Abbotts's trust-building in relation to climate change mainly focused on its effect on the economy and repealing the previous government's policies in this area. A theme throughout was an attempt to focus on the economic effects of climate change policies and build trust by protecting the economy first and foremost.

Abbott's trust-building with regard to MH17 focused heavily on competence, but integrity and responsiveness were also stressed. The comments on integrity focused on 'doing the right thing' for the victims:

Our objective is to ensure for the dead and for the living – dignity, respect and justice.

While competence focused strongly on the work done by Australian officials in response to the tragedy:

I can further inform you that a Department of Foreign Affairs and Trade consular officer has been dedicated to each of the family groups of the victims involved. Eleven Department of Foreign Affairs and Trade officials are in the process of being deployed to the Ukraine.

And furthermore:

There are now over 230 Australian officials who have been deployed or are being deployed to support Operation Bring Them Home. The 50 Australian Federal Police officers who had pre-deployed to London are moving forward to the Netherlands where they'll be joined by reinforcements from Australia. Some ADF [Australian Defence Force] support elements including a medical team are also beginning to pre-deploy.

Abbott displayed responsiveness through outlining how he communicated extensively with other world leaders on this matter:

Overnight, I have spoken with Prime Minister Rutte of the Netherlands, ... President Poroshenko of Ukraine, ... David

Cameron of the United Kingdom, with President Obama of the United States, with Prime Minister Razak of Malaysia, with Chancellor Merkel of Germany and with President Hollande of France. I've also spoken to Prime Minister Key of New Zealand. Also, overnight I spoke to President Putin of Russia.

Overall, Abbott attempted to build trust by focusing on competence and on negative responsiveness by claiming to 'fix' the problems in his view caused by the previous government. Integrity played a smaller part.

Malcolm Turnbull

Turnbull's trust-building with regard to asylum-seekers focused mainly on *integrity*:

> We're taking a number of steps to work closely with the Nauru Government to ensure the safety and security of all the refugees living in that community.

And, in particular, towards the children among the asylum-seekers:

> When we came into government. . . the one thing we know we must do is manage our border protection policies, yes, with compassion, yes, with humanity, yes with a deep concern about children.

Turnbull also took the opportunity to emphasise the compassion on the side of the government:

> I can assure you, we have big hearts on our side of politics in our Government, we do. Very big hearts but we have a very clear-eyed focus that ensuring our borders are secure is saving lives.

In relation to *competence*, Turnbull made a comment on the reduction of children in detention:

> When we came into government there were 2000 in detention, at its peak under Labor there were many more. There are now less than 100 in Australia.

And with regard to *responsiveness*, Turnbull aimed to reassure the public of the government's strict policies on asylum-seekers:

> Those who seek to come to Australia illegally on boats via people smuggling will not be resettled in Australia. . . I know that is a tough policy, but I can tell you it is the only one that works.

Over climate change, Turnbull attempted to build trust by focusing on competence and responsiveness. Only a brief comment in regard to *integrity*:

I take climate change very seriously. I take global warming very seriously. I take the challenge that the world faces to reduce emissions very seriously and that is why in Paris we committed, I committed to Australia reducing its emissions by 2030 by 26 to 28 per cent.

Turnbull focused much more on *competence* and mostly on a macro-level, aiming to reassure the public that his government were acting responsibly, stating:

Well I'm satisfied that the target of reductions by 2030 that we have committed to, that is to say 26–28 per cent reduction from our levels in 2005 is an appropriate one and comparable to similarly situated countries.

While showing flexibility within its policies:

So Greg has the measures in place to do that and we are going to review our measures in 2017 and, of course, if for whatever reason they're not tracking in the right direction, then we can adjust them. We always have the option of buying international credits, so there are many ways we can meet those emission reduction targets.

Later showing the practical aspects of his government's climate change policies:

And we are establishing a new $1 billion Clean Energy Innovation Fund and what that is going to do is every year invest $100 million in the smartest, most cutting-edge Australian clean-energy technologies and businesses to ensure that we not only drive jobs and innovation in Australia, but also play our part in cracking the very hard problems, the challenging technical difficulties, that we face in terms of reducing emissions.

In relation to *responsiveness*, Turnbull was keen to show that his government was responsible and taking climate change seriously:

The approach we're taking is a responsible one. Responsible for Australia, for jobs, for our economy and the environment so what will happen is there will be future conferences and I have no doubt emissions targets will move up into 2040 and 2050.

And, in a broader sense, making the point that the commitments will be followed through:

> You know Australia has, when Australia makes commitments to targets as we've done with the Kyoto targets, the first round of Kyoto targets and the second round, we have been, we have met those targets. So, when we make commitments to meet targets of this kind, we meet them.

And reassuring the public that the government was on track to meet their current emissions reduction targets:

> For Australia's part, our 2030 target represents real economic effort, and will halve our per capita emissions – one of the biggest reductions of any G20 country. We will meet and beat our 2020 emissions reduction target. We are committed to the cuts in emissions that we, as other countries did, committed to at Paris and we will deliver them.

Turnbull's trust-building, as regards the United States of America, focused on integrity and competence first and foremost, with only one comment on responsiveness. He approached integrity on both a macro-level and on a micro-level, stating on a macro-level:

> Our Alliance with the United States is vital. The commitment is so deep on both sides, it will survive many prime ministers and many presidents. That commitment is rock solid just as is America's commitment to security and stability in our region.

And on a micro-level:

> I do, I trust the judgement, the wisdom of the American Government, the President, the Vice President. I say to you, it is, the United States Government [that] will see changes of leader, of course, as indeed do all governments but the central national interest of the United States remains the same.

While emphasising the longstanding friendship and commitment by both nations to the alliance:

> Today, as 99 years ago, as 75 years ago, in all of those conflicts we have stood side-by-side because we are united by values. A commitment to freedom, democracy and the rule of law – our two great nations, we share so much.

In relation to competence, Turnbull emphasised his government's strong relationship with the Trump administration on many levels:

> We have a very warm and constructive relationship with the Trump Administration both at a head of government level between myself and President Trump and with my ministers and officials. It is a very deep and engaged relationship and very constructive and effective. We spent a lot of time together at the G20 in which we covered a lot of issues.

And also showing competence in practical outcomes:

> We have received confirmation from the White House this morning that Australian passport holders will be able to travel to and from the United States in the normal way.

Finally, Turnbull made one comment on responsiveness, emphasising the endurance and continued strong relationship with the United States of America:

> The President and I acknowledged the already strong and deep relationship between the United States and Australia and committed to making it stronger still.

Discussion

The unstable leadership situation in Australia made it immensely important for the three prime ministers studied in this chapter to re/build trust quickly with their colleagues and the public and, in turn, give themselves the best chance to remain as leader. The results in this study illustrate how they aimed to do so and how the circumstances in which they arrived at the position of prime minister contributed to how they attempted to re/build trust.

All three focused heavily on competence in their building of trust. It is the one feature that stands out throughout the case studies. Both Gillard and Turnbull needed to rebuild trust after having ousted their predecessor to become prime minister and portraying competence was vital to doing so, while Abbott had an interest in building trust and establishing his credentials as the newly elected prime minister and, in particular, to live up to his election promises to 'stop the boats' and eradicate the carbon tax.

Gillard, especially, had reason to focus on competence given the relentless criticism from OL Abbott on both asylum-seeker and climate-change policies. The only case study where competence was not represented was Turnbull on asylum-seekers: the likely reason being that the boats had already stopped under the previous government, hence he did not need to focus on competence as much as on the integrity that had been diminishing under Abbott.

Integrity featured prominently with Gillard and Turnbull, perhaps as a response to having ousted their predecessors and thus having to rebuild trust after the perceived loss of integrity in the process. Abbott, on the other hand, focused very little on integrity – only in a small manner in relation to MH17 – and negative integrity was indeed something Gillard had previously focused on when counter-attacking the then OL Abbott. It is also possible that, having the mandate of an election win, Abbott felt he was not required to focus as much on integrity in his trust-building exercise, since he may have had the belief that 'I'm fine now. Don't touch me'. Turnbull had reason to focus on integrity, since he had promised to deliver a different leadership style to Abbott when he ousted him. Abbott focused very little on integrity, so for Turnbull to do so helped contrast the two and could be seen partly as a way to justify the change in leadership.

Finally, responsiveness was apparent in seven out of nine policy instances examined and, after competence, seems to be an important part of building trust across all three prime ministers' terms of office. Abbott's responsiveness in regard to climate change is interesting to note as it can be labelled 'negative responsiveness', that is, focusing on removing the carbon tax and other climate change policies, rather than building something new.

The results presented here have important implications for the study of leadership in democracies. They illustrate how competence is regarded as crucial in building trust with colleagues and the public, while integrity is especially important for leaders who enter the job with less perceived legitimacy than a leader who was elected and hence has a mandate to implement their policy platform. Crucially, though, a leader who ignores integrity does so to their own peril, as it gives a potential challenger ammunition for a tilt at the leadership position. As Turnbull stated in his press conference, after having announced his challenge for the leadership against Abbott in 2015: 'The one thing that is clear about our current situation is the trajectory. We have lost 30 Newspolls in a row. It is clear that the people have made up their mind about Mr Abbott's leadership' (Sydney Morning Herald, 2015).

Conclusion

Building or rebuilding trust is essential in any relationship, but especially so today in terms of political leadership in liberal democracies. The circumstances in which one comes to the leadership position determines, to an extent, how trust-building is carried out. Focus on competence appears to be at the core of such an exercise, with responsiveness closely behind. Integrity became an integral part of the approach of leaders who had arrived at the prime ministership through a leadership coup in their own party, while a newly elected prime minister, to a certain extent, has received a mandate and has less reason to focus on integrity, so is thus able to concentrate solely on competence and responsiveness.

This paper, therefore, raises the question as to how important is integrity in building and rebuilding trust in the midst of Australia's political leadership crisis? The leadership needs to send positive messages of unity rather than of division and individual aspirations, if trust is to be built or rebuilt (Eidenfalk and Woodcock, 2019). If the lesson is not heeded, and the political leadership crisis continues, the risk of further damage to democracy is concerning. As the pace of politics gathers increasingly, building trust becomes more important than ever for political leaders, but, perhaps, also more difficult than ever.

We trust that we will have reason to return to this topic in the future.

REFERENCES

Badie, B. (2013). Transnationalizing diplomacy and global governance. In P. Kerr and G. Wiseman (Eds.), *Diplomacy in a globalising world*, pp. 85–102. New York, USA: Oxford University Press.

Beeson, M. (2014). Issues in Australian Foreign Policy: July to December 2013, *Australian Journal of Politics and History*, 60(2), 265–278.

Blind, P. K. (2010). Building trust in government: Linking theory with practice. In G.S. Cheema and V. Popovski (Eds.), *Building trust in government: Innovations in governance reform in Asia*, United Nations University Press, Tokyo.

Carlin, R. (2014). What's not to trust? Rubrics of political party trustworthiness in Chile and Argentina. *Party Politics*, 20(1), 63–77.

Davies, S. E. (2017). Asylum-seekers and Australia's security. In M. Beeson and S. Hameiri (Eds.), *Navigating the new international disorder: Australia in world affairs 2011–2015*, pp. 108–122. South Melbourne: Oxford University Press.

Eidenfalk, J. and Woodcock, S. (2019). 'I'LL BE BACK…': The chance of a political comeback as party leader, *Journal of Social and Political Psychology*, 7 (1), 402–422 doi:10.5964/jspp.v7i1.993

Elliott, L. (2017). The environment in Australia's foreign policy. In M.Beeson and S.Hamerri (Eds.), *Navigating the new international disorder: Australia in world affairs 2011–2015*, pp. 176–191. South Melbourne: Oxford University Press.

Evans, M., Halupka, M. and Stoker, G. (2019). Trust and democracy in Australia. In M. Evans, M. Grattan and B. McCaffrie (Eds.), *From Turnbull to Morrison: The trust divide*, pp. 17–35. Carlton Vic: Melbourne University Press.

Evans, M. and McCaffrie, B. (2014). 'Rudderless' – perceptions of Julia Gillard's domestic statecraft. In C. Aulich (Ed.), *The Gillard governments*, pp. 303–321. Carlton Vic: Melbourne University Press.

Foa, R. S. and Mounk, Y. (2016). The democratic disconnect. *Journal of Democracy*, 27(3), 5–17. doi:10.1353/jod.2016.0049

Gyngell, A. (2017). *Fear of abandonment: Australia in the world since 1942*. Carlton Vic: LA Trobe University Press.

Harris Rimmer, S. (2019). Foreign policy under the coalition: Turbulent times, dwindling investments. In M. Evans, M. Gratton and B. McCaffrie, *From Turnbull to Morrison: The trust divide*, pp. 59–74. Carlton Vic: Melbourne University Press.

Kim, P., Dirks, K., Cooper, C. and Ferrin, D. (2006). When more blame is better than less: The implications of internal vs. external attributions for the repair of trust after a competence- vs. integrity-based trust violation. *Organizational Behavior and Human Decision Processes*, 99, 49–65.

Lees-Marshment, J. (2012). Political marketing and opinion leadership: Comparative perspectives and findings. In L. Helms (Ed.), *Comparative political leadership*, pp. 165–185. Basingstoke: Palgrave Macmillan.

Linnane, K. (2015). Issues in Australian foreign policy: July to December 2015, *Australian Journal of Politics and History*, 62(2), 268–281.

Macintosh, A. and Denniss, R. (2014). Climate change. In C. Aulich (Ed.) *The Gillard governments*, pp. 195–219. Carlton Vic: Melbourne University Press.

McCaffrie, B. (2019). Trust me, I'm the prime minister: Prime ministerial statecraft under Malcolm Turnbull and Scott Morrison. In M. Evans, M. Grattan and B. McCaffrie (Eds.), *From Turnbull to Morrison: The Trust Divide*, pp. 354–369. Carlton Vic: Melbourne University Press.

—— (2016). Operation Sovereign Borders. In C. Aulich (Ed.), *From Abbott to Turnbull: A new direction?*, pp. 197–220. West Geelong: Echo Books.

Miles, M., Huberman, M. and Saldaña, J. (2014). *Qualitative data analysis: A methods sourcebook* (3rd ed.). Thousand Oaks, CA, USA: Sage.

Pew Research Center. (2019). Public Trust in Government: 1958–2019, www.pewresearch.org/politics/2019/04/11/public-trust-in-government-1958-2019/.

Phillips, J. (2015). Asylum seekers and refugees: what are the facts?, Parliamentary Library Research Paper, Parliament of Australia, https://parlinfo.aph.gov.au/parlInfo/download/library/prspub/HGNW6/upload_binary/HGNW6.pdf; fileType=application/pdf#search=%22asylum%20seekers%20and%20refugees%22.

Rudd, K. (2018). *The PM years.* Sydney: Pan McMillan Australia.

Sheridan, G. (2011). Gillard's No-Fly Mess Exposes Her Frailty, *The Australian*, 12 March.

Steketee, M. (2015, 9 October). Four-year terms could be the key to political stability. *Australian Broadcasting Corporation.* Retrieved from www.abc.net .au/news/2015-10-09/steketee-four-year-terms-could-be-key-to-political-sta bility/6839864.

Sydney Morning Herald (2015). Tony Abbott leadership challenge: Transcript of Malcolm Turnbull's blistering speech, (14 September 2015). *Sydney Morning Herald.* Retrieved from www.smh.com.au/federal-politics/politi cal-news/tony-abbott-leadership-challenge-transcript-of-malcolm-turnbulls blistering-speech-20150914-gjmace.html.

Talberg, A. (2016). The climate policy carousel. In C. Aulich(Ed.), *From Abbott to Turnbull: A new direction?*, pp. 145–170. West Geelong: Echo Books.

Tomlinson, E. and Mayer, R. (2009). The role of causal attribution dimensions in trust repair. *The Academy of Management Review*, 34(1), 85–104.

Walsh, M. (2014). The Gillard Government, the Coalition and Asylum Seekers. In C. Aulich (Ed.), *The Gillard governments*, pp. 125–140. Carlton Vic: Melbourne University Press.

Webb, P., Poguntke, T. and Kolodny, R. (2012). The presidentialization of party leadership? Evaluating party leadership and party government in the demo-cratic world. In L. Helms (Ed.), *Comparative political leadership*, pp. 77–98. Basingstoke: Palgrave Macmillan.

Weller, P. (2014). The variability of prime ministers. In R. A. W. Rhodes and P. 't Hart (Eds.), *The Oxford handbook of political leadership*, pp. 489–502. New York, NY: Oxford University Press.

Wile, R. (2013). Australia's New Prime Minister Wants to Immediately Dismantle His Country's Fight against Climate Change, *Business Insider Australia*, 13 September 2008, www.businessinsider.com.au/tony-abbott-cli mate-change-policy-2013-9?r=USandIR=T [Date accessed 12 April 2020].

CHAPTER 13

After the Party Is Over

Jane Roberts

Introduction

> You're in the middle of a party, you're talking to a lot of very interesting people and a few people have started to leave and you're getting a little bit drunk, you're beginning to get a little bit tired, you're beginning to get a bit loose with your tongue and so you decide perhaps it's time to go home.
>
> (Roberts, 2017)

This metaphor for standing down sums up the reflections of a former prominent council leader on his decision to resign. However, the transition from political office turned out not to be the simple process that he had anticipated, despite the fact that his exit had been long planned. And what of those former politicians who do not get to decide when to leave, but instead get thrown out at the height of the party? Or, indeed, what of those politicians who do not want the party ever to end, and seek to remain in office past their expected term, perhaps even for life?

Losing political office – whether by standing down or by electoral defeat – is a more complicated process than is often recognised. Often dislocating, it can be devastating for the individual (Opik, 2015). Even a cursory consideration might suggest this would be the case when political exit entails the potentially sudden loss of a role that encompasses cherished values and meaning as well as status, attention, structure and friendship groups – quite aside from income. And, yet, there is little spoken or written about it, despite the inevitability of losing political office. Paxman (2002) was puzzled by how unprepared politicians themselves are for their end, writing about ministers who 'do not seem to realise that just as one day they are elevated, so another they will be jettisoned'. Runciman (2019, p. 161) puts in pithily, 'The "Impermanence of Importance" is one of the brute facts of political life'.

Given that representative democracy depends on politicians losing office – indeed, democracy has been described as a mechanism for de-selecting leaders – the relative silence about its impact – except for a brief media salacious savouring immediately following defeat – is curious. What are we – and they, the politicians – so frightened of? After all, it is not as though the need to constrain power, including temporally, has been missing from vigorous debate by political philosophers since Ancient Greek and Roman times. However, for individuals making the journey from political office, it is a different matter: it is as though they are not to be mentioned in polite company. Even political memoirs rarely cover the actual experience of leaving political office. Ed Balls (2016), a former MP and senior UK government minister, was an exception. He confronted the issue head on in his valedictory book, writing: 'The end of your career is treated like a death'. It is indeed about political mortality; and mortality is deeply uncomfortable to us all.

This chapter will start with an overview of the literature on the loss of political office both from the UK and wider afield. It goes on to consider the key themes that emerge from the literature from a psychological and a sociological perspective, including my own empirical research. The chapter goes on to explore the impact of losing political office, not only for the individuals concerned but for their partners, their families, employers and wider civic society. It concludes on a cautionary note about the implications of not addressing how problematic political exit can be, for representative democracy and for us all as citizens.

What We Know about Losing Political Office

In short, we do not know a great deal. Scholarly work on the exit from political roles has been sparse, in striking contrast to a plentiful literature on how to gain and sustain such office – including famously by Machiavelli (2009) as well as, in the modern day, by scholars (e.g. Wren, 2007) and scores of political biographers (Walter, 2016). There is little consideration of routes out of political office, when and how to relinquish political leadership roles and what conditions facilitate politicians to leave, should either they or the electorate deem that it is time for them to go (Byrne and Theakston, 2016).

The literature on transitions generally offers rich insights, particularly Ebaugh's (1988) work on 'exes'. A former nun turned academic, Ebaugh became interested in the notion of 'role exit', that is 'the process of disengagement from a role that is central to one's self-identity and the re-establishment of an identity in a new role that takes into account one's ex-role' (p. 1). Her 'exes' did not, however, include any former politicians. The literature on retirement, redundancy and unemployment helpfully illustrates how the transition from work is a process over time with multiple meanings and impact – emotional and practical – not only for individuals, but also for their families (e.g. Beehr, 1986; Gabriel, Gray and Goregaokar, 2013; Hartley, 1987; Jahoda, 1982; Wang, 2013). However, few jobs have the all-consuming combination of personal demands and challenges that face politicians, not least from a hostile media and an increasingly sceptical electorate (Roberts, 2017).

Professional athletes share some similarities with politicians (and perhaps also the clergy and the military) in that they have a relentlessly demanding role where deeply held values, beliefs and identity are entwined, yet it may suddenly come to an end. However, in contrast to the loss of political office, there is a burgeoning literature on athlete retirement, whether planned or forced by injury (e.g. Cecić Erpič, Wylleman and Zupancic, 2004; Lally, 2007; Menke and Germany, 2018; Taylor and Ogilvie, 1994) that suggests the degree of voluntariness in retiring, the level to which identity is wholly consumed by sport and the subjective perception of athletic achievement all influence adjustment to retirement. Despite this knowledge, 62 per cent of former professional rugby players surveyed in the UK were found to have experienced mental health problems within two years of retirement (Kitson, 2019). In contrast to athletes, the clergy and the military, elected politicians have a representative function. Citizens elect politicians to represent them, which means we have a relationship with politicians, whether we like it or not.

What is known about the transition from political office is mostly about those who have been heads of government (Theakston and de Vries, 2012). The focus, beginning in the early twentieth century, was originally on US presidents, but most studies have looked at what former presidents have gone on to do after leaving the White House rather than examining their experience of transition from office. The interest in US Commanders-in-Chief sparked an interest in UK prime ministers (Just, 2004; Theakston, 2010) and heads of governments in other Western-style democracies (Theakston and de Vries, 2012). Few government leaders leave on their own terms. Harold Wilson was the only UK prime minister of modern times to leave at a time of his choosing, in 1976 (Richards, 2019). John Keys, New Zealand Prime Minister, was a more recent exception: a popular leader at the time of his resignation in 2016, who was determined not to find himself, 'in the position many leaders around the world find themselves, which is disgruntled and unhappy,' (Manhire, 2016). However Adonis (quoted in Runciman, 2019, p. 105) advises that there are no dignified prime ministerial exits, 'just exits and transitions, all more or less ragged and unsatisfactory'.

What of politicians in less prominent positions: party leaders, cabinet members, parliamentarians and local government leaders? They may be less in the public eye, but commitment to their political role may be no less intense. While there is some literature on party leader succession, ministerial sackings and resignations, the career pathways of ministers (for example, Bynander and 't Hart, 2008; Dowding and Kang, 1998; Dowding and McLeay, 2011; Ennser-Jedenastik and Muller, 2013), political ambitions (Allen and Cutts, 2018), the influence of gender on exits (O'Neill, Pruysers and Stewart, 2019) and on why elected representatives choose to retire (for example, Karol, 2012; Kerby and Blidook, 2011; Raymond and Overby, 2019), there is little systematic research on the experience of the transition from office. Meanwhile, political memoirs are mostly preoccupied with setting the record straight (in the eyes of the author), e.g. Hillary Clinton's sobering account of the 2016 US presidential election recalls Bill Clinton as 'so depressed he practically couldn't get off the floor' when he failed to be re-elected as Arkansas governor in 1980 (Clinton, 2017, p. 20). Canada, however, offers a relatively rich seam of documented experience of political exit (Doherty, 2001; Ignatieff, 2013; Paikin, 2003; Shaffir and Kleinknecht, 2005; Williams, 2011). Ignatieff reflects on the devastating defeat of the Canadian Liberal Party – and the humiliating loss of his own seat – while he was at the helm in 2011, in unsparing detail: he 'pursued the flame of power and saw hope dwindle to ashes', (Ignatieff, 2013, p. 3). Shaffir and Kleinknecht (2005, p. 715) specifically explore the experience of defeat among former federal and provincial parliamentarians and, from interview data, highlight the imagery of death invoked by a number, e.g., 'It's a different death. It's a death that no-one grieves with you.'

In the UK, thoughtful chapters by political commentators Riddell (1996, 2019) and Paxman (2002), more recent academic studies in the UK primarily using survey data (Byrne and Theakston, 2016; Theakston, Gouge and Honeyman, 2007) and Kwiatkowski's (2015) reflective piece having interviewed a number of Westminster MPs, demonstrate the difficulties experienced by many in adjusting to non-parliamentary life. Kwiatkowski (2015, p.37) highlights the 'inevitable period of mourning for that they have lost, and can never have again'. Hardman (2018, p. 33) highlights the devastation of many ex-MPs on losing their seat and the 'emotional trauma' it can inflict, even on their children.

Theakston and his colleagues' (2007) earlier survey portrays how the effect of electoral defeat or de-selection can endure for a number of years, with many former MPs both missing the buzz of the House of Commons but also welcoming more time with family. Many had continued to be active in public life, but over half felt that their skills could have been better put to use. It is noteworthy that an unusually high number of their respondents (25 per cent) had been appointed to the House of Lords. Byrne and Theakston's (2016) later paper illustrates the profound effect of the 2009 expenses scandal, with a relatively high number of MPs choosing to stand down, albeit some under pressure from unwelcome publicity, but others with considerable relief. Of those who had been defeated, a number commented on the sense of grief or loss of identity that they experienced as a result. Over two-thirds of the group who were under the age of sixty-five had taken up paid employment subsequently, but it had taken some time to find a job, with 11 per cent of the total still unemployed a year after leaving the House of Commons. Byrne and Theakston (2016, p. 706) concluded that 'the transition out of political office needs to be made less problematic, perhaps through the efforts of parliamentary authorities and political parties to help departing MPs navigate the labour market'.

My own work (Roberts, 2017, 2019) draws on empirical research in which over forty in-depth interviews were conducted with a diverse mix of former and current Westminster MPs and local authority leaders in England and a number of their partners. Given the scant attention paid to local government politicians in the UK – despite the increasing number of powerful full-time city mayors – leaders of major councils were included. Former MPs were interviewed about two years after leaving office at the General Election in 2010. Council leaders had left office between 2008 and 2012 and were interviewed mostly between twelve to eighteen months later.

In my study, the manner of exit was an element in the experience of transition from political office, but, in contrast to the assumptions of many, there was not a simple division between those who had stood down and those who had been defeated. Most, whether they had chosen to go or not, had grieved their loss of political office, acknowledging the emotional impact was more complex than anticipated. One former senior MP had chosen to go voluntarily, but recognised that it 'was still a huge loss because it's what I loved doing and had always wanted to do, and there was also a sense of I will never again have such a big job.' It is noteworthy that this describes a loss, not only of what had been, but the loss of a future, of what might have been, and this MP was unusually reflective about the transition from office and how it could best be managed. Curiously, few others, even if they had stood down, had made plans, either for the future or for the immediate transition. It had been, at the very least, a dislocating time for most: having had to make their staff team redundant at the same time as struggling with their own identity, as they sought to find a new narrative about who they were and what they did; how to structure the vast amount of time that had suddenly opened up; coming to terms with no longer mattering to others in the same way and – again, contrary to the assumption of many – a number had struggled hard to find employment, despite an impressive range of skills. Many were unfamiliar with newer methods of job recruitment, compiling a curriculum vitae or being interviewed.

The obvious distinctions between those who stand down and those who are defeated are the certainty of the exit of the former, the time that is available to plan for the future (even if it is not made use of) and the degree of control over the decision to leave – although the decision to stand down may not be entirely voluntary if there are external pressures such as likely de-selection or personal embarrassment. Even so, the experience of those standing down in this study was far from straightforward. Many had agonised over their decision to leave and even those MPs who had disliked their time in Parliament could still acknowledge that they needed some time to adjust to the transition, given the major changes to their identity. One MP who had stood down came to recognise how he had had, 'Quite a rational way of looking at things but the actual experience of doing it was a whole different matter... a bleak time... [and I] became quite depressed'. In standing down, a politician will have brought about their own demise: a potential complicating factor. He or she makes the decision: the electorate cannot be held responsible.

The Power of Emotions

For many of those who had been defeated at the ballot box – an event that may well be greeted all too gleefully by the public – it had been a time of emotional turmoil with a profound sense of personal failure. There were powerful and moving stories: of hurt, humiliation, betrayal, shame and of being avoided by those still in office, for fear of the contagion of failure. It was not just the individuals leaving office who were affected, but their partners and families and, for MPs, their staff too. Council leaders' income immediately ceased without even the statutory minimum redundancy pay and (now) no pension – and yet the public have no idea that this is so. A politician's job, role, social networks and status all vanish overnight with little sense of what the future might hold. Many former politicians felt as though they had had simply to disappear – both avoiding others and actively being avoided. Many felt deeply hurt and angry at the lack of acknowledgement from the political party they had served so loyally for so long. The door was simply slammed shut. One described it as, 'Like a bereavement – and it was – but there was no funeral'. Partners' anger was expressed with a notable rawness and intensity, and some had left the party as a result. Notably, their lives were often turned upside down as well. Observed one partner of her spouse, 'He lost a sense of who he was. . . lost a sense of having a future ahead, a political future. . . somebody whose past was now sealed off. . . the death of a future'. The struggle between the rational recognition that defeat is an integral and desirable part of the electoral process, and the lived experience of being crushed emotionally, was powerfully portrayed.

There was a deep sense of frustration that there was so little interest in the skills, knowledge and experience gained in political office. Although former senior ministers do not generally struggle to the same extent as backbenchers to find employment, even among those formerly employed in other professions, it is now harder to keep up the requisite level of skills necessary while in Parliament. On the other hand, four former MPs had been hugely relieved to leave, raising cogent questions about the environment into which we now elect our parliamentary representatives, echoing the findings of Weinberg (2012). The coarseness of what passes for debate on social media and the abuse many prominent politicians face, particularly women, is deeply inimical.

Current politicians were remarkably reluctant to think about how long they might seek to remain in office, the transition from office or planning for succession, even if they represented a marginal seat. Many had witnessed the difficulties experienced by former colleagues as they had left office. It was an unappealing prospect and not one to be dwelt upon. There was a notable exception: for one thoughtful MP, who had been deeply scarred by the previous loss of a parliamentary seat, the experience had been bottled up for years and the research interview was the first time this MP had been able to have a frank conversation about it with anyone.

Exploring the transition over the next two years or so revealed a mixed picture. There were both commonalities and, inevitably, given the widely different personalities and experiences, many differences. Perhaps unsurprisingly, former senior MPs gained employment more easily than their more junior colleagues, many of whom continued to struggle hard and long to find a job. The manner of exit – voluntary, involuntary or varying shades in between – again accounted for some of the differences, but by no means all. Depression was not confined to those who had been defeated. Many were ambivalent: a rational and ready acceptance of what they or the electorate had dealt, but still a yearning for elements of what had been and a sense of dislocation. Most acknowledged that the transition from political office had been a major life transition, less straightforward than anticipated, and a profound loss of both what had been and what might have been. Finding a new narrative about who they now were and what they did was the key issue for nearly all.

Despite an impressive array of skills, knowledge and experience that had been gained in political office, very few former politicians had been asked to contribute subsequently either to their political party or to wider civic society. In spite of the formidable responsibilities of the role, council leaders' skills appeared barely recognised. Both they and especially their partners were deeply frustrated at what seemed to be such a profligate waste of a valuable resource that could have been of benefit to both party and civic society.

It's About Loss – of Course

For the majority of those leaving political office, whether voluntarily or involuntarily, the experience is one of significant loss: loss of status, meaning, purpose, identity, friendship, income, media attention – just mattering.

Freud (1917) recognised that the loss of anything that is cherished, 'a loved object', and not just the death of someone close, can provoke a grief reaction – a profound sorrow and distress that perturbs individuals' relationships with the world around them. Grief can be better understood by the recognition that it involves a loss, not just of the other, but a loss within the self (Marris, 1993). Any significant loss disrupts an individual's 'assumptive world', that is, the internal representations of personally salient parts of the external world (Murray Parkes, 1971). Drawing on attachment theory, Marris argues that any significant loss perturbs how individuals construe themselves, the meaning of their experiences and their relationships with others and the world around them. Such a loss provokes both an attempt to recover what has been lost and a wish to avoid painful reminders of what has been lost, with grief being the process of psychological integration in which these contradictory desires can be reconciled. Marris is clear that such a crisis can arise from both involuntary *and* voluntary losses.

Kets de Vries suggests that leaders in any sector may find job loss especially difficult, having to relinquish the 'essential nutrients' of power (Kets de Vries, 2003, p. 708), influence and constant affirmation, and instead potentially facing 'the experience of nothingness' (p. 711). With the intoxicating nature of elected office for many, leaving may be even more unappealing for political leaders, particularly those in high-profile national positions, some of whom may have succumbed to Owen's (2006) 'hubris syndrome' – where behaviours such as excessive self-confidence, messianic zeal and the conflation of self with nation or organisation can be seen. Non-human primates are little different in this respect, as the evolutionary underpinning of attachment theory suggests. De Waal graph-ically describes the powerful reaction of a chimpanzee after losing top spot in his social group, who, 'Would often sit staring into the distance after a fight, an empty expression on his face. He was oblivious to the social activity around him and refused food for weeks... a mere ghost of the impressive big shot he had been' (de Waal, 2006, p. 50). De Waal explains how humans and apes are 'obligatorily gregarious', constantly fearing being cast out and ostracised: 'Evolution has instilled a need to belong and to feel accepted' (p. 220).

In losing political office, former politicians may, however, be very publicly cast out (if not formally ostracised, as in Ancient Greece [Keane, 2009]). The 'Portillo moment'[1] is now part of British electoral folklore. Yet, at a time when former politicians most need social support, they may be deprived of it. Their loss might well go unacknowledged, not least by national party leaders, further rubbing salt into the wound of defeat (Roberts, 2017). Something similar was seen in the fury of many of the forty-six Labour MPs who lost their seats after the 2019 UK General Election. Many attributed their loss to the political direction taken by the then Labour leader, Jeremy Corbyn, who retained his seat and staff team, but from whom they had no contact for some time post-election. This group may, however, be afforded some protection psychologically by the cohort effect of being part of a larger number of losing Labour MPs in demographically similar constituencies in the Midlands and North-East of England, rather like the cohort of losing Liberal Democrat MPs in 2015

---

[1] The unexpected defeat of Michael Portillo, a well-known MP and Cabinet member, by a relatively young Stephen Twigg, was widely broadcast after the General Election of 1997.

(Roberts, 2017). Seeking solace from within a losing group can help, but those whose social lives lie only within their political role, with little 'hinterland' outside politics (Healey, 1989), are likely to be particularly vulnerable. Given that politicians' values and identity may well be deeply bound up with holding elected office, many will experience a period of discombobulation at the very least, struggling to create new meaning about the self and its relation to the world, whether the loss of office arises voluntarily or involuntarily. Or, as Ignatieff (2013, p. 167) put it, 'The psychic challenge after defeat is to recover your standing'.

Implications for Representative Democracy

Other than on an individual human level, is there any reason to be concerned about how politicians leave elected office? I think that there is. Not only because the accumulated knowledge, skills and experience of former politicians are carelessly ignored by employers and civic society alike (Roberts, 2017) – as undoubtedly they are – but because political exit has wider repercussions for representative democracy.

Let us go back to Ancient Greece, when there were vigorous debates on the relationship between rulers and the ruled (Aristotle, 1992) that have continued ever since (Ruscio, 2004; Wren, 2007). The principle of 'democratic rotation' was crucial to Aristotle's understanding of the relationship between citizens of Athens (albeit restricted to men) and rulers, and the importance of both ruling and being ruled in turn. Rotation in office permitted more opportunity to serve in public office and thus enhance understanding of the public responsibilities of office more widely across the population. The idea was taken up later in England by Harrington and others, and later still in the United States of America by Thomas Jefferson (1807), who made clear, 'that I should lay down my charge at a proper period is as much a duty as to have borne it faithfully'. For Jefferson, an essential task of leadership was to be willing to go.

As then, I argue that any modern healthy system of representative democracy depends on a reasonable degree of 'fluidity' between those who are elected to serve in political office and those whom they represent. That is, citizens should have a reasonable chance of gaining positions of elected political leadership should they be able and motivated to do so, and not be precluded from seeking office by disproportionate risks that might be encountered through gaining, holding or leaving political office. However, in order for some to gain such office for the first time, others must leave. This may not appeal to those already in office, despite

Jefferson's 1811 dictum that, 'there is a fullness of time when men should go, and not occupy too long the ground to which others have a right to advance' (quoted in Keane, 2009, p. 280). Or, as Baturo (2017) puts it, political leaders who leave office and pursue their own careers reinforce, 'the rotation in office as norm and, in turn, strengthen democratic consolidation'.

Limiting terms has been seen both as a check on excessive power – a preoccupation of political philosophers – *and* an opportunity to enhance political participation.

The outlook for those leaders who seek to outstay their welcome can be bleak. The fate of presidents who entered office between 1960 and 2009 and sought to prolong their term in office was grim: a majority were assassinated or ousted (Baturo, 2014). Others have been more successful in clinging on to power, e.g., Pierre Nkurunziza in Burundi (who died in office in 2020) and Denis Sassou Nguesso in Congo-Brazzaville. The President of Belarus, Alexander Lukashenko, has sought to remain in the office since 1994, even though the constitution originally stipulated a maximum of two five-year terms, despite widespread street protests in 2020. Similarly, both Russia's Vladimir Putin and China's Xi Jinping have presided over changes to the constitution that, in Russia, will permit Putin to stand for two more six-year presidential terms and, in China, have abolished presidential term limits altogether. Giving up power is so very hard.

In the modern United States of America, democratic rotation has been instituted by means of term limits, both in the 22nd Amendment to the US Constitution in 1951 that limited the presidency to two terms, and in many states (Petracca, 1992). In parliamentary democracies where there is less separation between the executive and the legislature, term limits are more problematic. In addition, term limits have many detractors on grounds of fairness, loss of experience from legislatures and the potential of 'shirking' behaviour by politicians in their last term (Caress and Kunioka, 2012). It should be noted, however, that there is little evidence of shirking by MPs who have announced their retirement in the UK (Willumsen and Goetz, 2017).

Similarly, I argue that, in the absence of a reasonable degree of political fluidity, representative democracy is diminished because it reinforces the perception of a political class separate from the rest of the population; it may differentially exclude some groups who may otherwise come forward to serve in elected office; and, with prolonged incumbency, there are fewer opportunities for citizens to be able to represent others – arguably the deepest experience of political citizenship. Political participation itself has long been seen as an important element in sustaining a healthy democracy. Writing in the early nineteenth-century United States of America, de Tocqueville maintained that participation in public affairs drew members of a community away from narrow self-interest and into a wider appreciation of cooperative endeavour, thus re-invigorating civic virtue. It was necessary to, 'use Democracy to moderate Democracy' (de Tocqueville, quoted by Wren, 2007, p. 212).

These issues have become increasingly pertinent in the early twenty-first century, with evidence of profound disenchantment with representative democracy in many mature Western-type democracies (Mair, 2013; Stoker, 2006) and the rise of populism internationally. Many scholars have sought to disentangle the factors that account for the current degree of disaffection with representative democracy (summarised by Hay, 2007). Jennings, Stoker and Twyman (2016) suggest that a key element is the perception of the character and the behaviour of politicians themselves, rather than the political system. The nature, then, of the relationship between elected representatives and citizens, and the degree of meaningful connection between them, has a crucial part to play. As Stoker (2006, p. 15) highlights, 'Representative politics needs to be understood as a more active exchange between citizen and representative'. Yet Mair (2013, p. 18) observes, worryingly, 'an emptying of the space in which citizens and their representatives interact.'

In the absence of meaningful exchange between voters and representatives, citizens as a whole lose out: a relatively closed political class serves its population less well (Riddell, 1996), whether at local or national level. A distant political class – seen as a far cry from the lives of ordinary people and 'part of an external world which people view from outside' (Mair, 2013, p. 43) – risks precisely the disillusion with politics, not least in the UK following the 2016 referendum vote in the UK to leave the European Union (Evans and Tilley, 2017), upon which populists find it easy to prey. Echoing this view, Sarah Champion was reported as saying in 2015 that she planned to serve a maximum of two terms as an MP in the Westminster Parliament: 'I don't think it's healthy to be there for too long. Because the longer you're there, the more distant you get from reality.' (Pidd, 2017).

A more fluid system of political representation, with individuals serving time in elected office and then leaving with reasonable structures of support in place, increases the opportunity for a wider range of people to put themselves forward for election and facilitates a better understanding of the challenges of political office among a wider group. In this way, echoing de Tocqueville, there would be better understanding of the constraints encountered in political leadership (Jameson, 2019) and the relationship between leaders and citizens might be perceived as less distant. However, if the difficulties of gaining political office, holding that office and leaving political office are too great, the group of people who are able and motivated to stand as representatives will be narrowed. Indeed, King argues that the dominance of government by Britain's 'pan-party-political class is almost certainly a bad thing... deters some people from seeking a political career' (King, 2015, p. 295). In other words, fluidity into and out of office is reduced and the quality of political representation potentially diminished. Canada, in contrast to many other Western-type democracies, offers an interesting example where the turnover of MPs at federal level is high and the proportion of parliamentarians who have had previous political experience, so-called amateurs, is relatively low (Pow, 2018). It would be interesting to tease out what, if any, difference the high turnover of parliamentarians in Canada might make to the nature of the relationship between citizen and elected representative.

Political fluidity in the UK context concerns both access into office and exit from that office. We know that, after some opening up of elected political office to a broader range of people in the latter half of the twentieth century, access to the Westminster Parliament is now narrowing again (Roberts, 2017) with, in particular, the number of MPs from working-class backgrounds having steeply declined (Heath, 2019). The increasing professionalisation of politics seen now at all levels in the UK, and the predominance of career politicians in Westminster, further diminishes fluidity into and out of political office. Previously honed professional skills may be difficult to maintain with MPs frowned upon for having any other employment (with the curious exception of journalism), and directly elected mayors and, increasingly, even council leaders now working full-time. No wonder that, having gained political office, many are reluctant to leave – despite the intensity of the demands – such can be the risks of leaving. As one MP reflected to me, 'It's becoming harder and harder and why would people take those kinds of risks with their lives?' For some, it is too precarious even to embark on the journey of standing for office in the first place, given the risks involved. Might some not be tempted to seek to remain in office for longer than they might otherwise? Why would they go, given the prospect of potential oblivion, possibly to face unemployment and financial insecurity?

Politicians may shy away even from discussing the possibility of their eventual exit. One current MP described the thought of leaving Parliament as unbearably reminiscent of the sound of 'scratching my nails down a blackboard'. Sarah Champion, elected as an MP in 2012 and notwithstanding her intention quoted above, stood again (only just holding her seat) in the 2019 General Election. Letting go is so very hard. It is far from implausible that Conservative MPs' anxiety about losing their seats accounted for the result of the 2019 Conservative Party leadership election, despite the apparent long-held doubts by many of them about the eventual victor (Bush, 2019). Despite twenty-one usually loyal Conservative MPs having jeopardised their political careers by voting in the House of Commons against their government on the highly charged issue of a 'no-deal Brexit' in 2019, many more voted with the government despite their alleged profound misgivings because of the risks to their careers (Burt, 2019). Perhaps those twenty-one rebels had taken on board George Washington's lesson that enormous power can be gained by a readiness to give it up (Levitsky and Ziblatt, 2018). Indeed, only four of them were returned to the Commons in the 2019 General Election when the Conservative Party was re-elected with a handsome majority that few had predicted.

If the professionalisation of parliamentary office continues – with local government leadership hastening unchecked in the same direction – there is a compelling argument that the support available on exit to any professional losing their job should be available to elected representatives. Although a very few parliaments – the Norwegian Storting and the Welsh Senedd, for example – do have specific provision for departing members, most former MPs and council leaders have little of the support that is routinely offered in other occupations. Many politicians seem almost to 'disappear'. In democratic terms, that is just as it should be. However, if the personal struggle is made so unforgiving, we not only make the experience unnecessarily harsh for the individuals concerned, but we also quietly store up problems as described for our democratic system. If political exit could be managed more gracefully, as part of a broader appreciation of the importance of fluidity in political representation, representative democracy might be enhanced. Crafting 'a politics of retreat' (Keane, 2009, p. 283) – in which the transition from political office is thought about, talked about and better managed – would bring benefits, not just to individual politicians and their families, but also to representative democracy.

REFERENCES

Allen, P. and Cutts, D. (2018). An analysis of political ambition in Britain. *The Political Quarterly*, 89(1), 73–81.

Aristotle. (1992). *The Politics*. London: Penguin.

Balls, E. (2016). *Speaking out: Lessons in life and politics*. London: Hutchinson.

Baturo, A. (2017). Democracy, development, and career trajectories of former political leaders. *Comparative Political Studies*, 50(8), 1023–1054.

——— (2014). *Democracy, dictatorship and term limits*. Ann Arbor: University of Michigan Press.

Beehr, T. A. (1986). The process of retirement: A review and recommendations for future investigation. *Personnel Psychology*, 39, 31–55.

Burt, A. (2019). The One with Alastair Burt. *Political Thinking with Nick Robinson*. Podcast, 5 September 2019.

Bush, S. (2019). Tory MPs may despise Boris Johnson but he is the man they think can win an election. *New Statesman*, 5 June 2019.

Bynander, F. and 't Hart, P. (2008). The art of handing over: (Mis)Managing party leadership successions. *Government and Opposition*, 43(3), 385–404.

Byrne, C. and Theakston, K. (2016). Leaving the House: The experience of former Members of Parliament who left the House of Commons in 2010. *Parliamentary Affairs*, 69(3), 686–707.

Caress, S. M. and Kunioka, T. T. (2012). *Term limits and their consequences*. Albany: State University of New York.

Cecić Erpič, S., Wylleman, P. and Zupancic, M. (2004). The effect of athletic and non-athletic factors on the sports career termination process. *Psychology of Sport and Exercise*, 5, 45–59.

Clinton, H. R. (2017). *What happened*. London: Simon and Schuster.

de Waal, F. (2006). *Our inner ape*. London: Granta Publications.

Doherty, D. C. (2001). To run or not to run? *Canadian Parliamentary Review*, 24, 16–23.

Dowding, K. and Kang, W.-T. (1998). Ministerial resignations 1945–97. *Public Administration*, 76, 411–429.

Dowding, K. and McLeay, E. (2011). The firing line: When and why do Prime Ministers fire ministerial colleagues? In P.'t Hart and J. Uhr (Eds.) *How power changes hands: Transition and succession in government*, pp. 157–173. Basingstoke: Palgrave Macmillan.

Ebaugh, H. R. F. (1988). *Becoming an ex*. Chicago: The University of Chicago Press.

Ennser-Jedenastik, L. and Muller, W. C. (2013). Intra-party democracy, political performance, and the survival of party leaders: Austria, 1945–2011. *Party Politics*, 21(6), 930–943.

Evans, G. and Tilley, J. (2017). *The new politics of class*. Oxford, UK: Oxford University Press.

Freud, S. (1917). Mourning and melancholia In J. Strachey (Ed.), *The standard edition of the complete psychological works of Sigmund Freud*, pp. 243–258. Vol. XIV. London: The Hogarth Press.

Gabriel, Y., Gray, D. E. and Goregaokar, H. (2013). Job loss and its aftermath among managers and professionals: Wounded, fragmented and flexible, *Work, Employment and Society*, 27(1), 56–72.

Hardman, I. (2018). *Why we get the wrong politicians*. London: Atlantic Books.

Hartley, J. (1987). Managerial unemployment: The wife's perspective and role. In S. Fineman (Ed.), *Unemployment personal and social consequences*, pp. 118–137. London: Tavistock.

Hay, C. (2007). *Why we hate politics*. Cambridge, MA: Polity Press.

Healey, D. (1989). *The time of my life*. London: Penguin Group.

Heath, O. (2019). A growing class divide: MPs and voters. In (Eds.) P. Cowley and R. Ford, *Sex, lies and politics*, chapter 27. London: Biteback.

Ignatieff, M. (2013). *Fire and ashes. Success and failure in politics*. Canada: Random House Canada.

Jahoda, M. (1982). *Employment and unemployment: A socio-psychological analysis*. Cambridge, UK: Cambridge University Press.

Jameson, H. (2019). New Man in the chair. *The Municipal Journal*. 4 July 2019.

Jefferson, T. (1807). *Letter to the Legislature of Vermont. 10 December 1807*. Available at: http://teachingamericanhistory.org/library/document/letter-to-the-legislature-of-vermont/.

Jennings, W., Stoker, G. and Twyman, J. (2016). The dimensions and impact of political discontent in Britain. *Parliamentary Affairs*, 69, 876–900.

Just, P. D. (2004). United Kingdom: Life after number 10 – premiers emeritus and parliament. *The Journal of Legislative Studies*, 10(2-3), 66–78.

Karol, D. (2012). *Forcing their hands? Explaining trends in retirement announcement timing in the U.S. Congress. Paper prepared for presentation at the 2012 Annual Conference on Congress and History*, University of Georgia, Athens, Georgia.

Keane, J. (2009). Life after political death. In J. Kane, H. Patapan and P. t'Hart (Eds.), *Dispersed democratic leadership*, pp. 279–298. Oxford, UK: Oxford University Press.

Kerby, J. and Blidook, K. (2011). It's not you, it's me: Determinants of voluntary legislative turnover in Canada. *Legislative Studies Quarterly*, 36, 621–643.

Kets de Vries, M. F. R. (2003). The Retirement Syndrome: The psychology of letting go. *European Management Journal*, 21(6), 707–716.

King, A. (2015). *Who governs Britain?* London: Penguin.

Kitson, R. (2019). Rugby given warning over rising mental health issues. The *Guardian*, 21 August.

Kwiatkowski, R. (2015). Our House. *The House*, 37 (1513), 27 March.

Lally, P. (2007). Identity and athletic retirement: A prospective study, *Psychology of Sport and Exercise*, 8, 85–99.

Levitsky, S. and Ziblatt, D. (2018). *How democracies die: What history reveals about our future*. London: Random House.

Machiavelli, N. (1532/2009). *The Prince*. London: Vintage.

Mair, P. (2013). *Ruling the void: The hollowing of Western democracy*. London: Verso.

Manhire, T. (2016). Bloody hell, John Key just quit as prime minister. This is not how things happen! Available at: http://thespinoff.co.nz/politics/05-12-2016/bloody-hell-john-key-just-quit-as-prime-minister-this-is-not-how-things-happen/.

Marris, P. (1993). *Loss and change*, London: Routledge.

Menke, D. J. and Germany, M.-L. (2018). Reconstructing athletic identity: College athletes and sport retirement. *Journal of Loss and Trauma*, 24(1), 17–30.

Murray Parkes, C. (1971). Psycho-social transitions: A field for study. *Social Science and Medicine*, 5, 101–115.

O'Neill, B., Pruysers, S. and Stewart, D. K. (2019). Glass cliffs or partisan pressure? Examining gender and party leader tenures and exits. *Political Studies*, 1–21, doi:10.1177/0032321719880316

Opik, L. (2015). Losing badly takes a heavy personal toll on MPs – I should know. *The Guardian*, 9 May.

Owen, D. (2006). Hubris and nemesis in heads of government. *Journal of the Royal Society of Medicine*, 99, 548–551.

Paikin, S. (2003). *The dark side*. Toronto: Viking.

Paxman, J. (2002). *The political animal*. London: Penguin Books.

Petracca, M. (1992). Rotation in office: The history of an idea. In G. Benjamin and M. J. Malbin (Eds.) *Limiting legislative terms*, pp. 19–51. Congressional Quarterly Inc.

Pidd, H. (2017). The people's Champion. *The Guardian* 10 February.

Pow, J. T. (2018). Amateurs versus professionals: Explaining the political (in) experience of Canadian Members of Parliament. *Parliamentary Affairs*, 71, 633–655.

Raymond, C. D. and Overby, M. (2019). Calling it quits: Legislative retirements in comparative perspective. *Political Studies*. doi: 10.1177/0032321719865111

Riddell, P. (2019). *15 minutes of power: The uncertain life of British Ministers*. London: Profile Books.

(1996). *Honest opportunism: How we get the politicians we deserve*. London: Indigo.

Richards, S. (2019). *The Prime Ministers: Reflections on leadership from Wilson to May*. London: Atlantic Books.

Roberts, J. (2017). *Losing political office*. London: Palgrave Macmillan.

Roberts, J. E. (2019). The underappreciated loss of political office. *Journal of Loss and Trauma*. doi: 10.108015325024.20191617995

Runciman, D. (2019). *Where power stops: The making and unmaking of Presidents and Prime Ministers*. London: Profile Books.

Ruscio, K. P. (2004). *The leadership dilemma in modern democracy*. Cheltenham: Edward Elgar.

Shaffir, W. and Kleinknecht, S. (2005). Death at the polls. Experiencing and coping with political defeat. *Journal of Contemporary Ethnography*, 34(6), 707–738.

Stoker, G. (2006). *Why politics matters. Making democracy work.* Basingstoke: Palgrave Macmillan.

Taylor, J. and Ogilvie, B. C. (1994). A Conceptual Model of adaptation to retirement among athletes. *Journal of Applied Sport Psychology,* 6, 1–20.

Theakston, K. (2010). *After Number 10.* Basingstoke: Palgrave Macmillan.

Theakston, K., and de Vries, J. (2012). *Former leaders in modern democracies. Political sunsets.* Basingstoke: Palgrave Macmillan.

Theakston, K., Gouge, E. and Honeyman, V. (2007). *Life after losing or leaving. The experience of former members of Parliament.* A report for the Association of Former Members of Parliament. Leeds: University of Leeds.

Walter, J. (2016). Biographical analysis. In R. A. W. Rhodes and P. 't Hart (Eds.), *The Oxford textbook of political leadership.* Oxford, UK: Oxford University Press.

Wang, M. (2013). Retirement: An introduction and overview of the handbook. In M. Wang (Ed.), *The Oxford textbook of retirement.* Oxford, UK: Oxford University Press.

Weinberg, A. (2012). Should the job of national politicians carry a government health warning? The impact of psychological strain on politicians. In A. Weinberg (Ed.), *The psychology of politicians.* Cambridge, UK: Cambridge University Press.

Williams, L. M. (2011). The Queen's Park after-party: Post-cabinet life in the legislature. *Paper prepared for the Canadian Political Science Association Conference,* Waterloo, Ontario.

Willumsen D. M. and Goetz, K. H. (2017). Set free? Impending retirement and legislative behaviour in the UK. *Parliamentary Affairs,* 70, 254–279.

Wren, T. (2007). *Inventing leadership: The challenge of democracy.* Cheltenham: Edward Elgar.

PART III

For the People

CHAPTER 14

Democracy as a Moral Challenge

Gian Vittorio Caprara

About Democracy: A Moral Case for Its Defence

Democracy is usually associated with an ideal form of polity that aims at the broadest equal participation of citizens in government and at the full recognition and expression of their individualities (Sartori, 2007). It is a form of government whose most remote antecedents can be found in the assembly regimes of antiquity, among which Athenian democracy has been commonly indicated as an exemplary model of direct participation of ordinary people in collective self-governance. (Dahl, 1998; Hansen, 2006; Ober, 2012).

However, the assembly governments of the past and Athenian democracy itself can only be viewed abstractly as the original forms of modern democracy. The anthropological conceptions of individuals as social beings and of communities, which are at the basis of people's sense of belonging, participation and self-governance – in most cases implicitly as tacit knowledge and rules – were very different then from those of our times. The principle of the equal right of all human beings to be recognised and treated as humans became established later and only gradually. Slaves were not entitled to be treated humanely and women were not entitled to have a political voice.

Modern democracies are much more inclusive than those of the ancients, and the participation of the largest number of people in the governance of societies occurs through representation within the frame of a set of ideal principles, institutions and rules that solicit and guide individuals' actions and commitments. The extension of universal suffrage that grants the equal right of all citizens to express their voice has been achieved only in the last century in most democracies. Today's democratic ideals aim at guaranteeing to all citizens the greatest freedom of expression, the greatest equality of consideration and the widest participation in the choices that guide the government. As such, every person is viewed as the owner of his/her actions and deserves respect as a person. No one is entitled by nature to dominate others. Citizens are therefore free to express their worldviews, are morally responsible for the outcome of their actions, have equal rights and receive equal treatment from government and before the law.

The path towards this ideal type of democracy, to which the label 'liberal' is often associated, has been long, discontinuous and different across societies. At the beginning of the nineteenth century, only the United States of America and the United Kingdom, and only in part, showed the characteristics of a modern democracy. At the beginning of the twentieth century, there were no more than a dozen or so nations that could boast democratic governments. Even today, arguably no more than a third of the world's population can claim to live in political regimes that stand out as democratic because they aspire to guarantee to all citizens respect for their personal dignity; freedom to express their opinions on religion, values and ideologies; liberty of gathering together and to form associations in the pursuit of their ideas and interest; equal treatment before the law; equal access to public office; and equal opportunity to exercise control over the use of power. Although many countries claim the status of democracies, those that have lost and regained democracy in the last century are greater in number than those that can boast a prolonged and unbroken familiarity with it.

The ethos of liberal democracy has a clear impact at the level of the individual citizen. It requires that individuals perceive and treat each other equally in their right to express their opinions and preferences and to pursue living conditions that maximise their well-being. Recognition of everyone's right to self-determination and the pursuit of happiness is the condition for the full expression of their personality and common human-ity. Respect for the individuality and diversity of each person entitles everyone to fair treatment and to draw from the recognition of others the measure of his/her own value and the value of life itself.

The aims of democracy require citizens who feel responsible for the pursuit of public good. Representation and majority's rules are instrumen-tal to allow citizens to express their will and to self-governance under the assumption that public good is their common goal. Ideologies and parties serve democracy to the extent that they give voice to citizens' personal interests while pursuing the public good (Caprara and Vecchione, 2018).

These are ambitious goals that entail difficult challenges. In reality, individuals do not hold equal capacities to champion their opinions, nor is human life given equal value across social latitudes. On a formal level, the requirements that distinguish modern democracies are freedom of expression, of the press and of association, plurality of political offer, certainty and frequency of opportunities to express one's preferences and equal opportunities for access to political office. In essence, the various democracies differ in the degree to which all citizens are guaranteed equal recognition of rights and equal opportunities of realising their talents, through institutions capable of representing and reconciling competing interests and thus of orchestrating the best use of resources for the common good. Evidently, this includes and goes beyond the opportunities that citizens are given to vote periodically, to choose between different programmes and to run for government office.

In this chapter, I will address the psychosocial underpinnings of modern democracy and maintain that its realisation is conditional upon the moral development of citizens.

Democracy as a Moral Maze?

It is clear that the extension of universal suffrage is not enough – nor can constitutional charts and institutional solutions be enough – to achieve democracy in countries that are unfamiliar with any form of public debate, where traditional elites resist renouncing their privileges and where large sections of the population doubt that they may have any voice in government. Even in established democracies, one may doubt the realisation of democratic ideals, as citizens declare they are only moderately satisfied with the functioning of their institutions.

In this regard, my discourse about democracy and its challenges addresses themes that have long been the target of speculation and investigation, mostly among philosophers and political scientists. My aim, however, is to point out the special contribution of psychology to highlight the role that habits, beliefs and values exert in making democracy function and in realising its ideals. In this regard, I share most of the recent arguments advanced by Moghaddam (2016) about the actualisation of democracy in our societies, as dependent upon how people think and act and requiring a profound transformation of citizenry's psychology.

Today, one cannot ignore the widespread symptoms of malaise and unease of democracy attested by the falling levels of participation in voting, the fragmentation of political platforms and the erosion of confidence in political representation (Dalton, 2004; Torcal and Montero, 2006). Withdrawal from politics may result from the increased complexity of political issues, despite the increased information available to all and the higher levels of education of the electorate – or even from the conviction that democracy is not in danger, in any case, and the notion that it is good that others more competent and more motivated are dealing with it.

The fragmentation of political platforms may result from the waning of traditional ideological divides and by the need to make continuous compromises to ensure the necessary stability for ruling; or even from the difficulties of envisaging new visions of the future and of how to achieve more equitable societies. The erosion of confidence in political representation goes hand in hand with the volatility of political leadership and reflects the gap between what politicians promise and what they can deliver and, ultimately, their difficulties in meeting the moods and expectations of a composite electorate. These phenomena influence each other and fuel scepticism, dissatisfaction and resignation.

Scepticism can reflect the embarrassment of a citizen who is increasingly capable of managing his/her private life as (s)he believes and who is increasingly doubtful of his/her chances of influencing the management of public affairs. In the end, one can be convinced that there is no reason for rational people to devote intelligence, energy and passion in the pursuit of objectives that they do not perceive to be within their reach, and in the defence of systems that do not seem to need their commitment. Likewise, a great deal of dissatisfaction derives from higher expectations and more severe evaluations of politicians' performance. The more people become accustomed to thinking they can decide and choose for themselves, the higher their aspirations and expectations grow, and the more demanding it is for politicians to reconcile the interests of different social groups under common priorities and for the sake of public good. Resignation is the dead end in which trust, will and commitment are extinguished.

Evidently, much of the criticism of democracy comes from within and generally does not involve any nostalgia for past forms of government. Yet, such criticism can pose serious risks to democracy when it carries negative emotions such as anger, resentment, disappointment, despondency, apathy and powerlessness that undermine critical judgement and make one lose sight of the common needs and goals that underlie democracy. These risks become greater when the interests of new oligarchs manage to leverage the combined forces of misinformation and emotional manipulation to impose themselves on collective interests. In this respect, new communication technologies may offer powerful means of persuasion and deception at the service of a few, rather than opportunities aimed at extending the critical awareness of all.

In reality, the ideals of democracy cannot be achieved unless citizens are critically vigilant and fully committed to supporting its principles and institutions. As democracy aims to be the most far-reaching exercise of self-government, its proper functioning can only result from the degree to which citizens are convinced that it is possible and feel responsible for its realisation. This requires the commitment of all to regulate their conduct in accordance with the achievement of the common good. The functioning of democratic institutions, in fact, depends on the skills and honesty of the political elite no more than upon the virtues of citizens. Ultimately, the realisation of democratic ideals is a moral quest that depends upon the degree to which the pursuit of the common good remains at the apex of citizens' striving.

We can ascertain the state of health of various democracies by taking into account, not only the degree to which everyone is allowed to express and change their opinions and preferences, but also the extent to which citizens are convinced that their reason can influence political decisions and feel responsible for their outcomes. This cannot be given for granted, but is the result of democratic education and practice. People have reason to engage in politics and to commit themselves to the pursuit of the best governance in communities that encourage their participation and to the extent that political institutions and representatives value their opinions and aspirations.

Ideally, democratic laws and institutions should provide the most appropriate conditions for engaging all citizens in the pursuit of the common good. However, the reality suggests that laws and institutions are not sufficient to achieve the conditions of freedom of expression, equality of opportunities and mutual respect required by democratic ideals, unless sustained by appropriate world views, values, aspirations and habits. Knowing how people reason and what they value most is particularly necessary in an era such as the current one, in which the number of actors on the political scene has expanded and diversified while great changes have taken place at the level of affiliations and jurisdictions. At a time when political decisions take shape beyond the borders of local communities and are the result of negotiation among multiple interests, it is hard to justify the legitimacy of deliberations, to solicit the commitment and vigilance of citizens and to gain their consensus and trust.

How do we convince voters that their vote still counts, despite their distance from the centres where decisions are taken? Democracy requires, not only freedom of speech, but also the ability to listen and opportunities to make decisions: not only the right to express one's own ideas, but also the habits to debate, to understand others' opinions through confrontation, to grow through discussion, to participate in deliberative processes and to feel fully responsible for the functioning of institutions and good governance.

Promoting democracy means learning to value the mental capital of citizens and thus to promote their autonomy of judgement, critical thinking and accountability. For this reason, a major goal of democratic institutions is to capacitate citizens to govern themselves by making informed choices and by selecting their representatives in accordance with the pursuit of the public good. Making informed choice is particularly urgent in an era that celebrates knowledge and in which the greatest pitfalls may derive from the circumvention of truth. Improving the process of selection and turnover of political representation is equally urgent in a time in which the more politicians are morally trustworthy and possess the skills necessary for the exercise of government, the more they can sustain and strengthen the sense of fairness and collective efficacy, which are essential to the proper functioning of democracy.

To this end, knowledge of the personality of citizens, in all its different expressions of subjectivity and sociality, is no less important than knowledge of institutional and governmental practices.

Personalising Politics

Human beings carry extraordinary potential to grow and to develop capacities enabling the exertion of considerable influence over their experience and the course of their lives. However, the actualisation of this is mainly conditional upon the social and cultural environments they encounter.

One may argue that democratic ideals represent the apex of human thought and imagination about the ways people should live together and societies should be governed in order to actualise human potential. Moreover, modern democracy places the reflexive and responsible citizen at the core of the political scene under the assumption that the functioning of its institutions and, ultimately, its realisation depends upon the needs, the values and the habits of citizens: namely, their personalities. Personality, in fact, summarises the various components that account for being a person and allow us to distinguish one individual from another.

In this regard, the theme of the personalisation of politics has been recurring for years, but it has only partly done justice to the role of the person as the origin and end of politics, and has served to understand and thus appreciate how personality and politics influence each other. The word 'personalisation', in particular, has mainly been used to highlight the personality of leaders and focused upon the influence it can have in attracting and seducing voters. As a result, the interest in personality has been mostly instrumental in building and delivering the most captivating impressions that can extend consensus and strengthen the authority of leaders.

By using the word 'personalising', instead, it has been intended to reaffirm the central role of the person in politics and to point out the importance of citizens' personalities in making sense of their political choices and actions (Caprara and Vecchione, 2017). This occurs under the assumptions that: (a) the development of democracy and of citizens' personalities are mutually interdependent and (b) that the best politics is the one able to grant the full expression of citizens' personalities. I am convinced that this meaning of personalising may serve better than personalisation to value the extent to which democracy is the form of government most congenial to people of our times and the one that most can sustain human development.

The events of recent decades have brought about profound changes in the political orientations of citizens, in the selection of leaders and in the management of consensus. Traditional class constraints have been much lessened, ideological divides appear less polarised and socio-demographic factors such as age, gender, education and income affect political preferences much less than in the past. The grip of parties is also much less effective, and voting is volatile and increasingly uncertain (Dalton and Wattenberg, 2000; van der Brug, 2010).

Understanding personality, in particular, takes on greater importance the more the functioning of the political system depends on the active participation of citizens, their cognitive strategies and preferences, and the more their moral obligations replace the duties of in-group loyalties and socially ascribed roles. The more people become emancipated from scarcity and can afford greater mobility, the more traditional family, religious and class bonds are lessened and their social obligations are continually renegotiated.

The ethics of modernity claim the full realisation of individuals' potential and demand their widest responsibility as regards the course taken by their life. Likewise, self-interest is still the source of preferences and commitment in politics. However, self-interest includes a variety of intangible and symbolic assets such as self-esteem, recognition of others and the power to give voice to one's own ideas and aspirations, feelings of belonging and senses of personal and social identity, that in the past were mostly unknown or scarcely relevant to most people. These are goods that reflect shared values that significantly contribute to define individuals' personalities.

Values, in fact, are mental representations about desirable aims and priorities that operate as guiding principles in people's lives to the extent that their pursuit enhances one's own self-respect and others' acceptance. They reflect judgements about what is good and right and thus moral choices about the kind of life worth living and the kind of society worth pursuing. They guide people's actions the more they stay at the core of individuals' identity and the more their achievement is perceived as irremissible to preserve one's own integrity.

Democratic values like liberty, equality and justice represent major achievements upon which have converged different cultural traditions as the most compatible with human development. Yet, their realisation is conditional upon the moral development of citizens and, namely, to their readiness to embrace a view of self-interest that cannot be disjoined from what is good and right for all humanity. Whereas different views about ideal societies may compete with each other, it is reasonable to expect that an overlapping consensus can be ultimately achieved upon views that maximise all humanity welfare (Rawls, 1993). This, however, may occur to the degree that the structures of personality regulating and guiding behaviour – like needs, motives and values – operate in concert in the pursuit of goals that both satisfy and transcend individuals' private interests.

Personality's Determinants of Political Orientation and Participation

As stated above, personality summarises the various components that account for being a person and that allow us to distinguish individuals from one another. It concerns the organisation of structures and mental processes that regulate the relationship of the person with the world and account for the coherence and continuity of the experience from which each of us draws the sense of his/her or their individuality (Caprara and Cervone, 2000).

Such an organisation operates through a variety of bio-psychological systems that ensure the cognitive, motivational and executive functions necessary to interact effectively with the environment. It includes cognitive abilities such as intelligence and its various expressions, affective and cognitive dispositions such as traits, motives and values, and self-evaluations like self-esteem and beliefs about self-efficacy. To varying degrees, personality attests to how nature and culture co-act in making people what they appear to be and to how individuals themselves, through their experience, actively contribute to the course of their lives. Thus, people come into the world with a vast repertoire of potential that constitutes the basic equipment to cope with life's requirements. Evolution has selected the bio-psychological structures that predispose humans to interact with the environment, to give meaning and continuity to their experiences and to value life. Cultural and social contexts provide the conditions for potential to be translated and crystallised into skills, preferences and habits.

Compared to other living species, human beings are endowed with exquisitely mental properties and abilities that allow them to extend their control over their bodies and the environment. Self-reflection, intentionality and self-regulation are properties that allow people to appropriate their own experiences, to sift through their thoughts and feelings, to monitor their own reactions and to accord their conduct with the achievement of goals to which they attach value. Symbolisation, anticipation and learning skills allow people to encode their experiences into mental representations that guide their judgements and actions, to imagine and evaluate – in advance – alternative courses of action, and also to learn from their own experience and capitalise upon that of others.

These properties and capabilities are not fixed from the beginning and can vary significantly over the course of life, and across individuals. They develop gradually and are fully realised to the extent that they are properly cultivated depending upon the opportunities and conditions under which they can be practised. This is a source of diversities that maximise the capacities of humans to adjust to multiple environments.

Necessarily, genes play a decisive role in providing the primary instructions for the development and organisation of biological systems that lay the foundations of cognitive, motivational and behavioural structures. However, social and cultural environments are decisive in setting the conditions that upgrade biological structures into mental structures like traits, motives, attitudes, values and self-beliefs that account for individuals' behaviour and allow them to be distinguished from one another across domains of functioning, including politics. Culture, like nature, is also a source of diversities whose convergencies may ultimately operate in the service of human development.

The interest in personality in the political realm dates back a long time. Philosophers' thought has paved the way for social scientists in pointing to the importance of leaders and citizens' qualities for the achievement of effective governance. In recent decades, several research programmes have documented the special role of individual differences in personality to account for political preferences and participation. Alternative theoretical models have pointed to different constructs like traits, motives, social attitudes, values, moral intuitions and self-efficacy beliefs that, in varying degrees, have shown that individual differences in personality account for both preference and participation much more than traditional socio-demographic variables like sex, age and religion (Caprara and Vecchione, 2017; Duckitt and Sibley, 2009; Haidt, 2012; Jost, Federico and Napier, 2009; Mondak, 2010).

Despite reflecting different theoretical approaches, the above constructs are generally correlated. Thus, the issue one faces today concerns the added explanatory value of each model in comparison to the other, and the extent to which it is possible to pursue a comprehensive model capable of capitalising upon both the elements of convergency and diversity.

In this regard, Michele Vecchione and I developed a research pro-gramme that points to traits, basic values, political attitudes and self-efficacy beliefs as psychological structures of personality that, together, account for a significant portion of political orientation and participation. This research programme has unfolded over the years in collaboration with Shalom Schwartz and other colleagues around the world, providing most of the findings that we reported in *Personalizing Politics and Realizing Democracy* (Caprara and Vecchione, 2017).

In our reasoning, biology and experience predispose individuals to interact with the world in ways that turn into stable tendencies to think, feel and react in a consistent manner across time and situations, commonly called traits. These tendencies are seen in habits that allow us to distinguish individuals from one another and to predict their behaviour. Furthermore, most of these tendencies can be traced to a limited number of common dimensions that have proved to underlie and offer a common frame of reference, across cultures, to organise the various psychological qualities and individual differences to which people refer when describing one's own and others' personality. Over the last decades, the five-factor model (FFM; see Table 14.1) including Extraversion, Agreeableness, Conscientiousness, Emotional Stability and Openness to Experience, has gained growing consensus among personality scholars as the standard taxonomy of the basic traits of personality (Digman, 1990; Mc Crae and Costa, 1997).

It is likely nature equips humans with biological structures that, by encountering the environment, lead to the emergence and development of

Table 14.1. *Description of the Big Five personality factors.*

Extraversion: *the tendency to share one's experiences and to relate to others.*
Agreeableness: *the tendency to behave in a friendly manner and to show sympathy for others in need.*
Conscientiousness: *the tendency to behave diligently and to be well-organised and accountable.*
Emotional stability: *the tendency to behave calmly by keeping one's own emotions under control.*
Openness to experience: *the tendency to be attracted by new experience, habits and ideas.*

---

mental structures that predispose them to exert their agency (extraversion and openness) and to operate in communion with others (emotional stability, agreeableness and conscientiousness). Likewise, cultures equip people with internal systems of meaning and value attribution that shape their capacities and guide their conduct in the pursuit of goals that, in varying degrees, accord with the requirements of agency and communion. Values are cognitive representations of desirable aims that attest to these functions as guiding principles in people's lives.

Actually, one may enlist multiple value systems. However, over recent decades, the taxonomy proposed by Shalom Schwartz (1992) in the domain of values has achieved a large consensus across cultures, like the FFM in the domain of traits. This taxonomy includes ten distinct values associated with specific motivational goals: power, achievement, hedonism, stimulation, self-direction, universalism, benevolence, conformity, tradition and security. These values are commonly located around a circular model that shows the degree of their compatibility within a two-dimensional space in which values related to openness to change (self-direction, stimulation) oppose values related to conservation (conformity, tradition, security), whereas values related to self-enhancement (power, achievement) oppose values related to self-transcendence (universalism, benevolence) (see Chapter 3 by James Weinberg).

The ten values, like basic traits, can be traced to universal requirements of human conditions like agency and communion (Bakan, 1966). Achievement, hedonism, self-stimulation and self-direction are self-centred values that mostly rest upon the individuals' sense of their own agency and lead them to assign priority to self-enhancement goals. Universalism, benevolence, tradition, conformity and security, instead, are others-centred values that mostly rest upon the individuals' sense of communion and lead them to assign priority to self-transcendent goals. (Schwartz, 1992; see Table 14.2).

Table 14.2. *The motivational goals commonly associated with the ten basic values.*

Power: *social status and prestige, control and dominance over people and resources.*
Achievement: *personal success.*
Hedonism: *pleasure and sensuous gratification.*
Stimulation: *excitement and novelty.*
Self-direction: *independent thought and action.*
Universalism: *care for the welfare of all people and of nature.*
Benevolence: *protection of beloved people.*
Tradition: *endorsement and promotion of traditional customs and ideas.*
Conformity: *compliance with social norms and expectations.*
Security: *safety and stability.*

Basic Traits, Basic Values, Political Values and Political Orientation and Participation

In addressing political orientation, we considered Left/Right and liberal/ conservative as distinct ideologies able to account for the political offer that is made available and for the political preferences citizens can express in the Western democracies we examined (Caprara, 2020; Caprara and Vecchione, 2018). Findings have revealed that there is substantial congruency in how people present themselves as regards their behavioural tendencies, the values they prioritise and their political preferences.

First, basic traits have proved to account for significant variations in political orientation across established democracies, more than traditional socio-economic variables like gender, education and income. Left-leaning and liberal voters and politicians scored higher in openness than Right-leaning and conservative voters and politicians, who, instead, scored higher than the former in conscientiousness (Caprara et al., 2003). Then, basic values proved to account for significant variations in political preferences more than basic traits. Left-leaning and liberal voters and politicians assigned higher importance to universalism than Right-leaning and conservative voters and politicians. The latter, instead, assigned higher importance to conservation values than the former. In most cases, values entirely mediated the influence of the basic traits with regard to political orientation (Caprara et al., 2006; Caprara, Vecchione and Schwartz, 2009).

The influence of basic values, however, was largely mediated by values that were closely associated with core issues of current political debate like equality, free enterprise, traditional morality, civic liberties, law and order,

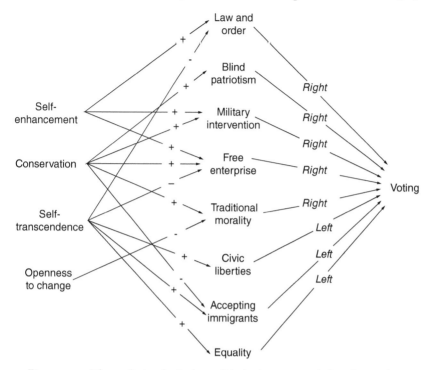

Figure 14.1   The mediational role that political values exert in linking basic values to voting.

accepting immigrants, military intervention and patriotism (see Figure 14.1). Political values accounted for a significant portion of variability in voting with Left and liberal voters showing greater preference for equality, civil rights and accepting immigrants than Right and conservative voters. Right and conservative voters, instead, prevailed over Left and liberal voters in traditional morality, law and order, free enterprise, military interventions and patriotism (Schwartz, Caprara and Vecchione, 2010).

As in the case of political orientation, even with regard to political participation, findings have shown that there is a substantial congruency in the beliefs people hold about themselves and their values. In general, extraversion, openness, self-direction and universalism are more associated with active engagement in politics than other traits and values. Yet, it is the degree to which citizens believe they have a voice and can affect the political system that mostly sustains their active participation in politics (Caprara et al., 2009; Vecchione and Caprara, 2009; Vecchione et al.,

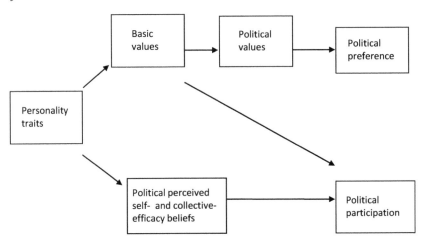

Figure 14.2   The hypothetical path of influence showing how traits, basic values, political values and self- and collective-efficacy beliefs may contribute to political orientation and participation.

2014). Indeed, people do not engage in politics unless they believe they hold the necessary capacities to voice their opinions and that the political system is receptive to them. Thus, both perceived self-efficacy and collective efficacy are needed to motivate people to take action and afford the cost that political activism may require. Perceived political self-efficacy is mostly due to experiences that lead individuals to master the knowledge and skills required to navigate through politics. Perceived political collective efficacy, instead, is a matter of trust since it depends, on the one hand, upon the confidence that citizens have in their fellow citizens' commitment to the pursuit of the common good and, on the other, upon the competence and integrity of politicians.

Likely self- and collective-efficacy beliefs operate as the gatekeepers through which traits and values may contribute to political participation (see Figure 14.2). It is, in fact, unlikely that people engage in politics, whichever their dispositions, values, orientation and ideology, unless they believe in the impact of their action.

The Moral Underpinnings of Democracy

Despite significant differences in value priorities among voters of competing ideologies such as Left/Right and liberal/conservative, a surprising convergence has been found in the priority given to a few basic political values across voters and in several democracies.

Among the basic values, self-direction featured among the two priori-tised values in most of the democracies we examined, as well as being the value most correlated with a country's level of democratisation (Caprara and Vecchione, 2015). Likewise, a large convergence was found in prior-itising equality and civil liberties among political values. Certainly, one cannot ignore that most of these findings derive from groups who were more conveniently accessible for researchers, showing higher levels of education than the average population. Yet, these results are encouraging in documenting the importance given to values crucial for the advance-ment of democracy, beyond diversities in ideological orientation. Self-direction attests to the importance of independent thought and action; civil liberties point to individuals' freedom as an inviolable value that finds a limitation only in others' right to freedom; equality claims fair treatment and proper opportunities to grow and realise one's own potential, for everyone.

In fact, one may wonder, not so much about the representativeness of the respondents, as to the extent to which the priorities they declare correspond to irremissible convictions that bind them to behave accordingly. This cannot be discounted. In reality, this may occur only in the degree to which the following conditions exist: (1) that people's value priorities are grounded in their moral judgements of true, good, right and just; (2) that people are aware of the obligations that derive from the endorsement of those values as regards their conduct; (3) that people feel capable of behaviour that con-forms with those obligations; (4) that people feel responsible for the achievement of those values and (5) that people cannot live comfortably with themselves unless they actively pursue those values, since their self-respect depends upon the actualisation of these values.

All these conditions require awareness, abilities and willpower that people hold in different degrees depending upon their moral development and experiences. In this regard, we do not have a universal theory of morality and of moral development upon which there is a general consen-sus as regards its biological underpinnings and the influence of social environment and culture. Considering morality as the domain of criteria that define what is good and evil, right and wrong, fair and unfair for individuals and society, one should be aware that plural ideas are held in different contexts and times regarding how people should treat each other in order to live well together. Pluralism, however, does not necessarily imply moral relativism since a convergence on basic principles about what is 'good' and 'evil' draw their universality from their evolutionary value. In fact, the added value to life and human development of caring for and not harming others is attested by population growth, rise in life expectancy and betterment of living conditions all over the world.

Indeed, most of our reasoning on morality reflects the achievements of civilisation as regards the view of human beings as responsible agents who live in communities under common rights and reciprocal obligations. However, most empirical investigations have been conducted under the assumptions of Western research traditions. These may have been sources of bias in accurately representing non-Western moral achievements, but, even in the domain of morality, one may acknowledge a kind of global convergence upon basic principles that advocate a major concern for the welfare of all humans.

For a long time, morality concerned prohibitions and sanctions aimed at refraining people from harming each other and at protecting the communities in which they lived. Moral imperatives geared to serving humanity require caring for others' well-being as one cares for one's own well-being. In this regard, the welfare of future generations and the safety of the planet have become matters of major moral concern in recent decades. The ideals of liberal democracy rest upon an idea of morality in which the private good cannot be disjoined from public welfare and that requires citizens to treat each other well as each of them would like to be treated.

The knowledge we have accumulated over the years leads us to view moral development as a process in which individuals gradually acknowledge and distinguish what is good and evil, and to align their feelings and actions to their judgements. While humans are biologically equipped to seek pleasure and to avoid pain, positive and negative effects resulting from the consequences of their behaviour and from reinforcements received from others set the premises for the discovery of 'good' and 'evil' in the first stages of development. This occurs in concomitance with the maturation and development of cognitive and affective structures that enable children to acknowledge the impact of their actions upon others and to conform their behaviour accordingly.

One cannot exclude that humans are predisposed by nature to behave morally, and, namely, not to harm but to care for others, through early emotions and intuitions that anticipate empathy and sympathy. Yet, the criteria of utility and social convenience are the ones that, at the beginning, chart the direction of moral development in concomitance with the emergence of self and the recognition of others. Gradually, children come to acknowledge that they are the owners of their actions and that it is beneficial and socially approved to refrain from behaviours that give pain to others and expose themselves to punishment, rejection and shame. Likewise, they come to acknowledge that doing good to others, telling the truth and being fair can be sources of others' commendation as well as sources of pleasure and pride in themselves.

Whereas moral development concerns learning, reasoning, feeling and behaving, moral functioning attests to the degree of integration and coherence of these factors. It is likely that moral behaviour largely depends upon obedience and then upon compliance in the early stages. Learning through reinforcements, about what is good and evil, sets the conditions for stable associations of actions with feelings and then for reasoning about the consequences of one's own actions. Only later are moral principles established as mental representations of thoughts and aspirations that guide people's thoughts, make sense of their feelings and predispose them to action under the direction of an internal system – the self – that grants coherence and continuity to individuals' experience.

The endorsement of moral principles from others and their appropriation, however, does not necessarily rest upon the same reasoning and carry the same investment of affect across contexts. Nor do care, truth and justice exert the same constraint upon all people's motivations to become stable behaviours. People may accord their beliefs and habits to moral principles because of obedience and compliance, and can dismiss them without particular discomfort when they no longer match their interests. One may expect a congruency between thought, affect and action only when people really take up moral principles: namely, when the pursuit of the good and fair, for their own sake, is perceived as irresistible 'oughts'. This occurs when moral values become core components of an individual's identity as obligations that condition their self-respect and well-being (Blasi, 2004).

The extent to which higher levels of moral judgement transcend obedience and convenience in pursuit of good, truth and fairness for their own sake, in accordance with a view of morality as an asset that operates at the service of all humanity, is a matter of debate. In fact, a narrow view of self-interest seems to bind most people's moral reasoning and action to conventional rules on the pursuit of what is good for the individual and for his/her community. In reality, the cultural and social environment have always exerted a decisive role in setting the values to achieve and in shaping the course of people's moral development by managing reinforcement and by providing the opportunities to achieve higher levels of moral functioning.

Thus, one may wonder about the extent to which our societies make people morally ready to meet the requirements of democracy. Much progress has undoubtedly been made at the level of declaration of principles as well as at the level of policies aiming to promote individuals' rights and defend human rights. The findings I reported above are encouraging with regards to the progress of democratic societies in the sphere of values that govern living together. Yet, one cannot take for granted that declared values are always grounded on moral convictions and matched by conforming conduct, even in the most socially advanced societies.

In reality, there is often a gulf between what people declare as morally desirable and what they do in their daily lives, as well as a kind of inattention regarding how to reduce the gap. Valuing liberty, equality and justice counts as a guide for action to the extent that they are ingrained in individuals' identities as moral agents firmly committed to their pursuit. Behaving consistently with one's own moral reasoning and convictions, however, requires capacities and willpower that need to be learned and practised. A morality guided by criteria of mere personal utility and convenience continues to prevail when the observance of moral norms entails costs and sacrifices that people consider difficult to sustain. Powerful mechanisms of self-deception make it possible to proclaim the values of truth, honesty, integrity and fairness, and to preserve an image of oneself conforming to their observance, despite the fact that one's conduct is in clear contrast with them. Mechanisms of moral disengagement abound: moral justification; euphemistic labelling; displacement and diffusion of responsibility; distortion of the consequences of one's own actions; and attribution of blame to others. Losing sight of the humanity of others allows people to detach their conduct from their judgement, to avoid shame and guilt, and to live in peace with themselves while damaging others (Bandura, 2016). These mechanisms operate pervasively across all walks of life and unavoidably undermine the reciprocal obligations that democracy entails.

Much of citizens' disappointment with democracy concerns the moral accountability of politicians. In reality, much of the malaise with democracy reflects the moral leniency of citizens. As stated above, democracy can be realised to the extent that its goals are grounded in people's moral priorities as regards good, truth and right. Likewise, democracy may effectively work and develop under the condition that citizens and their representatives operate as moral agents committed towards an ethic of public good and equipped with mindsets necessary to treat each other with the same respect as one would like to be treated.

To this end, citizens should be made aware of the obligations that derive from the endorsement of democratic values, enabled to behave in conformity with those values and feel responsible for their observance. This does not occur without great investments in people's development and education.

In this regard, psychological research should document the degree to which the capacity for autonomy, critical judgement and responsibility is decisive in appropriating values, exerting rights, practising freedom and pursuing the public good. The same research should indicate how to generate and cultivate virtues like honesty, truthfulness, fairness, generosity, loyalty and courage, while warning against the obstacles that preclude ways of thinking, desiring and acting that would allow everyone to live a better life (Blasi, 2013).

Inequality as a Major Obstacle to Democracy

A large number of human achievements depend upon the opportunities to discover and to nurture the potential given to individuals by nature. Humans, in fact, can be the governors of their own lives to the extent that their potentials turn into capacities that allow them to choose and transform the environments in which they live in accordance with their welfare.

The realisation of human potential in the domains of capacities and values is both an aim and a condition of democracy. It requires acknowledging the diversity of each individual and the equal rights of all individuals to grow and to be treated as unique persons worthy of respect. It points to the resources and to the opportunities that are necessary to be granted in order to make the qualities that make human life worth living achievable. Nowadays, increased economic resources, wider access to knowledge and broader recognition of individual rights have increased the opportunities to cultivate one's talents and have extended the control that citizens of many nations may exert over their lives.

However, even in the most socio-economically developed countries, it does not seem that equal opportunities to realise their own potential have yet been granted to all, despite the decisive role that is attributed to mental capital for social and economic development in a changing world (Beddington et al., 2008). Many are the merits of Amartya Sen (2009) and Martha Nussbaum (2011) for having placed at the centre of their analyses of human, economic and social development, the interdependence of capacities and dignity. Psychological research can document how self-worth, mutual respect and capacities are closely intertwined and crucial for the practice of democracy.

Democracy is commonly associated with freedom of speech and of choice. In reality, there is no real freedom unless all citizens' potential has equal consideration in politics. Democracy may claim that individuals' freedom finds its limits in others' freedom, to the extent that citizens are convinced that this requires granting equal rights to freedom to all. Likewise, democracy may advocate that citizens should treat each other as well as each would like to be treated, to the extent that citizens are convinced that caring for others' good and living well together are interdependent. Both these convictions require levels of moral reasoning in which the realisation of others' personality is worthy of the same value as the realisation of one's own personality and in which the pursuit of the common good subsumes individuals' self-interest. Both these convictions turn into effective practices to the extent that people are equipped with the necessary capacities.

As I stated above, it cannot be taken for granted that most people attain these levels of moral functioning spontaneously. In reality, the levels of moral functioning people achieve largely depend upon the opportunities people have been given to know, to think and to behave in ways that lead to ingrained moral values as basic components of their own identity. Psychological research may help to identify the abilities and the conditions that foster moral development, and then to indicate how desirable skills can be cultivated; and, also, how to deal with the obstacles that preclude some people from achieving ways of thinking, desiring and acting that would allow them to live a better life.

To this end, psychology has pointed to the role that social environments and interpersonal relations play in promoting capacities of self-reflection and regulation that enable people to express and cultivate their best. Since human development depends on prolonged early care, individuals' emotional and cognitive growth is largely dependent upon parental and care-givers' investments that, in turn, depend upon the family's and community's resources. Primary care lays the foundation for the trust that children can have in themselves and in the world. The conditions under which they are accepted shape their personal identity. The exchanges they establish, the models they are exposed to and the treatment they receive define the horizons of their desires and aspirations and, thus, what they can do and who they can become.

Stress and poverty are the main causes of early disruptive effects due to rejection, maltreatment and lack of cognitive stimulation and emotional support. Social environments can be harmful, both because of the lack of material and emotional resources and because of abusive experiences. Lack of means in combination with lack of care inevitably compromise self-respect, trust in others and attachment to life. When the family environment does not provide the conditions to develop the primary skills necessary to communicate with others, to regulate one's emotions and to conform one's conduct to the standards commonly expected, children bring a heavy inheritance of incapacity and insufficiency to school, which may be further exacerbated by difficulties in dealing with teachers, conflict with peers, rejection of others and self-exclusion.

It is not difficult to imagine how early deprivation can trigger circuits in which rejection and failure form a sort of perverse multiplication, which can lead to trajectories with inauspicious outcomes. Nor is it necessary to reiterate the arguments of a vast literature that documents how hindrances to entry into the world of work derive from the lack of opportunities to test and realise one's potential. It is more likely that children growing up in poverty have greater difficulty in realising their full potential (Nisbett et al., 2012; Turkheimer et al., 2003). Disadvantaged environments have the potential to undermine development of cognition, motivation and judgement where there is a scarcity of opportunities needed to promote and exercise the relevant skills (Cunha and Heckman, 2009).

Although the adverse effects of early experiences can be attenuated later, the prolonged combination of cognitive and affective deficits throughout childhood and adolescence can affect individuals' self-concept, view of others, levels of aspiration and skills. These often accord with wider relations as a competitive arena where the need to survive prevails over the desire to live well together. The costs that society ends up paying in terms of crime, illness, low productivity and unhappiness are enormous.

Likewise, the cost for democracy is enormous should a situation arise where large sections of the population lack the mindsets needed to make democracy work. In fact, it is unlikely that people deprived of the opportunity to fully express their talents will be able to play the role in politics that democracy requires, basically due to a lack of knowledge, skills and motivation. Empirical research data consistently show negative relationships between poverty, on the one hand, and education, civism and political participation, on the other. The more people live in poverty and the less they have access to education, the less their active participation in political life (Welzel, Inglehart and Klingemann, 2003).

Civic virtues require adequate opportunities for recognition and development. Democracy that does not invest in the moral education and civic engagement of its citizens is like an economy that does not invest in talents and innovation. Democratic participation rests upon the citizen's appropriation of values that must be cultivated as regards the importance of saying and pursuing the truth, behaving honestly, according to others the same respect one considers one deserves and caring for the public good. The functioning of democratic systems, on the other hand, depends fundamentally on the degree to which equal consideration, equal opportunities and fair treatment by the institutions is guaranteed to all.

In this regard, much of the malaise of contemporary democracy reflects a deficit of equality that is only partly documented by the most miserable conditions. In reality, a major matter of concern for the functioning of democracy in several economically developed countries is not the inequality between those who have and those who have not, but that between those who have too much and those who have much less than they believe they deserve. It is reasonable to expect that progress raises all people's levels of aspiration, but not that only a few will benefit from its advantages. Although the levels of aspiration of most people may rise beyond their possible satisfaction, what makes the mismatch intolerable is the sense of injustice that derives from comparing the attainments of the most with the privileges of the few.

Disadvantageous upward comparison, as it occurs when people compare themselves to others who are treated better than they are, does not help to promote the conviction that one should treat each other well, as each would like to be treated, in order to live well together. Nor does advocating merit help to justify inequalities when the criteria by which merit is assessed do not correspond to what consensually could be viewed as worthy of recognition and reward for the pursuit of public good (Sandel, 2020).

In reality, one has many reasons to doubt the degree to which equal respect and equal opportunities may hold sway when people consider that others start with major assets, gain access to better opportunities and enjoy the cumulative effects of privilege over time. Furthermore, new inequalities may derive from selective access to innovations that allow forms of empowerment in the domain of education and health that further amplify the initial divide. While democracy requires citizens to subsume and transcend their contingent self-interest in the pursuit of the common good, this becomes more of a challenge when society seems to function the other way around. Envy, anger, discomfort, distrust and resignation may easily accord with self-centred and conventional modes of moral reasoning, paving the way to corruption, resignation, withdrawal and cynicism.

For this reason, I believe that inequality of opportunities is the major problem precluding the full actualisation of individuals' potential and which undermines the realisation of democracy. Diversity, on the other hand, is the major asset of the human condition to the extent that it paves the way to multiple possible achievements.

Democratic governments should, therefore, ascertain whether everything possible is being done to ensure equality as regards the capacity to reason critically, to discern the truth, to behave honestly and fairly, and to pursue the common good through all available and legitimate means. To this aim, health and education are primary goods to be equally and unconditionally granted to all. After granting these conditions, one may expect to ground the proper functioning of democratic institutions upon citizens' talents and to move beyond counting upon their confidence in the law, their vigilance and their zeal.

Democracy is destined to stagnate and fail when critical judgement and moral conduct do not operate as multipliers of rationality, commitment and civil virtues.

Conclusions

I am convinced that democracy is among the main expressions of human development. The benefits of the spread of democratic ideals are documented by the potential benefits to quality of life in countries where democratic institutions have been established earlier and had the opportunities to improve. Health, education, security and greater freedoms document the merits of democracy. Moreover, I am convinced that democracy is, above all, an achievement of moral psychology that can be realised to the extent that citizens are fully committed to the achievement of the values it entails with regard to mutual respect and the pursuit of the common good.

However, persisting inequalities represent major obstacles to the realisation of democratic ideals and are common sources of dissatisfaction. In reality, democratic ideals of liberty and self-government cannot be attained unless equal opportunities for growth and fair conditions of life are granted to all citizens. Democratic institutions should enable citizens to be equally responsible in contributing to the pursuit of common good. Since democracy will struggle to function if citizens do not have the necessary mindsets to treat each other well and to live well together, democratic virtues must be nurtured and greater investment in moral education should be made in order to put democracy into practice.

REFERENCES

Bakan, D. (1966). *The duality of human existence*. Chicago: Rand McNally.
Bandura, A. (2016). *Moral disengagement*. New York: Worth Publishers.
Beddington, J., Cooper, C. L., Field, J., Goswami, U., Huppert, F. A., Jenkins, R., Jones, H. S., Kirkwood, T. B. L., Sahakian, B. J. and Thomas, S. M. (2008). The mental wealth of nations. *Nature*, 455, 1057–1060.

Blasi, A. (2013). The self and the management of the moral life. In F. Oser and T. Lowat (Eds.), *Handbook of moral motivation: Theories, models and applications*, pp. 229–248. Rotterdam: Sense.

(2004). Moral functioning: Moral understanding and personality. In D. K. Lapsley and D. Narvaez (Eds.), *Moral development, self and identity*, pp. 335–347. Mahwah, NJ: Lawrence Erlbaum Associates.

Caprara, G. V., Barbaranelli, C., Consiglio, C., Picconi, L. and Zimbardo, P. (2003). Personality of politicians and voters: Unique and synergistic relationships. *Journal of Personality and Social Psychology*, 84, 849–851.

Caprara, G. V. and Cervone, D. (2000). *Personality: Determinants, dynamics and potentials*. Cambridge, UK: Cambridge University Press.

Caprara, G. V., Schwartz, S. H. Capanna, C., Vecchione, M. and Barbaranelli, C. (2006). Personality and politics: Values, traits and political choice. *Political Psychology*, 27, 1–28.

Caprara, G. V. and Vecchione, M. (2018). On the left and right ideological divide: Historical accounts and contemporary perspectives. *Advances in Political Psychology*, 39, 49–83.

(2017). *Personalizing politics and realizing democracy*. New York. Oxford University Press.

(2015). Democracy through ideology and beyond: The values that are common to the right and the left. *Cesckolovenska Psychologie*, 59 (Suppl.1), 2–13.

Caprara, G. V., Vecchione, M., Capanna, C. and Mebane, M. (2009). Perceived political self-efficacy: Theory, assessment and applications. *European Journal of Social Psychology*, 39, 1002–1020.

Caprara, G. V., Vecchione, M. and Schwartz, S. H. (2009). The mediational role of values in linking personality traits to political orientation. *Asian Journal of Social Psychology*, 12, 82–94.

Cunha, F. and Heckman, J. J. (2009). The economics and psychology of inequality and human development. *Journal of European Economic Association*, 7, 320–364.

Dahl, R. (1998). *On democracy*. New Haven, CT: Yale University Press.

Dalton, R. J. (2004). *Democratic challenges, democratic choices: The erosion of political support in advanced industrial democracies*. New York: Oxford University Press.

Dalton, R. J. and Wattenberg, M. P. (2000). *Parties without partisans*. Oxford, UK: Oxford University Press.

Digman, J. M. (1990). Personality structure: Emergence of the Five Factor Model. *Annual Review of Psychology*, 41, 417–440.

Duckitt, J. and Sibley, C. G. (2009). A dual process motivational theory of ideology, politics and prejudice. *Psychological Inquiry*, 20, 98–109.

Haidt, J. (2012). *The righteous mind: Why good people are divided by politics and religion*. New York: Pantheon Books.

Hansen, M. H. (2006). *Polis: An introduction to the ancient Greek city-state*. New York: Oxford University Press.

Jost, J., Federico, C. M. and Napier, J. L. (2009). Political ideology: Its structure, functions, and elective affinities. *Annual Review of Psychology*, 60, 307–337.

McCrae, R. R. and Costa, P. T. (1997). Personality trait structure as a human universal. *American Psychologist*, 52, 509–516.

Moghaddam, F. M. (2016). *The psychology of democracy*. Washington, DC: American Psychological Association Press.

Mondak, J. (2010). *Personality and the foundations of political behavior*. Cambridge, MA: Cambridge University Press.

Nisbett, R. E., Aronson, J., Blair, C., Dickens, W., Flynn, J., Halpern, D. F. and Turkheimer, E. (2012). Intelligence: New findings and theoretical developments. *American Psychologist*, 67, 130–159.

Nussbaum, M. C. (2011). *Creating capabilities: The human development approach*. London: Harvard University Press.

Ober, J. (2012). Democracy's dignity. *American Political Science Review*, 106, 827–846.

Rawls, J. (1993). *Political liberalism*. New York: Columbia University Press.

Sandel, M. (2020). *The tyranny of merit: What's become of the common good?* London: Penguin Books.

Sartori, G. (2007). *Democrazia: cosa è?* (Democracy: What is it?) Milano: Rizzoli.

Schwartz, S. (1992). Universals in the content and structure of values: Theoretical advances and empirical tests in 20 countries. In M. Zanna (Ed.) *Advances in experimental social psychology*, vol. 25, pp. 1–65. New York: Academic Press.

Schwartz, S. H., Caprara, G. V. and Vecchione, M. (2010). Basic personal values, core political values, and voting: A longitudinal analysis. *Political Psychology*, 31(3), 421–452.

Sen, A. (2009). *The idea of justice*. Cambridge, MA: Harvard University Press.

Torcal, M. and Montero, J. R. (Eds.) (2006). *Political dissatisfaction in contemporary democracies: Social capital, institutions and politics*. London: Routledge.

Turkheimer, E., Haley, A., Waldron, M., D'Onofrio, B. and Gottesman, I. I. (2003). Socioeconomic status modifies heritability of IQ in young children. *Psychological Science*, 14, 623–628.

Van der Brug, W. (2010). Structural and ideological voting in age cohorts. *West European Politics*, 33, 586–607.

Vecchione, M. and Caprara, G. V. (2009). Personality determinants of political participation: The contribution of traits and self-efficacy beliefs. *Personality and Individual Differences*, 46, 487–492.

Vecchione, M., Schwartz, S. H., Caprara, G. V., Schoen, H., Cieciuch, J., Silvester, J., Bain, P., Bianchi, G., Kirmanoglu, H., Baslevent, C., Mamali, C., Manzi, J., Pavlopoulos, V., Posnova, T., Torres, C., Verkasalo, M., Lönnqvist, J. E., Vondráková, E., Welzel, C. and Alessandri, G. (2014). Personal values and political activism: A cross national study. *British Journal of Psychology*, 106, 84–106.

Welzel, C., Inglehart, R. and Klingemann, H. D. (2003). The theory of human development: A cross-cultural analysis. *European Journal of Political Research*, 42, 341–379.

CHAPTER 15

'Can I Trust My Future?'

Youth Civic Engagement, Civic Identity and Dystopias

Benjamin Bowman, Thalia Magioglou and Helen Haste

Introduction

Addressing the goals and methods of civic education and preparing young people for citizenship, in any society, rests massively on assumptions about power: who should hold it, for whose benefit should it be exercised and by which mechanisms should those in power be held accountable? This includes what skills are deemed necessary for the individual citizen to contribute to that accountability; in representative democracies, this means voting and exercising voice in defined ways. The margins of empowerment, and therefore the skills designated for appropriate education, are moderated variably – by definitions of what is necessary for 'maintaining social order', by discourses on what constitutes 'healthy democracy' and the routes and means for societal improvement, and by discourses about which groups, or value positions, are entitled to be respected and heard. Also behind civic education are key assumptions concerning the cultural, pedagogic and developmental processes that will equip the young person for whatever version of citizenship their society mandates.

Culture is a dialogic process; the growing individual makes sense of, and engages in, interaction with social structures and norms that convey frames of meaning and permit, or not, access to voice, dialogue and understanding (Haste and Bermudez, 2017). The structures, roles, normative practices and values of every aspect of school life, along with the family, are the most proximal sources, but young people encounter myriad wider discourses that offer options, constrictions and imaginaries. Bourdieu (2020) also highlights the entanglement of the socio-political and economic context with the 'habitus', or our construction of reality. In this context, 'subjectivisation', a term coined by Wieviorka (2012), reflects the creation of social identities specific to a particular socio-cultural and political context. Youth identity as 'citizens' and 'persons' is framed through these dialogues, which frame also the extent of their sense of efficacy. Does the cultural discourse offer efficacy or not? Even if it does, how do experience and social context affirm that potential, or not, and for whom?

Defining the goals of civic education, and how it is delivered, has changed (Carretero, Haste and Bermudez, 2016). A few decades ago, many versions of 'social studies' in different countries drew on mainstream political science definitions of 'citizenship' and focused on the knowledge and skills believed to be required for 'conventional' participation – primarily voting. The not so hidden agenda was to promote values and beliefs that sustained active support for the status quo. Education institutions reproduced both structural hierarchies and forms of discourse that reflected the social system (for example, how leadership and team cooperation were trained through school activities). Inevitably, these marginalised those young people who lacked social and economic capital, and so further contributed to social inequality. In more authoritarian societies, they also suppressed voices that resisted the orthodoxies. With the emergence of a wide range of civil rights movements in the late twentieth century, it became clear that 'civic participation' alongside 'democratic goals' had to expand to recognise the way that social change actually occurs, particularly when majority discourses have to be challenged to achieve social improvement (Gutmann, 1999; Haste, 2004; Kahne and Westheimer, 2004). This had the effect of widening the research base for participation, to explore what facilitated efficacy and voice as well as the emergence of new narratives and values that supported change. With regard to civic education, this meant a shift to exploring how youth experience, as well as youth values and beliefs, contributed to their efficacy and their motivation, and how this might be harnessed in pedagogy, formal and informal (Flanagan and Christens, 2011; Sherrod, Torney-Purta and Flanagan, 2010).

The current model of the 'effective citizen' is well-informed, tuned into appropriate values, capable of critical thinking and examining social, political and economic structures, skilled in formal and informal means of participation, with a sense of personal responsibility and the efficacy to engage in systemic change (Apple, 2010; CIRCLE, 2003; Gordon, 2009; Hess, 2009; Hess and McAvoy, 2015; Kennedy, 2007; Levinson, 2012; Westheimer and Kahne, 2003). Many education agendas have expanded to articulate these attributes, but only a few have equipped young people with the knowledge, skills and dispositions for action. In this chapter, we want to consider some of the more problematic aspects of youth efficacy – including a focus on studies in Greece and the UK – and to go in some depth into some less optimistic perspectives around social change and voice. In an era characterised by widening inequalities, precarity and austerity, transition to adulthood is profoundly influenced by tension between a hegemonic narrative that hard work and good moral conduct will lead an individual to success and prosperity and personal experiences of uncertainty, inequality, discrimination and marginalisation.

Change and Rupture

The general tone of research on youth civic engagement, and on democracy broadly, implies, we argue, an optimistic progressive perspective: current global trends are moving gradually towards more ethical, more sustainable and more democratic systems (Haste and Chopra, 2020). There is an implicit narrative that the current modes of civic education are contributing to this. We want to argue that this tone is problematic on two grounds. First, there is plenty of evidence that large parts of the world are threatened by potential political, economic and environmental disruptions that need to be anticipated if they are to be managed or averted; accordingly, there are many doubts about the extent that liberal principles and practices suffice.

Second, the progressive and gradualist model ignores the fact that the impetus for social change, and especially the impetus for the changing values, explanations and narratives that are fundamental to social change, frequently are precipitated by sudden surprising or even cataclysmic events. These are 'ruptures', breakages in norms and normative assumptions that create a new threshold, both unexpected and surprising (Kay and King, 2020; Stenner, 2017). They can be about beliefs and perspectives; powerful images, often dystopian, that reframe narratives. The 1962 book about pesticides by Rachel Carson, *Silent Spring*, was, for example, a highly significant 'rupture' that began public eco-awareness, and the many vivid images and accounts of subsequent environmental disasters – most recently Sir David Attenborough's 2020 film *Extinction* – have been the successive shocks that have moved forward our commitment to sustainability. Climate change debate has forced us to recognise that it is not just a matter of cumulative action such as recycling, but that we have to *think* very differently about the future because of the realities of massive geographical change, loss of coastal habitation and migration from uninhabitable regions (McKibben, 2020). The violent deaths of young Black men and women in the United States of America at the hands of law enforcement agencies have precipitated, not only outrage at local injustice and significant action for change, but also had spin-off effects globally for scrutinising how racial inequality is embedded in cultural history and symbols. As is clear from the resistance to it, this is provoking a major shift in cultural identities

In 2020, perhaps the biggest 'rupture' has been COVID-19. First, it 'came from nowhere'; there was no widely-discussed *public* narrative about pandemics even happening, let alone how to respond to them. Second, for everyone, worldwide, all areas of life are impacted and, most important, it is impossible to avoid the need to acquire new skills and practices. We are all 'ruptured'. However, things eventually stabilise to a 'new normal', as we have all experienced the reality of responding to uncertainty and the shattering of our 'gradual progressive' narratives. This is a new cultural frame that must, perforce, enter into how we structure civic education. But ruptures and unexpected developments also highlight another factor; when we envisage the future, we do not only build on consolidating the values of the present, we have an 'imaginary' – a framing scenario that represents and, indeed, directs our goals. Utopias and dystopias always act as critical lenses on the present – what is desired, what is feared (de Saint-Laurent, Obradovic and Carriére, 2018; Levitas, 2013). Literary utopias and dystopias, for example, of Wells, Huxley and Orwell, were significant political critiques. Similarly, young people's images of the future are strong indicators of their present values (Haste and Hogan, 2012; Hicks and Holden, 2007).

In this chapter, we argue that a common implicit theme of civic education has been to empower young people to become 'active' and a major goal has been to close the 'empowerment gap' between the more and less privileged (Levinson, 2012). Largely, the emphasis has been on current liberalising values and the skills and knowledge needed to implement them. Less research attention, we argue, has been placed on the longer-term scenarios within which these current values are embedded. Where there has been such work, it has mainly been on positive, utopian perspectives – the 'ideal' society that reflects the solutions to contemporary problems and also reflects a quality of future life for young people to which they can optimistically aspire. Such utopian thinking aligns with empowerment and a positive civic identity. We do know, however, that those young people who are actively involved in civic participation that represents dissent do express more negative, indeed dystopian, future scenarios, in combination with a strong sense of personal efficacy (Carretero et al., 2016). This negative perspective motivates commitment, often focusing on morally charged single issues. They have been extensively researched. One group who are, however, more neglected in research are the 'alienated'; those who are civically inactive or, indeed, socially disruptive, often

marginalised economically and educationally and, in particular, lack a
sense of personal efficacy (Torney-Purta and Barber, 2011).

In this chapter, we want to focus on the role of dystopian narrative in
the formation of young people's civic identities. In particular, we want to
explore how the young person's dialogue with cultural civic and economic
narratives is interwoven with their personal lives and aspirations for
making sense and for well-being. We argue that young people frequently
conceive of their transitions to adulthood as a pragmatic process of the
narrowing of hopes in response to precarity and enduring socio-economic
inequalities. This narrowing of hopes contributes to the tendency we
identify among young people to make sense of the world as a dystopia.
We examine how the dystopian sense among young people can inform our
concept of the role young people play in contemporary democracies.

Crises, Contention and De-Politicisation

Young people are making sense of the world in an era of successive global
and intersecting crises. These crises include a global crisis of political
inefficacy and distrust, sometimes called the 'democratic recession' (Della
Porta, 2013; Diamond, 2015; Ercan and Gagnon, 2014), the 2008 world
financial crisis and its continuing aftermath (Scarpetta, Sonnet and
Manfredi, 2010; Stanley, 2014; Verick, 2009), the accumulation and
acceleration of the impacts of climate change (Hagedorn et al., 2019;
Holmberg and Alvinius, 2019; Kaijser and Kronsell, 2014) and, more
recently, the global pandemic of SARS-CoV-2 or 'coronavirus', the
COVID-19 disease and associated regimes of outbreak control (Fauci,
Lane and Redfield, 2020; Reicher and Stott, 2020). These crises intersect
with political and social crises at global, national and local levels, and not
least the challenges posed to young people by austerity programmes that
have cut state provision, made communal and social infrastructure contingent on profit, and rendered futures unclear and precarious (Bramall,
2013; Della Porta, 2013; Heyes, 2013). Aside from arguments for or
against austerity policies, these measures have coincided with 'widening
class, gender and race inequalities, and opening divisions between and
within communities' (Durbin, Page and Walby, 2017, p.1). For instance,
in the UK, the recession of 2008 was associated with a devastating upturn
in suicides and deterioration in many indicators of mental health; unlike in
previous recessions, these impacts were not reversed as the economy
recovered and, indeed, continued to deteriorate (Barr, Kinderman and
Whitehead, 2015, p.324). Economic, social and political crises come

together to produce enormous turmoil, as in Greece, where the deterioration of healthcare provision and, especially, the widening inequality gap in health coverage has coincided with successive national elections, a referendum, the Eurozone membership crisis and a political crisis linked to the movement of documented and undocumented refugees fleeing the civil war in Syria (Karanikolos and Kentikelenis, 2016). The UK and Greece are examples of the many countries where young people are living through crisis after crisis as impacts accrue.

During the contemporary era of intersecting crises, the dominant approach to young people's politics has been the consideration of young people's participation in – and disengagement from – politics and democratic institutions (Banaji, 2008; Edwards, 2007; Grasso, 2018). Falling living standards and downward social mobility for this generation in Europe – the first since World War II who can expect worse economic prospects than their parents and grandparents – have profound impacts on political attitudes (Mitrea, Mühlböck and Warmuth, 2020). The impact of crises on young people's political psychology is complex and varied across social, geographic and other variables. Young people are diverse and their diverse experiences lead to divergent political attitudes in a given context. Overall, politically, this generation is socialised in an era of dissent. Pessimism towards political efficacy and distrust of political elites, as well as democratic institutions, have gone hand-in-hand with scepticism about the social contract and anxiety about well-being and economic security (Antonucci and Hamilton, 2014; Bessant, Farthing and Watts, 2017; Stanley, 2014).

Politically, it has been an era of local and global social movements for systemic change. This has included several cycles of movements against contemporary capitalism from the anti-globalisation protests of the 2000s and the Occupy movement, to anti-austerity protests (Della Porta, 2013). They have included global movements for structural change to address enduring systemic racism – especially, but not only, in the justice system – including Black Lives Matter (Rickford, 2016). Particularly since the mid-2010s, an influential movement in which young people are prominent has called for action on climate change (Bowman, 2019; Curnow et al., 2016). These and other developments at local, national, world-regional and global levels have established 'a long-term cultural trend toward horizontal, non-institutional movements' (Tufekci, 2014, p.203) and characterise a call for systemic change. Young people making transitions to adulthood in this era do so at a time of more or less constant, global action by social movements that do not demand piecemeal reform: these are times in which people are calling for intersectional, wide-reaching and systemic change, oriented at a 'system of interlocking oppressions' (Roberts, 2012).

In an intensive political atmosphere of crisis, conflict and contention, young people have continued to experience a depoliticisation of the transition to adulthood. Depoliticisation is the process by which the political becomes 'technocratic, managerial or disciplined towards a single goal' (Wood and Flinders, 2014, p. 161), as opposed to politicisation, in which issues become public where 'competing interpretations exist as choices'. Depoliticisation, in this period, is part of a broader framework for transitions to adulthood based on the 'market mentalities and moralities' of neoliberalism (Giroux, 2014).

The Meaning of 'Democracy' in Greece and Individual Aspirations

David Held (2006) has highlighted the existence of multiple models of democracy – in different or the same historical periods – associated with different economic and socio-cultural contexts. Democracy, as a hegemonic social representation, may allow conflicting representations, positions and actions. It covers a set of principles and values, used to describe different political and economic models, relationships and moulding social identities in different ways. Democracy was reinvented after the French Revolution and the Enlightenment, combining rationalism, science and enlarged participation of different groups of unequal societies in decision-making. However, the ways in which it is interpreted, both as a system and as a goal, are embedded variably in young people's experience and aspirations.

Magioglou has conducted research over two decades on the meaning of democracy and its relation to the future with young Greeks from different social and political backgrounds (Magioglou, 2017). Overall, the future appears either as an 'individual achievement' attainable for the minority of participants, or as collective distraction and fear for the majority. There have been changes. In the early 2000s, young participants expressed a feeling of lack of efficacy, unable to influence the public sphere. However, after ten years of financial crisis, the majority of participants in Magioglou's 2015–2016 study were politically active, informed and invested in the national public debates. The financial crisis of 2008, and its disastrous effect in Greece, brought consecutive Greek governments to the decision to accept a bailout, borrowing funds from the International Monetary Fund, the European Central Bank and the Eurogroup, and to accept a series of sudden reforms and extremely painful austerity measures for the population. This austerity decimated the country's GDP and resulted in a humanitarian crisis. It is also associated with one of the longest recessions of an advanced capitalist economy. Hundreds of thousands of educated young adults left the country and youth unemployment reached 50 per cent according to OECD data (2016). Young people who stayed held very strong positions regarding the Memoranda of Understanding linked to the financial bailouts and, in their majority, were against it in 2015, which allowed the Syriza-Anel government to rise to power in January 2015. However, after a referendum at the end of 2015, the newly elected government signed a third Memorandum of Understanding with its creditors, which shattered the confidence of its young supporters. The young participants positioned themselves for or against the Memorandum and there is a clear divide present in the 2015–2016 interviews. Yet, at the same time, there was no sign of any global common future unless it was seen as a dystopia.

Magioglou's argument is twofold. On the one hand, social representations of democracy in Greece are anchored in the existing intergenerational conflict between youth and previous generations. On the other hand, the representation of democracy for Greek youth correlates with the way they anticipate their personal future, in particular, the hope, or not, to become financially and socially integrated. Arguably, both these dimensions concern young adults in other Western countries, as consolidated social inequalities have made upward social mobility difficult (Lebaron and Blavier, 2017). Within these frames, for a majority of young people, democracy is either considered an idealised and impossible 'Platonic' dream, or, in a Marxist sense, as an ideological construction of the powerful to manipulate the masses. In the early 2000s, until 2008, the present state of affairs was judged as unacceptable for a majority of young Greeks, but they felt unable to make any significant change in the public sphere or in their own future. For others, there was still hope to succeed individually, in an idealised well-paid job and an affluent lifestyle, similar, for example, to those of young celebrities portrayed in the media.

On the other hand, democratic values such as freedom, equality and justice, in the form of having a voice, real options to choose and the means to take action, permeated everyday life and became important as part of family and social interactions. Democracy became part of the private sphere, something we can or cannot find in our everyday relationships and, even more, a desirable character trait for a romantic partner or a close friend.

> ... *democracy doesn't exist, nowhere, nowhere, nowhere, I am telling you, nowhere, for me. Ok, maybe what I say is pessimistic, it is, but I think that those who pretend democracy exist, just lie. If you asked my father if democracy exists, he will tell you 'it exists in general, nevertheless, in certain cases it doesn't'. This*

is not right. What does it mean in this case it exists and in the other it doesn't? Either democracy exists everywhere and always, or it doesn't exist at all. Democracy doesn't exist.

By the time of Magioglou's 2015–2016 study (Magioglou, 2015, 2017), after eight years' turmoil of the financial crisis, the majority of young people were well-informed on local politics and politically active. They had voted in the last elections and the referendum regarding the Memorandum. Their positions were conflicting and, for some of them, both on the Right and the Left of the political spectrum, democracy was identified with the representative political system that brought the Syriza-Anel government into power. This was 'populist' according to those on the Right and the liberals, or, for those on the Left, it betrayed the people by altering the result of the referendum and signing yet another exploitative memorandum.

> *Democracy what could I say, ha ha, . . . I think in general that democracy could only be practised in societies where people would have a very high education level, access (in English) to quality information yes, I don't know, . . . finally I think that it is more an illusion (in English) that everyone is equal in a democracy, and not a reality, yes, ha ha, what else to say? . . . on the other hand they say that it is more just as a system, because who could say who has a bigger say (in English) and who has a smaller, . . . eh. . . for example, whose opinion has more importance and whose has less, . . . personally, I wouldn't mind if I didn't have the right to vote for example ha ha, of course, it doesn't sound that nice, ha ha. . . but I think that if you give the right to participate to everyone and they don't respect their right I don't think that this produces what is best for a society. . . yes. . . despite this, maybe. . . a form of aristocracy would be better. . . (Xenophon, twenty-six-year-old).*

In a 2019 study, Magioglou, Sciplino and Riva (forthcoming),[1] gathered data in London, England on the future aspirations of young adults aged eighteen to thirty years from different social backgrounds. The participants' aspirations were mainly individually focused. Any common aspirations were limited to exercising philanthropy and alternated with fears of financial insecurity.

> *I want to **help** people. . . at the end of the day I don't think it should be just about making money it should be about what you are set out to do which is helping people. . . Main reason people go into some jobs is because of the money and it shouldn't be. . . I think there should be a balance because when I was*

---

[1] 'The study was planned as part of the methodology module at St Mary's University, Twickenham, Middlesex'.

looking what to do at University, I was thinking at the end what job I am going to do... how much money, because obviously with the inflation and prices and everything, that's what people worry about but then you're not gonna do what you like and you're not gonna do what you're interested in (Daisy).

My parents have hustled a lot in life to provide me what I have right now, so I need and I must, it's like a responsibility for me and morally and in every aspect that you take it... to pay for what they've done for me (Dee).

I want to bring someone joy... to be a role model... some teachers told me I couldn't make it, I would like to prove them wrong (Alice).

I want to help children with special needs (Joy).

Coaching, the idea of making people better (Lucy).

However, working in education as a teacher, which would be helping others, is considered against the individual's best interests, because it corresponds to a lower salary. This, in turn, is associated with devaluation of jobs in this sector and a lifestyle where the participants' needs may not be met – thus leading to individual unhappiness.

*I mean I would be happy helping those people I set out to help however I don't think I'd be getting my aspirations in my home life, as I don't think I'd be able to afford having a brand new car and a brand new house and all these things I aspire to have so... I'd be happy teaching people and making people appreciate education but then at the same time I probably wouldn't be happy about my home life ... * (Bill).

The following extract recognises the need for a societal goal, but it is limited to being less selfish and to caring for other people's problems, and it is far from a civic social identity:

I would like to be less selfish in how driven I am I need to be aware that there are other people in this world and it isn't just me wailing down a straight line to my goal. ... but everyone has shit in their lives and I just think people need to get on with it... So I aspire not to be the person that doesn't care about other people's problems (Mark).

In these data from young adults, we see a tension between the desire for a 'safe and secure' individual future and the fears of a dystopic collective future, for those who are not engaged in any form of activism, associated with stress and insecurity. How is it possible to be hopeful as an individual when the world's future is perceived as dystopic? The rational thing to do would be to fight or flee in the face of a perceived threat. However, the possibility to reach financial security and abundance is not presented as completely illusory since there are representations of individual success in content circulated by the media and in the social media that young adults consume. There is a form of individual 'utopia' available, towards which they aspire, in other words the possibility to be successful, if you follow the 'right' path. However, this path is not very clear.

Young People's Everyday Politics of Dystopia in the UK

In the UK, youth is socially constructed as a transition between childhood and adulthood, and typically considered in public discourse as an economic transition from dependence to independence. If youth is a process of becoming independent, then, in the UK, this process is profoundly a matter of arguing oneself to be independent. Young people must construct, argue and advocate for themselves as independent, economically competitive individuals in curricula vitae (CV), job applications, the agorae of public life, and so forth. Specifically, young people, through education and employment, engage in the reflexive construction of the future self as their intended destination. Young people in the UK are in the process, not just of becoming adults, but of arguing, through discourse, argumentation and CV-building, that they are on the way to being the adults they wish to be. In policy, one common indicator of problematic youth is the NEET – Not in Education, Employment or Training – label. In the UK, young people who are not seen to be fulfilling their potential tend to be problematised as 'unskilled, unemployable, redundant youth' (Nayak and Kehily, 2008, p. 40); the focus in governing young people is, in the words of former Prime Minister David Cameron, that young people must be 'nagged, pushed and guided' into employment and training (BBC, 2013).

In Bowman's work with young people in the UK, spanning twelve years from 2008 to 2020, he argues that young people experience everyday life as a constant conceptual disruption, and a dissonance between what Flanagan calls public hopes and private anxieties (Flanagan, 2008). Young people in the UK are encouraged to market themselves as having qualities of flexibility and self-led success as they negotiate unstable employment pathways through job seeking, joblessness, employment and underemployment, promotion and demotion. They often shift careers through precarious jobs and zero-hour contracts, while continually accumulating qualifications and credentials that can help them in future employment negotiations. More deeply, young people do not undertake transitions to adulthood as a linear, teleological pathway to a better future: youth is, rather, a constant process of reinventing the self in expectation of failure and in awareness of the absence of safety nets. Young people, in other words, must be outwardly positive, despite inward insecurity. As one young research participant, a student at a vocational college in southern England in 2011, put it, 'you hit the age when you've got to earn and it's not as easy as you think. . . it hit me hard. . . I've been looking [for a job] for a couple of years [and] I've only just got a job'.

Young people's experience of transitions to adulthood are, precisely, experiences of dystopia. The promise that study and hard work will be rewarded by success, stability and happiness is revealed through the process of becoming an adult to be an inaccurate, utopic vision. At the same vocational college, two other students explained that they had seen others who 'don't get the grades' in school were actually favoured, because 'it's not what you know, but who you know'. In the classroom discussion, peers agreed that their experience of young adulthood was 'shit', 'disheartening' and 'you just want to give up. I just go sign on' – the latter a colloquial term for applying for jobseeker's allowance.

In terms of their political subjectivity, young people often experience dystopia in the UK as a process of fracturing, mutual competition and loneliness. In the same way that UK society celebrates the concept of self-creation and independence, young people find themselves demonised for failure and dependence by a hegemonic discourse that states those who do not succeed did not work hard enough (Mendick, Allen and Harvey, 2015). It is a neoliberal common sense that people can be divided between 'strivers' and 'skivers', and that the latter is a 'figure of social disgust' and the subject of political arguments against social welfare (Jensen, 2014, p. 2). For young people, the social disgust surrounding economic failure is unsettling in times of immense economic precarity. In one focus group, held in 2011 with students at a technical college in rural England, Bowman explains that participants engaged with some gusto in a conversation about 'social housing as a deleterious influence on society in general' (Bowman, 2016, p. 190), particularly blaming young mothers who have children, as one young person in the group put it, 'to get benefits'. 'What's the point?' the young person asked the group, 'if you're just going to live off the dole, get housing and get benefits. . . it's ridiculous?' This conversation became a conflict when a young person in the group spoke up bravely in defence of young mothers and others in the group, who were mothers themselves, explained how difficult it was to get housing. The group resolved, in an outwardly good-natured way and with 'laughter throughout', that they had really been reproducing an opinion they saw on television, read in newspapers and heard from their parents. In their lived experiences, they shared an opinion that their town was 'too far gone': 'just go out into [town] and you'll see what we mean'.

The everyday politics of dystopia is a term Bowman uses, in his work in the UK, to encapsulate the lived experience of young people during transitions to adulthood. In dystopia, young people must really navigate two parallel transitions to adulthood. On the one hand, they must negotiate an outward, public and reflexive narrative of the self that is based in a utopian, neoliberal vision. On the other, they must make inward sense of their own precarity, ongoing and intersecting economic, social and political crises, and often loneliness and other forms of suffering. In Bowman's work with young activists, he identifies the ways that the complex, interweaving experiences of hope and despair come through in the experiences of young people who are organising for social and political change.

In Bowman's work with climate activists, for instance (2019, 2020), he uses findings to problematise a dominant concept of young political activism with respect to climate change. For instance, while studies of the school climate strikes make note of the coincidence of grief and joy in youth-led activism (as in Wahlström et al., 2019), the typical conceptualisation of young environmentalist activism remains top-down and negative – emphasising existential threats to humanity – and focused on young people's policy demands of adult policymakers. On the contrary, as Bowman demonstrates, the climate strikes – as youth-led and youth-centred forms of political activism – are resolutely joyful, playful and characteristically horizontalist. Young people's political activism in the climate strikes typically functions through emerging awareness of systemic injustice, alongside opportunities to shatter dystopian assumptions in everyday practice:

> My parents aren't exactly too happy about all this, so it's kind of, every night after everyone had gone to bed I'd get it out, do a bit more work on [my protest sign] . . . they don't quite understand the importance of what we're doing today. They think that me getting this day of education will be more important than making a stand against the systematic oppression that is happening. . . I think it's really important to do this because if we are successful and, say, however many years in the future I have all these amazing stories to tell my grandchildren about what I did to help (Mickey, age 17).

In times of crisis, young people in the UK tend to engage in democracy 'on a case-by-case basis in issues that hold meaning for their everyday lives'

(Sloam, 2020), but the search for meaning in the everyday is also, Bowman argues, a reflection of young people's disillusionment with politics, democratic institutions and political parties. This disillusionment must be understood within a wider reading of young political psychology as young people undertake transitions to adulthood in dystopia. Young people's disillusionment is not merely a function of perceived inefficacy, but also a lived experience of precarity and abandonment amid narratives of self-possession, meritocracy and success. It is characteristic of contemporary transitions to adulthood in the UK that young people are socialised to the civic domain as a place where one narrates public hopes while experiencing private anxiety. For this reason, the young person's sense of the civic is profoundly dystopian. A sense of hopelessness, grief and loss for towns that are 'too far gone' and for lives that turn out 'shit' and 'disheartening' must coexist with the constant reinvention of the self as a striver in the employment market. The revealing of 'systematic oppression' and the hope that 'however many years in the future I have all these amazing stories to tell my grandchildren about what I did to help' must coexist with the lived experience of growing up with parents who want you to attend school dutifully.

Future Thinking

The current crisis of COVID-19 has impacted on all these issues in ways that we cannot yet fully appreciate, and we cannot yet envisage what will be the long-term effects. Currently COVID-19 is wholly dystopic globally; whether a utopian scenario may emerge that enables a positive future on which to build identity is unknown. Young people worldwide have been particularly affected as their education and career entry trajectories have been sabotaged; their transition to adulthood has had to find new paths. Magioglou and Coen (2020) argue that the 'crisis' has led to a realisation of a common 'destiny', but the construction of a collective social identity in order to act in a coordinated way is still an unfulfilled objective (Jetten et al., 2020). Multiple divisions and power differences at the global, national and community level may result in a 'battle' of signification, where opposing groups fight to determine labelling and action at an unprecedented global level. This is an ongoing process. On the one hand, the experience of COVID-19 may raise civic awareness and efficacy or lead to influencing policy-making towards environmental protection and a new form of globalisation and democracy (with regional and global political power stepping in to support people and communities). However, on the other hand, will such notions of empowerment stimulate fragmentation and hateful and stigmatising forms of action – or, indeed, a combination of both? Jetten et al. (2020) argue that a 'we' social identity is the key to success in facing this new global challenge. However, intergroup relations and social identity theory have, in the past, shown that creating 'we' too often only happens in opposition to 'they'.

The question we raise is in what ways civic education, both in and out of the traditional educational systems, could empower young people so that they become 'effective' local and global citizens, confident that they matter and creators of meanings and narratives instead of meaning-consumers and subjects. The question is also how the feeling of inefficacy could be overcome in a way that respects 'democratic values' and does not lead to the physical or symbolic destruction of self and others in order to feel empowered. The current climate of civic education – that which does incorporate the wider scope of civic participation – has been termed 'New Civics', and is directed to creating the kind of effective citizen we describe (Carretero et al., 2016; Guérin, van der Ploeg and Sins, 2013). The agendas for pedagogy build on what evidence shows to be effective: developing critical thinking through dialogue and debate about controversial issues (Hess, 2009; Hess and McAvoy, 2015), creating a democratic classroom and school structure (Torney-Purta, Wilkenfeld and Barber, 2008), encouraging wide-ranging perspective-taking, especially across cultures, understanding the role of history in national identities (Carretero, Berger and Grever, 2017) and promoting young people's involvement in community action for change.

Arguably, such procedures and structures are within the existing system, however, for young people who feel marginalised these may not meet their needs. Characteristic of both Bowman's and Magioglou's young respondents is a *lack of trust*. First, in the political and social system in general, it does not meet their needs and aspirations as they transition to adulthood and, second, the ideas and values with which they engage are not represented, indeed these are dismissed or rejected. We have long known that very politically active young people tend to have low trust in the government combined with a fairly high sense of efficacy – believing that they, at least with others, can have an effect. We also know that such young people tend to express anger and their goals are morally charged (Haste and Hogan, 2006). Frequently, this civic action is oriented to single issues rather than party politics and the aetiology of engagement derives from an event or experience that prompts in them a moral or value-laden reaction that, importantly, generates a sense of *personal responsibility* to become engaged. It is from this that the commitment derives; not only 'I agree with this,' but 'I must support this'. This goes beyond endorsing an attitude; it is about *ownership and identity*.

We want to argue that the dimension of ownership and identity is missing from the profile of pedagogy for effective citizenship as we have reported it. In part, this is because there are numerous problematic issues around educating for passion, especially within the mainstream school curriculum – though many are happy to advocate for strongly committed national identity. We want to argue that the data we have presented about the role of dystopian perspectives in giving marginalised young people a personal stake, a goal and a sense of hope illuminates some of the motivation behind commitment to causes or ways of thinking. In particular, by owning a point of view and incorporating it into one's identity, there is also a sense of creation; 'my' beliefs. Of course, the young climate-change activists did not invent their ideology, nor did they individually choose which evidence or arguments to support it, but their commitment and motivation derive from sharing in the 'new' ideas and being part of innovation. Such a sense that one is part of creating new ways of thinking, analysing and building is characteristic of social movements in general – which is why utopias and dystopias are key elements.

We would argue that mainstream civic education, even in its 'new' version, does not take enough account of the kind of personal engagement and identity that we see in the dystopic constructions and meaning-making above. The one area in which these dimensions are evident is post-Freirean activism, where the young people involved are the initiators and drivers. The field of YPAR – Youth Participatory Action Research – captures these processes. Here we see how young people generate the ideas, goals and methods for their activities, and in particular how it is an iterative process, in dialogic interaction with their ongoing experience of the task. Central to this is the 'research' element – with or without the 'external' researcher – in that constant reflection and adaptation go on among the participants. Reports of YPAR activities substantially include accounts of participants' evolving consciousness, critical perspectives and growing efficacy, and social media frequently play a crucial role (Cammarota and Fine, 2008; Gordon, 2009; Jenkins and Shreshtova, 2016; Kirshner, 2015; Kreikemeier, 2021; Seif, 2011; Tausch et al., 2011). This is particularly true where part of the agenda is to consider and challenge cultural assumptions, for example, about authority and power (Bickmore, 2017; Zembylas and Bekerman, 2013).

YPAR contexts tend to incorporate elements of dystopia or utopia for the reasons described above. Having a future scenario – whether positive or negative – frames an agenda; this is what we want to achieve, this is what we want to avoid. It also inevitably feeds back to the present: what must we build upon, what must we now tackle to avoid future catastrophe? Finally, agendas for change must build in assumptions about how change occurs and how the actors can impact change, so that future scenarios very much reflect current concerns and anxieties. If we are to understand the roots of commitment and perhaps find ways to feed that understanding into broader civic education and democracy, we need to start from the factors that engage the identity of young people (Haste and Chopra, 2020).

REFERENCES

Antonucci, L. and Hamilton, M. (2014). Youth transitions, precarity and inequality and the future of social policy in Europe. In Antonucci L., Hamilton M., Roberts S. (Eds.), *Young people and social policy in Europe: Dealing with risk, inequality and precarity in times of crisis, work and welfare in Europe*, pp. 256–265. London: Palgrave Macmillan.

Apple, M. W. (Ed.) (2010). *Global crisis, social justice, and education*, New York: Routledge.

Banaji, S. (2008). The trouble with civic: A snapshot of young people's civic and political engagements in twenty-first century democracies. *Journal of Youth Studies*, 11(5), 543–560.

Barr, B., Kinderman, P. and Whitehead, M. (2015). Trends in mental health inequalities in England during a period of recession, austerity and welfare reform 2004 to 2013. *Social Science and Medicine*, 147, 324–331.

BBC (2013). David Cameron suggests cutting benefits for under-25s. 2 October. www.bbc.co.uk/news/uk-politics-24369514

Bessant, J., Farthing, R. and Watts, R. (2017). *The precarious generation: A political economy of young people*. Abingdon: Routledge.

Bickmore, K. (2017). Conflict, peace building ad education; rethinking pedagogies in divided societies, Latin America and around the world. In K. Bickmore, R. Hayhoe, C. Manion, K. Mundy and R. Read (Eds.). *Comparative and international education*, pp. 268–299. Toronto: Canadian Scholars Press.

Bourdieu, P., (1979/2020). *Habitus and Field. Sociology*, Vol. 2. Cambridge, MA: Polity Press.

Bowman, B. (2020). 'They don't quite understand the importance of what we're doing today': The young people's climate strikes as subaltern activism. *Sustainable Earth*, 3(1). doi.org/10.1186/s42055-020-00038-x

(2019). Imagining future worlds alongside young climate activists: A new framework for research. *Fennia*, 197(2), 295–305. doi:10.11143/fennia.85151

(2016). *'They don't know what's going on': Exploring young people's political subjectivities during transitions to adulthood in the UK. PhD Thesis*. Bath: University of Bath.

Bramall, R. (2013). *The cultural politics of austerity: Past and present in austere times*. London: Palgrave Macmillan.

Cammarota, J. and Fine, M. (2008). *Revolutionising education: Youth Participatory Action Research in motion*, New York: Routledge.

Carretero, M., Berger, P. and Grever, M. (2017). *International handbook of research in historical culture and education; hybrid ways of learning history*. Basingstoke: Palgrave Macmillan.

Carretero, M., Haste, H. and Bermudez, A. (2016). Civic education. In L. Corno and E. Anderman (Eds.), *Handbook of educational psychology*, 3rd edition, pp. 295–308. Abingdon, UK: Routledge.

Carson, R. (1962). *Silent spring*. New York: Houghton Mifflin.

CIRCLE: Carnegie Corp. of New York, N.Y. (2003). *The Civic Mission of Schools*. Center For Information And Research On Civic Learning And Engagement (CIRCLE), www.carnegie.org/publications/the-civic-mission-of-schools/.

Curnow, J., Gross, A., Connor, J. and Rosen, S. M. (2016). Injustice is not an investment: Student activism, climate justice, and the fossil fuel divestment campaign. In Conner, J. and S. Rosen (Eds.), *Contemporary youth activism: Advancing social justice in the United States*. Westport: Praeger.

De Saint-Laurent, C., Obradovic, S. and Carriére, K. R. (Eds.) (2018). *Imagining collective futures*. Basingstoke: Palgrave Macmillan.

Della Porta, D. (2013). *Can democracy be saved? Participation, deliberation and social movements*. Cambridge, MA: Polity Press.

Diamond, L. (2015). Facing up to the democratic recession. *Journal of Democracy*, 26(1), 141–155.

Durbin, S., Page, M. and Walby, S. (2017). Gender equality and 'austerity': Vulnerabilities, resistance and change. *Gender, Work and Organization*, 24 (1), 1–6.

Edwards, K. (2007). From deficit to disenfranchisement: Reframing youth electoral participation. *Journal of Youth Studies*, 10(5), 539–555.

Ercan, S. A. and Gagnon, J.-P. (2014). The crisis of democracy: Which crisis? Which democracy? *Democratic Theory*, 1(2), 1–10.

Fauci, A. S., Lane, H. C. and Redfield, R. R. (2020). Covid-19 – Navigating the Uncharted. *New England Journal of Medicine*, 382(13), 1268–1269.

Flanagan, C. A. (2008). Private anxieties and public hopes: The perils and promise of youth in the context of Globalization. In J. Cole and D. Durham (Eds.), *Figuring the Future: Children, Youth and Globalization*, pp. 125–150. Santa Fe: SAR Press.

Flanagan, C. A. and Christens, B. D. (Eds.) (2011). *Youth civic development: Work at the cutting edge. New directions for child and adolescent development, 134*, San Francisco: Jossey Bass.

Giroux, H. A. (2014). The swindle of democracy in the neoliberal university and the responsibility of intellectuals. *Democratic Theory*, 1(1), 9–37.

Gordon, M. (2009). *Reclaiming dissent; civics education for the 21st century*. Rotterdam: Sense Publishers.

Grasso, M. (2018). Young people's political participation in Europe in times of crisis. In S. Pickard and J. Bessant (Eds.), *Young people re-generating politics in times of crises*. Cham: Springer International Publishing.

Guérin, L. J. F., van der Ploeg, P. A. and Sins, P. H. M. (2013). Citizenship education: The feasibility of a participative approach. *Educational Research*, 55(4), 427–440.

Gutmann, A. (1999). *Democratic education*, Princeton, NJ: Princeton University Press.

Hagedorn, G., Kalmus, P., Mann, M., Vicca, S., Van den Berge, J., van Ypersele, J.-P., Bourg, D., Rotmans, J., Kaaronen, R., Rahmstorf, S., Kromp-Kolb, H., Kirchengast, G., Knutti, R., Seneviratne, S. I., Thalmann, P., Cretney, R., Green, A., Anderson, A., Hedberg, M., Nilsson, D., Kuttner, A. and Hayhoe, K. (2019). Concerns of young protesters are justified. *Science*, 364 (6436), 139.2–140.

Haste, H. (2004). Constructing the citizen. *Political Psychology*, 25(3), 413–440.

Haste, H. and Bermudez, A. (2017). The power of story: History, narrative and civic identity. In M. Carretero, S. Berger and M. Grever (Eds.), *International handbook of research in historical culture and education; Hybrid ways of learning history*, pp. 427–448. Basingstoke: Palgrave Macmillan.

Haste, H. and Chopra, V. (2020). *The futures of education for participation in 2050: Educating for managing uncertainty and ambiguity*. Paper commissioned for the UNESCO Futures of Education report

Haste, H. and. Hogan, A. (2012). The future shapes the present; scenarios, metaphors and civic action. In M. Carretero (Ed.), *History education and the construction of identities*, pp. 311–326. NC: Information Age Publishing.

(2006). Beyond conventional civic participation, beyond the moral-political divide; young people and contemporary debates about citizenship. *Journal of Moral Education*, 35(4), 473–493.

Held, D. (2006). *Models of democracy*. Cambridge, MA: Polity Press.

Hess, D. (2009). *Controversy in the classroom: The democratic power of discussion*. New York: Routledge.

Hess, D. E. and McAvoy, P. (2015). *The political classroom: Evidence and ethics in democratic education*. New York: Routledge.

Heyes, J. (2013). Flexicurity in crisis: European labour market policies in a time of austerity. *European Journal of Industrial Relations*, 19(1), 71–86.

Hicks, D. and Holden, C. (2007). Remembering the future: What do children think? *Environmental Education Research*, 13(4), 501–521.

Holmberg, A. and Alvinius, A. (2019). Children's protest in relation to the climate emergency: A qualitative study on a new form of resistance promoting political and social change. *Childhood*, 27(1), 78–92.

Jenkins, H. and Shreshtova, S. (2016). *By any media necessary; the new activism of American youth*. New York: New York University Press

Jensen, T. (2014). Welfare commonsense, poverty porn and doxosophy. *Sociological Research Online*, 19(3), 277–283.

Jetten, J., Reicher, S., Haslam, A. and Cruwys, T. (2020). Introduction. In J. Jetten, S. Reicher, A. Haslam and T. Cruwys (Eds.) *Together, apart: The psychology of COVID-19*, pp. 3–12. London: Sage.

Kahne, J. and Westheimer, J. (2004). Educating the 'good' citizen; political choices and pedagogical goals. *Political Science and Politics, 37(2)*, 241–247.

Kaijser, A. and Kronsell, A. (2014). Climate change through the lens of intersectionality. *Environmental Politics*, 23(3), 417–433.

Karanikolos, M. and Kentikelenis, A. (2016). Health inequalities after austerity in Greece. *International Journal for Equity in Health*, 15(1). doi.org/10.1186/s12939-016-0374-0

Kay, J. and King, M. (2020). *Radical uncertainty: Decision-making for an unknowable future*, New York: Norton.

Kennedy, K. (2007). Student constructions of 'active citizenship': What does participation mean to students? *British Journal of Educational Studies*, 55(3), 304–324.

Kirshner, B. (2015). *Youth activism in an age of education inequality*, New York: New York University Press.

Kreikemeier, A. (2021). Youth research in community: How Critical Pedagogy, collaboration, and art-making inspires social engagement. *Teachers College Record*.

Lebaron, F. and Blavier, P. (2017). Classes et nations : Quelle articulation à l'échelle européenne ? *Actes de la Recherche en Sciences Sociales*, 4(219), 80–97.

Levinson, M. (2012). *No citizen left behind*, Cambridge, MA: Harvard University Press.

Levitas, R. (2013). *Utopia as method; the imaginary reconstitution of society*. Basingstoke: Palgrave Macmillan.

Magioglou, T. (2017). Intergenerational inequality and Young adult's representation of Democracy. *GreeSe Papers, Hellenic Observatory Papers on Greece and Southeast Europe, LSE*.

(2015). Les représentations des jeunes Grecs à propos de la démocratie et de l'Europe. *Etudes Balkaniques, Cahiers Pierre Bélon*, 1 (21), 67–91.

Magioglou, T. and Coen, S. (2020). The construction of a hegemonic social representation: Climate crisis and the role of Covid-19 in defining survival. *European Psychologist*, 26(3), 230–240.

Magioglou, T., Sciplino, C., Riva, S. (forthcoming). Young adults' future aspirations and research oriented learning in higher education. *Qualitative Research*.

McKibben, W. (2020). *Falter; has the human game begun to play itself out?* New York: Holt.

Mendick, H., Allen, K. and Harvey, L. (2015). 'We can get everything we want if we try hard': Young people, celebrity, hard work. *British Journal of Educational Studies*, 63(2), 1–18.

Mitrea, E. C., Mühlböck, M. and Warmuth, J. (2021). Extreme pessimists? Expected socioeconomic downward mobility and the political attitudes of young adults. *Political Behaviour*. 43, 785–811.

Nayak, A. and Kehily, M. J. (2008). *Gender, youth and culture: Young masculinities and femininities.* Basingstoke: Palgrave Macmillan.

OECD (2016). OECD Economic Surveys: Greece. March, OECD. Accessed at: www.oecd.org/economy/surveys/GRC%202016%20Overview%20EN.pdf.

Reicher, S. and Stott, C. (2020). On order and disorder during the COVID-19 pandemic. *British Journal of Social Psychology,* 59(3), 694–702.

Rickford, R. (2016). Black Lives Matter: Toward a modern practice of mass struggle. *New Labor Forum,* 25(1), 34–42.

Roberts, D. E. (2012). Race, gender, and the political conflation of biological and social issues. *Du Bois Review: Social Science Research on Race,* 9(1), 235–244.

Scarpetta, S., Sonnet, A. and Manfredi, T. (2010). Rising Youth Unemployment During the Crisis: How to Prevent Negative Long-Term Consequences on a Generation? *OECD Social, Employment and Migration Papers* 106.

Seif, H. (2011). Unapologetic and unafraid: Immigrant youth come out from the shadows. *New Directions in Child and Adolescent Development,* 134, 59–75.

Sherrod, L. R., Torney-Purta, J. and Flanagan, C. A. (Eds.) (2010) *Handbook of research on civic engagement in youth.* Hoboken, NJ: John Wiley and Sons.

Sloam, J. (2020). Young Londoners, sustainability and everyday politics: The framing of environmental issues in a global city. *Sustainable Earth,* 3(14), doi.org/10.1186/s42055-020-00036-z

Stanley, L. (2014). 'We're reaping what we sowed': Everyday crisis narratives and acquiescence to the Age of Austerity. *New Political Economy,* 19(6), 895–917.

Stenner, P. (2017). *Liminality and experience: A transdisciplinary approach to the psychosocial,* Basingstoke: Palgrave Macmillan.

Tausch, N., Becker, J. C., Spears, R., Crist, O., Saab, R., Singh, P. and Siddiqui, R. (2011). Explaining radical group behaviour; Developing emotion and efficacy routes to normative and non-normative collective action, *Journal of Personality and Social Psychology,* 101(1), 129–148.

Torney-Purta, J. and Barber, C. (2011). Fostering young people's support for participatory human rights through their developmental niches. *American J. Orthopsychiatry,* 81(4), 473–481.

Torney-Purta, J., Wilkenfeld, B. and Barber, C. (2008). How adolescents in 27 countries understand support and practice human rights. *Journal of Social Issues,* 64(4), 857–660.

Tufekci, Z. (2014). The medium and the movement: Digital tools, social movement politics, and the end of the Free Rider Problem: The End of the Free Rider Problem. *Policy and Internet,* 6(2), 202–208.

Verick, S. (2009). Who is hit hardest during a financial crisis? The vulnerability of young men and women to unemployment in an economic downturn. *IZA Discussion Papers.* Bonn: International Labour Organization.

Wahlström, M., Kocyba, P., De Vydt, M., de Moor, J., Wouters, R., Wennerhag, M., van Stekelenburg, J., Uba, K., Saunders, C., Rucht, D., Mikecz, D., Zamponi, L., Lorenzini, J., Kołczyńska, M., Haunss, S., Giugni, M., Gaidyte, T., Doherty, B. and Buzogany, A. (2019). *Protest for a future:*

Composition, mobilization and motives of the participants in Fridays For Future climate protests on 15 March, 2019 in 13 European Cities. Keele: Keele University e-Prints.

Westheimer, J. and Kahne, J. (2003). Reconnecting education to democracy. *Phi Delta Kappan online*, www.pdkintl.org/kappan/k0309wes.htm.

Wieviorka, M., (2012). *Du concept de sujet à celui de subjectivation/dé-subjectivation*, Paris, Fondation Maison des sciences de l'homme (Working Papers Series; 16), accessed at https://halshs.archives-ouvertes.fr/halshs-00717835/document.

Wood, M. and Flinders, M. (2014). Rethinking depoliticisation: Beyond the governmental. *Policy and Politics*, 42(2), 151–170.

Zembylas, M. and Bekerman, Z. (2013). Integrated education in conflicted societies; is there a need for new theoretical language? *European Educational Research Journal*, 12(3), 403–415.

CHAPTER 16

Religious Identity Politics and Genuine Support for Democracy

Gizem Arikan and Pazit Ben-Nun Bloom

Introduction

Is group identity associated with pro- or anti-democratic orientations? Recent political developments such as the rise of Right-wing populism, Islamic fundamentalism and increasing partisan polarisation in several countries have revitalised debates about the role of identities and identity politics in democracies. Classic democratic theory places groups at the heart of the democratic process and views the essence of democracy in the formation of self-organising groups that seek to pursue particular interests (Linz and Stepan, 1996). In a similar vein, theories of participatory and deliberative democracy view group activities in civil society as an opportunity for democratic deliberation, the exchange of arguments between groups with competing interests and the refinement of preferences through this process. In this sense, group action and group identities can help people understand the true essence of the democratic process.

Some current works on identity politics beg to differ with this view. Most notably, Francis Fukuyama and Kwame Anthony Appiah have expressed pessimistic views about the effects of group identities on the democratic process. Fukuyama has argued that identity politics is among the 'chief threats' facing liberal democracies, as identities create grievances that only too often evolve into a demand for recognition of the group's superiority and that divert citizens' attention away from crucial political issues such as income inequality (Fukuyama, 2018). Similarly, Appiah has contended that group identities exaggerate our differences with others and our similarities with in-group members (Appiah, 2018). Thus, this recent strand of the literature suggests that group identities tend to divert citizens from the genuine norms of pluralistic democracy, prevent mutual tolerance among groups and often lead to anti-democratic orientations.

In this work, we contribute to the debate about the role of identities in the democratic process by focusing on the relationship between religious identity and democratic orientations in a comparative setting. We argue that the effect of religious identity on a genuine understanding of democracy, which is defined as citizens' endorsement of norms and procedures associated with democratic governance, is neither positive nor negative. Rather, it depends on the context, particularly whether individuals belong to a religious majority or religious minority tradition, and on the relationship between the state and religious groups. Drawing on data from the most recent two waves of the World Values Survey (WVS) and using involvement in religious social activities as a proxy for the strength of religious identity, we show that, while the strength of religious identity is generally associated with reduced genuine support for democracy, this negative effect is less pronounced for members of minority religious traditions, especially when these minority traditions face differential treatment. We also illustrate that members of minority religions become more committed to democratic norms as their group identity becomes stronger and as government treatment of minority religions becomes more discriminatory. Overall, our work contributes to these important recent debates in the literature by identifying some boundary conditions for how identities are connected to democratic attitudes.

Dimensions of Democratic Support: Overt Versus Genuine

Public opinion studies acknowledge that citizens may entertain a mix of competing democratic ideals and that they may express general support for the democratic system while simultaneously rejecting or failing to identify some of its core principles (Schedler and Sarsfield, 2007). Support for democracy requires, not only expressed backing of a democratic regime, but also commitment to liberal principles such as the protection of minority rights, individual freedoms and tolerance (Welzel and Alvarez, 2013). Accordingly, the current literature conceptualises democratic support as consisting of overt and genuine support dimensions. 'Overt' or 'abstract' support of democracy involves an endorsement of the democratic regime and the view that it is desirable for one's country (Norris, 2011; Welzel, 2007). Major cross-national surveys show that citizens indeed express a strong desire for democracy. For instance, more than 80 per cent of respondents in seventy-eight out of the eighty countries included in the 1999–2000 wave of the WVS described 'having a democratic political system' as either 'good' or 'very good' (Inglehart, 2003, p. 52). Similarly, almost nine out of ten respondents who participated in the 2005–2009 wave of WVS viewed democratic governance as either a 'very' or 'fairly' good political system for their own country (Norris, 2011, p. 142). However, this type of support may not necessarily entail a genuine understanding of what constitutes the principles of democratic regimes (Inglehart, 2003; Schedler and Sarsfield, 2007). In fact, citizens may express support for democracy without even knowing its real content in terms of norms or procedures (Norris, 2011; Schedler and Sarsfield, 2007). Therefore, scholars have distinguished overt support from 'intrinsic' or 'genuine' support for democracy.

At the very basic level, genuine support comprises *endorsing a procedural understanding* of democracy, including the endorsement of democratic procedures and norms such as free elections, civil rights, gender equality and freedom of speech. At the same time, individuals are expected to be able to identify and reject *authoritarian interpretations* that contradict democratic procedures or ideals, such as religious leadership or military rule as alternative ways to govern the country. Researchers also suggest that citizens may voice support for the democratic regime for *instrumental* reasons – for example, because they associate democracy with law and order, economic growth or redistribution of wealth. Instrumental support does not necessarily mean that citizens hold an illiberal interpretation of democracy (Schedler and Sarsfield, 2007; Welzel and Alvarez, 2013), yet it may be limited and conditional on the regime's ability to deliver material benefits, especially in non-consolidated democracies (see Bratton and Mattes, 2000; Norris, 2011). It may also indicate that citizens value democracy, not necessarily as an end in itself, but because of the potential services and benefits associated with it (Bratton and Mattes, 2000). As a result, scholars argue that citizens' ability to distinguish instrumental benefits as not constituting an integral and essential characteristic of democracy provides a more stringent and rigorous test of their genuine commitment to democracy (Norris, 2011).

Thus far, most works on religion and support for democracy have focused on the overt support dimension. Numerous studies have tested the implications of Huntington's Clash of Civilization thesis, which maintains that some religious traditions, such as Islam or Eastern Orthodoxy, have belief systems that are inherently anti-democratic and have found little evidence for these claims (for a review, see Arikan and Ben-Nun Bloom, 2020). Others have focused on the effects of different dimensions of the individual religious experience, such as religious belief or religious social behaviour (Ben-Nun Bloom and Arikan, 2012, 2013a, 2013b), but these studies have also generally considered overt support for democracy (although see, for example, Ben-Nun Bloom and Arikan, 2013a). Thus, studies examining the effects of individual religiosity on genuine support for democracy are limited. This present study, which focuses on religious group identities, therefore fills another gap in the literature by simultaneously considering the effect of other religiosity dimensions on genuine commitment to democracy.

Religious Identity and Genuine Support for Democracy: Contextual Boundary Conditions

Religious identity is one of the most relevant and politicised identities in many societies (Fearon and Laitin, 2000). Identity politics around religious groups is strongly tied to religious social involvement (Maliepaard, Gijberts and Phalet, 2015). This social facet of religion overcomes collective action problems for groups, highlighting shared interests and grievances, and offering opportunities for political mobilisation. Indeed, much research emphasises that religious social involvement makes religious group interests salient and contributes to group consciousness (Hoffman, 2019; Jamal, 2005). Places of worship and religious social networks often facilitate discussion around common goals and struggles and support the development of shared identity and solidarity (Jamal, 2005; Putnam and Campbell, 2010). The salience of group interests may also be enhanced through the political information members receive in these communities and organisations (Djupe and Gilbert, 2009). For minority groups in particular, houses of worship often serve as important places for uniting social capital and in-group trust and for creating a strong sense of community (Allen, 2010; Maliepaard et al., 2015).

Regarding how religious identity is connected to support for democracy, as discussed above, scholars such as Fukuyama (2018) and Appiah (2018) have argued that narrowly defined identities often highlight and exaggerate differences between one group's interests and those of others. Identities tied to ethnic or religious groups have a stronger likelihood of being connected to such exclusionary and antagonistic orientations (Del Sarto, 2019). In fact, religious social involvement and religious identity are often connected to prejudice, intolerance and xenophobia (Ben-Nun Bloom, Arikan and Courtemanche, 2015; Djupe and Calfano, 2013; Gibson, 2010). However, some scholars have suggested that a strong sense of identity may be associated with stronger endorsement of democratic principles, especially for underprivileged groups (Sides, Tessler and Vavreck, 2019). According to these authors, identity politics allows marginalised groups to overcome barriers to participation and mobilises them around a common cause, which consequently strengthens group members' endorsement of democratic principles (Abrams, 2019).

We contend that not all identities are equal in terms of their impact on attitudes and behaviour and that the effect of religious identity is contingent on the context. We suggest two key boundary conditions: whether individuals are members of minority religious groups (type of religious identity) and the extent to which these minority religious groups are subject to mistreatment and exclusion by the state (state–religion relations). We claim that it is generally those with a minority religious affiliation who are likely to develop pro-democratic orientations compared to those with a majority religious affiliation. We further suggest that the relationship between identity strength and pro-democratic orientations will be stronger for members of minority traditions when the state treats such identities in an unfair manner.

Contemporary identity politics is at least partly driven by the quest for equal recognition by marginalised groups. Identifying with a minority religion is typically associated with greater deprivation and, thus, a more pressing need for recognition. In fact, research in social psychology has found that persistent social disadvantage and unfair treatment by mainstream society often lead minorities to rally around their ethnic or religious identity as a response (Portes and Rumbaut, 2001). Such 'reactive' identities empower minority group members by restoring their sense of dignity and offering an effective source of social support and in-group solidarity (Portes and Rumbaut, 2001). This empowerment is crucial in overcoming barriers to participation and in voicing group interests and demands for recognition. These aspirations and activities may lead minorities with strong group identities to internalise liberal-democratic elements since demands such as equal recognition, tolerance and respect lie at the core of democratic ideals. Such demands are key to the religious group members' possibility of maintaining and expressing their own distinctive religious identity and obtaining a more equal social status (Verkuyten and Yildiz, 2009). A stronger identity among minority groups is also associated with more positive attitudes towards other minority groups. For example, Knoll (2009) has found that members of minority religions in the United States of America are more likely to empathise with immigrants, while Mustafa and Richards (2019) have reported highly religious Muslims in Europe to be more supportive of immigration. Moreover, Verkuyten (2010) has found that group essentialism – that is, perceiving groups as homogenous and inherently different from others – is associated with a stronger endorsement of multiculturalism among ethnic minority groups in the Netherlands. Verkuyten (2010) has suggested that cultural essentialism could be an important political tool for minorities, one that leads to questioning and challenging the status quo under which the majority group dominates minorities. Thus, to the extent that they organise and mobilise their shared grievances and develop stronger group identities, we may expect religious minority groups to espouse democratic ideals more than the majority. Accordingly, our first hypothesis is that *the effect of religious identity on genuine support for democracy is moderated by belonging to a minority versus majority group in one's country (H1).*

While our focus is on the effect of religious identity strength on genuine commitment to democracy, we also consider the role of affiliation with a minority tradition in the discussion of the model results. The effect of minority affiliation on support for democracy has received much consideration, but most existing works have focused on the effects of belonging to an ethnic minority group. These works have reported belonging to an ethnic minority group to be negatively associated with overt support for democracy (Dowley and Silver, 2002) and political participation (Anwar, 2001; Sandovici and Listhaug, 2010). Concerning religious minorities, most studies have focused on immigrant attitudes, and these works have yielded conflicting findings: for example, Gundelach (2010) has found that Muslim immigrants and their descendants in Denmark scored slightly lower on support for democratic principles than the religious majority, in line with Eskelinen and Verkuyten's (2018) findings, which are based on data from a more diverse sample of European countries. However, there is also evidence to the contrary: for example, Grundel and Mariepaard (2012) have reported no differences in democratic orientations between minority Muslims and majority Christians in the Netherlands. These works have almost always focused on the effect of identifying with a minority religious tradition (nominal affiliation with a religious group) rather than the *strength* of this identification. Based on our discussion above, we expect minority group members with a stronger sense of subjective identification to develop more pro-democratic orientations than those with a weaker sense of religious group identification, since such group identities help minority group members internalise democratic orientations via mobilisation to achieve group interests.

Our second boundary condition for the religious identity–democratic commitment relationship is the extent to which minority groups are marginalised by the state. As discussed above, an identity that is not recognised or respected results in grievances that can translate into a demand for compensation. While we expect religious minorities to hold more disadvantageous positions in their respective societies in general, political systems, including democracies, vary in the extent of differential and discriminatory treatment of minority religious groups (Fox and Akbaba, 2015). Where the differential treatment is more pronounced, we expect minority religious groups to be more involved in actions demanding equal treatment, which we argue is the key to the internalisation of democratic group ideals by group members. Thus, in such contexts, religious group identity is more effectively connected to democratic commitment among the members of minority religious traditions. For example, historically persecuted groups such as the Alevis in Turkey or Ahmadis in Pakistan have stronger pro-democratic orientations compared to the Sunni majority in these countries (see, for example, Banfi, Gianni and Giugni, 2016). We, therefore, hypothesise that *the effect of religious social identity on genuine support for democracy is moderated by whether an individual is a member of a minority religion and the extent to which that minority religion is subject to unequal treatment by the state (H2).*

In our analysis, we focus on two types of unequal treatment of religious groups by the state: first, *government favouritism of the majority religion* (also called state support for the majority religion) refers to various legal privileges and financial support provided to select majority groups or organisations (Finke and Martin, 2014). Where government favouritism exists, the state typically supports a single religion or a small group of religions with explicit endorsements and funding and/or favoured treatment in state institutions, such as regarding how religion is presented or taught in schools (Finke and Martin, 2014). Government favouritism of the majority religion(s) is also one of the most robust predictors of minority discrimination (Finke, Martin and Fox, 2017). Second, we consider *minority discrimination*, which is the restriction of religious practices or institutions of religious minorities that does not apply to the majority religion, including but not limited to restrictions on building, maintaining or repairing places of worship; restrictions on clergy; restrictions on conversion to minority religions or their proselytising activities; and surveillance of minority religious activities (Fox and Akbaba, 2015). Both types of differential treatment are related, but they are also distinct in that the first reflects differential support that privileges the majority religion (or select groups within the majority religion) and the second reflects the institutional and legal restrictions placed on the freedom of religion of minority groups.

Again, we also discuss this relationship from the perspective of religious minority support for democratic principles. Following the arguments above, we expect the effect of minority group membership (nominal affiliation) to be moderated by both the strength of one's level of subjective identification with that religious group and the extent of government favouritism and minority discrimination. Thus, for minorities, stronger group identity should lead to greater support for genuine democracy since differential treatment should lead to a stronger connection among group identities, group mobilisation and the consequent internalisation of democratic norms.

Findings from Fifty-Eight Nations

The data came from Waves 5 and 6 of the WVS. We included all countries in Wave 6 of the survey (conducted between 2010 and 2014) and those countries that were in Wave 5 (conducted between 2005 and 2009), but that were not surveyed in Wave 6. A major advantage of Wave 6 is that it covered a large number of non-Western countries that were not covered in earlier waves. By adding countries from Wave 5, which included countries from Western and Eastern Europe, we substantively increased the country-level degrees of freedom and obtained a diverse set of countries that differ regarding a wide range of indicators, such as the condition of political rights and civil liberties, economic development and religious heritage. Our final analysis includes 80,423 observations from fifty-eight countries.[1]

The dependent variable was *genuine support for democracy*. As discussed above, genuine support includes the simultaneous endorsement of liberal-democratic principles and the ability to identify authoritarian and instrumental interpretations as not constituting an integral part of democracy (Norris, 2011). The WVS includes a battery of items that ask respondents to rate the importance of several possible desirable outcomes that may be associated with democracy on a scale of 1 (not an essential characteristic of democracy) to 10 (an essential characteristic of democracy). In line with existing practice (Norris, 2011; Welzel and Alvarez, 2013), we added the three items that are indicative of a liberal and procedural understanding of

---

[1] The countries included are Algeria, Armenia, Australia, Azerbaijan, Brazil, Bulgaria, Burkina Faso, Canada, Chile, Colombia, Cyprus, Ecuador, Estonia, Ethiopia, Finland, France, Georgia, Germany, Ghana, India, Indonesia, Iraq, Japan, Kazakhstan, Kyrgyzstan, Lebanon, Malaysia, Mali, Mexico, Moldova, Netherlands, New Zealand, Nigeria, Norway, Pakistan, Peru, Philippines, Poland, Romania, Russia, Rwanda, Serbia and Montenegro, Slovenia, South Korea, Spain, Sweden, Switzerland, Taiwan, Trinidad and Tobago, Tunisia, Turkey, Ukraine, the UK, the United States of America, Uruguay, Yemen, Zambia and Zimbabwe.

democracy: 'People choose their leaders in free elections', 'Civil rights protect people's liberty against oppression' and 'Women have the same rights as men'. We then subtracted this score from the score for items indicative of authoritarian and instrumental interpretations of democracy: 'Religious authorities interpret the laws', 'The army takes over when government is incompetent', 'Governments tax the rich and subsidise the poor' and 'People receive state aid for unemployment'. Thus, the resulting measure indicates the extent to which citizens emphasise the procedural interpretations of democracy over the alternative interpretations. Higher scores indicate greater endorsement of genuine democratic principles. Final scores were recoded to range from 0 to 1.

However, a caveat is in order. All major religious faiths emphasise helping the poor and the needy, although not all religious groups or individuals may want the state to be responsible for redistribution and aid to the poor (Van Kersbergen and Manow, 2009). In fact, the relationship between religiosity and, especially, between religious belief and support for redistribution of wealth is not straightforward (Malka et al., 2011) and is conditional on religion-state arrangements (Arikan and Ben-Nun Bloom, 2019a). Still, religious individuals, and particularly those with stronger religious convictions, may be more likely to associate democratic governance with state aid and redistribution, which may result in a negative association between religiosity and genuine commitment. We further raise this point in the discussion of results.

Our measure of identity strength was the level of religious social involvement of the respondents. This variable is not an ideal measure of identity, but, since the WVS did not include any items assessing the strength of religious identity, we used the extent of involvement in religious social activities as a proxy measure of identity strength. As discussed above, visiting places of worship and being involved in social religious networks increase group consciousness and make group identity and interests salient (Hoffman, 2019). In fact, attendance at places of worship is highly correlated with religious identification (Jamal, 2005; Maliepaard et al., 2015). Accordingly, our measure of religious identity strength combined the two aspects of religious social behaviour: the frequency of attending religious services (an eight-category variable) and status regarding membership in a religious organisation (active or inactive). Each item was weighted equally to form an additive index in which higher values indicate stronger identification with the religious group.

To code the religious membership of respondents, we first recoded the sectarian or denominational subcategories in our dataset as nine main religious traditions, based on Arikan and Ben-Nun Bloom (2019b). We consulted Barro's religious adherence dataset (Barro, 2003) and the CIA World Factbook (The World Factbook, 2016) to determine which religious tradition had the most adherents in each country, and we then coded respondents who were part of the majority tradition as the *majority*. This category served as the baseline in the analysis. Those respondents who did not belong to the majority tradition were coded as *minority* if they reported belonging to any other religious tradition, and those who indicated that they did not belong to a tradition were coded as *unaffiliated.*

We also included a control for religious belief, which was an additive index that included the two items available in both waves: whether the respondent considered her/himself a religious person and the importance of God in the respondent's life (Ben-Nun Bloom and Arikan, 2012, 2013a). All items were given equal weight and the final index was rescaled to range from 0 to 1 where higher values indicate higher levels of religious belief. In addition, we controlled for sex (1 = male, 0 = otherwise), age, level of education (two dummy variables: low and medium education), income (ten categories), ideological orientation (1 = Left, 10 = Right), life satisfaction (four categories) and satisfaction with one's financial situation at the individual level. All models also controlled for level of democracy. We used the Polity IV measure of democracy and autocracy, which ranges from −10 to +10 with values between −10 to -6 corresponding to autocracies, −5 to 5 corresponding to anocracies and 6 to 10 to democracies.

There were two key independent variables at the country level. The first was government favouritism of religion as indicated by the Pew Research Center (2019). This measure captures the degree of friendliness of the state towards one or more religions through funding for religious education, property and clergy, as well as laws or regulations that recognise a favoured religion or religions. This variable ranges from 0 to 1, with higher values indicating greater levels of favouritism. A second country-level independent variable we considered was the measure of religious discrimination against minority religions from the Round 3 of the Religion and State (RAS) Project, which captures the extent of restrictions on religious institutions and leadership, along with limitations on religious activities directed towards minority religious groups. The original index ranges from 0 to 108, with higher values indicating higher levels of discrimination. The Russian Federation had the highest index value in our dataset (48), followed by Pakistan (43).

The Effect of Minority Status and Religious Identity Strength on Genuine Support for Democracy

Table 16.1 shows the results of random intercept models that tested for the effects of religious identity strength and minority status (Model 1) and the interaction of these two variables (Model 2) along with the other variables measured.[2] Our measure of religious identity strength was negatively related to the measure of genuine support for democracy (c.f. Norris, 2011) in both models, which seems to support the argument that identities may be detrimental to democracy. For Model 1, neither minority status nor an unaffiliated status had a statistically significant effect on genuine support for democracy. However, the findings for Model 2 demonstrate that the effects of both of these variables were conditional on our measure of religious identity strength. The coefficient of the interaction was positive and statistically different from zero for minorities, meaning that belonging to a minority religious tradition reduced the negative effect of religious identity strength. This finding provides empirical support for H1, which expects the effect of religious identity to be moderated by minority status.

To facilitate the interpretation of interaction effects, Figure 16.1 plots the predicted marginal effect of religious identity strength on genuine support for democracy conditional on minority status from Model 2. These predicted effects illustrate that the negative effect of religious identity was less pronounced for respondents affiliated with a minority religion than for those who were affiliated with a majority religious tradition. Thus, while the effect of religious identity on genuine support for democracy is generally negative, affiliation with a minority religious tradition attenuates this negative effect.

Next, we consider the effect of minority status on genuine support for democracy, conditional on religious identity strength. The results for Model 1 show that being a member of a minority religious tradition (nominal affiliation) did not have an effect on genuine support for democracy, and the positive interaction coefficient for Model 2 suggests that the effect of minority group status on genuine support for democracy was conditional on religious identity strength. Accordingly, Figure 16.2 plots the predicted marginal effect of minority status conditional on different levels of religious identity strength based on this interaction coefficient. While the effect of minority status on genuine support for democracy was

---

[2] The number of individual-level observations included in the final analysis is reduced due to listwise deletion.

Table 16.1. *Religious identity, minority status and genuine support for democracy: random intercept models.* *

	Model 1		Model 2	
	Coeff.	Std. error	Coeff.	Std. error
Constant	0.604	0.055	0.603	0.055
Individual-level effects				
Demographic variables				
Gender (male = 1)	0.004	0.001	0.004	0.001
Age	0.000	0.000	0.000	0.000
Low education	−0.047	0.002	−0.047	0.002
Medium education	−0.034	0.001	−0.034	0.001
Income	0.012	0.002	0.012	0.002
Political orientation				
Ideology (right = 10)	−0.010	0.002	−0.009	0.002
Quality of life variables				
Life satisfaction	0.022	0.003	0.022	0.003
Satisfaction with financial situation	−0.003	0.002	−0.003	0.002
Religiosity variables				
Religious belief	−0.007	0.002	−0.005	0.002
Religious identity strength	−0.024	0.002	−0.025	0.003
Minority status	0.003	0.002	−0.004	0.003
Unaffiliated	0.047	0.052	−0.051	0.053
Catholic	0.042	0.053	0.042	0.053
Protestant	0.052	0.053	0.052	0.053
Independent	0.048	0.053	0.048	0.052
Evangelical	0.039	0.053	0.037	0.053
Orthodox	0.040	0.053	0.041	0.053
Muslim	0.024	0.053	−0.024	0.053
Buddhist	−0.045	0.053	0.047	0.053
Hindu	0.026	0.053	0.026	0.053
Jewish	0.046	0.053	0.049	0.053
Interactions				
Minority status × religious identity strength	–	–	0.011	0.004
Unaffiliated × religious identity strength	–	–	−0.028	0.007
Country-level effects				
Polity IV index	0.005	0.001	0.005	0.001
Pew government favouritism	−0.040	0.021	−0.040	0.021
RAS minority discrimination	−0.000	0.000	−0.000	0.000
Variance components				
Random intercept variance	0.034	0.004	0.037	0.004
Residual variance	0.118	0.000	0.118	0.000

Table 16.1. (cont.)

	Model 1		Model 2	
	Coeff.	Std. error	Coeff.	Std. error
Model fit indices				
−2 × **log likelihood**	−77,491.72		−77,521.58	
N level-one observations	54,013		54,013	
N level-two observations	58		58	

*Entries are unstandardised coefficients and standard errors. Bold entries indicate p < 0.05.

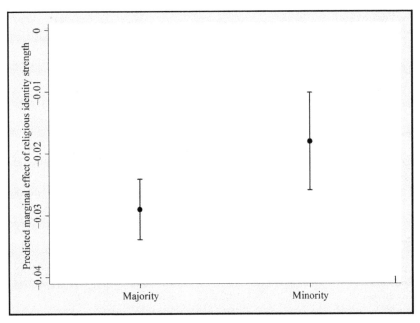

Figure 16.1   Predicted marginal effect of religious identity strength conditional on minority status, with 95 per cent confidence intervals.

statistically indistinguishable from zero for lower levels of religious identity strength, minority status had a positive and statistically significant effect on genuine support for democracy at higher levels of religious identity strength. Thus, a stronger sense of religious identity leads minority group members to show greater support for liberal-democratic regime principles. This outcome seems to run counter to the argument that identity politics

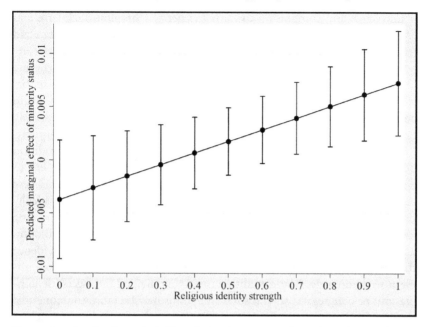

Figure 16.2   Predicted marginal effect of minority status conditional on religious identity
strength, with 95 per cent confidence intervals.

is detrimental to democracy since it shows that, for religious minorities,
stronger religious identity may lead to stronger genuine support
for democracy.

Before moving to the next set of analyses, we discuss the effects of other
religiosity variables. For both Model 1 and Model 2, religious belief was
associated with reduced genuine support for democracy, as shown by the
negative and statistically significant coefficients for this variable (see
Table 16.1). Research has found religious belief to be associated with
lower levels of overt support for democracy due to its connection with
traditional (as opposed to rational-emancipative) and survival/security (as
opposed to self-expression) values. Since these values are often incompatible with liberal-democratic values that emphasise freedom of choice, self-
expression and tolerance of behaviours that run counter to social order
(Ben-Nun Bloom and Arikan, 2013a), it is not surprising that religious
belief is also associated with reduced support for genuine democracy (also
see Arikan and Ben-Nun Bloom, 2020). In addition, given that most
religious traditions emphasise helping the poor and the needy, the belief
dimension of religiosity is also associated with pro-social values like

benevolence and compassion towards the needy (Saroglou, Delpierre and Dernelle, 2004), which influences support for redistribution and state aid (Arikan and Ben-Nun Bloom, 2019b; Malka et al., 2011). It is, therefore, possible that individuals with higher levels of religious belief are also more likely to see redistribution of wealth and aid to the poor as an essential characteristic of democracy. If this is the case, negative relationship between religious belief and genuine commitment could also be partly explained by the association of religious belief with instrumental support.

Holding all other variables constant, belonging to a religious tradition does not have a statistically significant effect on genuine commitment to democracy, compared to the baseline condition of no religion. These results are also in line with some studies that do not find statistically significant differences in levels of overt support for democracy among identifiers of major religious traditions (see Arikan and Ben-Nun Bloom, 2020 for a review). Of course, this finding should not be taken as evidence that religious belonging is irrelevant when considering genuine commitment to democracy. Major traditions are often divided into sects, denominations or congregations, and such affiliations may be more consequential for genuine support for democracy. Since cross-national datasets such as the WVS do not have information about the specific denominational or sectarian membership of respondents, we were unable to capture the diversity of viewpoints within the major religious traditions.

With the next set of models, we tested whether the effect of religious identity strength was conditional on both minority status and state–religion relationships in a country, as suggested by H2. For this, we specified three-way interactions among minority status, strength of religious identity and measures of differential treatment of the minority religion: in Model 3, we used the religious favouritism index and, in Model 4, we used the RAS minority discrimination index as indicators of differential treatment. The three-way interactions were positive and statistically significant for minority status and government favouritism (Model 3: β = 0.036; p = 0.030), but failed to achieve statistical significance for minority status and minority discrimination (Model 4: β = 0.001; p = 0.058). We turn to conditional effect plots to interpret the three-way interaction coefficients and facilitate the discussion. Figure 16.3 plots the conditional effects graphs from Model 3 (Table 16.2).

Figure 16.3 shows the predicted marginal effect of religious identity strength on support for democracy conditional on minority status and levels of government favouritism. The upper left- and right-hand side panels illustrate this conditional effect for low levels of government

Table 16.2. *The effects of religious identity and minority status conditional on religion–state relationships: random coefficient models.* *

	Model 3		Model 4	
	Coeff.	Std. error	Coeff.	Std. error
Constant	0.589	0.054	0.589	0.054
Individual-level effects				
Demographic variables				
Gender (male = 1)	0.005	0.001	0.005	0.001
Age	0.000	0.000	0.000	0.000
Low education	−0.047	0.002	−0.047	0.002
Medium education	−0.034	0.001	−0.034	0.001
Income	0.012	0.002	0.012	0.002
Political orientation				
Ideology (Right = 10)	−0.009	0.002	−0.009	0.002
Quality of life variables				
Life satisfaction	0.021	0.003	0.021	0.003
Satisfaction with financial situation	−0.003	0.002	−0.003	0.002
Religiosity variables				
Religious belief	−0.003	0.002	−0.003	0.002
Religious identity strength	−0.016	0.009	−0.012	0.007
Minority status	−0.002	0.004	0.004	0.004
Unaffiliated	0.051	0.053	0.058	0.053
Catholic	0.042	0.053	0.040	0.053
Protestant	0.052	0.053	0.048	0.053
Independent	0.048	0.053	0.046	0.053
Evangelical	0.039	0.053	0.033	0.053
Orthodox	0.043	0.053	0.037	0.053
Muslim	0.029	0.053	0.020	0.053
Buddhist	0.046	0.053	0.044	0.053
Hindu	0.028	0.053	0.023	0.053
Jewish	0.051	0.053	0.046	0.053
Country-level effects				
Polity IV index	0.006	0.001	0.005	0.001
Pew government favouritism	−0.053	0.018	–	–
RAS minority discrimination	–	–	−0.001	0.000
Interactions				
Pew government favouritism × religious identity strength	−0.025	0.016	–	–
Pew government favouritism × minority status	0.003	0.011	–	–
Minority status × religious identity strength	−0.007	0.007	−0.002	0.006
Pew government favouritism × religious identity strength × minority status	0.036	0.016	–	–

Table 16.2. (*cont.*)

	Model 3		Model 4	
	Coeff.	Std. error	Coeff.	Std. error
Pew government favouritism × unaffiliated	0.011	0.009	–	–
Unaffiliated × religious identity strength	**−0.051**	**0.011**	**−0.042**	**0.009**
Pew government favouritism × religious identity strength × unaffiliated	**0.055**	**0.024**	–	–
RAS minority discrimination × religious identity strength	–	–	**−0.001**	**0.000**
RAS minority discrimination × minority status	–	–	−0.000	0.000
RAS minority discrimination × religious identity strength × minority status	–	–	0.000	0.000
RAS minority discrimination × unaffiliated	–	–	**−0.001**	**0.000**
RAS minority discrimination × religious identity strength × unaffiliated			0.001	0.001
Variance components				
Random intercept variance	**0.032**	**0.004**	**0.040**	**0.004**
Residual variance	**0.117**	**0.000**	**0.118**	**0.000**
Model fit indices				
−2 × log likelihood	−77,682.80		−77,668.50	
N level-one observations	54,013		54,013	
N level-two observations	58		58	

*Entries are unstandardised coefficients and standard errors. Bold entries indicate p < 0.05.

favouritism (no favouritism on the upper left-hand side and low favouritism on the upper right-hand side). As the plots demonstrate, the marginal effect of religious identity strength was not very different for minority and majority respondents at these low levels of government favouritism. However, the effect of religious identity strength was less negative in relation to democracy for minorities than majorities at moderate or high levels of state support for the majority religion (lower left- and right-hand side panels in Figure 16.3). Overall, the negative effects of religious identity strength were less pronounced for minority respondents in

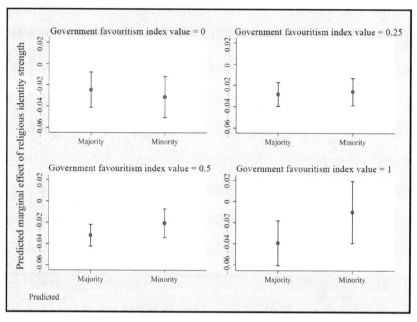

Figure 16.3   Predicted marginal effect of religious identity strength conditional on minority status and government favouritism, with 95 per cent confidence intervals.

contexts where minorities were treated differently, suggesting that the effect of identity on democracy is conditional on contextual variables and that broad generalisations about the relationship between religious identity and democracy may be misleading.

Again, we also interpret this interaction when considering the predicted marginal effect of minority status on support for democracy. Figure 16.4 shows this marginal effect for different levels of religious identity strength and state support of the majority religion based on Model 3. As the upper left- and right-hand side plots demonstrate, the effect of minority status on genuine commitment to democracy was not conditional on one's religious identity strength when government favouritism was non-existent or very low. However, as the predicted effect plots in the lower left and right components of the figure show, the effect of religious minority membership on genuine support for democracy was conditional on religious identity strength at moderate and high levels of government favouritism. As the state's differential treatment of the minority religion or religions increases, minority group members become more supportive of liberal-democratic regime principles conditional on their subjective group

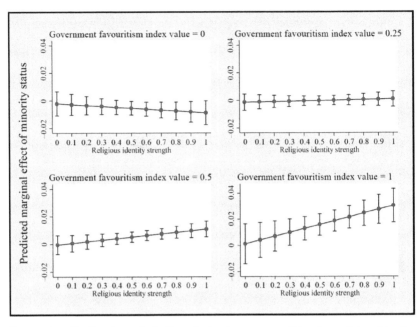

Figure 16.4   Predicted marginal effect of minority status conditional on religious identity strength and government favouritism, with 95 per cent confidence intervals.

identity. In fact, in such contexts, being a religious minority member with strong religious identity – regardless of affiliation to any religious grouping – is associated with stronger genuine support for democracy.

As mentioned above, the three-way interactions are statistically significant for the government favouritism variable, but not for the minority discrimination variable. This may be because government favouritism captures the differential treatment between the majority and minority religious groups more accurately than the minority discrimination variable. Higher levels of government favouritism indicate strong state support and privileges granted to some majority groups and this unfair treatment may lead to grievances among minority religious group members, while not necessarily suppressing their mobilisation potential. As discussed above, mobilisation around shared grievances is important for the internalisation of democratic ideals among disadvantaged groups. However, discrimination against minorities limits the expression of minority religious identities as well as minority group action (Arikan and Ben-Nun Bloom, 2019b), leaving less room for minority mobilisation and weakening the link between religious identity and the internalisation of democratic norms.

Conclusions

This chapter has considered a recent debate in the literature about whether identity politics is detrimental to democracy. We have focused on a specific type of identity – religious identity – and considered its effects on one aspect of democratic politics: citizens' support of liberal-democratic regime principles. Using data from fifty-eight countries that vary in terms of political, economic and religious variables, we have shown that the effect of religious identity on democratic commitment is conditional on meso- and macro-level factors and that strong religious identities may, in fact, have positive effects on attitudes towards democracy for marginalised minority groups. Thus, the findings demonstrate that generalisations about the role of identity politics in democracies may be misleading and that identity politics may, in fact, lead disadvantaged groups to internalise democratic norms and values.

These findings also contribute to the broader literature on the effect of different dimensions of religion on democracy. Thus far, most studies have considered overt support for democracy. We have illustrated that, as in the case of overt support, religious belief per se is associated with a decreased genuine commitment to democracy. By also considering the religious status of respondents, we contribute to existing research on minority status and support for democracy. To date, this research has been limited to ethnic minority support for democracy, and studies considering minority religious status have yielded conflicting findings. Our results indicate that these conflicting findings may be due to the fact that these studies considered nominal religious affiliation by showing that the effect of this variable is conditional on whether minority group members also have a subjective sense of belonging to their in-group and the extent to which these groups are differentially treated.

That said, our study has barely scratched the surface regarding the conditional role of identities in the democratic process. We used a large cross-national dataset, which improves the generalisability of our findings. Yet, that dataset is not quite fit to test various nuances concerning how identities within religious subgroupings may be linked to democratic commitment and to test for mechanisms underlying the relations between minority identity and democratic norm commitment. Future work could consider other types of marginalised identities and different dependent variables measuring commitment to democracy and they could also assess various hypotheses concerning the mechanisms and other types of boundary conditions for these effects.

REFERENCES

Abrams, S. (2019). E pluribus unum? The fight over identity politics. *Foreign Affairs*, 98(2), 160–163.

Allen, R. (2010). The bonding and bridging roles of religious institutions for refugees in a non-gateway context. *Ethnic and Racial Studies*, 33(6), 1049–1068.

Anwar, M. (2001). The participation of ethnic minorities in British politics. *Journal of Ethnic and Migration Studies*, 27(3), 533–549.

Appiah, K. A. (2018). *The lies that bind: Rethinking identity: Creed, country, class, culture*. New York: Liveright.

Arikan, G. and Ben-Nun Bloom, P. (2020). Democratic norms and religion. In P. Djupe, M. J. Rozell and T. G. Jelen (Eds.), *The Oxford encyclopedia of politics and religion*, pp. 241–261. Oxford, USA: Oxford University Press.

———(2019a). 'I was hungry and you gave me food': Religiosity and attitudes toward redistribution. *PLoS ONE*, 14(3), e0214054.

———(2019b). Religion and political protest: A cross-country analysis. *Comparative Political Studies*, 52(2), 246–276.

Banfi, E., Gianni, M. and Giugni, M. (2016). Religious minorities and secularism: An alternative view of the impact of religion on the political values of Muslims in Europe. *Journal of Ethnic and Migration Studies*, 42(2), 292–308.

Barro, R. J. (2003). Religion adherence data. Retrieved from http://scholar.harvard .edu/barro/publications/religion-adherence-data. (Accessed 28 October 2019).

Ben-Nun Bloom, P. and Arikan, G. (2013a). Religion and support for democracy: A cross-national test of mediating mechanisms. *British Journal of Political Science*, 43(2), 375–397.

———(2013b). Priming religious belief and religious social behaviour affects support for democracy. *International Journal of Public Opinion Research*, 25(3), 368–382.

———(2012). A two-edged sword: The differential effect of religious belief and religious social context on attitudes towards democracy. *Political Behavior*, 34(2), 249–276.

Ben-Nun Bloom, P., Arikan, G. and Courtemanche, M. (2015). Religious social identity, religious belief, and anti-immigration sentiment. *American Political Science Review*, 109(2), 203–221.

Bratton, M. and Mattes, R. (2000). Democratic and market reforms in Africa: What the 'people' say. Working Paper no.5. Afrobarometer. Accessed at: https://afrobarometer.org/publications/wp5-democratic-and-market-reforms-africa-what-people-say.

Del Sarto R. A., Malmvigand, H. and Soler i Lecha, E. (2019). Interregnum: The regional order in the Middle East and North Africa after 2011. MENARA Final Reports, no. 1. Accessed at: www.iai.it/en/pubblicazioni/interregnum-regional-order-middle-east-and-north-africa-after-2011.

Dowley, K. M. and Silver, B. D. (2002). Social capital, ethnicity and support for democracy in the post-Communist states. *Europe-Asia Studies*, 54(4), 505–527.

Djupe, P. A. and Gilbert, C. P. (2009). *The political influence of churches.* New York: Cambridge University Press.

Djupe, P. A. and Calfano, B. R. (2013). Religious value priming, threat, and political tolerance. *Political Research Quarterly,* 66(4), 768–780.

Eskelinen, V. and Verkuyten, M. (2018). Support for democracy and liberal sexual mores among Muslims in Western Europe. *Journal of Ethnic and Migration Studies.* doi:10.1080/1369183X.2018.1521715

Fearon, J. D. and Laitin, D. D. (2000). Violence and the social construction of ethnic identity. *International Organization,* 54(4), 845–877.

Finke, R. and Martin, R. R. (2014). Ensuring liberties: Understanding state restrictions on religious freedoms. *Journal for the Scientific Study of Religion,* 53(4), 687–705.

Finke, R., Martin, R. R. and Fox, J. (2017). Explaining discrimination against religious minorities. *Politics and Religion,* 10, 389–416.

Fox, J. and Akbaba, Y. (2015). Restrictions on the religious practices of religious minorities: A global survey. *Political Studies,* 63(5), 1070–1086.

Fukuyama, F. (2018). *Identity: The demand for dignity and the politics of resentment.* New York: Farrar, Straus and Giroux.

Gibson, J. L. (2010). The political consequences of religiosity: Does religion always cause political intolerance? In A. Wolfe and I. Katznelson (Eds.), *Religion and democracy in America: Danger or opportunity?,* pp.147–75. New York and Princeton: Russell Sage Foundation and Princeton University Press.

Grundel, M. and Maliepaard, M. (2012). Knowing, understanding and practising democratic citizenship: An investigation of the role of religion among Muslim, Christian and Non-religious adolescents. *Ethnic and Racial Studies,* 35(12), 2075–2096.

Gundelach, P (2010). Democracy and denomination: Democratic values among Muslim minorities and the majority population in Denmark. *Ethnic and Racial Studies,* 33(3), 426–450.

Hoffman, M. (2019). Religion, sectarianism and democracy: Theory and evidence from Lebanon. *Political Behavior.* doi:10.1007/s11109-019-09538-9

Inglehart, R. (2003). How solid is mass support for democracy – And how can we measure it? *PS Political Science & Politics,* 36(1), 51–57.

Jamal, A. (2005). The political participation and engagement of Muslim Americans: Mosque involvement and group consciousness. *American Politics Research,* 33(4), 521–544.

Knoll, B. R. (2009). 'And who is my neighbor?' Religion and immigration policy attitudes. *Journal for the Scientific Study of Religion,* 48(2), 313–331.

Linz, J. J. and Stepan, A. (1996). *Problems of democratic transition and consolidation: Southern Europe, South America, and post-Communist Europe.* Baltimore, MD: Johns Hopkins University Press.

Maliepaard, M., Gijsberts, M. and Phalet, K. (2015). Islamic gatherings: Experiences of discrimination and religious affirmation across established and new immigrant communities. *Ethnic and Racial Studies,* 38(15), 2635–2651.

Malka, A., Soto, C. J., Cohen, A. B. and Miller, D. T. (2011). Religiosity and social welfare: Competing influences of cultural conservatism and prosocial value orientation. *Journal of Personality*, 79(4), 763–92.

Mustafa, A. and Richards, L. (2019). Immigration attitudes amongst European Muslims: Social identity, economic threat and familiar experiences. *Ethnic and Racial Studies*, 42(7), 1050–1069.

Norris, P. (2011). *Democratic deficit: Critical citizens revisited*. Cambridge, MA: Cambridge University Press.

Pew Research Center (2019). A closer look at how religious restrictions have risen around the world. 15 July.

Portes, A. and Rumbaut, R. G. (2001). *Legacies: The story of the immigrant second generation*. Berkeley: University of California Press.

Putnam, R. D. and Campbell, D. E. (2010). *American grace: How religion divides and unites us*. New York: Simon and Schuster.

Sandovici, M. E. and Listhaug, O. (2010). Ethnic and linguistic minorities and political participation in Europe. *International Journal of Comparative Sociology*, 51(1-2), 111–136.

Saroglou, V., Delpierre, V. and Dernelle, R. (2004). Values and religiosity: A meta-analysis of studies using Schwartz's model. *Personality and Individual Differences*, 37(4), 721–734.

Schedler, A. and Sarsfield, R. (2007). Democrats with adjectives: Linking direct and indirect measures of democratic support. *European Journal of Political Research*, 46(5), 637–659.

Sides, J., Tesler, M. and Vavreck, L. (2019). Identity politics can lead to progress. *Foreign Affairs*, 98(2), 163–166.

The World Factbook (2016). Washington, DC: Central Intelligence Agency.

Van Kersbergen, K. and Manow, P. (2009). *Religion, class coalitions, and welfare states*. Cambridge, NY: Cambridge University Press.

Verkuyten, M. (2003). Discourses about ethnic group (de-)essentialism: Oppressive and progressive aspects. *British Journal of Social Psychology*, 42 (3), 371–391.

Verkuyten, M. and Yildiz, A. A. (2009). Muslim immigrants and religious group feelings: Self-identification and attitudes among Sunni and Alevi Turkish-Dutch. *Ethnic and Racial Studies*, 32(7), 1121–1142.

Welzel, C. (2007). Are levels of democracy affected by mass attitudes? Testing attainment and sustainment effects on democracy. *International Political Science Review*, 28(4), 397–424.

Welzel, C. and Alvarez, A. M. (2013). Enlightening people: The spark of emancipative values. In R. J. Dalton and C. Welzel (Eds.), *The civic culture transformed: From allegiant to assertive citizens*, pp. 59–89. New York: Cambridge University Press.

CHAPTER 17

Psychology, Democracy and the Media
Are Citizens Learning from the News? A Self-Regulated Learning Perspective

Sharon Coen and Karl Turgut Maloney Yorganci

One of the key functions of media is to transmit information. Indeed, this is a key attraction of the Internet. Research adopting a 'Uses and Gratifications' perspective brings a psychological approach to the study of media in recognising the importance of goals and motivations in considering how people interact with it (e.g. Rubin, 2002) and has shown that the acquisition of goods and information is one of the fundamental reasons for people using the Internet (Weiser, 2001). It is not surprising, therefore, that scholars have explored whether, how and to what extent we learn from information gathered online. This chapter is dedicated to a particular type of learning: developing knowledge and expertise about issues that are important to us as citizens.

One of the key assumptions in this chapter is that democracy is at its best when citizens are informed. We therefore see political knowledge as essential for the health of our democratic society. We also claim (and will try to justify later in this chapter) that news plays an important role in fostering and maintaining an informed citizenship, and that the Internet plays an important role in providing access to the news. We will, therefore, begin the chapter arguing for the importance of media in informed citizenship by discussing the democratic value of news and contextualising it in the current evolving media landscape, characterised by the steady growth of the Internet as a source of information. We will then hone in on the issue of transmission of knowledge. In order to do that, we will first focus on the definition of political knowledge, drawing on the way in which knowledge has been operationalised in the extant work on this issue. In particular, we will look at knowledge as ability to recall or recognise factual information (verbal and non-verbal), knowledge as ability to draw inferences about the world and knowledge as construction – thus adopting a perspective that recognises an increasingly central role of the audience in the knowledge-making process. In view of this discussion, we will revisit the idea of learning from the media, and how learning has been conceptualised in educational psychology.

377

We will propose that a self-regulated learning approach to understanding the way in which citizens learn from the media could prove fruitful in providing a theoretical framework that would help with organising extant work in the area, as well as identifying useful avenues of future research and development. We will argue that psychology in general, and particularly media psychology, can help shed light on the processes underpinning learning matters that are relevant for the health of our democracies in the context of the media landscape in the twenty-first century.

Overall, it is our hope that, while the chapter will likely raise more questions than answers, it will nonetheless provide important pointers to the ways in which psychology can fruitfully contribute to the debate concerning the role of media in democratic societies.

Why Is News Important?

Stephen Cushion's (2012) *The Democratic Value of News* reviews an extensive amount of work that demonstrates how the 'public service' function of journalism – so crucial in fostering informed citizenship – is often lost in media systems in which market-driven, commercial logic prevails. From a 'public service' perspective, he argues, news should deliver information on issues relevant to making informed decisions about social issues, e.g., politics, business, economics and international affairs, in an accurate and unbiased way. By presenting evidence from several studies in media and political communication, Cushion illustrates how systems in which there is a strong public service mandate and strong public service media (PBS – Public Broadcast Systems) are ultimately more successful in contributing to democracy as understood in Western democratic societies. Indeed, when it comes to knowledge, a series of comparative studies combining content analysis of news with surveys in representative samples of the population (Curran et al., 2009, 2012, 2014) suggested that participants in up to eleven countries, studied across four continents, tend to be more informed about current national and international affairs (as measured by multiple-choice questions concerning issues covered in the periods of data collection). Furthermore, Curran et al. (2014) provide initial correlational evidence that exposure to television news that provides ample representation of 'democratic' (non-state) voices is able to reduce (or indeed close) the gap in political self-efficacy among individuals with different levels of formal education. In this context, therefore, reliable and unbiased news is vital for the health of democracies (McGraw and

Holbrook, 2003) as it allows citizens to be sufficiently informed to make sound judgements and decisions (Trappel and Nieminen, 2018).

In today's media landscape, news is more readily available than ever and up-to-date information can be received almost instantly from a wide selection of different sources (Cushion, 2012). Technological transformations have led to an endless choice of online media, through easier and cheaper content production and distribution. The rise of 'do-it-yourself media' has led to an increasingly participatory media culture where members of the general public can be producers and contributors to news rather than merely consumers (Jenkins, 2006).

Most importantly, the Internet has become an important platform for (intentional and accidental) news consumption (Molyneux, 2018). The potential of this new medium to contribute to democratic processes, by allowing new forms of interactions and information gathering and sharing, has opened up a debate concerning the role of the Internet as a source of political knowledge.

Defining Political Knowledge

The previous section highlighted the importance of news (and online deliberation associated with it) as a tool to provide information and increase citizens' knowledge and awareness of social issues and current affairs. We discussed how news plays an important role in providing information, but also how the move to online media has been characterised by a debate concerning whether – and to what extent – media can function as a public sphere, i.e. intended as a realm of social life where access is guaranteed to all citizens with the freedom to express opinions on matters of general interest with the goal of forming something close to public opinion (Habermas, Lennox and Lennox, 1974).

In order to articulate an informed answer to the question of online news' role in democratic knowledge, we need to define what is meant by knowledge. A significant quantity of research on media effects concerning political issues has focused on the question of whether exposure to news media can increase public levels of knowledge and awareness of public affairs. Scholars in media and political science interested in the knowledge gap (i.e. To what extent do media help close the gap in knowledge between those who did versus did not receive formal education?) have developed a series of measures of knowledge, most of which have been widely adopted in the literature since the 1970s.

Political Knowledge as 'Factual' Knowledge

'Factual Knowledge' of People, Places and Policies

Studies in this area often rely on 'objective' issues such as, 'What is the name of Country X's prime minister?', 'What happened in Country Y?', 'What is Policy Z about?', etc. as indices of news-induced knowledge that is independent from broader civic education. An example of this is Curran et al. (2009)'s study of public knowledge and media, which combined a content analysis of media with a survey in representative samples of the population in four countries. Knowledge here was assessed by asking questions concerning both national and international current affairs that had been covered in the media in the sampled period. Advantages of adopting this method include its speed and ease of administration, as well as consistency throughout the sample – which allows ready comparisons. While there is a solid rationale for this type of measure, there are also issues associated with it. First, as Grabe and Bas (2021) explain, recognition should not be limited to verbal recognition, but also audio-visual[1]. Second, this measure does limit the definition and scope of political knowledge as a construct. Indeed, Delli Carpini and Keeter (1993) reviewed the extant literature on political knowledge grounded in models derived from political psychology and argue that this approach permits measurement of knowledge as factual information available to the audience. Importantly, the authors argue that one of the fundamental indicators of political knowledge should be citizens' awareness of what a government is and does.

'Factual Knowledge' of Institutions and Processes

When it comes to citizen's political knowledge, Delli Carpini and Keeter (1993, p. 1,182) state:

> We found considerable agreement that the core should be, in Barber's words, 'what government is and does' (p. 38). Neuman operationalises the notion of 'what government is' as 'the basic structure of government, its basic values, such as citizen participation, majority rule, separation of powers, civil liberties, and its basic elements, such as the two-party system, the two houses of Congress, the role of the judiciary, and the organization of the cabinet' (1986, p.186). A citizen's knowledge of what the government does is well described by Berelson, Lazersfeld, and McPhee: 'The

---

[1] Curran et al. (ibid) did use pictures to assess knowledge, but this is done inconsistently and videos as well as audios could improve recognition rate.

democratic citizen is expected to be well-informed about political affairs. He [S/he, nda] is supposed to know what the issues are, what their history is, what the relevant facts are, what alternatives are proposed, what the party stands for, what the likely consequences are (1954, p. 308).

In this sense, political knowledge not only incorporates awareness of salient issues, people and places, but also civic knowledge (see also Barrett and Zani, 2014). In 1996, Delli Carpini and Keeter published a landmark book in which they summarised survey data from a number of national surveys in the United States of America. They showed how American citizens were better at recognising institutions and processes than people and policies. Interestingly, exposure to television news was negatively correlated to knowledge.

Moreover, Galston (2001) stresses how, in order for people to be effective citizens, they need to have a basic level of civic knowledge, otherwise they will form their political judgements on the basis of what Popkin and Dimock (1999) define as 'personal character' rather than 'political character'. In other words, it is possible that – in the absence of knowledge concerning the way in which the political system works, and decisions are made and implemented within their institutions – people will attribute individual public figures' behaviours to their personal character-istics rather than to the political system, or their political persona. This evidence draws our attention to another important element of knowledge: the ability to make attributions and draw inferences on the basis of the factual information provided by news.

Knowledge as Ability to Draw Inferences

Scholars have gone beyond exploring whether news can provide novel information that people can recall and explored also whether the informa-tion gathered from the news is related to people's estimations concerning political issues. For example, Tichenor, Donohue and Olien (1970) famously reported an analysis of the extent to which issues covered in the news could inform audience members' evaluations of the likelihood that cigarettes cause cancer or of Man reaching the moon. Methodologically, the rationale is that, if there is a relationship between levels of exposure and perception of the issue, we would find evidence of an association between news and knowledge. In other words, what is being measured here is how the information provided in the news supports (or helps shape) people's views of relevant current affairs. Indeed, this definition and way to measure knowledge, as a body of information shaping our view of the world, is not only more comprehensive, but it also allows us to test another important theoretical development in the study of media effects: that of Cultivation Theory.

In Cultivation Theory (Gerbner, 1969), media in general (and news media in particular) have an influence on their viewers because these contribute to creating a particular view of the world. In a typical study based on this theory, for example, concerning media and crime, participants are asked to estimate the occurrence of crime (or the risk of them being victims of crime), and this will be correlated with the exposure to media (or specific genres/outlets). In other words, a cultivation perspective would suggest that media inform how we see the world around us, and we develop a worldview grounded in the content provided by media. However, Potter (2014) notices that – while Cultivation Theory has had success in promoting an impressive amount of research – in general it accounts for only about 1 per cent of variance in cultivation indicators (i.e. knowledge, attitudes and emotions being among the most common indicators). Therefore, additional approaches are required to understand the role played by media in political understanding.

An alternative explanation of the role of media in promoting (or hindering) people's ability to draw inferences concerning the preponderance of a phenomenon, or indeed to formulate accurate evaluations, is that of *accessibility bias*. Iyengar (1990) reports a series of studies showing how television news coverage influences people's political beliefs and attitudes by rendering some information more salient and readily accessible. This information is then used by citizens to inform their political attitudes and opinions concerning political actors and policies. However, while Iyengar and others often explain this phenomenon in terms of *priming* (i.e. information contained in the media activates and renders salient particular aspects of reality, which are then used to inform judgements and draw inferences), others view it as evidence of *learning* (e.g. Lenz, 2009). In other words, news content provides novel information that citizens draw upon when making inferences. Indeed, the learning perspective moves the emphasis from a passive audience 'primed' by media content, to a more active audience engaging with media in order to gather political information.

Knowledge as Construction

With the emergence of the 'Active Audience' perspective, that is, the idea that people are not passive recipients of media messages, but actively engage with its content (e.g. encoding/decoding, Hall, 1980) to achieve a goal or attain some gratification (McLeod and Becker, 1981), researchers have started viewing knowledge as the result of a process of construction, in which media messages are not simply absorbed passively, but elaborated and modified by the recipients of the message. This constructivist perspective has been explored mainly within qualitative traditions, for example, adopting methods derived from Social Representations (Bauer and Gaskell, 1999; Höijer, 2011) or discursive psychology (e.g. framing analysis, Giles and Shaw, 2009; or microanalysis of online data, Giles et al., 2015). For example, Schrøder and Phillips (2007) report three studies in Denmark: one analysing the discursive properties of media text concerning politics (discursive analysis), one looking at how citizens select media to gather information about politics (focus groups) and one looking at how people talk about politics (focus groups). Importantly, the authors state, 'We ascribe to the consensus view in media studies today that audience members are active meaning-makers, that media texts are polysemic and that texts set limits for meaning-production' (p. 893). In their analysis, the authors therefore explored how discourses in the media related to consumption choices and discourses about politics in the audience, while relinquishing claims about causality. What is interesting in their study is the analysis of interpretive repertoires offered by media and participants respectively, and in particular the preponderance of populist repertoires among both mainstream media and users. However, while the most prominent repertoire in the media was 'parliamentary democracy in action', focus group participants focused instead on a view of parliamentary democracy and politics as 'dirty deals'. The authors propose the differences in the preponderance of discourses in media and among the participants as evidence against a direct causal relationship between the content of media and people's knowledge about – and perception of – the world. It is important to notice, however, that the active audience perspective has been criticised for overestimating the agency of citizens while underestimating the role played by political, economic and media structures in shaping the information available in the news (e.g. Deacon, Fenton and Bryman, 1999). Indeed, back in 1935, Cantril and Allport stated that – when exploring the impact of media on the public – social psychologists should consider three levels that closely resemble the approach taken in this volume: the first is concerned with the structural characteristics of the broadcast institutions and their regulations; the second concerned the medium characteristics and its content; while the third concerned users' tastes and habits. The assumption – in our interpretation of this work – is that, in order to account accurately for the 'effects' of news on knowledge, we would need to consider all three of these levels, and how they impact individuals' subjective experiences in relation to the particular product of interest (in this case, news). Similarly, recognising the active role of the audience in constructing meaning does not – in itself – deny the influence broader societal, economic and political factors play in influencing what individuals will learn from the news. Rather, it takes a stance against the idea that individuals absorb content uncritically from the media. Indeed, for example, in the introduction of her book on the *Psychology of Political Communication*, Crigler (1998) explains how, in order to understand political sense-making, it is important to consider processes of construction of the message by politicians and media producers (what Hall would call the Encoding process), as well as the complex and varied interpretative work by the audience. In other words, a psychological approach to mediated knowledge construction acknowledges that, while learners do play an important and active role in meaning-making, this occurs within the boundaries of the tools in which learning occurs, and these tools in turn shape individuals' thinking and sense-making (Vygotsky, 1978).

Setting the Agenda

In recognition of the active role played by the audience in interpreting and extracting meaning from news, McCombs and Shaw (1972) stated famously that, while media might not be effective in telling us *what* to think, they are successful in telling us what to think *about*. From this viewpoint therefore, the measures of knowledge proposed above might fail to accurately capture 'knowledge' derived from media. Scholars within this tradition have, therefore, focused on 'issue salience'. The basic assumption is that media coverage of a specific issue will influence people's perception of what is deserving consideration in that moment. For example, Iyengar and Kinder (1987) showed that political candidates' performance is evaluated on the basis of issues that were deemed important (and thus covered extensively) in the media. According to McCombs (2005), the finding that public affairs seen to be of the highest importance by the media are also seen to be of high importance by the public has been replicated in hundreds of studies worldwide. However, it is important to stress that, when it comes to knowledge, not all coverage is the same, and that it is not sufficient for events to appear in the media to guarantee people will learn from it. Two empirical contributions can illustrate this point.

First, in a meta-analysis, Zoizner (2018) showed how strategic news coverage (or 'horse race coverage', which focuses on how individual politicians perform in polls, how they strategically use particular policy issues to gain consensus, what their popularity levels are, etc) actually hinders what he defines as *substantial political knowledge*, i.e. the extent to which participants could recall facts, relevant arguments and answer questions concerning specific issues presented in the news item. The author also included in this variable much rarer questions measuring *perceptual learning*, i.e. the extent to which participants think they learned something from the news.

The second study was conducted by Delli Carpini and Williams (1996) and focused on people's views regarding environmental issues and toxic waste. While the study's findings were in line with the agenda-setting theory (McCombs and Shaw, 1972) – because they suggested that the media has an impact on what citizens talk about and how they talk about it – they also revealed that some media messages are resisted by individuals. Delli Carpini and Williams (1996) revealed that television viewers construct and re-construct their opinions in a non-uniform and inconsistent manner by drawing on personal experiences and pre-existing beliefs as well as the views of others and information presented by the media. The study, which comprised nine focus groups with a total of thirty-four participants, also demonstrated that messages received by media audiences can bear little resemblance to the intended message of those who create them. Discussions following viewing of television programmes highlighted how some participants consciously ignored or rejected media messages as being illegitimate. One example of this rejection is visible in the reaction of a born-again Christian participant who stated that environmental problems are being overblown by the media, who are trying to attract greater interest in order to make a larger profit (Delli Carpini and Williams, 1996). This process of appropriation, framing and transformation of content becomes even more visible online, where individuals select, share – and provide context by adding text that effectively functions as a frame – and comment on news (cf. Kümpel, Karnowski and Keyling, 2015; Lewis, Pea and Rosen, 2010).

The Rise of the Internet and Implications for Research on Informed Citizenship

In the UK, the 2020 report on news consumption conducted by OFCOM (the UK's communications regulator) shows that 65 per cent of participants access news online. The rise of the Internet, and of social media, has allowed scholars to explore, not only the 'agenda-getting' (i.e. choices about news consumption), but also the 'agenda-setting' role of ordinary citizens. For example, Neumann et al. (2014) conducted an elaborate analysis testing alternative accounts of who 'sets the agenda', as well as the direction of influence of framing. Agenda Setting Theory (McCombs and Shaw, 1972) does not necessarily attribute to media the power to influence our opinion on political matters. Rather, it looks at the role media play in determining the salience of political topics (what we think about) and collocating an issue within a particular area of relevance (second-level agenda-setting – McCombs, Shaw and Weaver, 2014), e.g., is this an isolated event or something linked to a wider context/trend, or is this something that pertains to the environmental sphere or the economic sphere? Adopting a big data approach, the authors analyse online and mainstream media mentions of particular issues, as well as the frequency of appearance of a selection of frames across time. Results showed how the often-hypothesised unilateral direction of influence (from media to audience) is not an accurate reflection of what appears to be happening. The authors show instead that there is a bi-directional relationship, where issues spill from media to audience in some cases, from audience to media in others, and sometimes the influence seems to go in both directions in a mutually reinforcing cycle. This initial evidence shows how the change in the media landscape might be affecting journalistic practices. Moreover, it suggests that – at least when it comes to online media – the direction of influence might be reversed. An optimistic view could interpret this as evidence of the power of the Internet as a democratising force.

Moreover, while traditional media rely extensively on official communications from PR and press agencies to source the news (Lewis, Williams and Franklin, 2008), a growing amount of research is showing how social media are frequently used as 'beats' (i.e. sources of a story) in modern journalistic practices. For example, in a series of studies, Broesma and Graham (2012, 2013) showed how tweets are incorporated in journalistic practice in the UK and the Netherlands. The first (2012) study looked at how tweets were used as sources during the British and Dutch elections. Results showed significant differences in whose tweets were sourced (with a predominance of Vox Pop, especially in the tabloid publications for the UK compared to the Netherlands), which tended to rely on politicians' tweets as sources. Once again, therefore, we see an interaction between different levels: on the one hand, the introduction of new media – and their affordances – in journalistic practice, on the other, different ways in which these are used within different professional and cultural contexts.

A Psychological Approach

So, what can psychology add to this already impressive body of knowledge? First, in our opinion, a psychological approach can help by focusing on the subjective experience of interacting with media in context. In other words, as psychologists we are interested in understanding how individuals experience this interaction, and how it is incorporated in their subjective experience of the world. In this sense, while research looking at media systems will tell us how different organisation and regulation of the media environment is related to different offers in terms of frequency and type of news (Aalberg and Curran, 2012), a psychological approach will tell us how individual producers, editors, journalists or audience members experience this environment and how psychological processes will contribute to the way in which they act within it (see, e.g. Coen and Bull, 2021). Second, we argue, literature on educational psychology can help us redefine what we mean by knowledge and how learning happens, especially when it comes to adult learning. In the next section, we argue that learning from the news is a form of self-regulated learning.

Learning from the News as Self-Regulated Adult Learning: A GAMES Approach

In the first instance, we think educational psychology can give us useful insights into what knowledge is. Most media research is focused on knowledge interpreted as the ability to recall factual information, and use it (we have added) to make inferences about the world. A psychological perspective would widen this definition to include the ability to apply this information in practice. In this sense, therefore, we would argue that providing information that people can later recognise or recall is not sufficient to argue that news contributes to informed citizenship. Rather, adapting Boekaerts (1996), we argue that adequate news coverage is not simply aimed at transferring information to the audience's memory, and adequate learning from the news is not simply equated to the amount of accurate information people can remember from it. In this sense, 'factual knowledge' is only an aspect of what we consider as knowledge in this chapter, that is, the acquisition of information, skills and beliefs that allow citizens to perform their role in society. And, indeed, we have seen scholars in the media field (e.g. Curran et al., 2014) moving from a model where knowledge (measured as factual knowledge) was the main outcome of news exposure, to one where factual knowledge is only part of the 'learning' process, which also includes increased levels of political efficacy and increased interest in politics. From an educational psychology perspective, knowledge comprises all these elements (and more).

Indeed, back in 2001, Albert Bandura proposed a Social Cognitive perspective to account for learning from (mass) media. In this theory, learning is the outcome of several sequential processes: attention, retention, production and motivation. Particularly interesting for the current news landscape (especially online), he states: 'People seek information that may be potentially useful to them from different sources. [. . .]. How extensively different sources are used depends, in large part, on their accessibility and the likelihood that they will provide the kinds of information sought.' (p. 284). In other words, the search for information is goal-oriented, and the goals will determine where and what information will be considered. Based on the above, one can expect, for example, that a prospective student would look at several sources of information to make sure they get an accurate picture of which university they would like to attend, or that, before moving home, an individual will strategically seek and select information that would help them choose the area in which they are going to live.

More importantly for our proposal of applying self-regulated learning (SRL) theories to our understanding of news' contribution to informed citizenship, Bandura stresses how the ability to self-regulate, self-reflect and learn vicariously are at the heart of the socio-cognitive theory of learning.

Schunk and Zimmermann (1994) define self-regulated learning (SRL) as 'the process whereby students activate and sustain cognitions, behaviours and affects which are systematically oriented toward the attainment of their goals'. The literature in this area identifies a few characteristics that we think are relevant and applicable to understanding the role news plays in informed citizenship, which we summarise below. Accordingly, SRL can be considered within the following 'GAMES' model:

– **Goal-Oriented**. Pintrich (2000) defines goals as: 'cognitive representations of what individuals are trying to accomplish and their purposes or reasons for doing the task.' (p. 96). SRL literature places emphasis on goals as determinants of the outcome of learning. Evidence in support of this comes from different theoretical traditions, for example, Zimmermann and Kitsantas (1999) showed how high-school girls' performance improved when they shifted from an outcome goal (i.e. focus on getting a good outcome) to an accuracy goal (i.e. focus on being accurate). Boekaerts is acknowledged as the theorist whose work focused on explaining the role of goals in learning and putting emphasis on the role of emotions in the process (Panadero, 2017).

– **Active**. At the most basic level of being able to retain factual knowledge, Bandura (2001) states: 'Retention involves an active process of transforming and restructuring information conveyed by modeled events into rules and conceptions for memory representation'. From an SRL perspective, learners are active in that their learning is instrumental to the achievement of goals, and they actively monitor and direct their actions in pursuit of the goal.

– **Motivated**. We define motivation as the psychological 'push' to engage in an activity (or indeed avoid it). Pintrich (2000) identifies several motivational constructs that play an important role in education. Among these: goals, attributions, efficacy beliefs, interest and intrinsic motivation are represented in most SRL theories (e.g. Rheinberg, Vollmeyern and Rollett, 2000). Moreover, literature on motivated cognition shows how our motivations have a significant effect on the way in which we select, attend to, recall, feel and act in our social context (e.g. Madan, 2017).

– **Emotion-Laden**. Op't Eynde, De Corte and Verschaffel (2007) begin their chapter on the role of emotions in SRL with the following quote: 'Emotions are not just the fuel that powers the psychological mechanism of a reasoning creature, they are parts, highly complex and messy parts, of this creature's reasoning itself' (Nussbaum, 2001, p. 3). In the chapter, they present a reading of SRL through a socio-constructivist perspective on learning. Within this perspective, 'learning is characterized by a reflexive relation between *the context and the individual*' (p. 186). The authors further report a series of studies showing how emotions in learning are often the result of an interaction between the student and the environment, and that students often adopt coping strategies to regulate their emotions in the context of learning. Indeed, this echoes the original work of Vygotsky (1962).

– **Situated**. Boekaerts (1996) proposes that a psychological perspective on learning – and adult learning in particular (Bruscaglioni and Gheno, 2000) – views learning *in context*. In other words, educational psychologists realised that students' perceptions, thoughts and behaviours are highly situated. Indeed, she notices how while educators often work on the assumption that 'learning has been achieved when students have retrieved or used information sometime after it has been read, heard or discussed [...] Yet it has become apparent that many students experience difficulties in applying the knowledge and skills acquired in the classroom to everyday situations' (p. 101). Similarly, one can argue, the simple ability to recall information relevant to citizenry (at least in the eyes of the journalist) does not necessarily translate in its application to the practice of being a citizen (see e.g. Brown, Collins and Duguid, 1989).

Research in political psychology shows how similar processes are in play when we move outside the classroom to the context of informed citizenship. In the next section, we discuss how key aspects of learning, identified above in the context of educational psychology, can be applied to understanding media contributions to generating and reinforcing citizens' learning about politics and public affairs.

News and Self-Regulated Learning

Considering the contribution of news to informed citizenship through the lens of the SRL approach helps us to identify several factors likely to influence the quantity and quality of learning citizens can attain through the media.

In adherence with a socio-constructivist approach to SRL, we see learning from the news as an interactive process between the media user and the environment (intended in terms of the cultural, social and historical context as well as in terms of specific media and their affordances). In this sense, existing research on the effects of key psychological constructs on the way in which both journalists and audience make sense of news can help in identifying important processes that play a role in determining the contribution of news to information processing.

Personal Identity and Roles

How journalists and news producers see their role in society can often play an important part in determining news values and coverage, i.e. which information is available in the news and how it is discussed. For example, Hardy (2021) explains how changes in the structure, regulation, resource allocation and environment in which news is produced have raised important questions concerning the professional standing of journalists: who they are, what their function is in society, what expectations the public and media industry have of them. Olawale (2021) further explains how this can impact on the way in which these roles are enacted. For example, a journalist may adopt a delivery style more attuned to capturing attention if they think their role is to make sure as many people as possible are exposed to their message, but what is the consequence for knowledge? Grabe, Lang and Zhao (2003) have shown how the public tend to pay more attention to content delivered in a 'tabloidised' manner (i.e. big, sensationalistic headings and sensationalised, highly emotional delivery), and they remember it better. However, they judge it as less trustworthy. Therefore, if we measured knowledge as the ability to recall information, this study would suggest 'tabloidised' content would serve better the purpose. However, a self-reflective learning perspective highlights the study also showed people judged the content as less trustworthy.

From a GAMES perspective, we can expect that people who are motivated to draw an accurate picture of what is going on in the world, in order to inform their thinking, feelings and actions as citizens, might not use information provided when constructing an argument. It is possible they might not use that particular source, either, when trying to achieve those goals. Indeed, research has illustrated a tendency for the 'most liked' and 'most viewed' articles to be typically those media communication experts call 'soft' and weird stories (e.g. Boczkowski and Michtelstein, 2013). It is important, however, to note that Boczkowski and Michtelstein (2013) show how – in line with the context dependence claim in SRL (see the 'situated' aspect of GAMES) – both journalists' and audience's content choices vary corresponding to what is happening in the political scene. Accordingly, during significant political events, such as elections, people do opt for 'harder' content, and the offer of such content increases in news outlets. Similarly, regardless of the 'popularity' of individual news items, research has shown that people are still very aware of 'what news should be about', in terms of informing citizenship and providing 'solid' information (Schrøder, nd). Therefore, the evidence seems to suggest people may use news as a form of entertainment (Thussu, 2008), but they know when it is time for them to use it for different purposes, that is – we argue – when they are thinking of their 'informed citizen' identity.

From an SRL perspective, we argue that media can be a source of learning for citizens, who will use it strategically when seeking information as part of that role.

Social Identity

Identity-related issues do not only concern personal identity and role conceptions: a long tradition in social psychology demonstrates how the social groups to which we belong are indeed part of our social identities and have a significant effect on how we think, feel and act (Tajfel, 1981; Tajfel and Turner, 1979). Research has shown how the same processes identified as key motivators to join and identify with particular groups – or to think of our present, desired and future selves (for identity motives – see, e.g. Vignoles, 2011) – can explain the extent to which we use social media (Manzi et al., 2018). So, while access to news can be seen as a way to gather information we find relevant to our role as citizens, sharing news via social media can be part of our identity work. In other words, news sharing can be seen as a bonding activity that helps both claiming and reinforcing one's membership position in a particular group (e.g. Dwyer and Martin, 2017). Indeed, theories and evidence in social psychology suggest that online activities in which one engages can facilitate the emergence of new social identities, such as opinion-based groups (see, e.g. Thomas et al., 2015). News sharing and commenting can certainly be a powerful democratic tool, which allows for people who belong to marginalised and minoritised groups to come together, learn from each other, share and discuss their experiences (for an identity-related perspective on online forums, see, for example, David Giles' work on Pro Ana websites, Brotsky and Giles, 2007; Giles, 2006). On the other side, however, the same activities can be an obstacle to democratic dialogue, with people interacting mainly with others who share similar opinions and thereby creating echo chambers, where one rarely gets to have positive interactions with people who share different opinions. Within these echo chambers, discussions tend to reinforce, rather than challenge, one's existing views and, even when information from other groups is shared, this is used to reassert the groups' initial values (for an interesting parallel on how sources of criticism inform groups' reactions in an intergroup context, see Hornsey, 2005). Scholars have suggested that this can be the mechanism underlying polarisation online (see, e.g. Wojcieszak and Garret, 2018).

From an SRL perspective, we can therefore derive that affirmation and maintenance of a positive social identity affects learning. Indeed, the evidence presented above suggests that social identity processes influence the way in which people share, select and discuss the news. In other words, identity appears to be a goal, a driver for activity and a motivator for learning from the news.

Motivation

As discussed in the previous section, most of the literature on SRL acknowledges the important role played by motivational factors in determining learning. Similarly, the literature in media and communication has explored how motivation impacts individuals' media choices and effects. Media have been extensively explored within the Uses and Gratifications (UandG) perspective. In our opinion, the UandG perspective is a deeply psychological one, as it acknowledges that media messages are not received by every member of the audience in the same way. Rather, what one learns from a particular message depends on reasons for accessing the message and the gratifications sought by this activity (e.g. Rubin, 2009). For example, David (2009) argues that motivations and goals play an important role in determining the extent to which people will learn from the news. In her study, she analysed data from existing large studies – Electronic Dialogue 2000 (ED2K) and Healthcare Dialogue (HCD) projects – and showed how the motivations driving exposure to news (in terms of need for cognition and need for evaluation) were related to participants' interest in politics, exposure to news, attentiveness to political content and knowledge (measured in terms of both civic knowledge and issue-specific knowledge).

Research in the area of motivated reasoning further expands this point by showing how ideology can also function as a key motivator in determining the way in which citizens learn from news. For example, Nisbet, Cooper and Ellithorpe (2015) showed how accurate knowledge concerning climate change decreases for conservatives attending political news, but increases when conservatives attend science news.[2] Kahan et al. (2012) further show how differences in concern about climate change cannot be accounted for by differences in factual knowledge and comprehension of science: in their study, those with the highest level of scientific literacy and numeracy were, in fact, the most divided in this respect. Indeed, Xue et al. (2014) conducted a meta-analysis exploring the effect of cultural worldviews (i.e. individuals' 'distinct preferences for how society should be structured', p. 249) on environmental concerns, showing how these play a(n overall modest) role in determining citizens' perceptions of environmental risk.

Therefore, from an SRL perspective, we can conclude that motivational factors – such as ideological positions, worldviews and task orientation – will influence the way in which citizens draw on information to form beliefs about the challenges faced by the society they live in.

---

[1] No change is reported for liberals and moderates.

Emotions

The fundamental structural changes faced by news media, with an ever-increasing competition for attention (Nixon, 2020), have implications for how journalists try and capture people's attention and for the extent to which these 'tricks' may actually be effective (Thompson and Coen, 2021). For example, psychological research suggesting that negative information tends to be more attended to than positive information applies also to news (Soroka, 2014). Bachleda and Soroka (2021) clearly show how emotions are featured in journalistic content and in people's reaction to the content. Applying an automated content-analytic strategy to analysis of the *New York Times* from 1980 to the present day, the authors showed how news reports frequently include expression of emotions and that this practice has increased in recent times. Moreover, the authors' analysis shows how the presence of emotional content increases public attentiveness to news. Similarly, Grabe's work (see, e.g. Grabe et al., 2003) shows that emotionally charged coverage (typical of tabloids) attracts more attention, but also hinders information processing. In this sense, leveraging on emotions entails clear risks when it comes to informed citizenship.

Despite this, Bas and Grabe (2015) clearly show that informative content does not need to be dull. They presented participants with news stories concerning issues deemed important for informed citizenship (e.g. corruption, child labour, industrial practices), which featured (versus not featured) an emotional testimony. Results showed how the presence of emotional personalisation, not only improved ability to memorise and recall information, but also reduced the knowledge gap, by improving knowledge (at least in the short term) among those with lower levels of educational qualification.

Literature in psychology shows how emotions also play an important role in susceptibility to misinformation. Porter et al. (2014) show that, when individuals are primed with emotional content on exposure to 'neutral' images (e.g. people queuing at an airport), they become more susceptible to misinformation and false memories in a subsequent recall task.

The evidence proposed, therefore, suggests that emotions do play a role in determining the selection, interpretation and knowledge citizens derive from interacting with news content in different contexts. Nonetheless, the link between emotions and learning is not as straightforward as one would hope, with emotional content appearing as fostering – and at times hindering – learning from the news (see also Grabe and Bas, 2021). An SRL perspective can help further clarify the role played by emotion in civic engagement and identify ways in which emotions can be harnessed to foster the development of learning, engagement and dialogue in a democratic society.

Conclusion

While there is evidence supporting the idea that media can contribute to knowledge by providing citizens with information concerning current affairs, this connection is much less straightforward than previously imagined. Contrary to suggestions in early research on media effects research, media 'consumers', their social groups and the environment in which they interact, their motivations and goals all play an active role in shaping whether and how the message will be received, evaluated and considered. The current media landscape, and in particular the online environment, offers novel opportunities for learning and for citizens to encounter news – for example, on social media – even where they are not actively looking for it. Indeed, research suggests that even this type of exposure leads to increased knowledge, where this is defined as the ability to recognise correct information (Lee and Kim, 2017). In this sense, one could argue that the Internet offers novel and unique ways in which citizens can engage with news, and learn about the world around them from a wider variety of sources.

However, it is important to resist temptation to underestimate the important role played by media providers in shaping public debates about social issues. For example, Curran, Fenton and Freedman (2016) warn against the optimistic view of the Internet as an open, free platform of information sharing. They highlight how information online is subject to political and economic controls, which often re-create the same dynamics as those observed in traditional media – and in the broader societal landscape. For example, Curran et al. (2012) report on a content analysis of news appearing on the landing pages of the most popular online news sources in nine countries. Contrary to what could be expected, the news provision of these online outlets focused on domestic issues (or international issues with a direct involvement of the home-nation) and were still over-reliant on official sources. Moreover, the twenty-four-hour cycle of news, the growth of media conglomerates and increased popularity of the Internet have seen the erosion of rigorous reporting in favour of dubious practices that increase speed and quantity of production, such as the over reliance on PR and wires (e.g. Johnston and Forde, 2017). In the face of such decline in the quality of the offer (which is mostly due to the media landscape fostering a view of news as a product – or even as a form of entertainment – rather than a public service), evidence suggests that citizens are still very well aware – and demanding – of 'quality' journalism (Schrøder, nd).

From a (media) psychological perspective, the Internet offers opportunities for scholars to test the effectiveness and quality of information available to citizens adopting both large (big data) and small (micro-analysis) scale studies of online content, and explore the processes of sense-making in which individuals engage when consuming news. Moreover, research in psychology can highlight ways in which key psychological processes, such as identity – both personal and social – motivation and emotions, influence whether, how and what people will learn from (news) media.

We hope this chapter also provided a persuasive argument as to why moving away from a 'traditional' definition of learning, into a self-regulated learning perspective, would provide new and (possibly) more fruitful ways to consider the role of media in a democratic society. From this perspective, learning is: (a) driven by individuals' goals when consuming news; (b) determined by individuals playing an active role; and (c) influenced by the motivations, (d) emotions and (e) situational factors in which it occurs.

We argue that reconceptualising learning from the news in terms of the GAMES approach offers a theoretical framework that can fruitfully account for the extant work on how media can be used to promote informed citizenship (cf. Grabe and Bas, 2021). Moreover, a vision of learning from the news informed by the literature on self-regulated learning will allow scholars to evaluate and redefine the type and quality of political knowledge and skills modelled in news media and propose strategies to help journalists create – and educators help citizens navigate – a news environment that fosters the development of knowledge and skills necessary to contribute to modern societies. Put simply, in order to understand the complex process of learning from the news, research in media, journalism and psychology need to start where the individual is and understand where they are trying to go, and why.

REFERENCES

Aalberg, T. and Curran, J. (2012). *How media inform democracy: A comparative approach.* New York: Routledge. doi:10.4324/9780203803448

Bachleda, S. and Soroka, S. (2021). Emotion. In S. Coen and P. Bull (Eds.), *The psychology of journalism.* New York: Oxford University Press.

Bandura, A. (2001). Social cognitive theory: An agentic perspective. *Annual Review of Psychology,* 52(1), 1–26. doi:10.1146/annurev.psych.52.1.1

Barrett, M. and Zani, B. (Eds.). (2014). *Political and civic engagement: Multidisciplinary perspectives.* New York: Routledge.

Bas, O. and Grabe, M. E. (2015). Emotion-provoking personalization of news: Informing citizens and closing the knowledge gap? *Communication Research*, 42(2), 159–185.

Bauer, M. W. and Gaskell, G. (1999). Towards a paradigm for research on social representations. *Journal for the Theory of Social Behaviour*, 29(2), 163–186. doi:10.1111/1468-5914.00096

Boczkowski, P. and Mitchelstein, E. (2013). *The news gap: When the information preferences of the media and the public diverge.* Cambridge, MA; London, UK: The MIT Press. doi:10.2307/j.ctt9qf7t3

Boekaerts, M. (1996). Self-regulated learning at the junction of cognition and motivation. *European Psychologist*, 1(2), 100–112. doi:10.1027/1016-9040.1.2.100

Broersma, M. and Graham, T. (2013). Twitter as a news source, *Journalism Practice*, 7(4), 446–464. doi:10.1080/17512786.2013.802481

(2012). Social media as beat, *Journalism Practice*, 6(3), 403–419, doi: 10.1080/17512786.2012.663626

Brotsky, S. R. and Giles, D. (2007). Inside the 'pro-ana' community: A covert online participant observation. *Eating disorders*, 15(2), 93–109.

Brown, J. S., Collins, A. and Duguid, P. (1989). Situated cognition and the culture of learning. *Educational Researcher*, 18(1), 32–42.

Bruscaglioni, M. and Gheno, S. (2000). *Il gusto del potere. Milano, FrancoAngeli srl.* Cambridge, MA: Harvard University Press.

Cantril, H. and Allport, G. W. (1935). *The psychology of radio.* New York: Harper and Brothers.

Coen, S. and Bull, P. (2021) *The psychology of journalism.* New York: Oxford University Press.

Crigler, A. N. (1998). *The psychology of political communication.* Ann Arbor: University of Michigan Press.

Curran, J., Coen, S., Aalberg, T. and Iyengar, S. (2012). News content, media consumption, and current affairs knowledge. *How media inform democracy: A comparative approach*, 1, 81–97.

Curran, J., Coen, S., Soroka, S., Aalberg, T., Hayashi, K., Hichy, Z., Iyengar, S., Jones, P., Mazzoleni, G., Papathanassopoulos, S., Rhee, J. W., Rojas, H., Rowe, D. and Tiffen, R. (2014). Reconsidering 'virtuous circle' and 'media malaise' theories of the media: An 11-nation study. *Journalism*, 15(7), 815–833.

Curran, J., Fenton, N. and Freedman, D. (2016). *Misunderstanding the Internet.* London: Routledge. doi:10.4324/9781315695624

Curran, J., Iyengar, S., Brink Lund, A. and Salovaara-Moring, I. (2009). Media system, public knowledge and democracy: A comparative study. *European Journal of Communication*, 24(1), 5–26.

Cushion, S. (2012). *The democratic value of news: Why public service media matter.* Basingstoke: Macmillan Education.

David, C. C. (2009). Learning political information from the news: A closer look at the role of motivation. *Journal of Communication*, 59(2), 243–261.

Deacon D, Fenton N and Bryman A. (1999). From inception to reception: The natural history of a news item. *Media, Culture and Society*, 21(1): 5–31. doi:10.1177/016344399021001001

Delli Carpini, M. and Keeter, S. (1993). Measuring political knowledge: Putting first things first. *American Journal of Political Science*, 37(4), 1179–1206. doi:10.2307/2111549

Delli Carpini, M. and Williams, B. (1996). Methods, metaphors, and media messages: The uses of television in conversations about the environment. In A. Crigler (Ed.), *Political communication and public understanding*, pp. 149–176. Ann Arbor, MI: University of Michigan Press.

Dwyer, T. and Martin, F. (2017). Sharing news online, *Digital Journalism*, 5(8), 1080–1100. doi:10.1080/21670811.2017.1338527vv

Galston, W. A. (2001). Political knowledge, political engagement, and civic education. *Annual Review of Political Science*, 4(1), 217–234. doi:10.1146/annurev.polisci.4.1.217

Gerbner, G. (1969). Toward "cultural indicators": The analysis of mass mediated public message systems. *AV Communication Review*, 17(2), 137–148.

Giles, D. (2006). Constructing identities in cyberspace: The case of eating disorders. *British Journal of Social Psychology*, 45(3), 463–477.

Giles, D. and Shaw, R. (2009). The psychology of news influence and the development of media framing analysis. *Social and Personality Psychology Compass*, 3, 375–393. doi:10.1111/j.1751-9004.2009.00180.x

Giles, E. L., Holmes, M., McColl, E., Sniehotta, F. F. and Adams, J. M. (2015). Acceptability of financial incentives for breastfeeding: Thematic analysis of readers' comments to UK online news reports. *BMC Pregnancy and Childbirth*, 15(1), 116. doi:10.1186/s12884-015-0549-5

Grabe, M. E. and Bas, O. (2021). Reconsidering informed and participatory citizenship in the current media ecosystem. In S. Coen and P. Bull (Eds.), *The psychology of journalism*. New York: Oxford University Press, pp.87–110.

Grabe, M. E., Lang, A. and Zhao, X. (2003). News content and form: Implications for memory and audience evaluations. *Communication Research*, 30(4), 387–413. doi:10.1177/0093650203253368

Habermas, J., Lennox, S. and Lennox, F. (1974). The public sphere: An encyclopedia article (1964). *New German Critique*, No. 3 (Autumn, 1974), 49–55.

Hall, S. (1980). Encoding/Decoding. In S. Hall, D. Hobson, A. Lowe and P. Willis (Eds.), *Culture, media, language*, pp. 117–127. London: Hutchinson/CCCS.

Hardy, J. (2021). Journalism in the 21st century. In S. Coen and P. Bull (Eds.), *The psychology of journalism*, pp. 18–52. New York: Oxford University Press.

Höijer, B. (2011). Social representations theory: A new theory for media research. *Nordicom Review*, 32(2), 3–16.

Hornsey, M. J. (2005). Why being right is not enough: Predicting defensiveness in the face of group criticism. *European Review of Social Psychology*, 16(1), 301–334.

Iyengar, S. (1990). The accessibility bias in politics: Television news and public opinion. *International Journal of Public Opinion Research*, 2(1), 1–15.

Iyengar, S. and Kinder, D. R. (1987). *American politics and political economy. News that matters: Television and American opinion.* Chicago, IL: University of Chicago Press.

Jenkins, H. (2006). Convergence culture: Where old and new media collide. *New York: New York University Press*; London: Eurospan distributor.

Johnston, J. and Forde, S. (2017). Churnalism: Revised and revisited. *Digital Journalism*, 5(8), 943–946.

Kahan, D. M., Peters, E., Wittlin, M., Slovic, P., Ouellette, L. L., Braman, D. and Mandel, G. (2012). The polarizing impact of science literacy and numeracy on perceived climate change risks. *Nature Climate Change*, 2(10), 732–735.

Kümpel, A. S., Karnowski, V. and Keyling, T. (2015). News sharing in social media: A review of current research on news sharing users, content, and networks. *Social Media and Society*, 1(2), 2056305115610141.

Lee, J. K. and Kim, E. (2017). Incidental exposure to news: Predictors in the social media setting and effects on information gain online. *Computers in Human Behavior*, 75, 1008–1015.

Lenz, G. S. (2009). Learning and opinion change, not priming: Reconsidering the priming hypothesis. *American Journal of Political Science*, 53(4), 821–837. doi:10.1111/j.1540-5907.2009.00403.x

Lewis, J., Williams, A. and Franklin, B. (2008). A compromised fourth estate? UK news journalism, public relations and news sources. *Journalism Studies*, 9(1), 1–20.

Lewis, S., Pea, R. and Rosen, J. (2010). Beyond participation to co-creation of meaning: Mobile social media in generative learning communities. *Social Science Information*, 49(3), 351–369.

Madan, C. R. (2017). Motivated cognition: Effects of reward, emotion, and other motivational factors across a variety of cognitive domains. *Collabra: Psychology*, 3(1), 24.

Manzi, C., Coen, S., Regalia, C., Yévenes, A. M., Giuliani, C. and Vignoles, V. L. (2018). Being in the social: A cross-cultural and cross-generational study on identity processes related to Facebook use. *Computers in Human Behavior*, 80, 81–87.

McCombs, M. E. (2005). A Look at agenda-setting: Past, present and future. *Journalism Studies (London, England)*, 6(4), 543–557. doi:10.1080/14616700500250438

McCombs, M. E. and Shaw, D. L. (1972). The agenda-setting function of mass media. *Public Opinion Quarterly*, 36(2), 176–187. doi:10.1075/asj.1.2.02mcc

McCombs, M. E., Shaw, D. L. and Weaver, D. H. (2014). New directions in agenda-setting theory and research. *Mass Communication and Society*, 17(6), 781–802.

McGraw, K. M. and Holbrook, R. A. (2003). Democracy and the Media. In *Encyclopedia of international media and communications* (Vol. 1). Cambridge, MA: Academic Press.

McLeod, J. M. and Becker, L. B. (1981). The uses and gratifications approach. In D. D. Nimmo and K. R. Sanders (Eds.), *Handbook of political communication*, pp. 67–100. Beverly Hills, CA: Sage.

Molyneux, L. (2018). Mobile news consumption: A habit of snacking. *Digital Journalism*, 6(5), 634–650.

Neuman, W. R., Guggenheim, L., Mo Jang, S. and Bae, S. Y. (2014). The dynamics of public attention: Agenda-setting theory meets big data. *Journal of Communication*, 64(2), 193–214.

Nisbet, E. C., Cooper, K. E. and Ellithorpe, M. (2015). Ignorance or bias? Evaluating the ideological and informational drivers of communication gaps about climate change. *Public Understanding of Science*, 24(3), 285–301.

Nixon, B. (2020). The business of news in the attention economy: Audience labor and MediaNews Group's efforts to capitalize on news consumption. *Journalism*, 21(1), 73–94.

Nussbaum, M. (2001). *Upheavals of thought: The intelligence of emotions.* Cambridge, MA: Cambridge University Press. doi:10.1017/CBO9780511840715

Olawale, O. (2021). Norms and Roles. In S. Coen and P. Bull (Eds.), *The psychology of journalism*, pp.128–167. New York: Oxford University Press.

Op't Eynde, P., De Corte, E. and Verschaffel, L. (2007). Students' emotions: A key component of self-regulated learning? In P. A. Schutz and R. Pekrun (Eds.), *Emotion in education*, pp. 185–204. Cambridge, MA: Academic Press.

Panadero, E. (2017). A review of self-regulated learning: Six models and four directions for research. *Frontiers in Psychology*, 8, 422, doi:10.3389/fpsyg.2017.00422

Pintrich, P. R. (2000). *The role of goal orientation in self-regulated learning.* In M. Boekaerts, P. R. Pintrich and M. Zeidner (Eds.), *Handbook of self-regulation*, (pp. 451–502). San Diego, CA: Academic Press. doi:10.1016/B978-012109890-2/50043-3

Popkin, S. L. and Dimock, M. A. (1999). Political knowledge and citizen competence. In S. L. Elkin and K. Soltan (Eds.), *Citizen competence and democratic institutions*, pp. 117–46. University Park: Pennsylvania State University Press.

Porter, S., ten Brinke, L., Riley, S. N. and Baker, A. (2014). Prime time news: The influence of primed positive and negative emotion on susceptibility to false memories. *Cognition and Emotion*, 28(8), 1422–1434.

Potter, W. J. (2014). A critical analysis of cultivation theory. *Journal of Communication*, 64(6), 1015–1036.

Rheinberg, F., Vollmeyer, R. and Rollett, W. (2000). Motivation and action in self-regulated learning. In M. Boekaerts, P. R. Pintrich, and M. Zeidner (Eds.), *Handbook of self-regulation*, pp. 503–529. San Diego, CA: Academic Press.

Rubin, A. M. (2009). Uses-and-gratification: An evolving perspective of media effects. In J. Bryant and M. B. Oliver (Eds.), *The Sage handbook of media processes and effects*, pp. 147–159. Los Angeles: SAGE.

(2002). The uses-and-gratifications perspective of media effects. In J. Bryant, D. Zillmann and M. B. Oliver (Eds.), *Media effects*, pp. 535–558. New York: Routledge.

Schrøder, K. C. (2019). What Do News Readers Really Want to Read About? How Relevance Works for News Audiences. Available online at: www .digitalnewsreport.org/publications/2019/news-readers-really-want-read-rele vance-works-news-audiences/#1-recent-research-on-news-preferences.

Schrøder, K. C. and Phillips, L. (2007). Complexifying media power: A study of the interplay between media and audience discourses on politics. *Media Culture and Society*, 29, 890–915. doi:10.1177/0163443707081693

Schunk, D. H. and Zimmerman, B. J. (Eds.). (1994). *Self-regulation of learning and performance: Issues and educational applications.* Lawrence Erlbaum Associates, Inc.

Soroka, S. (2014). *Negativity in democratic politics.* New York: Cambridge University Press. Accessed at: Online ISBN: 9781107477971. doi:10 .1017/CBO9781107477971.

Tajfel, H. (1981). *Human groups and social categories – studies in social psychology.* Cambridge, UK: Cambridge University Press.

Tajfel, H. and Turner, J. C. (1979). *An integrative theory of intergroup conflict.* In W. G. Austin and S. Worchel (Eds.), The social psychology of intergroup relations, pp. 33–37. Monterey, CA: Brooks/Cole.

Thomas, E. F., McGarty, C., Mavor, K. (2016). Group interaction as the crucible of social identity formation: A glimpse at the foundations of social identities for collective action. *Group Processes and Intergroup Relations*, 19(2): 137–151.

Thompson, C. and Coen, S. (2021). The importance of visual attention and perception in journalism. In S. Coen and P. Bull (Eds.), *The psychology of journalism*, pp.53–86. New York: Oxford University Press.

Thussu, D. K. (2008). *News as entertainment: The rise of global infotainment.* London: Sage.

Tichenor, P. J., Donohue, G. A. and Olien, C. N. (1970). Mass media flow and differential growth in knowledge. *Public Opinion Quarterly*, 34(2), 159–170. doi:10.1086/267786

Trappel, J. and Nieminen, H. (2018). Media and democracy: A couple walking hand in hand? In L. d'Haenaens, H. Sousa, and J. Trappel (Eds.), *Comparative media policy, regulation and governance in Europe*, pp. 185–206. Bristol, UK: Intellect.

Vignoles, V. L. (2011). Identity motives. In K. Luycke, S. J. Schwartz and V. L. Vignoles (Eds.), *Handbook of identity theory and research*, pp. 403–432. New York, NY: Springer.

Vygotsky, L. S. (1978). *Mind in society: The development of the higher psychological processes.* Cambridge, MA: Harvard University Press.

(1962). *Thought and language.* Cambridge, MA: MIT Press. (Original work published in 1934).

Weiser, E. B. (2001). The functions of internet use and their social and psychological consequences. *Cyberpsychology and behavior*, 4(6), 723–743.

Wojcieszak, M. and Garrett, R. K. (2018). Social identity, selective exposure, and affective polarization: How priming national identity shapes attitudes toward immigrants via news selection. *Human Communication Research*, 44(3), 247–273.

Xue, W., Hine, D. W., Loi, N. M., Thorsteinsson, E. B. and Phillips, W. J. (2014). Cultural worldviews and environmental risk perceptions: A meta-analysis. *Journal of Environmental Psychology*, 40, 249–258.

Zimmerman, B. J. and Kitsantas, A. (1999). Acquiring writing revision skill: Shifting from process to outcome self-regulatory goals. *Journal of Educational Psychology*, 91(2), 241–250. doi:10.1037/0022-0663.91.2.241

Zoizner A. (2018). The consequences of strategic news coverage for democracy: A meta-analysis. *Communication Research.* doi:10.1177/0093650218808691

CHAPTER 18

A Social Psychological Approach to Understanding China's Democratisation

Yida Zhai

Introduction

During the past seventy years, we have witnessed the dynamics of the Chinese party-state system. This political system has undergone countless setbacks and challenges. These issues include the catastrophic failures in the Great Leap Forward (1958–1961) and the Cultural Revolution (1966–1976); progressive student movements in the 1980s, which peaked with the 1989 Tiananmen protests; social uprisings and protests by workers laid off from state-owned enterprises; protests by peasants, whose interests had been violated in land expropriations and village corruption; and protests by citizens from both rural and urban polluted environments. China experts and observers boldly predicted an immediate collapse of the Chinese Communist Party (CCP) when the party took office in 1949, but the predictions have yet to come true. The Chinese party-state system actively seeks to adapt to the changing domestic and global environment and consolidates its rule by various means. To this day, its survival has not encountered fundamental challenges even during the 1989 crisis.

Against the background of the CCP's continuous rule, a paradigm shift is needed to broaden the examination of China's politics in the area of democratisation. There are various approaches taken to explain democratisation of authoritarian regimes. One is the structural approach, which attempts to explain the transition through socio-economic modernisation (Lipset, 1959; Rueschemeyer, Stephens and Stephens, 1992). Economic development and modernisation are widely considered as important driving forces for democratisation. The structural approach describes the macro-environment of democratisation, but it is unable to explain how it takes place. Another example is the elite-centric approach, which emphasises the role of elites and argues that political actors promote and determine the process of democratisation (Linz and Stepan, 1996; O'Donnell, Schmitter and Whitehead, 1986). In fact, the success of democratisation is associated with the attitudes ordinary people have toward it. Without pressure from the bottom of the political hierarchy, it is unlikely that authoritarian leaders will voluntarily give up their monopoly of power and agree to political reforms: structural and elite-centric approaches fail to realise the roles of ordinary people in democratisation. Therefore, more attention should be paid to the social bases of politics, because the attitudes and values of the masses affect and shape the dynamics of politics (Qi and Shin, 2011; van de Walle, 2002; Zhai, 2016, 2017a).

The social psychological approach is an alternative to the structural and elite-centred approaches. This approach can be traced back to the pioneering studies of civic culture by Almond and Verba (1963), which attempted to explain the 'rise and fall of political constitutions in social psychological terms' (Almond and Verba, 1989, p. 2). Their works aimed to study the political system 'without losing the benefits of individual psychology' (Pye and Verba, 1965, p. 9). The social psychological approach places the masses at the centre of analysis and brings ordinary people back into the studies of democratisation (Welzel and Inglehart, 2008). Pye's (1968) pioneering study examined a psycho-cultural dimension in Chinese politics and found that paternalism is the highest ideal of government in China (Pye, 1968, p. 19). The social psychological approach builds upon such insights that advocate the importance of the attitudes, values and behaviour of ordinary people in politics (Inglehart, 1990; Inglehart and Welzel, 2005; Moghaddam, 2016). Popular beliefs and attitudes toward the legitimacy of regimes have been viewed as critical elements in determining the maintenance, transformation and breakdown of a political system (Chu et al. 2008; Dahl, 1971; Linz and Stepan, 1978).

Differing from the line of research that focuses on the Chinese government, this chapter will apply a social psychological approach to understanding China's democratisation by analysing the attitudes that ordinary Chinese people have toward politics. The Chinese government has long been the focus of political studies. Whether the narratives are praise for its achievements in developing the country's economy or criticism of its ruthless oppression of human rights and abuse of power, limited attention has been paid to ordinary Chinese people. Nevertheless, the social psychological approach aims to examine how ordinary Chinese people evaluate the current regime and think about their political rights and democracy. Do they trust the authoritarian governments? What kind of democracy do they want? How will changes in their attitudes towards democracy and the current political regime take place? Answers to these questions will provide

Table 18.1. *Attachment to democracy in East Asian societies.*

	Preference	Suitability	Favourability
Mainland China	57.34	76.12	86.09
Japan	74.67	75.56	95.17
South Korea	65.23	88.19	89.31
Taiwan	47.34	79.18	88.22

Source: The Asian Barometer Survey (2014–2016)

valuable clues to understanding China's politics. The social psychological approach helps unveil the Chinese public's attitudes towards the government and popular preferences to political systems, which are the most critical factors in China's democratisation.

A Paradox in China's Politics

How do ordinary Chinese people think of democracy and the current regime? Cross-national surveys consistently reveal that the Chinese public is supportive of it to the same extent as citizens support their governmental systems in democratic societies. According to measures of attachment to democracy (Chu et al. 2008; Mishler and Rose, 2005; Shin and Wells, 2005), pro-democratic orientations can be measured by the following three indicators: preference, suitability and favourability. The Asian Barometer Survey (ABS)[1] asked three questions corresponding to these different elements of attachment to democracy: (1) Preference for democracy. 'Do you agree democracy is preferable to any other kind of government in any circumstances?' (2) Suitability of democracy. 'Do you think democracy is suitable for our country?' (3) Favourability of democracy. 'Do you agree democracy is the best form of government in spite of some of its problems?' Table 18.1 shows the levels of attachment to democracy in China and three other East Asian democratic societies. The results indicate that Chinese citizens are as supportive of democracy as people in these other three democratic societies.

[1] Data analysed in this article were collected by the Asian Barometer Project (2013–2016), which was co-directed by Professors Fu Hu and Yun-han Chu and received major funding support from Taiwan's Ministry of Education, Academia Sinica and National Taiwan University. The Asian Barometer Project Office (www.asianbarometer.org) is solely responsible for the data distribution. The author appreciates the assistance in providing data by the institutes and individuals aforementioned. The views expressed herein are the author's own.

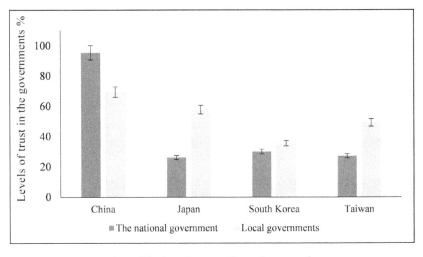

Source: The Asian Barometer Survey (2014–2016)

Figure 18.1   Public trust in governments in East Asian societies.

Intuitively, people in a liberal democracy may believe that authoritarian governments cannot obtain public trust and have to maintain rule by means of oppression. However, various surveys show that the current authoritarian regime obtains fairly high levels of political trust among the Chinese public (Chen, 2004; Dickson, 2016; Tang, 2005, 2016). As Figure 18.1 shows, both the national and local governments in China have higher levels of public trust than their counterparts in the other three East Asian societies featured. In particular, the national rather than regional government is more trusted among the Chinese people. Previous studies have proved that political fear is not the major reason for the high levels of public trust (Manion, 2010; Shi, 2008).

The evidence of high levels of public trust in the Chinese government indicates that, at present, ordinary Chinese people are not particularly motivated to topple the current regime. First, the older generations, who experienced the Cultural Revolution, have appreciated the socio-economic modernisation since the 1980s (Shi, 2008). The CCP claims that remark-able improvements in standards of living are due to the merits of the current political system. Second, the younger generations in China have internalised patriotic sentiments and materialist values in the process of socialisation (Zhai, 2016; Zhao, 1998). The political psychological char-acteristics of Chinese youth are manifest in two ways. First, they are emotionally mobilised by patriotism to defend China's national interests when it comes to territorial disputes or diplomatic disagreements with other countries. Second, Chinese youth are apathetic to politics, partially because of the authoritarian political system. They are immersed in entertainment, consumerism and enjoyment of their lives (Zhai, 2016; Zhao, 1997). Another factor is that the disadvantaged and the rising middle classes resort to the authorities for benevolent care when they encounter problems (Shi and Lu, 2010; Zhai, 2017a). Even if there are protests in mainland China, their aims are pragmatic rather than challenging the political system (Zhang, 2013).

The evidence shows that there is a paradox in China's politics. Although Chinese people are pro-democratic, they also trust the current regime, which is normally regarded as non-democratic (Shi, 2008). This paradox in China's politics is not covered by modernisation theories, which assume there is a congruent relationship between socio-economic modernisation and democratic transition. A systematic investigation of pro-democratic attitudes among the Chinese public and their trust in the current regime will help to explain why the majority of them have not fought enthusiastically for democracy, even though the authoritarian political system is viewed as cruel and inhuman by people in democratic societies. To try and solve this puzzle, a theoretical framework is developed and utilised in this chapter that will explore the political attitudes of Chinese people towards democracy and their trust in the current regime (see Figure 18.2). This will provide social psychological insights into prospects for China's democratisation.

This theoretical framework incorporates three main pillars: political psychological impact of economic modernisation, political culture and popular perceptions of democracy. Theories of modernisation and political culture are useful in explaining why pro-democratic Chinese citizens trust an authoritarian regime. Popular perceptions of democracy show how the Chinese public views it. The following sections will discuss these social psychological elements underlying China's politics and any potential future democratisation.

Public Support for the Current Regime

The Political Psychological Consequences of Economic Modernisation

Modernisation theory attempts to bridge economic modernisation with political liberalisation and democratisation. It assumes that economic development leads automatically to social and political changes. In

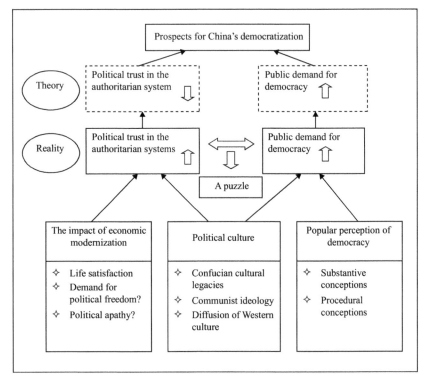

Figure 18.2   A social psychological approach to understanding China's democratisation.

particular, it presupposes that civic society will develop and a democratic transition will take place after economic modernisation from a linear, evolutionary perspective (Deutsch, 1963; Huntington, 1968; Pye and Verba, 1965; Stinchcombe, 1965). A revised version of modernisation theory is a combination of theories of post-materialist and self-expression values. It inherits the modernisation theory's evolutionary views by contending that socio-economic modernisation brings about a subsequent rise in interpersonal trust, post-materialist values, social tolerance, and political activism, which in turn will drive a transformation in political and cultural fields. A combined post-materialist/self-expression values theory argues that the value shift is the key factor in assessing the impact of modernisation on democratisation (Inglehart, 1990; Inglehart and Baker, 2000; Inglehart and Welzel, 2005; Welzel, Inglehart and Klingemann, 2003).

Does modernisation facilitate a democratic transition in China? One of China's most remarkable characteristics over the past few decades is its rapid economic development without democratisation. According to the

World Bank's statistics, the GDP per capita has risen from 194 US dollars in 1980 to 10500 US dollars in 2020, making China an 'upper-middle income' country. This shows that a market economy brings about affluence. The standard of living for the Chinese people has improved considerably. As their basic economic security has been satisfied, they are paying more attention to quality-of-life issues. More and more have a chance to travel or study abroad. In contrast to official propaganda, alternative information on the Internet has become accessible despite government censorship. As previously mentioned, socio-economic modernisation has changed the lives of ordinary Chinese people. However, the political outcomes of economic development do not match the predictions of modernisation theory. Research is needed to examine the effects of economic modernisation on the Chinese public's attitudes towards democracy and their trust in the current regime. After all, the political psychological impact of economic modernisation affects the potential for democratisation in China.

With economic modernisation, the Chinese government obtains public trust. According to survey data, government performance is positively correlated with public trust in the government (Chen, 2004; Tang, 2005). In addition, economic modernisation increases people's political satisfaction rather than their discontent. After Mao's death, Deng Xiaoping initiated economic reforms to bring China back into international society. While national economic growth increases ordinary people's life satisfaction, incredible improvements in life satisfaction fail to motivate ordinary Chinese people to actively struggle for political liberalisation and democratisation. Consumerism, individualisation of Chinese society and de-politicisation cause the Chinese to be divorced from politics. In spite of social protests, the discontent of the masses is centred on pragmatic and instrumental benefits rather than against the authoritarian political system. Most people are indifferent to politics and appear satisfied with low levels of civil liberties and political rights (Zhai, 2016). They do not demand democracy, but seek to build ties with the government; nor do they see fundamental changes in political institutions as necessary (Guan, 2018). The political psychological consequences of economic modernisation in this case are maintenance of trust by the Chinese public in the government and, at the same time, an absence of desire to eagerly pursue a liberal democracy.

The Impact of Political Culture

Study of political culture highlights the importance of the psycho-cultural dimension of political activities, such as experience within the political system; the perception and evaluation of one's own role in political life; and learning about various orientations to politics (Almond and Verba, 1963, p. 34). Political culture incorporates two aspects: one deals with cognition, feelings and the evaluation of output and performance of political systems. The other aspect deals with the perception and judgement of the role of oneself in politics. These two aspects are interconnected – the motivations of individuals and attitudes towards political systems co-existing in a political culture (Almond and Verba, 1963, p. 33). Ultimately, ordinary citizens form a 'subjective orientation to politics' and perception of the situation in which political actions take place (Pye and Verba, 1965, p. 513). The importance of political culture is manifest in its role as an engine of a political system: 'People's beliefs and values play an important role in how societies function' (Inglehart and Welzel, 2010, p. 563). The masses in any political context internalise their specific culture and subsequently form their political values and attitudes. Therefore, political activities are mediated by the embedded culture.

Chinese political culture provides a cultural explanation for the co-existence of trust in authoritarian governments and pro-democratic attitudes. Traditional Confucian values, Maoist communist ideology and the West's liberal ideas are three major elements in Chinese political culture (Hua, 2001, p. 9). Confucian cultural legacies maintain a long-term influence in China (Shi, 2014; Shi and Lu, 2010; Zhai, 2017a, 2017b). Traditional culture encourages conformity to authority in the family, community and political life (Hsu, 1949, 1981; Zhai, 2017a). The Chinese Communist Revolution and a number of campaigns afterwards attacked traditional culture, but selected some of its elements in order to strengthen blind loyalty and conformity to the CCP's leadership. Even though communism remains as the official ideology, its influence has largely weakened. Since the 1980s, China has returned to a global capitalist system and has allowed the importation of the West's liberal ideas into China. Consumerism and materialism have been rising since the 1990s. All of these forces shape Chinese political culture.

The Chinese government deftly manipulates and employs political culture to maintain its rule. Paternalism, obedience to authority and intolerance of political pluralism are still prevalent in China (Zhai, 2017a) and these political values have the effect of boosting public trust in the government (Chu, 2013; Shi, 2014; Zhai, 2018). Under the influence of political culture, the Chinese masses maintain their trust in authority and seek benevolent favour from the authorities rather than challenge it. However, Chinese political culture does not deter public support for democracy. Conventional wisdom regards Chinese political culture as incompatible with democracy and also as an impediment to democratisation (Huntington, 1996; Weatherly, 1999). However, Zhai (2017b) divided public support for democracy into attachment to it and an adherence to liberal-democratic values. Attachment to democracy indicates explicit support for it, while adherence to liberal-democratic values reflects implicit support for it. The empirical evidence shows that Chinese political culture does not inhibit the public's support for democracy, but it is negatively connected to liberal-democratic values, which are fundamental to the resilience and consolidation of a fledgling democracy.

Public Support for Democracy

With the collapse of the Soviet Union and the overwhelming third wave of democratisation, a number of cross-national surveys have revealed that democracy has earned global endorsement, even in post-communist societies, the Muslim Middle East, Africa, Latin America and Asia (Dalton, Shin and Jou, 2007; Diamond, 2008; Jamal and Tessler, 2008). Because democracy is popular and has a positive image, even dictatorships attempt to appeal to its rhetoric. However, 'democracy is a concept with a variety of potential meanings, and it is not simple to grasp or define' (Dalton et al. 2007, p. 143). The confusion over what democracy means stems from the long developmental history of the concept and from a variety of sources (Dahl, 1989).

Democracy is an elastic concept, and people in different cultures and countries view it in different ways (Bratton, Mattes and Gyimah-Boadi, 2005; Chu et al. 2008; Zagrebina, 2019). Its concepts are classified differently, according to distinct standards such as constitutional arrangements, procedural perspectives, liberties and rights, and outcomes of democracy. Two broad categories of democracy are procedural and substantive conceptions. The procedural conceptions of democracy prioritise civil liberties and political rights (Dahl, 1971); the minimum requirement of a democracy is that there are periodically fair and competitive multiparty elections (Schumpeter, 1976). In contrast, the substantive conceptions of democracy contend that socio-economic security and equality are pre-conditions for, as well as the essence of, democracy (Meyer, 2007).

Based on these two sets of assumptions, I investigated the Chinese public's perceptions of democracy. Democracy is not an alien idea for Chinese citizens. Appealing for democracy was one of the two key slogans during the May Fourth Movement in 1919. On 30 June 1949, before the

CCP took power, Mao delivered a speech on the CCP's policy on democracy, titled, 'On the people's democratic dictatorship'. The CCP later replaced the term 'people's democratic dictatorship' with 'socialist democracy', and claimed that its political regime was democratic. After careful scrutiny of China's traditional culture, Shi and Lu find that Chinese people's understanding of democracy is strongly influenced by Confucian *minben* thought (Shi and Lu, 2010). Basically, *minben* thought can be interpreted as advocating reciprocal relationships between the rulers and the ruled (Murthy, 2000). On the one hand, people remain loyal and deferential to the government in return for protection and welfare. On the other hand, the government should take care of the interests of the people and bring tangible benefits to them. Under the influence of Confucian tradition, Chinese people view democracy as a form of guardianship that brings benefits to the people (Shi and Lu, 2010). Their perception of it is close to substantive conceptions of democracy.

Popular perception of democracy reflects whether there is public demand for democratisation. If the Chinese public view democracy as a source of tangible benefits and benevolent care from the authorities rather than elections and political rights, there will be no formidable challenges facing the current Chinese political system. Empirical studies show that the majority of ordinary Chinese people view democracy as representing economic security and equality (Shi, 2008; Shi and Lu, 2010; Zhai, 2019a). Compared with elections and political rights, the Chinese seem to be more concerned about what democracy can bring to them economically as an instrument rather than viewed through procedural definitions. Popular perceptions of democracy make a difference in how (dis)satisfied people are with its current levels in China, and the extent to which they trust the political system. Empirical studies find that people who perceive democracy in terms of substantive conceptions are more satisfied with its current state than people who perceive it in a procedural manner (Zhai, 2019a). In addition, the effects of the public's assessment of government performance on political trust are conditioned by different patterns in the perception of democracy. A favourable assessment of government performance on economic and social policy leads to a high level of political trust in people who subscribe to substantive conceptions of democracy (Zhai, 2019b). Popular perception of democracy is, therefore, an important moderating factor that affects satisfaction with it and the effects of government performance on political trust, which explains the co-existence of pro-democratic attitudes among Chinese citizens and high levels of public trust in an authoritarian regime.

Prospects for China's Democratisation

Differing from the structural and elite-centred approaches, this chapter presents clues regarding the prospects for China's democratisation through a social psychological perspective. The bright side of China's democratisation lies in the power of ordinary Chinese people. Changes in the co-existence of the public's pro-democratic attitudes and their trust in the current regime indicate a possible trajectory by which democratisation would likely take place in China. Through empirical investigation of ordinary Chinese people's attitudes toward democracy and political trust, the vulnerabilities of the current regime have been revealed. A powerful authoritarian regime will lose its momentum when reaching its peak and, at that moment, countervailing forces will expand and democratisation break out. A democratic transition is not always smooth and it may produce a variety of dangers. A transition to electoral democracy may not meet the idealised expectations of the masses, such as a quick crackdown on corruption, enhancement of government accountability and responsiveness, and improvements in economic welfare and equality. All of these problems can disappoint the public and affect the survival of new democracies. Moghaddam (2016) examined the psychological characteristics of the democratic citizen and different types of political changes. Drawing insights from Moghaddam's work, the next section will discuss the prospects for democratisation in China by two ideal democratisation types: superficial and profound.

Superficial Democratisation in China

With superficial democratisation, the authoritarian political system would be replaced by an electoral democracy through democratic movements as a result of the eruption of discontent with either an economic crisis, abuse of power or corruption in politics. As the CCP monopolises strong military capabilities, such democratisation is more likely to happen by a split in the CCP leadership along with the pro-reform camp taking control of power. Institutional establishment, such as holding regular elections and the multi-party system, will be the major achievements that come from superficial democratisation. However, political liberalisation and protection of civil liberties and political rights are delayed in this type of democratisation. It takes time for ordinary people to acquire the social and psychological skills to become democratic citizens (Moghaddam, 2016).

First, the superficial democratisation of a multi-party electoral regime may occur due to severe economic stagnation or inflation. A pervasive economic crisis would cause the outbreak of widespread discontent, as a rocketing rate of unemployment and inflation threatens the lives of ordinary people. Previous studies have found that an economic crisis forces autocracies to adopt formal democratic institutions such as multi-party systems (Levitsky and Way, 2002). Government economic and social outputs are primary sources of political support for the current Chinese regime. A social psychological analysis shows that ordinary Chinese people are not concerned with how the government is organised and whether powers are separated and balanced. Instead, they care about the substantive benefits with which the government can provide them. This kind of performance-based political trust can only be maintained in a period of economic prosperity, as it would rapidly lose favour once the economy falls into recession. If economic and social well-being of the Chinese were to be severely jeopardised, political trust in the Chinese government risks decaying. As material interests are a major reason for public engagement in protests (Zhang, 2013, pp. 196–197), in an economic crisis, they could form a common goal of struggling for a living and connecting to each other.

In a democratic society, when a serious economic crisis occurs and governments are unable to deal with it, citizens can change the administration through elections. Even if the replacement of the ruling party may not immediately improve the situation, elections provide a channel for the public to express their discontent and bring about new hope. However, multi-party competition and a procedural way of government replacement are not available in China. Since the CCP is the dominant power in all policy-making processes, it is subject to strong criticism and pressure for any failures in economy. As a result, anti-regime forces could take advantage of an economic crisis and thus earn widespread public support and promote democratic reform.

Second, great discontent with rampant corruption and abuse of power can cause superficial democratisation. Empirical evidence shows that the government's political performance has a negative influence on the Chinese public's trust in the current regime; no matter how the Chinese masses perceive democracy, the assessment of government political performance invariably erodes political trust in the current regime (Zhai, 2019b). Corruption and abuse of power are the political deficit of the current regime. For example, the 1989 Tiananmen protests were associated with the corruption and abuse of power occurring at that time. The public raised doubts about the CCP's rhetoric of 'sincerely serving people' and expressed their strong discontent with the illegal possession of wealth by political elites. During the past few decades, discontent with corruption and abuse of power have surged (Saich, 2016; Zhai, 2019b). Any success-ful mobilisation of people in democratisation should provide a common target for the movement. The narrative that an authoritarian regime is a greenhouse of abuse of power and corruption that can be taken down via electoral democracy will become prevalent. Appealing for eradication of abuse of power and corruption by democratic movements can draw the utmost support and sympathy among the masses.

The aforementioned driving forces – economic and political crises – in superficial democratisation do not necessarily guarantee a successful tran-sition to liberal democracy in China. Superficial democratisation may turn out to be 'a mixture of democratic and authoritarian elements, openness and secrecy, idealism and selfishness, turbulence and stability' (Nathan, 1990, p. 209). Even if elections were held regularly in China, they could be controlled by the CCP, in which case elections would not provide a channel for the opposition to seek power, but merely serve as an instru-ment for the CCP's domination.

A social psychological approach takes into consideration whether the public shows persistent support for a democratic system during the process of democratisation. There is a tension between the aspirations of the masses and achievements of democratic movements with superficial democratisa-tion. As outcomes of democratisation, elections and multi-party systems would be established. However, the replacement of the authoritarian regime via superficial democratisation would have been originally promoted through discontent with economic crisis, abuse of power or corruption. No one can guarantee the newly elected government can effectively get rid of an economic crisis and control corruption. In fact, these problems are not managed well in many third-wave democracies (van de Walle, 2002). In these democracies, multi-party electoral institutions are built, but corrup-tion, abuse of power and economic crisis continue to exist. Democratic politics needs to be accepted as legitimate among the masses (Dahl, 1971). Therefore, it remains unclear whether ordinary Chinese people would remain attached to an electoral democracy and instead have nostalgia for the former authoritarian regime. Karl (1995) contends that policies con-cerning the reduction of poverty and income inequality affect the survival of democracy after transition to democracy. If the majority of ordinary Chinese people adhere to their substantive conceptions of democracy and a newly electoral government does little to satisfy their economic desires, the legit-imacy of the new democratic institutions could risk being challenged.

Even though flaws exist in superficial democratisation, there is no doubt that the establishment of democratic institutions would be a mark of progress in the history of China. At the very least, superficial democratisation grants universal suffrage and promotes elections as a basic method of government formation and the people would be able to change an administration they do not like. Democratic learning (both institutional and for ordinary citizens) could take place even if those processes are imperfect (van de Walle, 2002). As Rome was not built in one day, China should not be expected to become a fully-fledged democracy overnight. Time would be needed to improve the quality of democracy with the process of superficial democratisation.

Profound Democratisation in China

Profound democratisation in China assumes that a democratic transition would take place as the outcome of the prevalence of liberal-democratic values and the adherence of the majority of the Chinese people to procedural conceptions of democracy. In profound democratisation, political liberalisation takes priority over holding competitive elections and universal suffrage. In other words, electoral democracy is not the ultimate goal with regard to the idealised type of profound democratisation. Protection of civil liberties and political rights and flourishing liberal-democratic values give rise to a more healthy and effective democracy. Conventional views of democratisation can put excessive emphasis on elections, but the practice of an electoral democracy cannot succeed without the participation of its citizens. The 1989 Tiananmen democratic movement failed largely because it was made up 'almost entirely of students and intellectuals, a small minority within Chinese society' (Nathan, 1990, p. 173). Popular adherence to liberal-democratic values and prevalence of procedural conceptions of democracy would pave the way for profound democratisation to take root in the population. Liberal-democratic values would inspire more persistent demands for a liberal democracy and lead to a successful democratic transition and consolidation. Therefore, a social psychological approach to understanding democratisation tends towards the perspective that profound democratisation is more likely to earn solid public support as it entails a successful political transition.

When the majority of the Chinese view democracy in a procedural manner, incompatibility and tension between liberal-democratic ideals and authoritarian political reality will create intrinsic public desires for democratisation. The effects of popular perceptions of democracy on profound democratisation are manifested in two ways. On the one hand, procedural conceptions of democracy generate public discontent with the state of elections and people's liberties and rights in China. Despite high levels of satisfaction with democracy as an abstract concept in China at present, these are subject to change (Zhai, 2019a, 2020). Compared to those viewing democracy as constituting economic benefits and the benevolent care of the authorities, the Chinese who hold procedural conceptions of democracy, have low levels of satisfaction with its levels in China (Zhai, 2019a). On the other hand, procedural conceptions of democracy would erode political trust in the current Chinese regime, as popular perceptions of democracy affect evaluations of government performance and the effects of governmental performance on political trust are contingent on particular democratic perceptions (Zhai, 2019b). Even though government economic and social policy performance bolster public trust in political institutions in general, the favourable effects are attenuated among people who have procedural conceptions of democracy. When procedural conceptions of democracy become prevalent in the Chinese population, the public pressure for democratisation is likely to be formidable and irresistible. Violent oppression remains a choice, but its considerable costs would force political elites to reconcile and move forward with democratic reforms.

Moreover, liberal-democratic values contradict authoritarian politics. When the majority of the Chinese people adhere to liberal-democratic values, democratisation is more likely to occur. Liberal-democratic values underscore the rule of law, separation of powers, political pluralism, political freedom, etc., all of which are underdeveloped in the current Chinese political system. Empirical evidence indicates that liberal-democratic values have negative effects on the Chinese people's political trust (Zhai, 2018). In addition, the Chinese who adhere to liberal-democratic values have significant discontent with the state of democracy in China (Zhai, 2019a). Analysis of demographic structures indicates liberal-democratic values are higher in the younger generations (Zhai, 2019a). With an intergenerational shift, prevalence of liberal-democratic values will lead to increasing aspirations for democratisation. However, this change will be slow but steady. It will take a relatively long time for the diffusion of liberal-democratic values in China, as the CCP's dominant discourse competes to control the minds of the Chinese public. With the prevalence of procedural conceptions of democracy and liberal-democratic values among the Chinese public, profound democratisation of China would most likely occur.

The Relationship Between the Two Idealised Types of Democratisation

The relationship between superficial and profound democratisation in China lies in the dynamics of public attitudes toward democracy. It also relates to whether and how their co-existence will shift between the public's pro-democratic attitudes and their trust in the current regime. With regard to popular perceptions of what democracy means, previous studies have developed two theoretical models – democratic learning and diffusion (Rohrschneider, 1999; Sandholtz and Gray, 2003). The Chinese public's attitude toward democracy is not static, but it will change and affect the routes of future democratisation.

China may transform into an electoral democracy, even if the majority of its citizens adhere to the substantive conceptions of democracy. In the idealised type of superficial democratisation, the establishment of formal democratic institutions takes priority over political liberalisation. As discussed before, elections are held regularly in such democracies, but separation of powers, the rule of law, civil liberties and political rights are underdeveloped. It can be argued that, with superficial democratisation, the Chinese people can learn liberal-democratic values and improve the quality of democracy by practising it, i.e. a democratic learning process. The democratic learning model claims that people learn what liberal democracy means and acquire its values after their countries change to an electoral democracy. Previous studies have found that the public perception of democracy shifts to freedom and political rights with increasing democratic experience (Dalton et al. 2007). In addition, Shin (2012) discusses the democratic consolidation of the Confucian societies. He argues that the democratic learning model finds more convincing evidence in the cases of South Korea and Taiwan, in which their citizens define democracy in a liberal manner by learning its meaning through practising it.

However, a diffusion model contends that ordinary Chinese people can gradually acquire procedural conceptions of democracy and adhere to liberal-democratic values even within an authoritarian political system, in line with a global convergence of liberal democracies. A large proportion of the citizens in the third-wave democracies of Africa, Latin America and Eastern Europe view democracy in liberal-democratic terms (Dalton et al. 2007). The demographic attributes of popular perceptions of democracy in China indicate an increase in the younger population likely to adhere to the procedural conceptions of democracy in the future (Zhai, 2019a, 2020). This evidence indicates the future possibility of profound democratisation. The idealised type of profound democratisation assumes democratic transformation is more likely to take place when the majority of Chinese people make demands for political liberalisation. It is a diffusion process of liberal democracies, which is a system that states that procedural conceptions of democracy will spread because it is integrated with a human being's desire for freedom.

Regarding the prospects for democratisation in China, even though it is currently not an electoral democracy, democratic learning can take place in an indirect way. The Chinese people can learn procedural conceptions of democracy and liberal-democratic values from other democratic societies. Democracy has already obtained more legitimacy in the contemporary world compared to other forms of government (Dalton et al. 2007; Mainwaring and Bizzaro, 2019). The legitimacy of democracy puts enormous pressure on China to follow a path to democratisation. Pressure from the international community will not disappear, even though the international environment becomes more hospitable to the Chinese authoritarian regime because of its economic power (Chu, 2012). Meanwhile, the Chinese government spares little effort to control its people and resist the influence of democratic diffusion from the outside world. Changes in public attitudes towards the current regime and democracy will eventually predict the Chinese political future.

REFERENCES

Almond, G. and Verba, S. (1989). *The civic culture revisited.* Newbury Park, CA: Sage Publications.

(1963). *The civic culture: Political attitudes and democracy in five nations.* Princeton: Princeton University Press.

Bratton, M., Mattes, R. and Gyimah-Boadi, E. (2005). *Public opinion, democracy and market reform in Africa.* New York: Cambridge University Press.

Chen, J. (2004). *Popular political support in urban China.* Stanford: Stanford University Press.

Chu, Y. (2013). Sources of regime legitimacy and the debate over the Chinese model. *China Review,* 13(1), 1–42.

(2012). The Taiwan factor. *Journal of Democracy,* 23(1), 42–56.

Chu, Y., Diamond, L., Nathan, A. J. and D. C. Shin (Eds.). (2008). *How East Asians view democracy.* New York: Columbia University Press.

Dahl, R. A. (1989). *Democracy and its critics.* New Haven: Yale University Press.

(1971). *Polyarchy: Participation and opposition.* New Haven: Yale University Press.

Dalton, R. J., Shin, D. C. and Jou, W. (2007). Understanding democracy: Data from unlikely places. *Journal of Democracy,* 18(4), 142–156.

Deutsch, K. W. (1963). *The nerves of government*. London: Free Press.

Diamond, L. (2008). Introduction. In L. Diamond and M. F. Plattner (Eds.), *How people view democracy*, pp. ix–xxvii. Baltimore: Johns Hopkins University Press.

Dickson, B. (2016). *The dictator's dilemma: The Chinese Communist Party's strategy for survival*. New York: Oxford University Press.

Guan, Y. (2018). Demand for democracy in resilient authoritarianism: Evidence from rural China. *Democratization*, 25(7), 1073–1092.

Hua, S. (2001). *Chinese political culture 1989–2000*. New York: M. E. Sharpe.

Huntington, S. P. (1996). *The clash of civilizations and the remaking of world order*. New York, NY: Simon & Schuster.

(1968). *Political order in changing societies*. New Haven: Yale University Press.

Hsu, F. (1981). *Americans and Chinese: Passage to differences, third edition*. Honolulu: University of Hawaii Press.

(1949). *Under the Ancestors' shadow: Chinese culture and personality*. New York: Columbia University Press.

Inglehart, R. (1990). *Culture shift in advanced industrial society*. Princeton: Princeton University Press.

Inglehart, R. and Baker, W. E. (2000). Modernization, cultural change, and the persistence of traditional values. *American Sociological Review*, 65(1), 19–51.

Inglehart, R. and Welzel, C. (2010). Changing mass priorities: The link between modernization and democracy. *Perspectives on Politics*, 8(2), 551–567.

(2005). *Modernization, cultural change, and democracy: The human development sequence*. New York: Cambridge University Press.

Jamal, A. and Tessler, M. A. (2008). Attitudes in the Arab world. *Journal of Democracy*, 19(1), 97–110.

Karl, T. L. (1995). The hybrid regimes of central America. *Journal of Democracy*, 6(3), 72–86.

Levitsky, S. and Way, L. (2002). The rise of competitive authoritarianism. *Journal of Democracy*, 13(2), 51–65.

Linz, J. and Stepan, A. (1996). *Problems of democratic transition and consolidation: Southern Europe, South America, and post-Communist Europe*. Baltimore: Johns Hopkins University Press.

(1978). *The breakdown of democratic regimes*. Baltimore: Johns Hopkins University Press.

Lipset, S. M. (1959). Some social requisites of democracy: Economic development and political legitimacy. *American Political Science Review*, 53(1), 69–105.

Mainwaring, S. and Bizzarro, F. (2019). The fates of third-wave democracies. *Journal of Democracy*, 30(1), 99–113.

Manion, M. (2010). A survey of survey research on Chinese politics: What have we learned? In A. Carlson, M. E. Gallagher and K. Lieberthal (Eds.), *Contemporary Chinese politics: New sources, methods, and field strategies*, pp. 181–199. New York: Cambridge University Press.

Meyer, T. (2007). *The theory of social democracy*. Cambridge, UK: Polity.

Mishler, W. and Rose, R. (2005). What are the political consequences of trust? A test of cultural and institutional theories in Russia. *Comparative Political Studies*, 38(9), 1050–1078.

Moghaddam, F. M. (2016). *The psychology of democracy*. Washington, DC: American Psychological Association Press.

Murthy, V. (2000). The democratic potential of Confucian minben thought. *Asian Philosophy*, 10(1), 33–47.

Nathan, A. (1990). *China's crisis: Dilemmas of reform and prospects for democracy*. New York: Columbia University Press.

O'Donnell, G., Schmitter, P. and Whitehead, L. (1986). *Transitions from authoritarian rule: Tentative conclusions about uncertain democracies*. Baltimore: Johns Hopkins University Press.

Pye, L. W. (1968). *The spirit of Chinese politics: A psychocultural study of the authority crisis in political development*. Cambridge, MA: MIT Press.

Pye, L. W. and Verba, S. (1965). *Political culture and political development*. Princeton: Princeton University Press.

Qi, L. and Shin, D. C. (2011). How mass political attitudes affect democratization: Exploring the facilitating role critical democrats play in the process. *International Political Science Review*, 32(3), 245–262.

Rohrschneider, R. (1999). *Learning democracy: Democratic and economic values in unified Germany*. Oxford, UK: Oxford University Press.

Rueschemeyer, D., Stephens, E. H. and Stephens J. D. (1992). *Capitalist development and democracy*. Chicago: University of Chicago Press.

Saich, T. (2016). How China's citizens view the quality of governance under Xi Jinping. *Journal of Chinese Governance*, 1(1), 1–20.

Sandholtz, W. and Gray, M. (2003). International integration and national corruption. *International Organization*, 57(4), 761–800.

Schumpeter, J. A. (1976/1942). *Capitalism, socialism and democracy*. London: Allen and Unwin.

Shi, T. (2014). *The cultural logic of politics in mainland China and Taiwan*. New York: Cambridge University Press.

(2008). China: Democratic values supporting an authoritarian system. In Y. Chu, L. Diamond, A. J. Nathan and D. C. Shin (Eds.), *How East Asians view democracy*, pp. 209–237. New York: Columbia University Press.

Shi, T. and Lu, J. (2010). The shadow of Confucianism. *Journal of Democracy*, 21(4), 123–130.

Shin, D. C. (2012). *Confucianism and democratization in East Asia*. New York: Cambridge University Press.

Shin, D. C. and Wells, J. (2005). Is democracy the only game in town? *Journal of Democracy*, 16(2), 88–101.

Stinchcombe, A. L. (1965). Social structure and organizations. In J. G. March (Ed.), *Handbook of organizations*, pp. 142–193. Chicago: Rand McNally and Company.

Tang, W. (2016). *Populist authoritarianism*. New York: Oxford University Press.

(2005). *Public opinion and political change in China*. Stanford: Stanford University Press.

The Asian Barometer Survey dataset. (2016). Wave 4th survey. Available at: www
.asianbarometer.org/survey/wave-4th-survey.

van de Walle, N. (2002). Africa's range of regimes. *Journal of Democracy*, 13(2),
66–80.

Weatherly, R. (1999). *The discourse of human rights in China*. London: Macmillan
Press.

Welzel, C. and Inglehart, R. (2008). The role of ordinary people in democratization. *Journal of Democracy*, 19(1), 126–140.

Welzel, C., Inglehart, R. and Klingemann. H.-D. (2003). The theory of human
development: A cross-cultural analysis. *European Journal of Political Research*,
42(2), 341–380.

Zagrebina, A. (2019). Concepts of democracy in democratic and nondemocratic
countries. *International Political Science Review*, doi:10.1177/
0192512118820716

Zhai, Y. (2020). Popular perceptions of democracy in China: Characteristics and
longitudinal changes. *Asian Survey*, 60(3), 557–582.

(2019a). Popular conceptions of democracy and democratic satisfaction in
China. *International Political Science Review*, 40(2), 246–262.

(2019b). Popular democratic perception matters for political trust in authoritarian regimes. *Politics*, 39(4), 411–429.

(2018). Traditional values and political trust in China. *Journal of Asian and
African Studies*, 53(3), 350–365.

(2017a). Values of deference to authority in Japan and China. *International
Journal of Comparative Sociology*, 58(2), 120–139.

(2017b). Do Confucian values deter Chinese citizens' support for democracy?
Politics and Religion, 10(2), 261–285.

(2016). Remarkable economic growth, but so what? The impacts of modernization on Chinese citizens' political satisfaction. *International Political
Science Review*, 37(4), 533–549.

Zhang, M. (2013). *What kind of democracy do the Chinese want: Chinese 'Political
Man' 2012*. Beijing: Social Sciences Academic Press (in Chinese).

Zhao, B. (1997). Consumerism, Confucianism, communism: Making sense of
China today. *New Left Review*, 222, 43–59.

Zhao, S. (1998). A state-led nationalism: The patriotic education campaign in
post-Tiananmen China. *Communist and Post-Communist Studies*, 31(3),
287–302.

CHAPTER 19

The Psychology of Radicalised Conceptions of Democracy
Steps Too Far?

Roderick Dubrow-Marshall

> We have it in our power to begin the world over again. A situation, similar to the present, hath not happened since the days of Noah until now. The birthday of a new world is at hand...
> Thomas Paine, in Common Sense (1776).

Many of the most significant advances in social psychology during the second half of the last century emanated from researchers whose ideas were forged, literally in some cases, in the horrors of Nazism and the Holocaust. Through different means, a host of psychologists arguably shared similar motivations in seeking to understand and explain the psychology of totalitarianism and its barbarity. Whether in shedding light on conformity (Asch, 1956), cognitive dissonance (Festinger, 1962), obedience (Milgram, 1974), minority influence (Moscovici and Lage, 1976), learned helplessness (Seligman, 1972), the basis for conflict (Sherif, 1967), group identity and prejudice (Tajfel, 1978) or the situational factors leading to barbarism (Zimbardo, 1971), each provided a compelling diagnosis of the everyday psychology behind the destruction and bloodshed that they and countless millions had witnessed and suffered.

If social psychology provided a thorough-going analysis of the twentieth-century malaise, it was arguably less clear on the remedies for it and the potential cures. While this could indicate a healthy empirical detachment from advocating social change, others have argued that each body of empirical evidence, and the theories that emerged from it, tended to encapsulate an inevitability about the barbarity that it sought to explain (Parker, 1990). It could be argued that, as a collective corpus of work, the field took on – with no irony intended – an air of learned helplessness about the nature of humanity. Furthermore, it took some time before learned optimism (Seligman, 1990) and the heroic imagination (Zimbardo, 2008) were formulated as standard bearers for positive psychology and the hope of a new and hopefully more enlightened century to come.

In the aftermath of the Holocaust and War War II, it can also be argued that social psychology was, as with the world in which it operated, somewhat traumatised and blinking uncertainly as the smoke cleared to seek to answer the most heart aching question of all – why did this happen? In seeking overarching psychological explanations for barbarity and totalitarianism, there is a constant tug of reductionist logic that seeks to set aside the social, cultural and historical engines of radicalism and extremism of all forms and which leads to the inevitable conclusion that humans have an in-built and inevitable capacity to oppress and to destroy. As Primo Levi (1965) wrote, 'Monsters exist, but they are too few in number to be truly dangerous. More dangerous are the common men, the functionaries ready to believe and to act without asking questions (p. 228).'

Moreover, an historical vista and understanding tell us that the radical transformation of society has been an attractive proposition across the centuries since liberal democracies became established as Thomas Paine, among many others, advocated. Whether it is the allure of starting over with a utopian democracy somewhere new or turning the clock fast forward or back, radicalised conceptions of democracy are a constant presence on both the far Left and Right of politics (Tourish and Wohlforth, 2000). This chapter will provide an analysis of the operation of such radicalised movements and will show how psychology has contributed to understanding them.

Seeds of Extremism?

Health warnings about such conceptions are commonplace, however, and, on occasions, derive from revolutionary thinkers themselves, such as Frantz Fanon, whose maxim, 'Blind idealism is reactionary', sought to demonstrate how notions of utopian democracy need to be culturally located and applied, if they are to avoid colonial forms of oppression themselves. Within Fanon's wider tradition of revolutionary Marxism, there is often a delineation between those who believe that the 1917 Russian Revolution is a potential, yet contested, model for all countries – as demonstrated in the 100th anniversary celebrations in 2017 such as the 'Russian Revolution: Hope, Tragedy, Myths' exhibition at the British Library – and those who believe that nationalist liberation struggles can define new models of revolutionary change. Either way, these idealised conceptions of democracy on the far Left, whether traditionally 'young' Marxist, Stalinist or Trokskyist, or some other variant, can be advocated by groups whose actual body politic and practice are steeped in the same oppressive conditions as the world they so despise (Downes, 2017).

On the far Right, the folk myths of racial and ethnic purity from which society has supposedly retreated obscure the simultaneous mixing with and oppression of a myriad of cultural populations, not only across the panoply of history, but also within the very movements who claim that 'God' and Biblical righteousness is on their side, as the 2003 revelations about Strom Thurmond's daughter indicated (Clinton, 2010). 'Turning the other cheek' is demonstrably less common than turning one's head away from the smouldering residues left in the wake of the struggle by 'true' believers for a 'true' democracy as has been recorded in the aftermath of KKK insurgencies (McVeigh and Cunningham, 2012). It follows that radical pacifists (such as Martin Luther King) are, therefore, not only outstanding for their novelty, but are often seen as less zealous for 'true' change (in King's case, by Malcolm X).

In many respects, it can be argued that liberal democracies stand and fall on the underpinnings of the cliché that 'one person's terrorist is another person's freedom fighter'. If only we understood our enemies better, and all that they have been through, then their world, and ours, would be a much better place. Restorative justice would be neither restorative nor justice without such underpinning ideals (Young, 2003) Therefore, acceptance – or even advocacy – of violence in the cause of political freedom very much comes down to an individual's frame of reference about the injustice one is seeking to address. Nelson Mandela is not Timothy McVeigh[1] and Jeremy Corbyn[2] is not Donald Trump.

Therefore, an understanding of frame of reference is critical to understanding how people with the same neurological apparatus can perceive the world in radically different ways. Social psychology has, for many decades, sought to explain how polarised frames of reference provide the lens that creates these differences in perception (Hogg and Abrams, 1993).

Relativistic conceptions of radicalism automatically eschew clarity of definition, most of all to the benefit and comfort of the perceiver. The Kantian interpretation of perceptual reification can sit easily within, and is fertile ground for, liberal democratic notions of accepting other people's views, however obnoxious or abhorrent they are seen to be, as long as these do not hurt other people. Actions, after all, speak louder than words and,

---

[1] Timothy McVeigh was the Oklahoma City Bomber, who killed 168 people in 1995 and was executed for this crime in 2001, and who is often assessed as having far Right beliefs that motivated his actions.

[2] Jeremy Corbyn is a UK Member of Parliament and was the Leader of the Labour Party from 2015–2020 and is usually considered to be on the Left of the Labour Party and of politics generally.

sometimes, these are words that we cannot understand because we accept – and even celebrate – that others see the world differently from ourselves. This gap between the toleration of thoughts and behaviours can be seen to be a philosophical 'get out' clause that simultaneously tolerates racism and prejudiced views while also condemning racist lynching or the fascist's head hitting the pavement. Accordingly, this creates space for expressions like, 'The only good fascist is a dead fascist' as the non-ironic mantra of some peace-loving Leftists, while some pro-life Rightists proclaim the carrying out of the blood oath as an ultimate and necessary conclusion, as witnessed in cult-like groups such as the 'Fundamentalist Latter Day Saints' (Krakauer, 2003).

The Emergence of Radicalised Groups and Movements

Research and practice regarding radical groups and movements has, therefore, established over time the notion that it is the 'deed' and not the 'creed' that should be the focus of attention. This allows for freedom of belief and religion (whether in the European Convention of Human Rights or in the United States Constitution) to be upheld while some of the practices that are consistent with these beliefs are heartily condemned. Many concerned citizens are keen to help the police and other agencies in countering violent extremism. Few wish to join the Orwellian ranks of the 'thought police', as found by research on the implementation of the UK's Prevent strategy in schools (Busher et al., 2017). 'Die Gedanken sind frei (thoughts are free)' has become a focus of research regarding intrusions on privacy and free expression amid the battle against terrorism (Donner, 2004).

Radicalised groups and movements are commonly defined in terms of their actual or potential damage to wider society. For example, the Commission of the European Communities (2005) defines violent extremism or radicalisation as 'the phenomenon of people embracing opinions, views and ideas which could lead to acts of terrorism as defined in Article 1 of the Framework Decision on Combatting Terrorism' (p. 2). Likewise, the UK government's Prevent guidance (2011) is concerned 'with all forms of terrorism and with non-violent extremism, which can create an atmosphere conducive to terrorism and can popularise views which terrorists then exploit'.

Psychological research on radicalisation and extremism also examines the personal allure and importance of radicalised group membership for the individual and this is described by Kruglanski et al. (2009) as the 'personal significance of radicalised identity and ideology'. Such conceptions align with the Social Identity tradition in social psychology and the 'emotional and value significance' of group identity for the person (Tajfel and Turner, 1979).

More post-structuralist accounts of language, such as Discursive Psychology (Edwards and Potter, 1992), argue that words are also actions in and of themselves. Words 'do things' and hence the playground line that 'sticks and stones may break my bones, but words can never hurt me' is effectively consigned by this understanding to the equality and diversity training 'dustbin of history' (Trotsky, 1932). However, it is not merely the words, or the spoken creed, that inspires the deed. It is, instead, how people think about these concepts that is critical to explaining the attraction of the radical proposition and how people identify with groups, whose raison-d'être is often wholly at odds with liberal-democratic principles of the society around them. As Lifton (1961) explains about the Nazi doctors, it is only through an understanding of radicalised identity and its inherent splitting or doubling of identity that the loving father and physician by day could also be the eugenicist killer of children by night.

In striving for an ideal democracy, radicalised movements adopt the approach that the ends justify the means; the means are the ends in and of themselves (Bayes, 1970; Emerson, 1937). It is only when the political stakes are seen to be so high that everything else – family, friends, work and wider society – can so easily be set aside. An understanding of extremist or cultic thought process, as advanced by Lifton, is the psychological key to explaining how high functioning and intelligent people can become deeply embroiled, and identify so strongly, with groups whose beliefs are often so radical that they dare not speak their name (and, indeed, some are proscribed by law) (Dubrow-Marshall, van de Donk and Haanstra, 2019).

In order to illustrate the psychological processes involved in extreme political environments, the following sections consider examples from both ends of the spectrum, beginning with the far Left.

Building Political 'Cults'

The Marxist-Leninist theory of party-building, which is practised by many radical movements on the far Left, illustrates the concept and practice of democratic centralism. In and of itself, the term 'democratic centralism' can appear to be oxymoronic in that it combines, as stated by its adherents, maximum amounts of democracy with maximum amounts of centralism – i.e. a lot and a lack of democracy. This is predicated on the notion that the democratic centralist party is, in effect, a 'combat party', trained and prepared to lead the working class in revolutionary change against the bourgeoisie. In war time, and as historically in military and para-military organisations, there is often not time to argue and take votes. 'Command and control' is, therefore, used by far Left groups as a means to an end and becomes part of the body politic of the organisation. At the same time, and usually while waiting for the revolutionary period to come, these same groups spend countless hours in internal discussions and, in so doing, demonstrate to members and to others how democratic they are. In all endeavours, whether internal or external, the question of loyalty to the party and the cause is paramount. In this way, members of such groups can be seen to be subject to the same processes of cultic indoctrination and thought reform as in other extremist groups of different political or religious hues (Tourish, 2013).

Lifton's work on thought reform (1961), based originally on an analysis of Mao's political movement in China, defines the psychological process that people go through in extremist and radical environments to reach a polarised perceptual vantage point, which nevertheless makes complete sense to the individuals concerned because of the lived social reality of the perceiver (Turner and Oakes, 1997). In such movements and groups, the milieu is tightly controlled by the group leadership and the group member's whole life is a practical devotion to the group and its leader or past leaders (in the case of the far Left, Leon Trotsky perished many years ago, but his legacy lives on in a way akin to religious deities).

The leader of a radical group or cult will often claim special powers and will practise what Lifton terms 'mystic manipulation', to persuade group members of their amazing powers. On the far Left, the ability of leaders – a special cadre at the 'vanguard' of the working class – is nothing less than totally emancipatory for workers currently oppressed and largely unaware of their degree of bondage. In a polarised belief system, the language will become discursively 'loaded' to favour the group over all others and a very clear 'us and them' dichotomy will emerge, with total loyalty and a 'demand for purity' from group members. This is characterised by a disavowal of their former lives, loves and interests (if recruited in adult-hood), and of the rest of the world in general. Therefore, for the far Left, 'bourgeois deviations' abound and reformist politicians of the Left are seen as 'class traitors', no better and indeed sometimes worse than politicians of the Right, who are held literally beneath contempt.

On the far Left, and in all parties which have taken on board key aspects of Marxist-Leninist thought, the party is everything and individuals are at its disposal. In this sense, prioritising or even thinking about personal self-interest, career advancement and hobbies are precisely the forms of class betrayal that must be eliminated at all costs. Long internal debates about theory and the creation of debating factions only serve the purpose of elevating the ideological discourse above the needs of everyday lives. As such, both party members, and members of the wider working class, come to be seen as completely disposable. Strikes, demonstrations, pickets and the sacrificing of personal and professional life become grist to the mill of an ideology that sees capitalism as to blame for everything.

The 'Individual' Within the Extremist Group

Lifton argues that this 'dispensing of existence' for the group member is replaced by a total focus and dominance of the group, its leader and ideology. This has been termed as a 'totalistic identity' that exists when the group dominates the person psychologically and to the exclusion of other interests or identities (Dubrow-Marshall, 2010). Building on self-categorisation theory (Turner et al., 1987), the notion of a totalistic identity arose from analysis of group-related aspects of psychological distress, which indicated an unhealthy dominance of the group aspect of identity over every other aspect of self-identity. The usual cognitive process of moving psychologically between different self-categorisations is, in effect, put on hold and the extremist group identity is total in terms of focus, beliefs and practices.

In radicalised or extremist movements, as in groups generally, the group influence or pressure has become an internalised influence and pressure – what has been referred to as 'referent informational influence' (Turner et al., 1987). Every act on behalf of the group reinforces the group-based identity that is totally dominant for the person psychologically. This condition has also sometimes been referred to as 'brainwashing', but this term is potentially problematic, as it implies an emptiness or zombie-like indifference to events and the wider world. Politically inspired practice, including violence, is actually the very opposite: it is the very pinnacle and height of commitment in action for the cause that has become everything to the person and which the person believes in completely and totally – and they need very strongly to believe in it totally, as it is literally their everything (Dubrow-Marshall, 2010). This explanation of a radicalised and totalised identity sheds new potential light on the relationship between deed and creed by demonstrating that actions and practices are inherently as self-referential as beliefs and ideas (Turner, 1991).

This also accords with research that has shown that a radicalised or extreme perception of reality is not necessarily erroneous (Haslam and

Turner, 1995, 1998). The effect of a polarised frame of reference and the range of available social stimuli indicate that a radicalised perception can be an accurate representation of the inhabited social world. This explains how different sets of people can view the same stimuli differently – not because some are right and some are wrong in their perceptions, but because 'the shared ideas and actions of group members are intrinsically compelling as they imply a reality which explains them' and 'the shared world is psychologically experienced as the real objective world' (Turner et al., 1987, p. 81).

Members and supporters of radical groups are, therefore, responding to the social milieu in which they live and, to the extent that it is full of specific ideas and content, then their perception of those things will reflect that lived reality. Therefore, Lifton's (1961) description of 'milieu control' explains potentially more about the self-categorical judgements that group members will make, as much as it tells us about the specific level of coercion experienced. Furthermore, the normative actions of group members, while overtly pressured by leaders or fellow members, may not feel coerced to the individuals concerned as they are reinforcing the central part of their identity, which is dominated by the group. The influence is self-referential (Turner et al., 1987) and, therefore, seems as compelling as the shared reality that the influenced actions reinforce.

The 'veridical' nature of radicalised group perception and normative action does not, of course, justify violence or harm being inflicted (Haslam and Turner, 1995), nor does it mean that the perceptions and actions are not extreme or polarised compared to wider societal norms. While liberal democracies tend to support or even celebrate their ability to contain the latter, as evidence of a plurality and the right to political or religious beliefs, the former is often considered unacceptable and unlawful. Understanding how deeply meaningful the beliefs and actions are does not mean that the radicalised group identity is healthy or beneficial to the individual or wider society (Banisadr, 2009).

Kruglanski's (2019) work on the 'personal significance' of extremist ideologies sheds further light on how, as Haslam and Turner (1995) describe it, 'people's representation of others is inherently bound up with their representation of self' (citing Turner et al., 1994). In a similar vein, Post (2007) describes the 'continuing reinforcement by manipulative leaders by consolidating the collective identity and by externalising, justifying and requiring violence against the enemy'. The shared reality is, indeed, compelling and is encouraged by leaders who appear to find it the most compelling of all. In this way, then, proto-typical actions become a self-referential form of proof of well-being – in this case the well-being of the group or movement.

It is sadly ironic how radical groups who champion equality and human rights often eschew such principles when it comes to their own members and those around them. The notion of 'revolutionary defeatism' is a peculiar affliction whereby the biggest losses and defeats are considered valuable losses by revolutionary leaders and become a compelling argument for trying yet harder and sacrificing still more 'for the cause'. Like any self-fulfilling prophecy, Marxist-Leninist groups adopt what Lifton (1961) describes as a form of 'confession' for failures even when they could be, and indeed are, predicted. For example, on the far Left, there is a common call for a 'general strike' and members of such political groups become active trade union members who regularly encourage their members to 'walk out'. These actions are widely acknowledged as destined to fail and yet are tests of loyalty to the revolutionary creed, while seemingly providing more 'evidence' of exploitation of apathetic masses by exploitative employers. Despite the hopelessness of the cause, or even – in fact – because of it, members of Marxist-Leninist movements see this as a key reason for working even harder and sacrificing even more – there is no limit to what the party can expect of its members (Stein, 2002; Tourish, 2013): the party is everything and the individual is at its behest, apparently willingly and with the cause of workers' liberation at stake.

The Psychology of Coercive Control in Extreme Groups

Radicalised groups of all political hues and beliefs have a demonstrable ability and commitment to 'destroying the world to save it' (Lifton, 2000). Whether in terror attacks or in the countless lives sacrificed to the cause, the 'dispensing of existence' (Lifton, 1961) is all too plain to see. Yet, the shared reality means that members of such extreme groups validate each other's perceptions of the world around them. The tragic consequences of the creed and deed, as well as the self-referential sacrificial acts that perjure existence, seem to point to a perception that is so markedly different and barely recognisable to anyone outside of their hallowed circles. Former cult members testify to how the scales fell from their eyes and their powers of perception were renewed when they saw the self-referential self-defeating sham for what it really was (Lalich, 2000).

As much as anything else, there is clear and convincing evidence that former members of extremist groups are as much victims of psychological harm as survivors of a disaster, such as a train crash or tsunami (Aronoff,

Lynn and Malinoski, 2000; Dubrow-Marshall and Dubrow-Marshall, 2015). Self-referential influence in tightly controlled radical groups can also be explained as a pattern of trauma-coerced attachment (Herman, 2015), whereby the person takes on the identity of the leader and the group and acts on their behalf, while also being oppressed and abused by them. Drawing on instances popularised by the term 'Stockholm Syndrome' (such as Patty Hearst's kidnap and then active part in a bank robbery alongside her captors), trauma-coerced attachment has been shown to be a common feature in abusive relationships and groups of different kinds, including trafficking gangs (Doychak and Raghavan, 2020). Distinctions between victims and perpetrators become harder to discern and so do notions of personal responsibility for crimes committed.

Yet, if the defence plea of diminished responsibility in legal proceedings is applied fairly, then the mental health effects of membership of radical groups and movements provide prima facie evidence that 'mens rea' has its limitations, as conscious intent to commit a crime arguably becomes harder to discern. The consequences for health and well-being of such thought reform environments are significant (Dubrow-Marshall and Dubrow-Marshall, 2015), indicating that beliefs, sometimes also carried out as actions, can be devastating for the victims of extremist groups, as much as the psychological threats, intimidation and shaming that is manifest in controlling and coercive behaviour in intimate relationships (Stark, 2009). Moreover, the notion of 'totalistic identity' arose from evidence of a group-based form of psychopathology or psychological harm that could be uniquely treated by group-focused forms of therapeutic intervention (Dubrow-Marshall, 2010; West and Martin, 1996).

Far-Right and Religious Cults

Similar difficulties can be observed in radicalised movements on the far Right, as on the far Left. There is a tendency in ideological terms on the far Right to extend folk or 'volk' myths of a bygone age of purity and freedom, which 'can be returned to if the world is cleansed of the "others" that have be-spoiled it'. A sharp and highly polarised 'us and them' dichotomy is often carried along by popularist movements whose aims are broader. For example, in the UK, the campaign to leave the European Union, popularly referred to as the Brexit movement, has arguably provided a 'Trojan Horse' for the far Right in a similar way to which the Labour Party and trade unions have been the wider vehicles for far Left groups over many decades (Grant, 1959; Tourish, 2013).

Extremist political movements on the Right are sometimes more direct in the way in which they promulgate and enact their ideology. Thomas Mair, a member of the far-Right British group, National Action, murdered the British Labour Member of Parliament, Jo Cox, in 2016, bringing to fruition his long-held idea that the 'white race' was in a long and 'very bloody struggle' for its survival. Similar motivations have long been central to far-Right movements, ranging from the Ku Klux Klan to lone wolf terrorists such as Anders Brevik and the Nazi Third Reich.

With a more religiously inspired ideology, there is a proliferation of groups with lineage to the 'Fundamentalist Latter Day Saints' (FLDS) in the United States of America who practise a gang-based approach to their 'local turf'. One such example is the polygamous group led by Ervil LeBaron – who had thirteen wives and fifty children – whose group was responsible for at least twenty murders. LeBaron founded his destructive cult when he was ejected from his older brother's group; his daughter described how he was viewed by members as 'the one true prophet on earth'. He used the doctrine of 'blood atonement' – repudiated by mainstream Mormons as far back as 1889 – which supports the killing of sinners (including apostates or former members) in order to 'cleanse them of evil'. In such cases, Ervil claimed that God would reveal to him (as 'the one true prophet') the name of his next victim and he would then pick a team of close disciples to carry out the murder. Refusing to obey Ervil's commands was unthinkable – caught in the psychological trap and double-bind of a totalistic identity, members could no more deny their leader's wishes than deny the core of their own being and destiny – hence the use of Bateson's (1956) term 'double-bind' to describe the mental trap that some extremist group members find themselves in and its terrible effects.

Other movements, such as the Freemen and Sovereign Citizens, operating across part of North America (Kent, 2015), invent a latter-day libertarian opt-out from civil society that they appear to equate with a bygone age of freedom. Eschewing modern laws and, instead, espousing adherence to Biblical law, British Common Law and Maritime laws of past centuries, the Freemen and Sovereign Citizens effectively claim secession rights to an era of democracy that pre-dates modern civil society. As with LeBaron's blood atonement, these movements are not concerned with civil liberties more generally, but instead with its liberty to act as it sees fit according to a concoction of self-serving laws conveniently selected from history. In certain respects, such groupings can be seen to share an anarchistic disregard for norms and conventions, which locates them among a sea of libertarian movements who fundamentally see the state as the 'enemy within'. Idealised forms of democracy in these movements are almost akin to no democracy at all, at least unrecognisable by modern standards. This illustrates the ideological position of fascism in relation to modernist conceptions of democracy (Griffin, 2007).

Far-Right movements such as QAnon espouse a similarly libertarian ideology, while also illustrating the psychological 'double-bind', in which people can become ensnared, in an era when the social stimuli from the Internet and social media are omnipresent and ubiquitous. Utilising Cooper's (1998) 'triple A engine' of access, affordability and anonymity on the Internet, supporters of QAnon can immerse themselves in conspiracy theories that are self-fulfilling prophecies precisely because there is no real-world evidence to support them. For example, the belief that there is no effective democracy and that governments are in cahoots with organised crime is a deep well of despair in which popularist leaders readily cast their nets for supporters (Amarasingam and Argentino, 2020).

As with the Freemen and Sovereign Citizens, there is something psychologically comforting and reassuring for members in believing with certainty that doubts and frustrations about life are because the world is simply 'out to get you and good people like you'. For those whose introjects (ideas assimilated from others) involve a degree of paranoia, then an apparent recourse is to retreat as far away from reality and the constraints of modern life as possible. In this regard, QAnon and other conspiracy theory-focused movements can be seen as the ultimate rejection of the ethics of civil society and the notion of the 'commons' as a place for reasoned discourse and collective progress (Standing, 2019). It is, instead, to the pre-enlightenment period to which these movements look for dark-age inspiration and to pre-democratic conceptions of individual liberty, i.e. 'kings of their castle and no dirty democratic rascals in sight'.

What Is to Be Done?

Supporters of mainstream political parties often look aghast at radical movements and incorrectly assume that these dangerous phenomena arise as a combination of faulty thinking or personality disorders. While rehabilitation from the clutches of radicalisation is often a beneficial path for individuals (Langone et al., 1995), the more vexed question is how to address the democratic deficit in communities more widely that are the fertile ground (but not the excuse) for extremism. The need for critical thinking as an antidote to cult-like thinking is widely acknowledged, however, radical thought can also demonstrate its own critical credentials, as Thomas Paine would be the first to acknowledge – so, on its own, it is not enough as a form of inoculation. As such, it is also necessary to consider the forms of action-based learning and restorative justice that can be truly transformative and that tackle the interweaving of deed and creed in everyday life that lead people to radicalised conclusions and movements (Prilleltensky, 2014). Such transformational change for communities and genuine 'mattering' has been shown to happen despite conditions of economic 'austerity' (CLES and Preston City Council, 2019).

Social empathy requires a deep appreciation of others in group terms and an understanding of one's own position in relation to others (Segal, 2018). A reflexive understanding of intersubjectivity potentially allows for disagreements about ideas and the outcome of disputes to be appreciated as part and parcel of human existence. The material reality can make accepting those outcomes almost impossibly painful to bear and, yet, manifest inequality cannot alone explain why some become adherents to radical ideologies while others do not. The Northern Ireland peace process demonstrates the importance of social empathy in helping to overcome long-established and deep-seated sectarian violence and destruction (Powell, 2009). This illustrates that a commitment to empathic practice and understanding the position of others, whether or not we agree with it or not, allows for a kind of parallel thinking from which real progress can potentially be made (De Bono, 1994).

Positive transformations for individuals and communities can also be key to showing how well-intended preaching and practice can be brought into alignment and, for this, it may be helpful to turn to the World Health Organisation's (WHO, 2010) definition of a healthy workplace, which demonstrates how beliefs can guide actions for improved psychological and physical well-being. A core aspect of any functioning democracy or organisation is arguably the health and safety of its voters, workers or members, as with Article 4 of the European Convention of Human Rights, which prohibits slavery and forced labour, i.e. the very chains of servitude that extremist groups often manifest and embody for their members while simultaneously promising to break them for everyone else (Banisadr, 2014). WHO emphasise that:

> For a healthy workplace to create a workplace that protects, promotes and supports the complete physical, mental and social well-being of workers, an enterprise/organization should consider addressing content in four 'avenues of influence,' based on identified needs...: 1. The physical work environment 2. The psychosocial work environment 3. Personal health resources in the workplace 4. Enterprise community involvement. (p. 83)

On the opposite end of the spectrum, the WHO guidelines also offer examples of psychosocial hazards, some of which are pertinent to groups of all kinds. These speak clearly about organisational culture, command and control management style, a lack of awareness of and competence in dealing with mental health or illness issues, all of which are the ironically perennial features of radical groups and movements whose avowed aim is to create a paradise on earth. Realising that radical groups and conceptions of democracy are just as likely to harm their members as mainstream organisations is a further reminder that singling out the ideology or creed is unhelpful and counter-productive in seeking to redress the effects of abusive groups wherever they may be found on the political or religious spectrum (Langone, 2000).

Recognising and reflecting on one's own frame of reference – and the 'basket of deplorables'[3] to which one belongs – allows for a potential form of social empathy and intersubjectivity, whereby we can reflect on our interpretations of ourselves and others and recognise how others are doing the same. This is not a muddy commonality or abandonment of radicalised conceptions of democracy and not an outlawing or proscription of them either. Instead, it represents a fundamental commitment to using the science of psychology to transform our relations with one another, particularly those with whom we appear to disagree the most: based on principles of health and safety that safeguard and ensure well-being, these are rooted in the practice of social empathy. Now that really would be a truly radical form of democracy!

REFERENCES

Amarasingam, A. and Argentino, M.-A. (2020). The QAnon Conspiracy Theory: A security threat in the making? *Combating Terrorism Center Sentinel,* 13(7), 37–44.

Aronoff, J., Lynn, S. and Malinoski, P. (2000). Are cultic environments psychologically harmful? *Clinical Psychology Review,* 20(1), 91–111.

Asch, S. E. (1956). Studies of independence and conformity: I. A minority of one against a unanimous majority. *Psychological Monographs: General and Applied,* 70(9), 1–70.

---

[3] The term 'basket of deplorables' was used by Democratic Candidate for US President, Hillary Clinton, in a private meeting with supporters in 2016 and was later leaked to the media. The comment is often cited as a factor in the alienation of key voters in certain 'swing states' who felt psychologically boxed into this category and into voting for her opponent during the subsequent presidential elections.

Banisadr, M. (2014). *Destructive and terrorist cults: A new kind of slavery: Leader, followers, and mind manipulation*. London: Research Institute on Destructive Cults.

(2009). Terrorist organizations are cults. *Cultic Studies Review*, 8(2), 154–184.

Bateson, G., Jackson, D., Haley, J. and Weakland, J. (1956). Toward a theory of schizophrenia. *Behavioral Science*, 1, 251–264.

Bayes. W. W. (1970). *Ends and means*. New York: Foundation for Economic Education.

Busher, J., Choudhury, T., Thomas, P. and Harris, G. (2017). *What the Prevent duty means for schools and colleges in England: An analysis of educationalists' experiences*. Coventry: Centre for Trust, Peace and Social Relations, Coventry University.

CLES and Preston City Council (2019). *How we built community wealth in Preston – Achievements and lessons*. Available at: https://cles.org.uk/publications/how-we-built-community-wealth-in-preston-achievements-and-lessons/.

Clinton C. (2010). Breaking the silence: Sexual hypocrisies from Thomas Jefferson to Strom Thurmond. In B. J. Brooten (Eds.), *Beyond slavery: Overcoming its religious and sexual legacies*, pp. 213–228. New York: Palgrave Macmillan.

Commission of the European Communities (2005). *Communication from the Commission to the European Parliament concerning terrorist recruitment: Addressing the factors contributing to violent radicalization [Article 1, COM (2005) 313 final]*. Brussels, Belgium: European Commission.

Cooper, A. (1998). Sexuality and the Internet: Surfing into the new millennium, *Cyber Psychology and Behaviour*, 1, 181–187.

de Bono, E. (1994). *Parallel thinking*. London: Penguin Books Ltd.

Donner, M. (2004). Die Gedanken Sind Frei. *IEEE Security and Privacy*, 2, 53–55.

Downes, J. (2017). 'It's not the abuse that kills you, it's the silence': The silencing of sexual violence activism in social justice movements in the UK Left. *Justice, Power and Resistance*, 1(2), 35–58.

Doychak, K. and Raghavan, C. (2020). 'No voice or vote': Trauma-coerced attachment in victims of sex trafficking, *Journal of Human Trafficking*, (3), 339–357. doi:10.1080/23322705.2018.1518625.

Dubrow-Marshall, R. P. (2010). The influence continuum – the good, the dubious and the harmful – evidence and implications for policy and practice in the 21st Century. *International Journal of Cultic Studies*, 1(1), 1–13.

Dubrow-Marshall, R. P. and Dubrow-Marshall, L. (2015). Cults and mental health. In H. S. Friedman (Ed.), *The encyclopedia of mental health*, pp. 393–401. New York: Academic Press.

Dubrow-Marshall, R. P., van de Donk, M. and Haanstra, W. (2019). Lessons from adjacent fields: Cults and radical extremist groups. *ICSA Today*, 10(1), 2–9.

Edwards, D. and Potter, J. (1992). *Inquiries in social construction: Discursive psychology*. Thousand Oaks, CA: Sage Publications, Inc.

Emerson, R. W. (1937). 'Compensation', *Essays and English Traits*, vol. 5 of The Harvard Classics, C. W. Eliot (Ed.), LL.D., 51 vols. New York: P. F. Collier and Son Corporation.

Festinger, L. (1962). *A theory of cognitive dissonance.* Stanford, CA: Stanford University Press.

Gov.UK (2011). Prevent strategy. Accessed at: www.gov.uk/government/publica tions/prevent-strategy-2011.

Grant, T. (1959). *Problems of entrism.* Ted Grant Archive. Accessed at: www .marxists.org/archive/grant/1959/03/entrism.htm.

Griffin, R. (2007). *Modernism and fascism: The sense of a new beginning under Mussolini and Hitler.* Basingstoke: Palgrave.

Haslam, S. A. and Turner, J. C. (1995). Context-dependent variation in social stereotyping 3: Extremism as a self-categorical basis for polarized judgement. *European Journal of Social Psychology,* 25, 341–371.

(1998). Extremism and deviance: Beyond taxonomy and bias. *Social Research,* 65(2), 435–448.

Herman, J. (2015). *Trauma and recovery.* London: Pandora.

Hogg, M. A., and Abrams, D. (Eds.). (1993). *Group motivation: Social psychological perspectives.* Hemel Hempstead: Harvester Wheatsheaf.

Kent, S. A. (2015). Freemen, sovereign citizens, and the challenge to public order in British heritage countries. *International Journal of Cultic Studies,* 6, 1–15.

Krakauer, J. (2003). *Under the banner of heaven: A story of violent faith. 1st large print ed.* New York: Random House.

Kruglanski, A., Chen, X., Dechesne, M., Fishman, S. and Orehek, E. (2009). Fully committed: Suicide bombers' motivation and the quest for personal significance. *Political Psychology,* 30(3), 331–357.

Kruglanski, A., Jasko, K., Webber, D., Chernikova, M., Molinario, E. (2019). The making of violent extremists. *Review of General Psychology,* 22(1), 107–120.

Lalich, J. (2001). *Bounded choice: True believers and charismatic cults.* Oakland, CA: University of California Press.

Langone, M. (2000). The two 'camps' of cultic studies: Time for a dialogue. *Cultic Studies Journal,* 17, 55–68.

(1995). *Recovery from cults: Help for victims of psychological and spiritual abuse.* New York: W.W. Norton.

Levi, P. (1965). *The re-awakening.* New York: The Bodley Head.

Lifton, R. (2000). *Destroying the world to save it: Aum Shinrikyo, apocalyptic violence, and the new global terrorism.* New York: Henry Holt and Company.

(1961). *Thought reform and the psychology of totalism.* New York: W.W. Norton.

McVeigh, R. and Cunningham D. (2012). Enduring consequences of Right-Wing extremism: Klan mobilization and homicides in southern counties. *Social Forces,* 90(3), 843–862.

Milgram, S. (1974). *Obedience to authority: An experimental view.* New York: Harper and Row.

Moscovici, S. and Lage, E. (1976). Studies in social influence: III. Majority versus minority influence in a group. *European Journal of Social Psychology,* 6(2), 149–174.

Paine, T. (1776/1975). *Thomas Paine's Common sense: The call to independence.* Woodbury, New York: Barron's Educational Series.

Parker, I. (1990). Real things: Discourse, context and practice. *Philosophical Psychology,* 3, 227–233.

Post, J. (2007). *The mind of the terrorist: The psychology of terrorism from the IRA to Al-Qaeda.* New York: Palgrave Macmillan.

Powell, J. (2009). *Great hatred, little room: Making peace in Northern Ireland.* London: Vintage.

Prilleltensky, I. (2014). Meaning-making, mattering, and thriving in community psychology: From co-optation to amelioration and transformation. *Psychosocial Intervention,* 23(2), 151–154.

Segal, E. A. (2018). *Social empathy: The art of understanding others.* New York: Columbia University Press.

Seligman, M. E. P. (1990). *Learned optimism.* New York: Knopf.

——— (1972). Learned helplessness. *Annual Review of Medicine,* 23, 407–412.

Sherif, M. (1967). *Social interaction: Process and products.* Chicago: Aldine.

Standing, G. (2019). *Plunder of the commons: A manifesto for sharing public wealth.* London: Pelican.

Stark, E. (2009). Rethinking coercive control. *Violence Against Women,* 15(12), 1509–1525.

Stein, A. (2002). *Inside out – A memoir of entering and breaking out of a Minneapolis political cult.* North Star Press of St. Cloud.

Tajfel, H. (1978). *Differentiation between social groups: Studies in the social psychology of intergroup relations.* London: Published in cooperation with European Association of Experimental Social Psychology by Academic Press.

Tajfel, H. and Turner, J. C. (1979). An integrative theory of intergroup conflict. In W. Austin and S. Worchel (Eds.), *The social psychology of intergroup relations,* pp. 33–47. Monterey, CA: Brooks/Cole.

Tourish, D. (2013). *The dark side of transformational leadership: A critical perspective.* New York, NY: Routledge.

Tourish, D. and Wohlforth, T. (2000). *On the edge: Political cults of the right and left.* New York: Sharpe.

Trotsky, L. (1932, 1980). *The history of the Russian Revolution,* translated Eastman, M. New York, NY: Anchor Foundation.

Turner, J. C. (1991). *Social influence.* Milton Keynes: Open University Press and Pacific Grove, CA: Brooks/Cole.

Turner, J. C. and Oakes, P. J. (1997). The socially structured mind. In C. McGarty and S. A. Haslam (Eds.), *The message of social psychology,* pp. 355–373. Oxford, UK: Blackwell.

Turner, J., Hogg, M., Oakes, P., Reicher, S. and Wetherell, M. (1987). *Rediscovering the social group: A self-categorisation theory.* Cambridge, MA: Basil Blackwell.

Turner, J. C., Oakes, P. J., Haslam, S. A. and McGarty, C. (1994). Self and collective: Cognition and social context. *Personality and Social Psychology Bulletin,* 20, 454–463.

West, L. and Martin, P. (1996). Pseudo Identity and the treatment of personality change in victims of captivity and cults. *Cultic Studies Journal,* 13(2), 125–152.

World Health Organization (2010). Healthy workplaces: A model for action. Geneva: WHO. Accessed at: www.who.int/occupational_health/publica tions/healthy_workplaces_model_action.pdf.

Young, J. (2003). In praise of dangerous thoughts. *Punishment and Society,* 5(1), 97–107.

Zimbardo, P. (2008). *The Lucifer effect; How good people turn evil.* London: Ebury Publishing.

Index

9 781108 745091